REFORMS, OPPORTUNITIES, AND CHALLENGES FOR STATE-OWNED ENTERPRISES

Edited by Edimon Ginting and Kaukab Naqvi

JULY 2020

ASIAN DEVELOPMENT BANK

ADB

ISBN 978-92-9262-282-4 (print), 978-92-9262-283-1 (electronic); 978-92-9262-284-8 (ebook)
Publication Stock No. TCS200201-2
DOI: http://dx.doi.org/10.22617TCS200201-2

The views expressed in this publication are those of the authors and do not necessarily reflect the views and policies of the Asian Development Bank (ADB) or its Board of Governors or the governments they represent.

ADB does not guarantee the accuracy of the data included in this publication and accepts no responsibility for any consequence of their use. The mention of specific companies or products of manufacturers does not imply that they are endorsed or recommended by ADB in preference to others of a similar nature that are not mentioned.

By making any designation of or reference to a particular territory or geographic area, or by using the term "country" in this document, ADB does not intend to make any judgments as to the legal or other status of any territory or area.

Please contact pubsmarketing@adb.org if you have questions or comments with respect to content, or if you wish to obtain copyright permission for your intended use that does not fall within these terms, or for permission to use the ADB logo.

Corrigenda to ADB publications may be found at http://www.adb.org/publications/corrigenda.

Notes:
In this publication, "$" refers to United States dollars.

ADB recognizes "China" as the People's Republic of China; "Hong Kong" as Hong Kong, China; "Korea" and "South Korea" as the Republic of Korea; "Vietnam" as Viet Nam; "Hanoi" as Ha Noi; and "Saigon" as Ho Chi Minh City.

Cover design by Mike Cortes with photos from Mark Floro, Deng Jia, Nikita Makarenko, Zen Nuntawiny, and Ariel Javellana for ADB. All Rights Reserved.

Contents

Tables, Figures, and Boxes

Tables

Figures

Boxes

Preface

State-owned enterprises (SOEs) have played a significant role in promoting economic development worldwide. They have not only become global players, they are also an important part of the economic structure of the world's fastest-growing economies. Despite the rise of privatization over the past 20 years, SOEs are still prevalent in many countries, globally accounting for about 20% of investment, 5% of employment, and up to 40% of output. Despite their active participation, however, the general trend in overall state ownership has spiraled downward.

Governments in developing countries initially created SOEs to primarily achieve import–substitution industrialization and promote domestic production of industrial goods, in effect forming companies that produce steel, chemicals, and electricity.

Several arguments have been offered to justify or oppose state participation in economic affairs. Advocates claim that government involvement in the economy expedites the resolution of market failure. Some say that SOEs may be better placed to tackle the externalities associated with the provision of public goods. The social view underscores the achievement of societal objectives, which depart from purely profit-maximizing goals. Others favor SOE involvement in the production of basic commodities such as water, health care, and education while not necessarily providing them for profit. Governments also provide basic services on equity considerations, such as universal access to essential services, and create jobs in backward areas.

On the other hand, many argue against SOE involvement as well. The so-called principal–agent argument, for example, suggests that an SOE is not run by its owner, but by a manager who has less incentive to manage the enterprise efficiently. Others assert that SOEs are often statutory monopolies—their products are not subject to market competition, they have easy access to government finances, and they are not subject to market discipline.

Additionally, the lack of competition and frequent government bailouts during crises, they claim, may lead to inefficient performance and poor public service delivery.

Despite large-scale privatization in the 1980s and the 1990s, SOEs in emerging markets have remained active in domestic and global markets. Episodes of financial crisis have led some governments to expand the role of SOEs to further developmental and policy goals. But despite their involvement in different sectors, SOEs in emerging markets lag behind in the consistent application of corporate governance standards.

The prevalence of SOEs, however, has also raised concerns about a level playing field and their performance toward enhancing economy-wide productivity and growth. Given their large presence in economic activities, SOEs have the potential to influence policy and competition in individual sectors, not only through their physical presence, but also through their privileged access to government, as represented in the SOEs' board of directors. With no competition from the private sector, these companies may have few incentives to innovate. Consequently, many of them either deteriorate or perform poorly. And governments, especially in developing countries, continue to bail them out by providing financial help.

Poorly performing SOEs incur high financial and economic costs and impede competitiveness and growth, in many countries becoming a fiscal burden and a source of fiscal risk as they weaken the financial system. Continued lending to unprofitable companies can create contingent liabilities and is likely to destabilize the macro economy.

SOE policy is therefore a key component of any reform agenda, and it can take many forms—from outright divestment to partial divestment, and even privatization to improve efficiency. For example, after considering the adverse impacts of the financial crisis, some governments are reasserting ownership over strategic sectors. Also, because SOEs are active internationally, many countries employ them to reap the benefits of economies of scale in the race for finance, talent, and resources.

This study posits that government policy in developing countries should focus on reforming SOEs and making them an efficient driver of growth, particularly during Asia's transition to high-income status.

Chapter 1 provides a regional perspective of the importance of SOEs in developing Asia. It analyzes the role and performance of SOEs across a number of economies including developing member countries (DMCs) of the Asian Development Bank (ADB) such as the People's Republic of China (PRC), Indonesia, Kazakhstan, and Viet Nam, each one unique in development context, but together presenting a panoramic view of the SOE landscape in the region. The chapter also provides interesting insights from the Republic of Korea on the evolving role of the public sector in various stages of development. It examines the productivity and efficiency of SOEs and highlights their role in supporting productivity-led growth to facilitate Asia's transition to high-income status.

Chapter 2 recounts the successful development experience of the Republic of Korea and the contribution of public enterprises and the government in promoting economic development. It demonstrates the merits of a government's flexibility in adopting a different role at each phase of development—in this case, selecting the sectors to invest in during the early development stages, and then increasing the role of the private sector as the economy develops and modes of production become more complex.

Chapter 3 examines SOEs in Indonesia, briefly reviews past SOE reforms and performance, and considers the likely constraints on future reforms. It argues that maintaining Indonesia's development trajectory hinges on huge improvements in infrastructure and public services with SOEs still playing a key role. It suggests a pragmatic two-pronged approach: (i) adopt politically feasible reforms in the near term such as corporatization, listing, and improving corporate governance; and (ii) build awareness and consensus in the long term as the government adheres to the politically difficult requirements of the SOE Law, particularly in privatization, governance, and competition.

Chapter 4 discusses the role of the government and SOEs in the economic development of Kazakhstan, underscoring the need for improved corporate governance, a developed finance sector, a vibrant private sector, and restructured SOEs. It compares the efficiency of SOEs against private listed companies, examines the macroeconomic risks emanating from SOEs' poor performance, and highlights the need to modernize public sector management and make SOEs an efficient driver of growth. The chapter emphasizes the importance of engendering professionalism and infusing a sense of dynamism in managing state enterprises.

Chapter 5 discusses the evolving role of SOEs in the PRC and highlights the importance of reforms in promoting economic development. It compares the efficiency and productivity of SOEs vis-à-vis their private counterparts, analyzes the fiscal risks emanating from SOEs, emphasizes the need for better and professional management of public assets, and offers a brief but comprehensive review of SOE reforms and the evolution of the country's corporate governance structure. As the PRC is faced with the challenge of improving its corporate governance and the quality of the structure of its SOEs, the government will need to pay greater attention to enhancing the quality of public service delivery and moving the economy from the current investment-driven model to an innovation-driven growth model.

Chapter 6 describes the importance of SOE reforms in Azerbaijan and provides a detailed analysis of SOE performance in different economic sectors. It highlights the fiscal risks of underperforming SOEs and suggests ways to improve their performance. It also underlines the recent initiative of the government to improve corporate governance of SOEs, suggesting ways to align corporate governance with the Organisation for Economic Co-operation and Development guidelines, and provides a four-step approach to enhancing SOE reforms.

Chapter 7 discusses SOEs in Viet Nam and their role and contribution to economic development. While growth has been steady and impressive, Viet Nam must consider reforms to its SOEs as a consequence of rising public debt, significant levels of nonperforming loans and burgeoning SOE debt, and underperformance of many SOEs. Continuing with SOE reforms is essential in improving resource allocation and public service delivery.

This book provides an insightful understanding of the importance of SOEs in selected DMCs and an in-depth assessment of key issues relating to SOE reforms.

Yasuyuki Sawada
Chief Economist and Director General
Economic Research and Regional Cooperation Department
Asian Development Bank

Acknowledgments

This book, *Reforms, Opportunities, and Challenges for State-Owned Enterprises,* is a product of a study undertaken by the Asian Development Bank (ADB) as part of the project Research and Development Technical Assistance for Country Diagnostic Studies in Selected Developing Member Countries.

The study was carried out by a team of economists from the Economic Analysis and Operational Support Division (EREA) of ADB's Economic Research and Regional Cooperation Department (ERCD) and external experts. Project leader Kaukab Naqvi, senior economist at EREA, led the study team. Edimon Ginting, deputy director general, ERCD, supervised the team and provided valuable insights in finalizing the study. During the book's final stretch, the study also benefited from the advice of Rana Hasan, director, EREA, ERCD.

The study benefited from comments and inputs from ADB's Central and West Asia Department, East Asia Department, Southeast Asia Department, South Asia Department, and the Sustainable Development and Climate Change Department's Thematic Group on State-Owned Enterprises. The team acknowledges the valuable comments and contributions of Hal Hill, Yougesh Khatri, and Mohamad Ikhsan. The team would like also to thank the Korea Development Institute for facilitating the final workshop for the study, which provided a venue to brainstorm and enhance the quality of the project.

Amador Foronda, Rica Cynthia Maddawin, and Angelica Maddawin assisted the team with research. Lilibeth Poot ensured excellent product quality and overall coherence of the study and provided valuable comments and suggestions in finalizing the study. We would like to thank her for organizing the various workshops and steering the production and publication processes of the study. Tuesday Soriano edited and proofread the study, while Michael Cortes typeset the text and designed the cover. The Knowledge Support Division of the Department of Communications supported publishing. Roslyn Perez assisted in administrative matters.

The study draws extensively from a series of consultations with the governments of the selected countries. The team is grateful for their support and valuable comments.

Finally, the team appreciates the assistance and cooperation of ADB resident missions. We acknowledge in particular the excellent support of Country Directors Winfried Wicklein of the Indonesia Resident Mission, Nariman Mannapbekov of the Azerbaijan Resident Mission, Benedict Bingham of the People's Republic of China Resident Mission, Eric Sidgwick of the Viet Nam Resident Mission, and Giovanni Capannelli of the Kazakhstan Resident Mission, for facilitating dialogue and fostering collaboration with the respective government representatives and other stakeholders. This study would not have been completed without their insightful input and guidance.

Abbreviations

ADB	Asian Development Bank
ADY	Azerbaijan Railways
ASEAN	Association of Southeast Asian Nations
AZAL	Azerbaijan Airlines
CMSC	Commission for the Management of State Capital
DEA	data envelopment analysis
DMC	developing member country
EBIT	earnings before interest and taxes
EBITDA	earnings before interest, tax, depreciation, and amortization
EBRD	European Bank for Reconstruction and Development
EVN	Vietnam Electricity
FDI	foreign direct investment
GC	general corporation
GDP	gross domestic product
GLC	government-linked corporation/company
GSO	General Statistics Office
IBAR	International Bank of Azerbaijan
IBRD	International Bank for Reconstruction and Development
IMF	International Monetary Fund
IPO	initial public offering
JSC	joint-stock company
KPI	key performance indicator
LOI	letter of intent
MOF	Ministry of Finance
MPP	mass privatization program
MSOE	Ministry of State-Owned Enterprises
NBS	National Bureau of Statistics
NFRK	National Fund of the Republic of Kazakhstan
NPL	nonperforming loan

OECD	Organisation for Economic Co-operation and Development
POSCO	Pohang Iron and Steel Company
PPP	public–private partnership
PRC	People's Republic of China
PSO	public service obligation
R&D	research and development
ROA	return on assets
ROCE	return on capital employed
ROE	return on equity
SASAC	State Asset Supervision and Administration Commission
SBV	State Bank of Vietnam
SCIC	State Capital Investment Corporation
SEG	state economic group
SOCAR	State Oil Company of the Azerbaijan Republic
SOE	state-owned enterprise
SOSCEs	state-owned and state-controlled enterprises
SWF	sovereign wealth fund
UPCoM	Unlisted Public Company Market
US	United States
VAMC	Vietnam Asset Management Company
WTO	World Trade Organization

Contributors

Alexander Ewart is an international consultant specializing in state-owned enterprise reforms in Asian countries.

Edimon Ginting is deputy director general at the Economic Research and Regional Cooperation Department (ERCD) of the Asian Development Bank (ADB) in Manila.

Aziz Haydarov is a senior portfolio management specialist at ADB's Azerbaijan Resident Mission.

Mohamad Ikhsan is special advisor and chief economist at the Ministry of State-Owned Enterprises of Indonesia.

Hyung-Gon Jeong is a senior research fellow at the Korea Institute for International Economic Policy and a special senior research fellow at the Chinese Academy of Social Sciences.

Yougesh Khatri is an associate professor at the Nanyang Business School of Nanyang Technological University in Singapore, a senior international advisor at PROSPERA in Jakarta, and an associate fellow at Chatham House (The Royal Institute of International Affairs) in London.

Minsoo Lee is a senior economist at Central and West Asia Department of ADB in Manila and was previously head of the Knowledge Hub at ADB's People's Republic of China Resident Mission.

Kaukab Naqvi is a senior economist at ERCD of ADB in Manila.

Michael Schur is a former managing director at Castalia.

Vu Van Tuan is a managing director at T&C Consulting in Viet Nam.

CHAPTER 1

State-Owned Enterprises and Economic Development in Asia

*Kaukab Naqvi and Edimon Ginting**

1.1   Introduction

State-owned enterprises (SOEs) make up a significant part of the commercial and policy landscapes of developing economies in Asia. Despite the trend toward privatization and deregulation across the globe over the last 2 decades, SOEs have retained a strong presence in the global economy and play an important role in implementing public policy in many advanced and developing economies. By and large, these institutions have played a typically much larger role in the economic development of developing countries than developed countries.

In many countries, SOEs continue to provide vital infrastructure and public services, such as energy, transportation, water management, and exploration of natural resources. Governments also use them to pursue various economic, social, and political objectives particularly in regions where development has lagged; deliver services to the general population including the urban or rural poor; and address issues of national priority or heightened security.

Although SOEs remain active, the overall trend of state ownership is spiraling downward. State capitalism[1] has pretty much varied in degree and intensity across countries. On average, SOEs account for a higher share of gross domestic product (GDP) in developing countries than in developed countries. For example, in Central Asian countries, SOEs' share of GDP ranges from 10% to 40% compared with 5% in Organisation for Economic Co-operation and Development (OECD) economies (World Bank Group 2014). In Asia, SOEs account for about 30% of GDP in the People's Republic of China (PRC), 38% in Viet Nam, and 25% in Thailand. Globally, SOEs account for about 20% of investment and 5% of employment (Kim and Ali 2017).

---

[*]   Rica Cynthia Maddawin provided support in compiling data and performing data envelopment analysis.

[1]   State capitalism is an economic system in which the state plays a dominant role in different sectors through government ownership and control.

However, the prevalence of state ownership has also raised concerns about the performance of these enterprises which in certain circumstances may impede competitiveness and growth. For example, SOEs often have access to government support and enjoy soft budget constraint which, when combined with lack of competition and multiple competing objectives, result in low productivity and efficiency compared with private enterprises.

The impact of how well or how poorly these companies perform will inevitably have spillover effects on macroeconomic stability and economy-wide productivity. In many countries, underperforming SOEs have become a fiscal burden and a source of fiscal risk. Loss-making and ineffective SOEs weaken the financial system; and continued lending to unprofitable companies can create contingent liabilities and potentially destabilize the macro economy.

Many countries have taken significant steps to address corporate governance challenges and therefore improve SOE operations. Evidence across countries has shown that better governance and more efficient management lead to lower costs of capital and higher valuation, thus making investments more attractive. Consequently, the efficiency of SOEs and the economy as a whole improves, transactions become more competitive and transparent, and resources are allocated efficiently when the fiscal burden on SOEs is reduced and fiscal risk is managed.

Understanding governance challenges and addressing them is essential in boosting economy-wide productivity and growth. An SOE performs better if it is able to communicate its purpose and objectives and build its capacity to steer and manage resources efficiently. To enhance the delivery of public services and allocation of resources, the government must professionally manage SOEs on commercial terms and steer them away from markets where the private sector is better able to provide services more effectively.

This study explores the abovementioned issues in detail and addresses the policy questions on SOE reforms. It highlights the corporate governance framework of SOEs in selected countries, assesses SOE performance, and examines the implications for each country's productivity and growth over the long term. The study posits that SOEs will continue to make a significant contribution to economic development in developing countries. But their performance is crucial to economy-wide productivity and innovation-driven growth especially as Asia transitions from middle-income to high-income status.

1.2   Definition and Origin of SOEs

There is no universally agreed definition of an SOE.[2] However, a working definition is that an SOE is any commercial entity in which the government has significant control through direct and indirect ownership. An enterprise that is 100% government-owned is obviously categorized as an SOE. But other enterprises may also qualify as SOEs, such as (1) those in which the government has a majority equity stake; and (2) those in which the government owns a minority stake, but the government retains a controlling vote in major financial and management decisions—as is commonly the case. A variety of other organization models within the SOE sector also includes corporate and noncorporate structures.

SOEs have a diverse and expansive origin. Initially, SOEs were established to address market failure and capital shortfalls, promote economic development, provide public services, and/or ensure government control over the overall direction of the economy by infusing capital and technology into strategic areas or in areas lacking private sector capacity or interest (Chang 2007).

It is important to stress that SOEs basically reflect, and are deeply enmeshed in, the institutions, political history and ideology, commercial landscape, and technological trajectory of a country. These parameters dictate the political economy of SOE reforms. For example, in the centrally planned economy, the state owns not only the dominant or leading enterprises but also those in other sectors, including agriculture. In transition economies where the government plays a relatively dominant role, such as in the PRC, the SOE sector's symbiotic relationship with the government explains why the sector has remained unusually large. In addition, the perceived failure of privatization has caused many Asian economies to retain large state-owned sectors.

In countries where state-owned banks dominate the formal finance sector, as they typically do in many transition economies, the state directs much of private sector investment, and thus has a considerably wider reach than official statistics suggest. In many countries, subnational governments also own SOEs, which may be only partially recorded in national statistics.

Outside the transition economies, many countries have also favored a large SOE sector at the onset of their independence, for various reasons: (i) distrust of markets and capitalism (in India, for example); (ii) nationalization of

---

[2]   Throughout this study, the term "SOE" is defined in different ways across countries. In Malaysia and Singapore, for example, the term "government-linked corporation" (GLC) is widely used. In Viet Nam, the term "equitization" refers to SOEs that have been corporatized.

assets owned by companies under the former colonial power (in Indonesia); or (iii) concerns that indigenous capitalists are unable to undertake large-scale investments (in Singapore). In some cases, regional (subnational) development objectives also provided the impetus for SOE projects (in the PRC and Indonesia).

In others, state ownership is the result of the historical processes and inherited institutional conditions of a country. For example, it has been argued that poorly developed financial markets severely constrain investment. Often governments establish SOEs to build basic physical infrastructure; provide essential services such as finance, water, and electricity; generate revenue; control natural resources; address market failures; and curtail oligopolistic behavior. Public enterprises also purposefully promote social objectives—generating employment, enhancing regional development, and benefiting economically and socially disadvantaged groups of society.

1.3   Evolving Role of SOEs

The prevailing policy orthodoxies reinforced the important role of SOEs in at least two respects. First, many advanced economies had already very large SOE sectors, especially in continental Europe, where the state generally owned not only the major utilities (power, telecommunication, transport, and so on), but also banks, airlines, and industrial conglomerates. This model bolstered the ideological predisposition of newly independent countries in Asia and the Pacific. Second, this prevailing policy also embraced import substitution—as theorized by the so-called "Prebisch doctrine"[3] and the related "Prebisch-Singer declining terms of trade" hypothesis. According to this view, an activist industrial policy is required to guide economic actors toward the desired direction. This model employed tariffs and subsidies among others, as well as direct state ownership, especially in cases where the anticipated investments were not forthcoming, even after generous tariff support.

In certain circumstances especially in developing countries, state ownership can be the vehicle through which the state plays an active role in economic development. In several emerging markets for instance, governments have helped build much-needed physical infrastructure and bring about stability in times of crisis and across supply chains, thereby promoting social welfare. Development banks, sovereign wealth funds (SWFs), public holding

---

[3]   The Prebisch–Singer hypothesis argues that the price of primary commodities declines relative to the price of manufactured goods over the long term, which causes the terms of trade of primary-product-based economies to deteriorate.

companies, and many other vehicles of government capital have helped achieve developmental objectives. And when confronted with insufficient private capital base, governments have also used SOEs to promote economic development as well as industrial policy.

In addition to the declining trend in state ownership and presence in many emerging economies, there is also a tendency for governments to partially divest. Although this reduces government holdings to the degree that these companies no longer fall under the strict definition of SOEs, it does not necessarily imply a corresponding decrease in the ability of such governments to exert influence over these companies.

Moreover, episodes of financial crises have also led some governments to further expand the role of SOEs. For example, the governments of Iceland, the Netherlands, the United Kingdom, and the United States bailed out financial institutions through capital injections and partial or full nationalization to mitigate the adverse impacts of a crisis. It is, however, important to note that these interventions were mostly temporary in nature rather than permanent takeovers (World Bank Group 2014). Nevertheless, the ensuing episodes of financial crises underscored the importance of effectively managing these institutions and maintaining macroeconomic stability.

Following the global financial crisis, state development banks and development finance institutions in several countries also played a countercyclical role, providing credit to private firms that were unable to access funding through private banks and the capital markets. Such was the case in Malawi, Mozambique, and Serbia, wherein new development banks were established.

Some governments are explicitly pursuing policies to promote SOE internationalization. For example, the PRC's "Made in China 2025" strategy is designed to help improve the export capability of SOEs and make them more competitive globally. The PRC government has introduced measures such as easing red tape, introducing market practices, and consolidating selected SOEs to create larger and more efficient national champions. These companies are also empowered to make major decisions such as on cross-border mergers and overseas acquisitions (PwC 2015).

In 2019, 11 SOEs made it to the top 50 of the Fortune Global 500; of these 11 companies, 8 are from the PRC.[4] Meanwhile, SOEs have also been listed among the world's biggest capital markets. To raise capital, impose capital market

---

[4]   Fortune. Global 500. https://fortune.com/global500/2019/search/.

discipline on these enterprises, and dilute state ownership, some governments have listed large and important financial and nonfinancial SOEs in their respective stock exchanges. As a consequence, the initial public offering of these SOEs increased their contribution to capital market development—in 2014, for example, SOEs accounted for 20% of total market capitalization in India, about 30% in Malaysia and Indonesia; and 45% in the Middle East and North Africa (World Bank Group 2014).

In some resource-rich countries, SWFs rose to prominence during the financial crisis. For example, in the face of highly volatile commodity prices and growing current account imbalances in Azerbaijan and Kazakhstan, these funds have proved useful for maintaining macroeconomic stability. Thus, SWFs could also be viewed as a special group of SOEs. As major holders of government debt, these state-owned investment funds are used to mitigate external shocks, implying that SOEs, including SWFs, have also become active in global markets. Clearly, state ownership occurs in various forms: the state could be a majority shareholder, or it could be a minority shareholder and still influence the governance of SOEs (Musacchio and Lazzarini 2012).

These examples show the increasing role of the state in economic affairs and the importance of managing SOEs more effectively without compromising macroeconomic stability.

1.4   Stylized Facts and Data Set

This section presents the stylized facts of SOEs in six Asian countries: Indonesia, Kazakhstan, the PRC, the Republic of Korea, Sri Lanka, and Viet Nam, all of which have been selected largely for their diverse experience in SOE management. The Republic of Korea, representing an advanced economy, serves as a benchmark for how the role of SOEs can change effectively through the various stages of development.

Data are extracted from the Orbis database, which defines an SOE as a company in which the government shares 51% of total assets.[5] The data set covers the period 2010–2018, while the number of SOEs varies across countries. For purposes of analysis, however, we have confined our study to SOEs with available financial data.[6] It is, therefore, important to note that

---

[5]   The Orbis database provides a comprehensive, wide-ranging, and consistent data set for state-owned and private companies, thus making comparison across countries reliable.

[6]   Orbis covers all the listed companies. However, not all listed companies share information about their financial statistics. For consistency, analysis is limited to those SOEs for which financial data are made available to the Orbis database. The number of SOEs with financial data is much smaller than the number of listed companies.

despite the database's extensive coverage, the data set is by no means fully exhaustive. Hence, the statistics reflecting various aspects of SOE activities should be considered indicative and for illustrative purposes only.

The analysis shows that the prevalence of SOEs across sectors in the sample countries varies considerably. The largest concentration of SOEs is found in the services sector, including public utilities, financial and insurance activities, and in the trade and transport sectors. The significant presence of SOEs in manufacturing is due mainly to the large number of SOEs operating in the manufacturing sector of the PRC (Figure 1.1).

Figure 1.1: Distribution of SOEs by Sector, 2010–2018 (%)

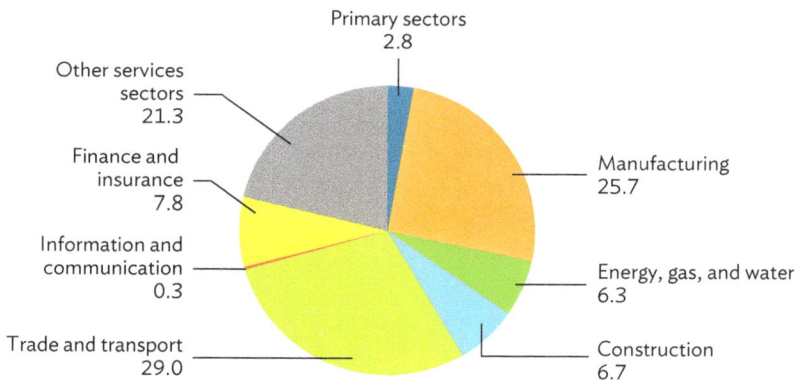

Primary sectors
2.8

Other services
sectors
21.3

Finance and
insurance
7.8

Information and
communication
0.3

Trade and transport
29.0

Manufacturing
25.7

Energy, gas, and water
6.3

Construction
6.7

SOE = state-owned enterprise.
Note: Primary sectors comprise agriculture and mining and quarrying with a share of 0.7% and 2.1%, respectively.
Source: Authors' calculations based on the Orbis database.

Next, we evaluate the contribution of SOEs by examining their equity. Total equity is the difference between a corporation's assets and its tenabilities.[7] Figure 1.2 breaks down by sector the total equity value of the countries in 2010–2018.

Distribution of equity depicts a dominance of SOEs in the primary sectors (agriculture and mining); manufacturing; and electricity, gas, and water supply. Collectively, these three sectors comprised about 70% of the SOEs' total equity

---

[7] In the world of finance, the term equity generally refers to the value of an ownership interest in a business, such as shares of stock held. On a company's balance sheet, equity is defined as retained earnings, plus the sum of inventory and other assets, and minus liabilities.

value. In other sectors during 2010–2018, construction, trade and transport, information and communication, and financial and insurance activities contribute 10.3%, 6.4%, 4.6%, and 4.7% of total equity value, respectively.

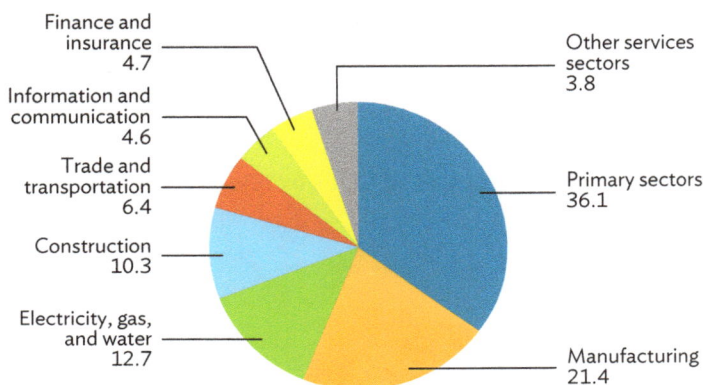

Figure 1.2: Sectoral Breakdown of Equity Value, 2010–2018
(%)

Finance and insurance 4.7
Information and communication 4.6
Trade and transportation 6.4
Construction 10.3
Electricity, gas, and water 12.7
Other services sectors 3.8
Primary sectors 36.1
Manufacturing 21.4

Note: Primary sectors comprise agriculture and mining and quarrying. The share of mining and quarrying is 36%, while the share of agriculture is 0.1%.
Source: Authors' calculations based on the Orbis database.

Next, we measure sectoral distribution of output through gross value added. Figure 1.3 shows that during 2010–2018, the primary sector alone accounts for 45.7% of total output. Similarly, the manufacturing; construction; electricity, gas, and water; and information and communication sectors' contribution to total output during 2010–2018 is estimated to be 12.7%, 13.2%, 7.5%, and 10.3%, respectively. Overall, the contribution of the services sector to SOE output remained around 21%.

In most of the selected developing member countries (DMCs) in our study, SOEs also provide employment opportunities to the labor force. The sectoral distribution of SOE employment shows that the manufacturing sector absorbs 30% of the labor force, followed by primary sectors which employ about 25% of workers. The construction, information and communication, trade and transport, and energy and water sectors also contribute a significant share in employment (Figure 1.4).

Figure 1.3: Distribution of Output by Sector, 2010–2018
(%)

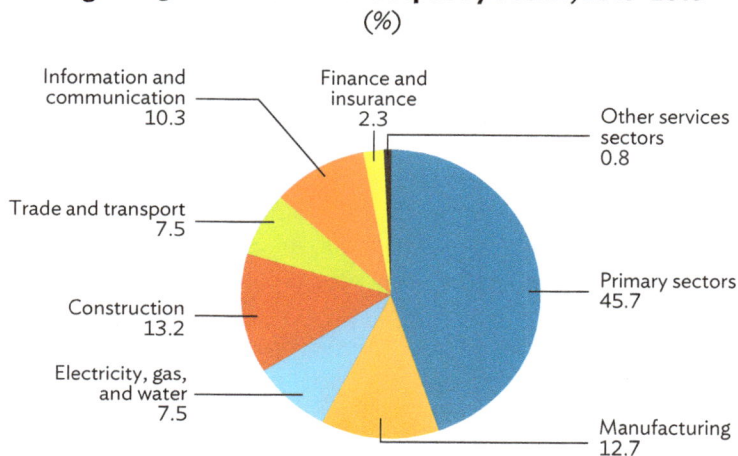

Information and communication 10.3
Finance and insurance 2.3
Other services sectors 0.8
Trade and transport 7.5
Primary sectors 45.7
Construction 13.2
Electricity, gas, and water 7.5
Manufacturing 12.7

Note: Primary sectors comprise agriculture and mining and quarrying. The share of mining and quarrying is 45.6%, while the share of agriculture is 0.1%.
Source: Authors' calculations based on the Orbis database.

Figure 1.4: Sectoral Distribution of Employment, 2010–2018
(%)

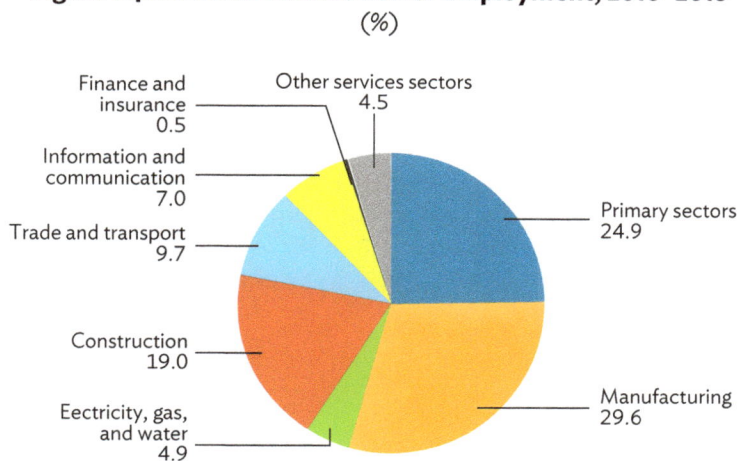

Finance and insurance 0.5
Other services sectors 4.5
Information and communication 7.0
Primary sectors 24.9
Trade and transport 9.7
Construction 19.0
Eectricity, gas, and water 4.9
Manufacturing 29.6

Note: Primary sectors comprise agriculture and mining and quarrying. The share of mining and quarrying is 24.8%, while the share of agriculture is 0.1%.
Source: Authors' calculations based on the Orbis database.

1.5   SOEs' Financial Performance and Objectives

In analyzing the various measures of efficiency and profitability of public enterprises, it is important to interpret SOE financial performance data with great caution. SOEs typically have public service obligations imposed on them, such as price suppression, servicing uneconomic markets, and various employment-related restrictions. They may not have full commercial freedom in their managerial appointments, capital acquisitions, and product mixes. More broadly, the government may regard them as "agents of development," which entails additional noncommercial obligations.

Viewed in this context, most public enterprises are not expected to be financially profitable since they provide crucial public goods and are engaged in promoting regional development. For example, the provision of public services in remote areas might not be as financially profitable as in urban areas; nevertheless, such services are equally important for inclusive and sustained development.

In many cases the financial analysis of SOEs is practically meaningless, because of the plethora of explicit and implicit subsidies and obligations affecting their operations (Box 1.1). Unlike private enterprises, the government provides various types of subsidy and capital injections to SOEs when their sources of revenue fall short of covering costs or when they are avoiding default. The subsidies may include privileged market power (i.e., restrictions on barriers to entry and other anticompetitive provisions), state-supported or guaranteed access to preferential finance, and sales/contract guarantees. These subsidies may be so large as to crowd out productive private sector investment, as appears to be the case in Viet Nam. Given these various considerations, on net, the profitability and efficiency of SOEs tend to be generally lower than their private counterparts.

Box 1.1: Soft-Budget Constraint and Implicit Subsidies

State-owned enterprises (SOEs) often enjoy implicit and explicit government guarantees for borrowing and preferential treatment to sustain their operations. Generally, these companies tend to have easy access to credit and capital injections, as well as various types of subsidies, which puts them at a clear advantage over private sector firms which generally do not have such privileges.

To perform a quantitative assessment of these preferential treatments, we compare SOEs' actual profits vis-à-vis their "potential profits," which is defined as the level of profits had these companies attained an "efficient" ROE*, i.e., the efficient risk-weighted cost of equity and basically the long-term average return on equity (ROE) for United States (US) and emerging market economies (PROSPERA unpublished). Typically ROE* turns out to be around 12%.

A finding that SOEs' actual profits are higher than potential profits suggests that public enterprises are getting an undue advantage from the government, which would explain their higher profits relative to their private counterparts—this can be treated as an implicit surplus. On the other hand, lower actual profits relative to potential profits would suggest forgone profits or the existence of an implicit subsidy. Accordingly, the implicit subsidy/surplus can be calculated using the following equation:

$$\text{Implicit Subsidy/Surplus} = \text{Profit} - [\text{Equity} \times \text{ROE}^*]$$

The estimated implicit subsidy (if negative) or surplus (if positive) is based on an assumed ROE* of 12%—which is the 10-year average of ROE on the US stock market (through 2018) and approximately the long-term average ROE for overall emerging markets.[a] A persistently large and positive (surplus) would suggest that the advantages enjoyed by SOEs (such as state monopoly or cheap financing) outweigh the drags on performance (such as unremunerated public service obligations and governance issues). On the other hand, a largely negative subsidy reflects the amount of "forgone profits" and implies that SOEs are, on net, underperforming. The forgone profits could be considered implicit subsidies.

The following graph provides a comparison of implicit subsidy/surplus for different countries covering the period 2010–2018 (Figure B1.1.1).

In Figure B1.1.1, the horizontal line signifies that actual profits of SOEs are equal to potential profits. Positive deviations from the horizontal line imply an implicit surplus while negative deviations suggest an implicit subsidy. Although SOEs' actual profits are cyclical in nature, for the purpose of analysis we are focusing on average implicit subsidy or surplus during 2010–2018.

Continued on next page

Box 1.1 continued

Figure B1.1.1: Implicit Subsidies, 2010–2018
(% of GDP)

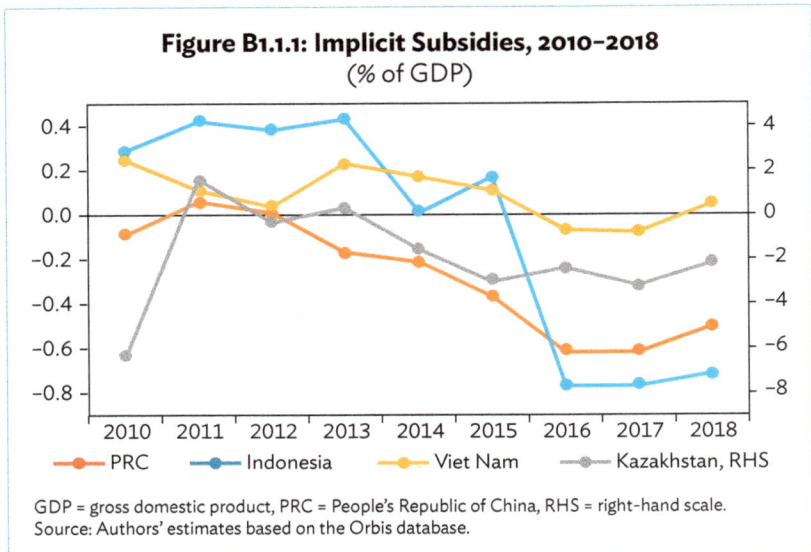

GDP = gross domestic product, PRC = People's Republic of China, RHS = right-hand scale.
Source: Authors' estimates based on the Orbis database.

The analysis suggests that in the People's Republic of China the total amount of implicit subsidies during 2010–2018 was 2.5% of gross domestic product (GDP). Kazakhstan follows at 2.4% of GDP, and Indonesia at 0.6% of GDP. On the other hand, SOEs in Viet Nam during the same period had implicit surplus (1.0% of GDP), indicating state monopoly or cheap financing was made available to these companies.

[a] The US and emerging market ROEs are from the Damodaran NYU Stern database. http://pages.stern.nyu.edu/~adamodar/ (accessed 8 January 2018).
Source: Authors.

1.6   Productivity and Efficiency Analysis

Improved productivity in providing goods and efficiency in delivering services remain the core issues of policy making in both developed and developing countries. Governments worldwide are increasingly under great pressure to upgrade the performance of the public sector and to identify best practices in delivering cost-effective public services.

Given the large presence of SOEs in some developing countries, there is considerable scope for these institutions to contribute to growth and efficiency. Since the public sector output makes up a substantial share of GDP in these countries, any effort to boost economy-wide productivity must also include measures to enhance the productivity and efficiency of these enterprises. However, improving efficiency does not only mean reducing spending; it also encompasses the entire process of delivering public services in a more cost-effective, efficient, and timely manner.

Governments will need to rely on several factors—there is no single key driver—to increase the efficiency of the public sector and SOEs. The efficiency with which an enterprise utilizes its resources is affected by market and incentive structure (Jakob 2017). For example, there is ample room for enhancing the efficiency and quality of public service delivery by improving service design and by using markets and competition and new technology. Since there is no one-size-fits-all formula to achieve efficiency, we draw valuable insights from the diverse approaches adopted by OECD economies since the early 1990s to introduce institutional reforms to the public sector. The main findings of the literature regarding public sector efficiency suggest that measures such as strengthening competitive pressures, transforming workforce structure, improving the size and skills of the workforce, and introducing results-oriented approaches to budgeting and management can be instrumental in enhancing SOE efficiency (Curristine, Lonti, and Joumard 2007).

In the subsequent section, we examine SOE productivity and efficiency by analyzing various measures, which provide valuable insights in understanding SOE underperformance and highlight the areas with significant scope for further improvement.

Productivity Analysis: First, we look at the results of sales per worker across countries. In this context, nominal sales of SOEs in each country are deflated by the respective index of GDP deflators (2010=100), giving us the series of real sales. In the second step, labor productivity is captured through the ratio of real sales to employment in different countries during 2010–2018 (Figure 1.5).

The analysis shows that productivity growth was highest in the Republic of Korea (13.3%) followed by the PRC (10.2%). In all other countries, labor productivity declined between 2010 and 2018. Changes in labor productivity can be attributed to either changes in labor productivity of the individual sectors or the structural shift in resources between contracting and expanding sectors. The results reveal that the growth in labor productivity mainly originated from productivity increases in individual sectors. On the other hand, the contribution of structural change, i.e., the movement of labor from low to high productivity sectors has remained limited (Table 1.1).

Figure 1.5: Trends in Labor Productivity of SOEs, 2010–2018
(2010=100)

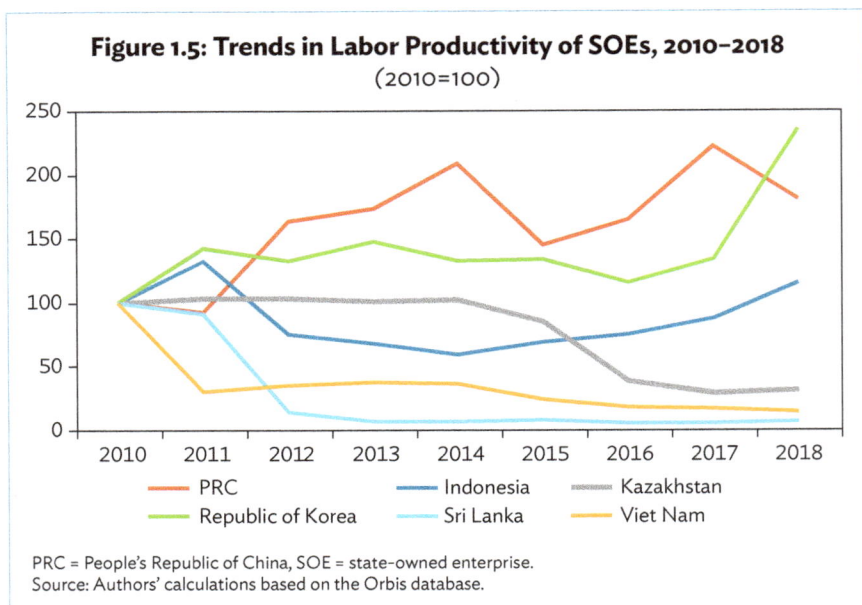

PRC = People's Republic of China, SOE = state-owned enterprise.
Source: Authors' calculations based on the Orbis database.

Table 1.1: SOEs' Productivity Decomposition, 2010–2018
(%)

	Static Shift Effects	Within Shift Effects	Dynamic Shift Effects	Productivity Growth
PRC	0.7	14.0	(4.5)	10.2
Indonesia	(5.1)	2.0	(0.2)	(3.4)
Republic of Korea	35.2	11.2	(33.2)	13.3
Kazakhstan	17.3	(8.2)	(17.8)	(8.6)
Sri Lanka	(11.6)	(0.5)	0.0	(12.1)
Viet Nam	1.3	(10.5)	(2.2)	(11.4)

( ) = negative, PRC = People's Republic of China, SOE = state-owned enterprise.
Source: Authors' calculations based on the Orbis database.

Efficiency Analysis: Governments across the world operate in an increasingly complex and unpredictable environment and are striving to improve access to and quality of public services while also ensuring value for money. Since SOEs are increasingly important actors in developing countries, more and more attention has been focused on the issue of SOEs performing efficiently. In the following section, we analyze various aspects of SOE efficiency.

Asset Turnover Ratio: To measure the efficiency with which SOEs in different sectors utilize their assets productively, we use the asset turnover ratio for the period 2010–2018. The asset turnover ratio measures the efficiency of a company's assets to generate revenue or sales. It is equal to net sales divided by total or average assets of a company. Table 1.2 presents the average assets turnover ratio during 2010–2018 for different sectors. A company with high asset turnover ratio operates more efficiently compared with other firms in the same industry. Hence, a higher ratio indicates a more efficient use of assets, while a lower ratio indicates that the firm in that industry is not utilizing its assets efficiently. Industries with low profit margins tend to generate a higher ratio, and capital-intensive industries tend to report a lower ratio.

Table 1.2: Average Assets Turnover Ratio, 2010–2018

	PRC	Indonesia	Kazakhstan	Republic of Korea	Sri Lanka	Viet Nam
Mining and quarrying	0.57	0.28	0.38	0.33		1.19
Manufacturing	0.66	0.09	0.58	1.28		0.60
Electricity and gas	0.50	0.04	0.40	0.36		1.15
Construction	0.75	0.58	0.18	1.21		0.45
Wholesale and retail trade	1.78	0.00	0.53	0.78		1.70
Transportation and storage	0.18	0.53	0.35	0.20		0.79
Accommodation and food services	0.42	0.06	0.09	0.33	0.20	0.61
Information and communication	0.41	0.59	0.68	1.23		0.53
Real estate activities	0.20	0.28		0.06		0.45
Professional activities	0.48	0.00	0.05	0.62		1.09
Public administration and defense	0.03			2.31		0.28
Education	0.25		0.20	2.46		3.34
Total	**0.52**	**0.25**	**0.34**	**0.93**	**0.20**	**0.76**

PRC = People's Republic of China.
Note: Turnover ratio = sales-to-assets ratio.
Source: Authors' calculations based on the Orbis database.

In the manufacturing sector, SOEs in the Republic of Korea have a higher assets turnover ratio (1.3) compared with similar firms in other countries. Companies engaged in providing construction, information and communication, public administration, and education services in the Republic of Korea also performed better during 2010–2018 compared with similar companies in other countries. On the other hand, SOEs in wholesale and trade performed well in the PRC and Viet Nam and have higher asset turnover ratios. Likewise, SOEs in sectors such as mining and quarrying, electricity and gas, transportation and storage, and accommodation and food services performed better in Viet Nam. As discussed earlier, a lower ratio of companies in the same industry indicates poor efficiency, which may be due to poorly utilized fixed assets or relatively poor inventory management.

Allocative Efficiency of Capital: To analyze the allocative efficiency of the capital employed by SOEs, we use return on capital employed (ROCE), a ratio that captures the profitability and efficiency with which SOEs use their capital. ROCE is the operating profit or loss before tax as a share of capital employed. Hence, this measure basically captures the efficiency by which the sum of shareholders' equity and debt are deployed to generate profits.

The analysis suggests wide disparity in the use of capital employed by SOEs in different sectors. For example, average ROCE during 2010–2018 ranges from 0.8% in financial and insurance activities to 11.8% in mining and quarrying sector. Prominent sectors with relatively higher ROCE are manufacturing (9.5%), electricity and gas (9.2%), construction (8.9%), information and communication (9.9%), and professional and administrative services (7.1%). On the other hand, SOEs operating in water supply and sewerage, accommodation and food services, and financial and insurance services have lower ROCE, implying less efficient use of capital (Figure 1.6).

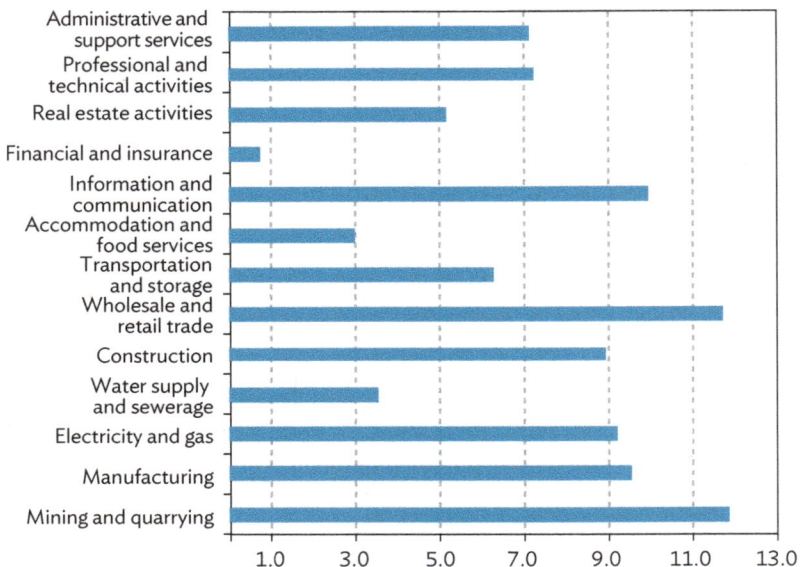

Figure 1.6: Return on Capital Employed, Average, 2010-2018, (%)

Source: Authors' calculations based on the Orbis database.

Allocative Efficiency of Labor: Next, we analyze the allocative efficiency of labor employed by SOEs in different countries and compare it with private firms. Allocative efficiency of labor captures how efficiently SOEs and private firms allocate labor for different activities. We basically compare the average cost of labor per capita in SOEs vis-à-vis private enterprises. The average cost of labor includes basic salary, taxes, benefits, allowances, contributions, and other perks and bonuses of all employees including top management. The analysis reveals that in general allocative efficiency of labor for SOEs across our sample countries is lower than their private counterparts. On average, cost of labor per capita in SOEs has remained higher than in the private firms (Figure 1.7).

Figure 1.7: Average Cost of Employees in SOEs
(percentage of cost in private firms)

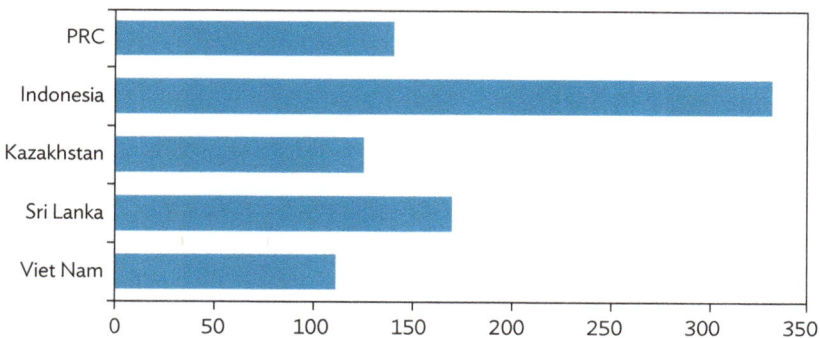

PRC = People's Republic of China, SOE = state-owned enterprise.
Note: Data set is the average for the period 2010–2018.
Source: Estimates based on Orbis (Bureau Van Dijk). https://www.bvdinfo.com/en-gb (accessed October 2019).

While SOEs incur larger labor costs than private firms in all countries, the difference is more pronounced in the PRC, Indonesia, and Sri Lanka where average cost of labor per capita is significantly higher than in private firms. On the other hand, in the case of Viet Nam, cost of labor is marginally higher than their private counterparts.

1.7   Return on Equity and Profitability

In this section, we examine the return on equity (ROE) and profitability of SOEs. A comparison of ROEs indicates that on average SOEs lag behind private firms in profitability, which implies that SOEs have not succeeded in generating profits from the money shareholders invested. The analysis shows that generally the rate of return for private firms is higher than public companies (Figure 1.8).

Figure 1.8: Average Return on Equity, SOEs versus Private Firms, 2010–2018

(%)

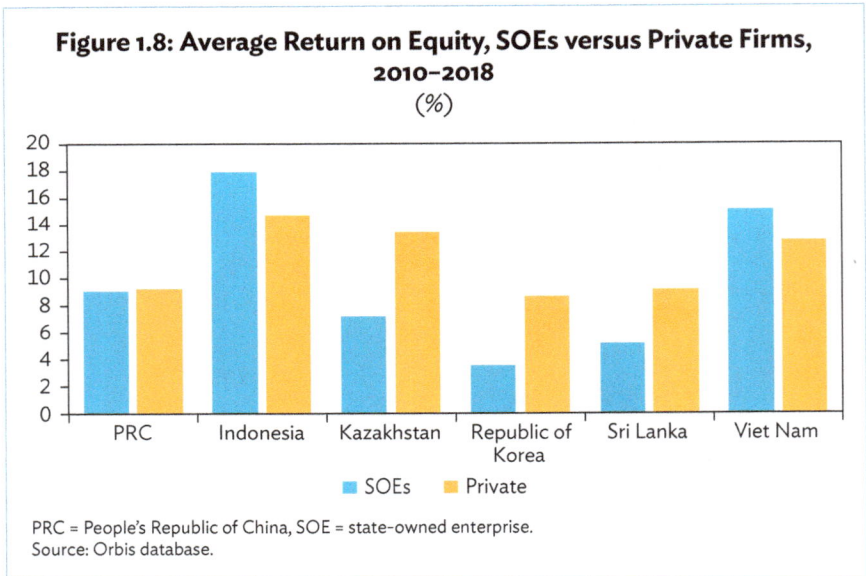

PRC = People's Republic of China, SOE = state-owned enterprise.
Source: Orbis database.

In the Republic of Korea, the ROE of private firms is substantially higher than that of SOEs. The average ROE during 2010–2018 for private firms was 8.6% compared with 3.5% for SOEs. A similar trend is observed in other Asian countries except for Viet Nam and Indonesia where the ROE of SOEs is higher than that of private firms. It is important to note that in most countries, SOEs are often privileged to have access to credit and receive various types of government subsidies, which precludes a level playing field for private firms. Hence, the higher ROEs of SOEs do not necessarily reflect good performance but may be a result of the advantages given to them by the government.

Next, we compare the ROE for SOEs and private listed companies across different sectors and countries. For this purpose, we compute the percentage-point differences between the ROEs of SOEs and private companies (Table 1.3).

Table 1.3: Average of Percentage-Point Differences between Return on Equity of SOEs and Private Listed Companies, 2010–2018
(%)

Sector	PRC	Indonesia	Kazakhstan	Republic of Korea	Sri Lanka	Viet Nam
Agriculture	5.1	(17.6)	(11.9)	(14.7)	(17.6)	(17.1)
Industry	1.2	1.8	(33.7)	(4.8)	(16.6)	1.2
Mining and quarrying	0.8	(6.0)	(53.5)	(13.5)	(13.3)	(2.5)
Manufacturing	(1.0)	(6.4)	(45.4)	(20.2)	(24.1)	(3.3)
Electricity, gas, and water	2.4	11.0	(2.1)	(0.3)	(18.8)	8.9
Construction	2.6	8.6		14.5	(10.3)	1.8
Services	(0.2)	(10.3)	(25.8)	(8.3)	(8.7)	(4.3)
Trade	1.4	(20.1)	(2.6)	(8.9)	(11.3)	(2.0)
Transport and communication	(0.2)	(45.0)	(13.8)	(10.2)	(15.7)	(4.5)
Hotels and restaurants	1.8	(6.5)	1.5	(9.8)	(5.0)	1.3
Financial services	2.9	(8.3)	(15.6)	(17.9)	(7.0)	(16.2)
Real estate activities	(4.6)	0.8	(64.9)	(8.5)	3.1	(8.9)
Business services	1.0	3.1	2.0	2.0	(14.2)	6.1
Public administration	5.2	0.0	0.0	0.0	(8.0)	(16.1)
Education and health	(14.6)	(14.0)	0.0	(8.2)	(19.9)	2.5
Other services	5.5	(2.9)	0.0	(12.7)	0.1	(0.8)

( ) = negative, PRC = People's Republic of China, ROE = return on equity, SOE = state-owned enterprise.
[a] Percentage-point difference between the ROEs of SOEs and private listed companies.
Source: Authors' calculations based on the Orbis database.

Generally, the analysis shows that SOE profitability is significantly lower than privately owned firms in similar sectors. For example, the ROE of SOEs in the agriculture sector is about 17.1 percentage points lower than privately owned firms in Viet Nam. Similarly, SOEs in other countries have shown varying degrees of underperformance. SOE underperformance is more pronounced in Kazakhstan where the industry sector ROE is about 33.7 percentage points and the services sector is 25.8 percentage points lower than private companies. However, services sector firms in the PRC have smaller differences in their ROEs relative to private enterprises. The analysis corroborates the viewpoint that generally SOE performance and efficiency lag behind their private counterparts. As discussed, SOE underperformance can be partly attributed to the government's provision of soft budget constraint and various types of subsidies which do not incentivize SOE management to work in a competitive environment. On the contrary, private enterprises often operate in a competitive market which helps improve their efficiency.

Next, we analyze the earnings before interest and taxes (EBIT) margin of SOEs. EBIT is operating earnings over operating sales, which enables entrepreneurs to understand the true costs of running their company. Lower EBIT margins indicate lower profitability, which could either be an outcome of the competitive landscape in which case all firms in an industry have lower profits or the result of lower sales and higher costs. Since taxes vary by location and are not part of day-to-day core operations, using EBIT allows the comparison of companies on a level playing field.

Table 1.4 provides sector-wise EBIT margins for different countries. For example, in the Republic of Korea, the EBIT margin is higher in construction, business services, and public utilities. Comparison across countries reveals that in financial services, real estate, public administration, and other services, EBIT is much higher in the PRC than in other countries.

Table 1.4: Average of Earnings Before Interest and Taxes Margins, 2010–2018
(%)

	PRC	Indonesia	Kazakhstan	Republic of Korea	Sri Lanka	Viet Nam
Agriculture, forestry, and fishing	6.0	0.0	0.0	6.8	0.0	(0.4)
Mining and quarrying	6.5	15.5		15.1	0.0	6.1
Manufacturing	6.2	12.9	(1.4)	0.0	0.0	7.7
Electricity and gas supply	20.2	25.6	8.8	29.0	0.0	16.7
Construction	4.7	9.3	15.5	0.0	0.0	10.5
Trade	5.9	0.0	0.0	0.0	0.0	2.4
Transportation and storage	7.9	22.2	0.0	27.9	0.0	6.4
Hotels and restaurants	10.6	15.4	0.0	0.0	10.1	3.1
Financial services	36.2	0.0	0.0	11.1	0.0	(110.7)
Real estate activities	23.2	21.1	0.0	(1.2)	58.3	0.0
Business services	11.6	21.4	12.3	0.0	0.0	10.2
Public administration	22.7	0.0	0.0	0.0	0.0	(17.0)
Education and health	0.0	0.0	0.0	0.0	0.0	11.7
Other services	31.8	0.0	0.0	0.0	0.0	6.5

( ) = negative values, EBIT = earnings before interest and taxes, PRC = People's Republic of China.
Source: Authors' calculations based on the Orbis database.

1.8   Quality of Output

This section evaluates the quality of output and public service delivery of SOEs across countries. In the absence of detailed data on SOEs' quality of output, we use infrastructure data. Additionally, since most SOEs are engaged in providing various infrastructure-related services, a comparison of infrastructure ranking across countries could provide some insight into the quality of the SOEs' output (Figure 1.9).

Figure 1.9 shows that in all aspects of infrastructure development, the Republic of Korea outperformed other countries. The higher quality of infrastructure could also indicate good performance of the public enterprises providing these services, which may partly explain the Republic of Korea's higher economy-wide productivity compared with other countries. One way to enhance output quality is to galvanize SOEs by promoting competition among public and private companies.

The evidence corroborates the view that competition is more important than ownership—in the 1980s for example, the Republic of Korea succeeded in improving quality of services by increasing competition among companies. In this context, the government set up a new state-owned telecommunication company which competed with existing SOEs in providing international call services, thus enhancing the quality of services. Competition could also be increased by liberalizing a sector dominated by private enterprises and letting it compete with SOEs that are supplying a partial substitute.

For example, in the United Kingdom, following the liberalization of bus services in the 1980s, the government allowed bus services to compete with the state-owned rail company thereby enhancing the quality of public services.

Another way to promote competition is to push SOEs to export and compete internationally and domestically, like the Republic of Korea did with the Pohang Iron and Steel Company (POSCO) in the 1970s. The company started production in 1973 and by the mid-1980s, it was considered one of the most cost-efficient producers of low-grade steel in the world (Chang 2013).

Figure 1.9: Quality of Output

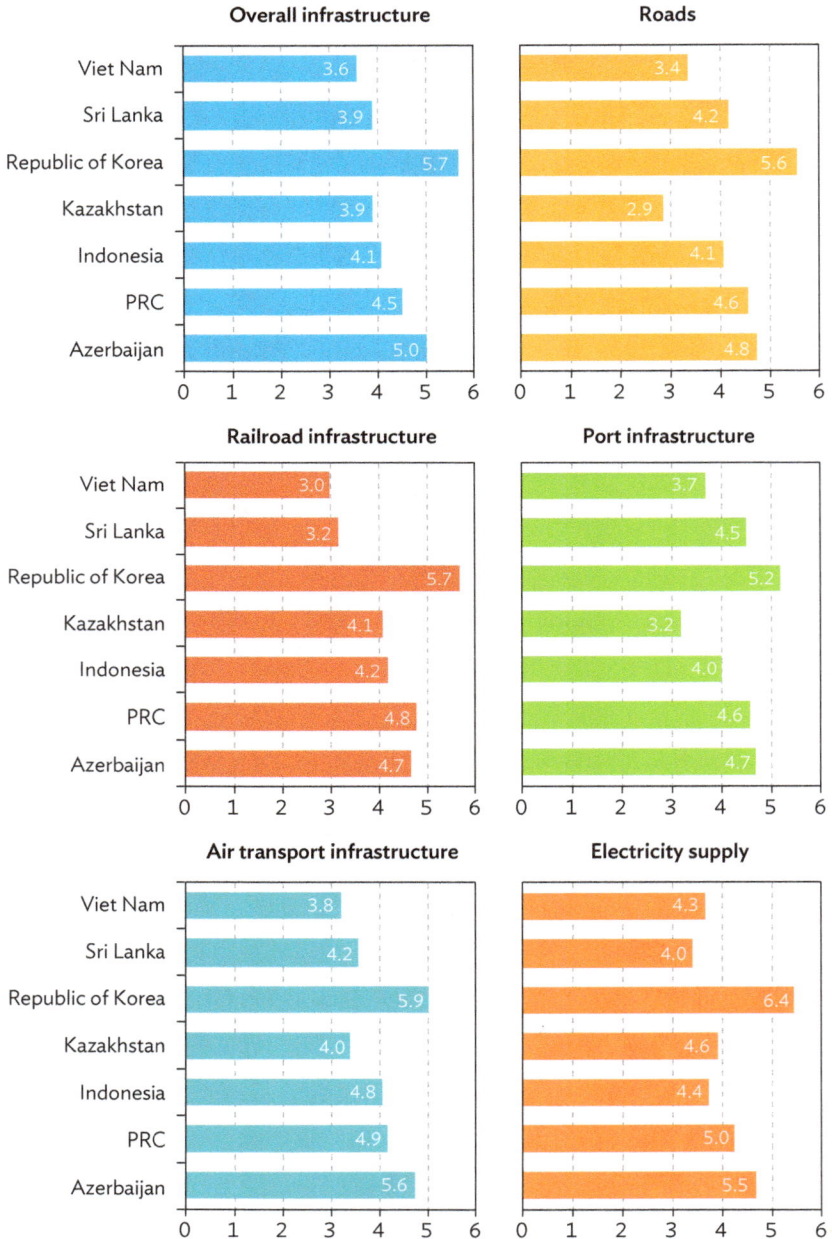

Overall infrastructure

Viet Nam	3.6
Sri Lanka	3.9
Republic of Korea	5.7
Kazakhstan	3.9
Indonesia	4.1
PRC	4.5
Azerbaijan	5.0

Roads

Viet Nam	3.4
Sri Lanka	4.2
Republic of Korea	5.6
Kazakhstan	2.9
Indonesia	4.1
PRC	4.6
Azerbaijan	4.8

Railroad infrastructure

Viet Nam	3.0
Sri Lanka	3.2
Republic of Korea	5.7
Kazakhstan	4.1
Indonesia	4.2
PRC	4.8
Azerbaijan	4.7

Port infrastructure

Viet Nam	3.7
Sri Lanka	4.5
Republic of Korea	5.2
Kazakhstan	3.2
Indonesia	4.0
PRC	4.6
Azerbaijan	4.7

Air transport infrastructure

Viet Nam	3.8
Sri Lanka	4.2
Republic of Korea	5.9
Kazakhstan	4.0
Indonesia	4.8
PRC	4.9
Azerbaijan	5.6

Electricity supply

Viet Nam	4.3
Sri Lanka	4.0
Republic of Korea	6.4
Kazakhstan	4.6
Indonesia	4.4
PRC	5.0
Azerbaijan	5.5

PRC = People's Republic of China.
Source: World Economic Forum (2018).

1.9   Public Asset Management and Macroeconomic Risks

In many developing countries, large deficits and contingent liabilities of SOEs are major reasons for high and rising government deficits. The global financial crisis was a painful reminder to governments to not only improve the effectiveness of SOEs but also to maintain ample fiscal space for applying an effective fiscal stimulus. As SOEs contribute significantly to economic development in emerging markets, their poor performance especially as they incur heavy losses, poses substantial macroeconomic risks to fiscal policy and financial stability. In some countries, SOEs have accumulated large amounts of debt particularly in the energy and transport sectors. Large debt and rising contingent liability along with a poorly regulated banking sector can potentially destabilize the finance sector, with negative spillovers likely affecting overall economic performance.

The quality of public asset management is one of the crucial building blocks that divide well-run countries from poorly governed countries. Better management is not just about financial returns, but other important social gains as well. It is worth emphasizing that a systematic assessment of the public sector's assets across countries can increase transparency and accountability and provide valuable insights into their evolution over time (Detter and Folster 2015).

Introducing international best practices, such as transparency, proper accounting, and realistic balance sheets,[8] can be particularly helpful in improving the quality and worth of public assets. Recent research by the International Monetary Fund (IMF) (2018) comprising 31 countries and covering 61% of the global economy suggests that with proper management, even a higher return of only 1% on public wealth worldwide can add about $750 billion annually to public revenues. Similarly, professional management of public assets such as SOEs among central governments can raise returns by as much as 3.5% and generate an extra $2.7 trillion worldwide. These are substantial gains and are more than the total current global spending on national infrastructure for transport, power, water, and communications combined (Detter and Folster 2015).

Recent episodes of financial crises have exposed many countries to external demand shocks and reemphasized the importance of effective management

---

[8]   The public sector balance sheet consists of the assets and liabilities of general government and public corporations, including the central bank. Hence, it brings together all of the accumulated government-controlled assets and liabilities (IMF 2018).

of public assets and SOEs. The huge size of public wealth across countries and the scars from the global crisis underline the necessity to effectively manage public assets. Further, it is also essential for governments to rebuild their balance sheets by reducing debt and investing in high-quality assets (Detter and Folster 2015). For example, once governments understand the size and nature of public assets and start managing them efficiently, the potential gains could be as high as 3% of GDP a year. These are quite substantial gains and roughly equal to annual corporate tax collections across advanced economies (IMF 2018).

It is, however, important to note that the long-term objective of governments is not merely to maximize the net worth of public assets, but to provide quality goods and services as well. Nevertheless, effective asset management allows governments to raise expenditures during times of crisis and help maintain macroeconomic stability. Viewed in this context, governments that believe their net worth is too low to ensure these objectives may choose to improve the net worth of public assets as one of their operational goals. Empirical evidence corroborates the fact that financial markets consider governments' asset positions in addition to debt levels when determining borrowing costs. One way to gain insight on the health of the government's public finance is to examine its public sector balance sheet. As empirical evidence shows (Figure 1.10) countries that have a strong balance sheet and professional management of public assets have had a quick economic recovery (IMF 2018).

Figure 1.10: Public Asset Management and Economic Recovery
(percentage change)

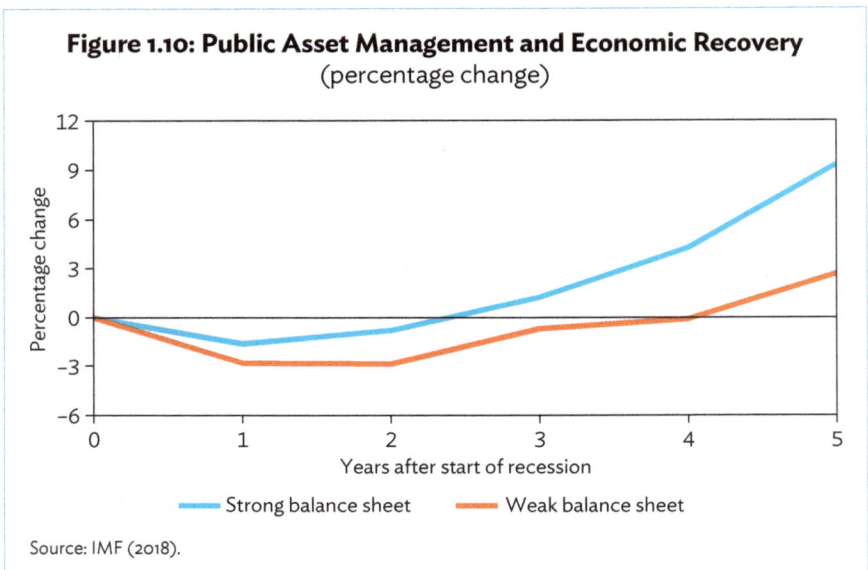

Source: IMF (2018).

Figure 1.10 shows that economies entering a slump with a strong balance sheet and with ample fiscal space are better able to mitigate the impact of the recession and are quick to recover. Economic recovery in these economies started approximately after the second year from the start of the recession. On the contrary, those with a weak balance sheet suffered the adverse impact of the recession on a relatively longer scale and started to recover only four years after the recession began.

This discussion shows that a systematic analysis of the public sector's balance sheet and that of its assets provides a broader fiscal picture beyond debt and fiscal deficits. As a result, governments and policy makers are in a better position to allocate resources optimally. Effective asset management enables governments to identify risks and take remedial measures in due time rather than deal with the consequences after problems occur. Hence, efficient management of public assets and SOEs not only help improve fiscal position but also quality of public service delivery.

1.10   Reforming and Restructuring SOEs

Early SOE Reforms and Privatization: Evidence from the 1970s and 1980s suggest that, on average, SOEs in many countries have performed poorly compared with private firms, partly because of the difficulty reconciling multiple policy goals. The ensuing heavy financial loss becomes an unsustainable burden on the public budget and banking system. Consequently, various governments since the 1980s have introduced reforms such as exposing SOEs to competition, imposing hard budget constraint, and introducing institutional and managerial changes. As a result, many SOEs were commercialized and eventually corporatized into separate legal entities, and governments developed performance contracts with SOEs to monitor performance and hold managers accountable for results (World Bank Group 2014).

Many developing countries have drafted laws to regulate SOE operations in an effort to improve SOE performance. But without meaningful corporate planning and independent management, many laws and regulations virtually proved to be a pro forma exercise not much relevant to enhancing the performance of public enterprises. In several countries, frequent transfers of managers, directors, and supervisors also diminished the commitment to meet the long-term needs of these enterprises. Even so, SOE managers generally had to face a number of disincentives to adapt to new challenges—especially as many of these companies were insulated from market signals, with their prices controlled, their market protected, and for whom government loans were readily available.

The early reforms introduced by governments across the globe produced some improvements but fell short in implementation. Generally, autonomy in commercial decision-making remained limited, and more importantly, employing financial discipline during a period of hard budget constraint proved difficult without the corresponding restrictions on SOE borrowing from the banking system and from state-owned banks in particular. Implementing performance contracts with SOE management also proved problematic and produced mixed results.

The modest outcome of reforms led many countries to privatize SOEs. During the 1990s and in the early 2000s, financial and nonfinancial SOEs were privatized through various means such as auctions, strategic sales, vouchers, public stock offerings, and management and employee buyouts. The privatization of SOEs was perceived to be a means to eliminate SOE deficits from the national budget, attract private investors with capital and managerial know-how, and achieve efficiency gains through SOE reforms. As a result, the number of SOEs globally declined.

However, privatization was often handled poorly, creating wealth for a few and sometimes leading to high prices for essential goods and services. In developing countries, privatization of SOEs raised concerns and roused sensitivities about foreign ownership of strategic enterprises, and generally proved to be unpopular with the public because of higher infrastructure tariffs and employment losses. As a consequence, widespread privatization stopped around 2000 (World Bank Group 2014).

In the aftermath of the 2007–2008 global financial crisis with capital markets in turmoil, investors' interests waned and SOE privatization slackened. Governments bailed out failed banks and public enterprises in emerging markets including the PRC, contributing to a dramatic increase in government purchases of corporate equity which had already started in 2008 (Reverditto 2014). Ironically, the crisis itself triggered a new debate on the effective role of government in economic affairs from which emerged a growing interest in public enterprises (World Bank Group 2014).

Modern SOE Reforms: Worth noting also from the viewpoint of improving the performance of public enterprises is that privatization is not the only option. Other intermediate solutions are available as well, such as for example: (i) the government can sell some shares of an SOE and still retain majority control; (ii) the government can retain its whole or majority ownership and contract out management only in certain sectors; or (iii) the government can restructure SOEs and make them more efficient drivers of growth. Indeed, evidence indicates that restructuring is often more important than privatization (Chang 2013). The Philippines' case study provides invaluable insights about the importance of private sector participation and reforms, which helped transform a loss-making public company into a commercially viable entity (Box 1.2).[9]

Box 1.2: SOE Reforms – Manila Water

The Metropolitan Waterworks and Sewerage System (MWSS), a state-owned enterprise (SOE) in the Philippines, tells the story of how improving governance and fostering competition have enhanced public service delivery. The MWSS is an interesting example of how the public–private partnership concept can be used to transform a once ailing public company into a commercially viable one.

Before the 1997 reforms, the underperforming MWSS was burdened by large debts. Unable to invest in much-needed water system improvements, it provided poor water quality and intermittent supply. System losses due to poor service and leaks in 1997 amounted to almost 60%, while water coverage was a mere 67%, of which only 26% had 24/7 water supply. In addition, non-revenue water hit almost 60%. The government was unable to increase water tariffs because customers were unwilling to pay for poor service. Furthermore, the MWSS suffered from poor financial performance. Eventually, the Philippines faced a severe water crisis triggered in part by the events that followed El Niño during the 1990s.

Prompted to resolve the crisis, the government selected the concession model to introduce reforms. This led to two separate concession agreements with Maynilad and Manila Water for waterworks rehabilitation, both spanning 25 years. It divided Metro Manila into two areas—east and west. The government assigned Manila Water to be responsible for the east zone and put Maynilad in charge of the west. It introduced reforms and brought in investments in both hard and soft infrastructure and adopted a corporate-style governance, aiming specifically to improve water delivery and wastewater services to existing customers, enhance operating efficiency, and expand service coverage.

As a result of the reforms, water coverage in 2002 increased to 82% for Manila Water and 78% for Maynilad from only 67% before the privatizations. Water availability rose to 21 hours from under 17 hours, and the quality of water improved significantly. The reforms also succeeded in bringing in efficiency gains while reducing operational costs. Likewise, the ratio of staff to 1,000 connections fell from 9.8 to 4.1.

Source: Authors, based on Chia et al. (2007).

---

[9] It is worthwhile to note that after 18 years of MWSS privatization, water supply has significantly improved. Nevertheless, the current arrangement is far from perfect, and Metro Manila still experiences water shortages. On top of that, the government has recorded about 38 million cases of diarrhea annually due mainly to poor sanitation and hygiene. Tap water is still not safe to drink. The government is once again considering to revisit the concession agreement and introduce further reforms to improve the quality and quantity of water.

In many developing countries, SOEs are generally attached to a sector ministry, with the Ministry of Finance often playing the key role. However, the oversight of sector ministries often appears to be questionable, and combined with rampant interventions, undermines the performance of public companies. These ministries are responsible for making decisions pertaining to SOE investments and expansion, which directly influence the quality of public service delivery. But, improving the oversight and the caliber of these ministries is a difficult and challenging task. Malaysia is an example of successful SOE restructuring where state investment funds oversee SOEs or government-linked companies (GLCs) (Box 1.3).

Box 1.3: SOE Restructuring – A Case Study of Malaysia

Malaysia's experience in restructuring and managing SOEs, or government-linked companies (GLCs) in Malaysian nomenclature, provides interesting insights in the use of key performance indicators (KPIs), linking the performance of SOEs to remuneration of management.

In 2004, the Government of Malaysia embarked on the Transformation Program, a comprehensive reform program of GLCs. The government aimed to improve the performance of GLCs and convert them into profitable, financially self-sufficient enterprises. The program adopted realistic objectives in line with international best practice.

Overall, five key factors contributed to the success of GLC transformation:

1. the establishment of a government body with a clear mandate and objectives in relation to enhancing the performance of GLCs;
2. development and monitoring of KPIs;
3. sound accountability framework for delivering results;
4. strong focus on profitability; and
5. appointment of qualified professionals.

A central body in the Transformation Program was the Putrajaya Committee on GLC High Performance chaired by the deputy finance minister and comprising representatives of all key SOE shareholders and experts. Shortly after its establishment in 2005, the committee produced in 2006 a guidebook, Blue Book: Guidelines on Announcement of Headlines KPIs and Economic Profit (OECD 2016). The book established KPIs to be reported by GLCs in a consistent manner, aligning expectations at all levels.

Continued on next page

Box 1.3 continued

The book tasked every GLC to annually file KPIs concerning its financial, nonfinancial, organizational, and operational goals, which were audited and benchmarked with comparable international peers. Based on the audit, the committee analyzed causes of underperformance and was able to mitigate weaknesses in a timely and targeted manner.

In addition to KPIs, the committee introduced performance-based contracts and compensation schemes, along with a change in the composition of GLC board members and senior management. The Malaysian government upgraded the legal and operational framework of the GLCs to corporatize them and infused into GLCs newer management practices from the private and public sectors. The new management received a clear mandate along with indicators to improve SOE performance. Performance-based contracts linked GLC performance to the remuneration of GLC management, which meant that management had similar incentives as those in the private sector.

These reforms helped instill a performance-based culture and improved GLC management, which subsequently translated into higher GLC profitability—between 2004 and 2014, 20 of Malaysia's largest GLCs operating overseas tripled their market capitalization.

Source: Authors, based on OECD (2016).

One way to improve oversight is to introduce a central SOE organization, while reforms are introduced to sector ministries. To minimize the ad hoc ministerial interventions in SOE matters, some developing countries have introduced a central oversight or coordinating organization. This central body typically reports only to the President or Prime Minister, the cabinet, or a special interministerial group. By breaking the one-on-one relationship between the sector ministries and the managing director, the central coordinating organization introduces a check and balance against political intervention. Despite rather mixed reviews of its track record, such an organization can be beneficial to improving the coordination between different stakeholders. Lessons from the experience of different countries suggest that the central oversight body would be more successful if it has a small and dedicated staff, the full support and backing of the competent authority, and a clear mandate to deal with relevant ministries.

To maintain a balance between autonomy and accountability, governments in some developing countries have established holding companies by creating conglomerates, thereby increasing the size and power of SOEs vis-à-vis ministries—this can work in favor of autonomy. However, there are certain pros and cons for such an arrangement. For example, by exploiting economies of scale, these holding companies can work more efficiently in the international capital and export markets than smaller companies. In such a setup, it is relatively easier to liquidate a nonviable subsidiary than a freestanding SOE; at the same time, these holdings also provide an effective buffer against political interference.

On the negative side, large holdings comprising mainly unrelated subsidiaries often tend to become very political and bureaucratic in nature. If there is still political interference, these huge conglomerates may promote monopolistic or oligopolistic behavior. Under such circumstances, instead of closing nonviable operations, these holdings may shift funds, inventories, and skilled staff from profitable units to nonperforming units, keeping alive nonviable firms and thus dragging down the performance of the holdings (Shirley 1989).

1.11 Relevance of SOEs in Asia's Next Transition

Developing Asia's economy has grown robustly at 6.9% per annum during 1970–2019. A comparison of per capita incomes across the region suggests that in the early 1960s, a majority of the population was living in low-income economies; however, by 2018, most of them lived in middle-income countries. This experience has motivated policy makers and governments to prepare for Asia's transition to high-income status. Can Asia's success guarantee a similar transition from middle income to high income and can the improved performance of SOEs facilitate the transition?

Experience across economies has revealed the structural difference of middle-income and low-income economies, and that graduation from middle income to high income can be quite challenging. An examination of the Asian economies that have transitioned successfully to high-income status suggests that improvement in productivity played an important role in their transition and in sustaining high growth over a longer period. For example, in Asia, Singapore; Hong Kong, China; the Republic of Korea; Taipei,China; and Malaysia are the only economies that have transitioned to high-income status (Figure 1.11).

Empirical evidence reveals that to meet the challenges of middle-income transition, countries need more cutting-edge technologies and frontier innovation to sustain knowledge diffusion as their income levels rise. This would

Figure 1.11: GDP per Capita (current $), 1960 and 2018

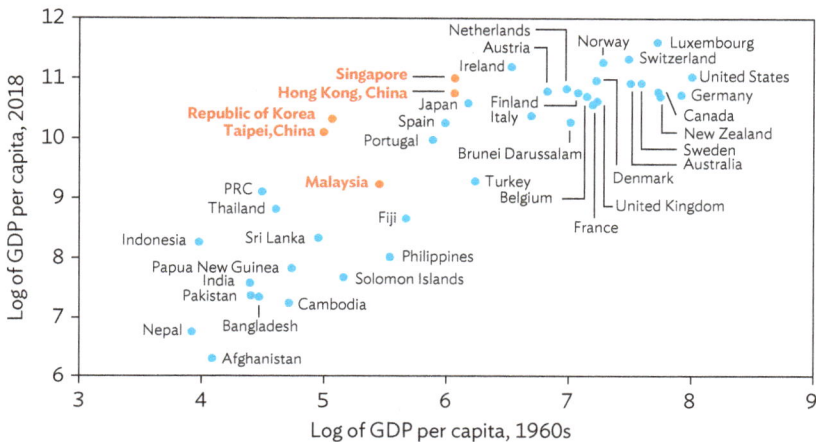

GDP = gross domestic product, PRC = People's Republic of China.
Notes: Data for Brunei Darussalam start in 1965; for Indonesia and Solomon Islands, 1967; for Germany, 1970; and for all others, 1960.
Sources: For Taipei,China: countryeconomy.com (accessed January 2020); and for all others: World Bank. World Development Indicators. https://datacatalog.worldbank.org/dataset/world-development-indicators (accessed January 2020).

require greater investments in human capital and research and development (R&D) thereby allowing countries to adopt globally existing technologies. Another priority would be to ensure that the relatively more productive enterprises in an economy are able to engage in and reap the benefits of the latest innovations.

In Figure 1.12, the comparison of per capita income and the innovation score reveals that economies already in advanced stages of development tend to score better on innovation. On the other hand, lower-income and middle-income economies also score lower on innovation. This suggests that economies that have adopted policies promoting competition and a level playing field perform better in producing quality products.

The capability to innovate and to bring innovation successfully to the market is crucial in improving the global competitiveness of DMCs. However, it is equally possible for economic growth and other macro factors to affect innovation activities, implying that in practice both innovation activities and economic growth can bring about the other, and therefore there is a potential for feedback relationship between the two (Maradana et al. 2017).

Figure 1.12: Innovation and Economic Growth

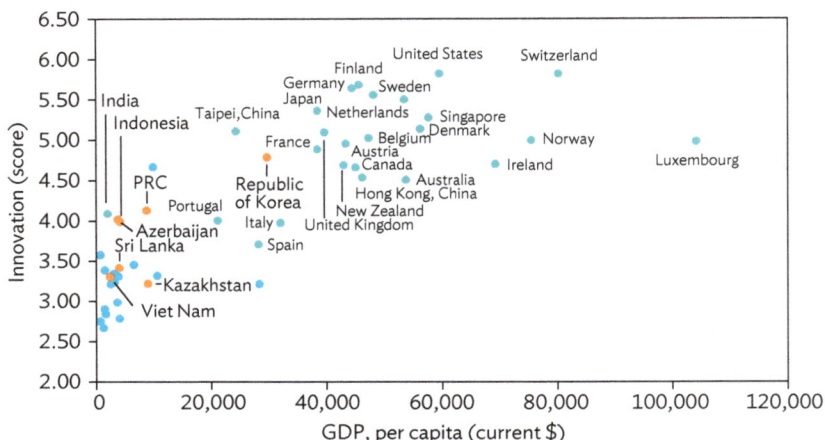

GDP = gross domestic product, PRC = People's Republic of China.
Sources: World Economic Forum. *The Global Competitiveness Report 2017–2018*. Geneva; and World Bank. World Development Indicators. Washington, DC.

To promote innovation-led growth, DMCs should ensure the growth of innovative enterprises to an efficient scale and also encourage the entry of new firms while discouraging the survival of less-productive entrepreneurs. The political economy and the quality of existing institutions will likewise play a more prominent role as a country approaches the technology frontier (Aghion and Bircan 2017).

The prevalence of SOEs and state ownership in developing countries suggests that governments should promote policies that create a level playing field and a sense of dynamism in public companies to foster innovation. This will require a balance between the SOEs' objectives and the services that private entrepreneurs are better able to produce. The idea is that policy objectives and instruments should be tailored to a country's level of development and the strengths and weaknesses of its innovation system. More importantly, governments need to increase R&D expenditure to promote a culture of innovation. DMCs can enhance such a transition through reforming SOEs and making them an efficient driver of growth.

An examination of economies that have transitioned successfully from low-income to high-income status reveals that the role and nature of the public sector changes in parallel with the stages of development. For example, at early development stages when the private sector is not yet fully developed, the public sector can play a significant role in promoting economic development. During this stage, governments often have relatively better human capital, and public policies and programs mainly focus on identifying key development bottlenecks and coordinating capacity-building efforts in infrastructure and human capital. With weak private financial institutions, it is also challenging to secure financing for large-scale projects, and private investors remain reluctant. In such cases, government financing and SOEs could take the lead in providing the necessary infrastructure for economic development. The Republic of Korea's experience emphasizes the importance of the changing role of the public sector in different stages of development (Box 1.4).

Box 1.4: The Role of the Public Sector – A Case Study of the Republic of Korea

The Republic of Korea is a classic case demonstrating the usefulness and merits of government flexibility in adopting a different role at each phase of development. In the early stages of development, governments typically select the sectors to invest in. However, as economies develop and modes of production become more complex, the role of the private sector increases.

Economic development in the Republic of Korea can be divided into three distinct phases. During the first phase (1962–1979), the government played a major role in leading development and mobilizing resources to promote economic development. In the second phase (1980–1989), government control became indirect and implicit, rather than explicit. At the same time, the private sector rapidly grew, increasing its investments especially in the finance sector. In the third phase (1990 to present), the government became a facilitator while the private sector took the lead. After the Asian financial crisis in 1997, it became clear that government failure brought more danger than market failure, thereby diminishing the government's role in the economy (Figure B1.4.1).

For example, in the early stages of development, the government was active in selecting sectors and supported economic growth mainly by increasing the inputs of labor and capital. Despite extensive state intervention in economic affairs, the government managed to contain corruption and rent-seeking. More importantly, as market capacity and the state and non-state actors changed, their respective roles began to shift as well. The 1997 economic crisis provided an opportunity to introduce market-based discipline, clean up massive nonperforming loans, improve corporate governance, promote competition, and strengthen the social safety net.

Continued on next page

Box 1.4 continued

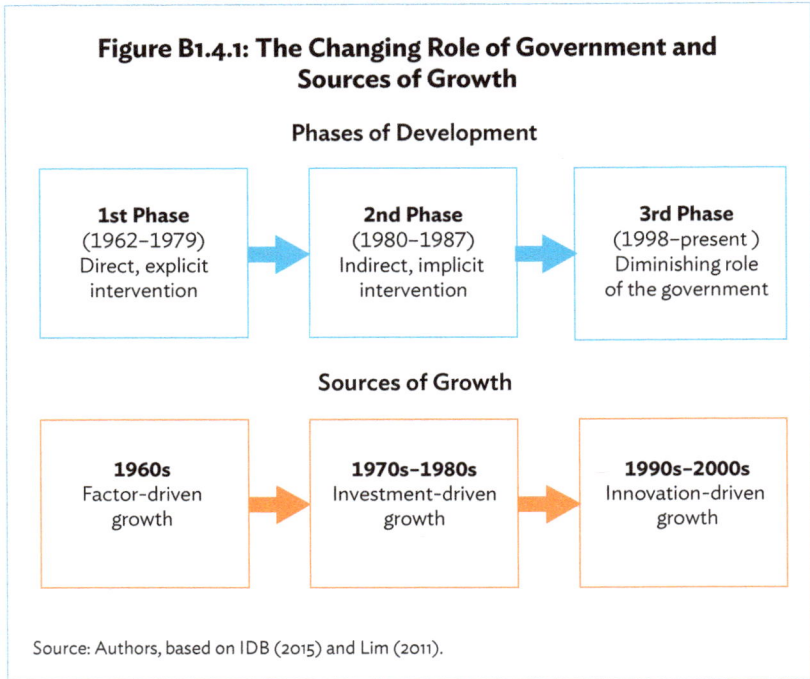

Figure B1.4.1: The Changing Role of Government and Sources of Growth

Phases of Development

1st Phase (1962–1979) Direct, explicit intervention	→	**2nd Phase** (1980–1987) Indirect, implicit intervention	→	**3rd Phase** (1998–present) Diminishing role of the government

Sources of Growth

1960s Factor-driven growth	→	**1970s–1980s** Investment-driven growth	→	**1990s–2000s** Innovation-driven growth

Source: Authors, based on IDB (2015) and Lim (2011).

As the private sector grew stronger, the focus of government support shifted to "indicative" targeted industries, and assistance was confined to research and development efforts and to promote private sector development. Additionally, the government invested massively in information technology and infrastructure and succeeded in improving science and technology capacity and in facilitating productivity-led growth.

The Republic of Korea's economy evolved throughout the development process—relying initially on factor-driven growth before transitioning to productivity-led growth in which the private sector played a more dominant role. More significantly, government policies instilled a sense of competition and dynamism, enabling the public sector to compete and improve its delivery of public services. The government provided a level playing field to promote the private sector, addressed the problems of innovation and coordination externalities through public–private partnership, and helped promote productivity-led growth.

Source: Authors, based on Lim (2011) and IDB (2015).

Empirical analysis[10] based on the Orbis database for the selected countries in our study also corroborates the probability of significant gains when factors of production are allocated more appropriately. The results reveal that with improved corporate governance and efficient utilization of resources, SOEs' output in Kazakhstan and Indonesia can be expanded by at least 17% and 32%, respectively. Similarly, in the PRC, at least 9% additional output can be produced with a similar level of input. On the other hand, both Sri Lanka and Viet Nam, which are far away from the efficient frontier, can substantially enhance SOEs' output with proper allocation of resources (Figure 1.13).

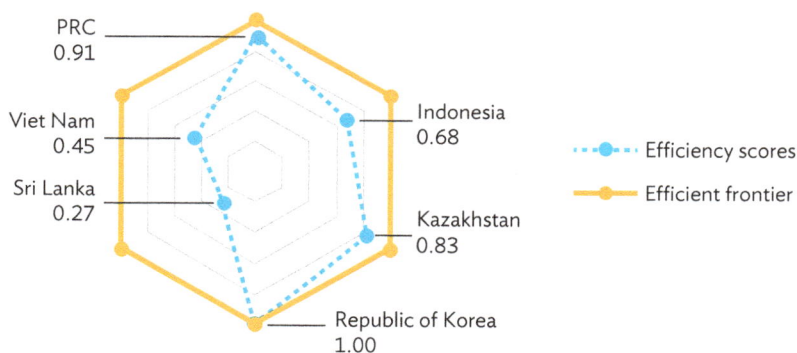

Figure 1.13: Efficient Frontier and Relative Efficiency, Average 2010–2018

PRC 0.91
Viet Nam 0.45
Sri Lanka 0.27
Indonesia 0.68
Kazakhstan 0.83
Republic of Korea 1.00

· · ·●· · · Efficiency scores
━━●━━ Efficient frontier

PRC = People's Republic of China.
Source: Authors' estimates derived from data envelopment analysis based on the Orbis database.

The foregoing discussion suggests that with proper allocation of resources, the output of SOEs and public service delivery can be improved substantially in countries within the efficient frontier. DMC governments should make best use of available resources to improve SOE performance, thus helping enhance the quality of public services. Productivity-induced growth is not only important in coping with the challenges of middle-income countries, it is also crucial in bridging the gap between nations.

[10] These results are based on the data envelopment analysis which captures the operational efficiency of SOEs in the selected countries. Appendix A1.2 provides more details.

Governments will need to employ state-of-the-art technology and find ways to make enterprises more efficient and innovative. Furthermore, a level playing field and a competition-oriented environment will encourage private sector entrepreneurs and new firms to come forward and help achieve innovation-led growth.

1.12 Pathways to SOE Reform

Countries have adopted different approaches to SOE reform, as dictated by political preferences, general economic conditions, institutional capacities, interactions with international development agencies, and several other factors. There is no "one-size-fits-all" approach to SOE reform. As noted, some countries have opted for a "big bang" approach to privatization during their transition from a planned to market-oriented economy. In other countries, external factors have been significant, such as the PRC's reforms as a condition of World Trade Organization entry, and Indonesia's reforms as part of its 1997–1998 IMF crisis rescue package.

What follows here are illustrations of various options drawn from country experiences and organized around the general objective of improved enterprise efficiency, consistent with the national development objectives of inclusive and sustainable growth.

1. Hard budget constraint. This option is an essential prerequisite for SOE reform—SOEs must manage their operations within defined financial parameters. Budget constraints impose a discipline on the management of SOEs. They also protect the country's fiscal position. The absence of hard budget constraint was the single most important explanation for the occurrence of hyperinflation in transition economies (such as Viet Nam), when SOEs, and state-owned banks in particular, accumulated very large deficits which in turn central banks monetized. An explicit provision for contingent liabilities is also essential, within and beyond the SOE sector.

2. Transparency. SOE operations are frequently not transparent. The direct subsidies they receive are often not reported in the government's budget, and the indirect subsidies are not costed. Politically, the absence of public accountability makes reform very difficult.

3. Explicit costing for public service obligations. SOEs typically carry many public service obligations (PSOs), which need to be explicitly costed and accounted for in any SOE performance evaluation. In most cases, such estimations are relatively straightforward. If a state-owned electricity utility is required to service customers (or a segment of them) at an uneconomic price, the difference between the market price and regulated price is the cost of the PSO. Similarly, if an SOE transport provider is required to provide below-cost services (for example, as an alternative to a congestion tax), this PSO can likewise be estimated.[11]

4. Public asset management. Professional and better management of public assets can increase transparency and accountability and lead to higher financial and social gains. Experience across countries suggest that professional management of public assets allows governments to raise expenditures during times of crisis and help maintain macroeconomic stability. Recent episodes of financial crises have further underscored the importance of effective management of public assets and SOEs. Hence, efficient management of public assets and SOEs not only help in improving the fiscal position but also in raising the quality of public service delivery.

5. The importance of competition. The regulation of SOEs that operate in competitive markets is relatively straightforward. The performance of SOEs can be benchmarked against private sector competitors, factoring in any subsidies and PSOs. As a corollary, it is important to remove any regulatory constraints on competition (e.g., barriers to private sector entrants). For tradable activities, this also includes ensuring that import competition operates without hindrance. This is an important area of work for the region's nascent competition commissions.

6. SOEs and "natural monopolies." SOEs are frequently found in sectors that may be described as having "natural monopoly" characteristics, that is, with a declining long-term average cost over all feasible levels of output. In practice, the definition of a natural monopoly is not straightforward. For example, electricity generation and transmission were once considered to be such a case, and therefore best suited to a sole supplier. However, new solar generation technologies are radically changing the sector's economics. The same applies to mobile telephony services.

For other cases of natural monopolies, mainly in the utilities sector, regulation is a key issue whether or not the sector is state-owned. The appropriate policy regime is one in which an independent, arms-length regulator monitors and, if necessary, determines pricing and service quality. Such a body of course

---

[11] It is important of course to benchmark the full cost of the service against some independently agreed figure, not the one a possibly inefficient SOE provides. In the case of incomplete markets (for example, information asymmetries), these prices may not be readily available. International benchmarks can be an option.

assumes high-level governance capabilities. To improve the public service delivery, governments should introduce professional management and enhance the corporate governance of SOEs.

7. Sequencing matters—getting privatization "right." As argued above, privatization is one possible SOE reform option. However, it should be regarded as the final step in the process, after all the preliminary reforms have been completed. These include establishing an appropriate regulatory/competitive framework, accurate and transparent financial reporting, and explicit costing of any remaining PSOs.

Privatization remains a politically controversial issue in several countries. In these cases, opening the SOE sector to private sector competition is a more palatable option, as in the case of the 1997 reform of Manila Water.

If privatization is to be pursued, it is also crucial to handle the process of divestment in an open, competitive, and nonpolitical environment that maximizes the return to the state. There are well-documented cases, mainly in the transition economies in which SOEs are disposed of at highly concessional prices to the politically well-connected (termed "insider privatization" in the PRC). In such cases, it is arguably preferable not to proceed with privatization.

1.13 Summing Up

SOEs are major commercial entities, invariably larger than commonly realized, and typically more important in developing Asia and Pacific economies than in the advanced economies. They are particularly important in sectors that have weak competitive pressures, and in sectors such as mining and natural resources that are commonly bedeviled by governance problems. Their size and their generally indifferent performance highlight the importance of reform.

There is no template or single path to reform, as approaches will differ depending on institutions, history, and political preferences. However, there are common elements of a reform agenda, including the importance of hard budget constraint, financial accounting transparency, competitive market structures, and a regulatory framework that protects the public interest. It may be the case that privatization is the preferred approach, but this will be effective only if the necessary prerequisites are in place.

Appendix A1.1: Labor Productivity Decomposition and Shift–Share Analysis

The changes in SOE labor productivity across countries can further be decomposed into different components. Following Ichihashi et al. (2013), changes in total labor productivity can be written as follows:

$$\frac{\Delta LP_i}{LP_i^o} = \sum_j (\Delta S_{ij}) \frac{LP_i^o}{LP_i^o} + \sum_j \frac{\Delta LP_{ij}}{LP_i^o} S_{ij}^o + \sum_j (\Delta S_{ij}) \frac{\Delta LP_{ij}}{LP_i^o}$$

where subscript "i" denotes a country, subscript "j" denotes a sector, LP is labor productivity, S is the share of sector in employment, a superscript "o" indicates the year 2009, and Δ indicates a change over 2009–2017. The first term in this equation is "static shift effect," which is followed by "within shift effect" and "dynamic shift effect":

(i) **Static Shift Effect:** Productivity growth due to relocation of labor between different sectors is measured through "static shift effect." A positive value of static shift effect would indicate that the share of high productivity industries in total employment increases at the expense of industries with low productivity. Hence, static shift effect measures the impact on total productivity resulting from the movement of labor between sectors.

(ii) **Within Shift Effect:** This component measures the impact of productivity growth within each sector on total productivity growth, assuming sector labor shares are unchanged. Hence, it is unaffected by changes in the employment share and thus isolates the contribution due solely to productivity improvement within a sector. It captures how much of the changes in aggregate productivity can be explained by the change in labor productivity within an individual sector.

(iii) **Dynamic Shift Effect:** The last component measures the change in both labor share and productivity in each sector. It therefore accounts for the impact of labor reallocation between sectors with varying productivity growth rates. A positive sign for "dynamic shift effect" implies that the fast-growing sectors in terms of productivity growth also increase their share of total employment.

Source: Authors', based on Ichihashi et al. (2013).

Appendix A1.2: Data Envelopment Analysis and Operational Efficiency

Data envelopment analysis (DEA) is a linear programming-based technique for measuring the relative performance of organizational units in which the presence of multiple input and output makes comparisons difficult. The usual measure of efficiency may be defined as the ratio of output to inputs; however, such a measure is often inadequate because of the existence of multiple input and output related to different resources, activities, and environmental factors.

The DEA model allows relative efficiency measures for multiple input and output. The measurement of relative efficiency where there are multiple possibly incommensurate input and output was addressed by Farrell (1957) and developed by Farrell and Fieldhouse (1962), who focused on the construction of a hypothetical efficient unit, as a weighted average of efficient units, to act as a comparator for an inefficient unit. A common measure for relative efficiency can be defined as follows:

Efficiency = weighted sum of outputs/weighted sum of inputs, which can be written as

$$\text{Efficiency of unit j} = \frac{u_1 y_{1j} + u_2 y_{2j} + \dots}{v_1 x_{1j} + v_2 x_{2j} + \dots},$$

where u_1 = the weight given to output i
y_{1j} = amount of output 1 from unit j
v_1 = weight given to input 1
x_{1j} = amount of input 1 to unit j

Efficiency is usually constrained to the range [0, 1]). Charnes, Cooper, and Rhodes (1978) have proposed that each unit should be allowed to adopt a set of weights which shows it in the most favorable light in comparison to the other units. Under these circumstances, the efficiency of a target unit j0 can be obtained as a solution to the following problem:

Maximize the efficiency of unit j0, subject to the efficiency of all units being < =1.

The solution of the equation produces the weights most favorable to unit j0 and produces a measure of efficiency. Linear programming is the underlying methodology that makes DEA particularly powerful compared with alternative productivity management tools. The solution to this linear programming provides a measure of the relative efficiency of the target unit and the weights leading to that efficiency.

Measuring Operational Efficiency

Operational efficiency is defined as the capability of an enterprise to deliver goods and services to customers in a timely and cost-effective manner using strategies and techniques. We capture operational efficiency of SOEs by using DEA. In measuring the efficiency of SOEs, the DEA method assesses the relative efficiency of public enterprises in countries including the People's Republic of China (PRC), Indonesia, Kazakhstan, the Republic of Korea, Sri Lanka, and Viet Nam. In this context, data on output and inputs of the SOEs were compiled for the years 2009–2017. For the purpose of analysis, gross profits and sales are treated as output while number of employees and capital used in the production process represent inputs.

The results of the analysis reveal that, during 2009–2017, SOEs in the Republic of Korea with an overall efficiency score of 0.88 are more efficient compared with those in other countries. This is followed by the PRC, Kazakhstan, and Indonesia with an efficiency score of 0.79, 0.73, and 0.59, respectively. On the other hand, SOEs in Sri Lanka and Viet Nam with an average efficiency score of 0.24 and 0.39, respectively, have the lowest efficiency ratings.

Next, in order to compare the performance of SOEs across different countries, we compute the relative efficiency scores. Since the Republic of Korea has the highest efficiency rating (0.88), we divide the efficiency scores of other countries by the efficiency score of the Republic of Korea, which gives us the relative efficiency rating. We then define an "efficient frontier"—with a maximum efficiency rating of 1.0—that can be achieved with optimal utilization of available resources. This "efficient frontier" is represented by the outermost polygon while the estimated efficiency scores are reflected by the vertex of the inner polygon in Figure 1.13 (in Chapter 1). The inefficiency of SOEs across countries is then measured through their relative distance from the efficient frontier.

The results of the analysis show that, during 2009–2017, the Republic of Korea with a relative efficiency of 1.0 lies on the efficient frontier. Other countries with efficiency ratings of less than 1.0 typically lie inside the efficient frontier, reflecting various degrees of inefficiency. For example, the PRC's relative efficiency of 0.91 implies an efficiency rating of 91%, suggesting that SOEs were using 9% excess resources compared with the efficiency threshold of 100%. This implies that with efficient resource allocation, at least 9% additional output can be produced with a similar level of inputs. On the other hand, the relative efficiency ratings for Kazakhstan and Indonesia are 0.83

and 0.68, respectively, suggesting that with improved corporate governance and efficient utilization of resources, SOEs' output in these countries can be expanded by at least 17% and 32%, respectively. Additionally, the analysis also reveals that both Sri Lanka and Viet Nam are far away from the efficient frontier, reflecting relatively poor performance of SOEs in these countries.

Source: Authors, based on Huguenin (2012).

References

Aghion, P. and C. Bircan. 2017. The Middle-Income Trap from a Schumpeterian Perspective. *ADB Economics Working Papers Series*. No. 521. Manila: ADB.

Chang, H.-J. 2007. State-Owned Enterprise Reform. National Development Strategies Policy Notes. United Nations: Department for Economic and Social Affairs. https://esa.un.org/techcoop/documents/PN_SOEReformNote.pdf.

_____. 2013. The Worst Business Proposition in Human History: The Appropriate Role of State-Owned Enterprises in Developing Countries. *Cuadenro De Economia*. Segunda Epoca (2). pp. 139–144.

Charnes, A., W. W. Cooper, and E. L. Rhodes. 1978. Measuring the Efficiency of Decision Making Units. *European Journal of Operational Research*. 2 (6). pp. 429–444.

Chia, P. et al. 2007. Water Privatization in Manila, Philippines: Should Water be Privatized? A Tale of Two Water Concessions in Manila. Economics and Management in Developing Countries. INSEAD.

Curristine, T., Z. Lonti, and I. Joumard. 2007. Improving Public Sector Efficiency: Challenges and Opportunities. *OECD Journal on Budgeting*. 7 (1). Paris: OECD.

Detter, D. and S. Folster. 2015. *The Public Wealth of Nations: How Management of Public Assets Can Boost or Bust Economic Growth*. London: Palgrave Macmillan.

Farrell, M. J. 1957. The Measurement of Productive Efficiency. *Journal of the Royal Statistical Society*. Series A (120 [III]). pp. 253–281.

Farrell, M. J. and M. Fieldhouse. 1962. Estimating Efficient Production Functions under Increasing Returns to Scale. *Journal of the Royal Statistical Society*. Series A (125). pp. 252–267.

Huguenin, J-M. 2012. *Data Envelopment Analysis (DEA): A Pedagogical Guide for Decision Makers in the Public Sector*. Lausanne: IDHEAP.

Ichihashi, M. et al. 2013. Structural Change, Labor Productivity Growth, and Convergence of BRIC Countries. Development Discussion Policy Paper. 3 (5). Japan: Graduate School for International Development and Cooperation, Hiroshima University.

Inter-American Development Bank (IDB). 2015. Governance, Performance, and the Best Reform Practices in State-Owned Enterprises in Latin America and the Caribbean and Korea. Forum Report and Proceedings from the International Symposium. Seoul, Republic of Korea. 5–8 November 2013.

International Monetary Fund (IMF). 2018. *Fiscal Monitor: Managing Public Wealth.* Washington, DC.

Jakob, B. 2017. Performance in Strategic Sectors: A Comparison of Profitability and Efficiency of State-Owned Enterprises and Private Corporations. *The Park Place Economist.* 25 (1). https://digitalcommons.iwu.edu/cgi/viewcontent.cgi?article=1458&context=parkplace.

Kim, C. J. and Z. Ali. 2017. Efficient Management of State-Owned Enterprises: Challenges and Opportunities. Policy Brief. No. 2017-4. Tokyo: ADBI. https://www.adb.org/sites/default/files/publication/390251/adbi-pb2017-4.pdf.

Lim, W. 2011. Joint Discovery and Upgrading of Comparative Advantage: Lessons from Korea's Development Experience. A presentation for the Korea Development Institute.

Maradana, R. P. et al. 2017. Does Innovation Promote Economic Growth? Evidence from European Countries. *Journal of Innovation and Entrepreneurship.* https://doi.org/10.1186/s13731-016-0061-9.

Musacchio, A. and S. G. Lazzarini. 2012. Leviathan in Business: Varieties of State Capitalism and Their Implications for Economic Performance. *Harvard Business School Working Paper.* 12–108.

Orbis. Bureau van Dijk. https://www.bvdinfo.com/en-gb/our-products/data/international/orbis (accessed 10 January 2019).

Organisation for Economic Co-operation and Development (OECD). 2016. *State-Owned Enterprises in Asia: National Practices for Performance Evaluation and Management.* Paris. https://www.oecd.org/ corporate/SOEs-Asia-Performance-Evaluation-Management.pdf.

PricewaterhouseCoopers (PwC). 2015. State-Owned Enterprises: Catalysts for Public Value Creation?. https://www.pwc.com/gx/en/psrc/publications/assets/pwc-state-owned-enterprise-psrc.pdf.

PROSPERA. Has the Private Sector Shrunk?. Unpublished paper led by Adhi Suputro and David Nellor.

Reverditto, X. B. 2014. Economic Development and State-Owned Enterprises. *Economic Development and SOEs.* SELA.

Shirley, M. 1989. The Reform of State-Owned Enterprises: Lessons from World Bank Lending. *Policy and Research Series.* No. 4. Washington, DC: World Bank.

World Bank Group. 2014. *Corporate Governance of State-Owned Enterprises: A Toolkit.* Washington, DC. https://openknowledge.worldbank.org/handle/10986/20390 License: CC BY 3.0 IGO.

World Economic Forum. 2018. *The Global Competitiveness Report 2017–2018.* Geneva.

CHAPTER 2

State-Owned Enterprises in the Republic of Korea

Hyung-Gon Jeong

2.1   Introduction

State-owned enterprises (SOEs) have played a major role in promoting economic development and in shaping the economic landscape of the Republic of Korea. During the initial stages of the country's development, one of the main roles of SOEs was to provide the necessary infrastructure that was vital to economic development and upscale private sector investments. Like many Asian economies such as Japan; the People's Republic of China; Singapore; and Taipei,China, the Republic of Korea has been successful in using state-led economic policies, especially during the start of its industrialization. SOEs became the means through which the government implemented its economic policies. In a short time, the Republic of Korea became an industrialized economy, with the state intervening in the market to establish large corporations with economies of scale.

As a consequence, many chaebols[1] and SOEs were created. Lacking the typically large initial capital stock required to establish a network of industries, developing nations may choose to establish large corporations in the form of an SOE. With a high entry barrier preventing competition, industry remained inevitably in a state of monopoly or oligopoly for a fair amount of time. In such a state, the most efficient way to operate a network of industries would be for the state to establish and run a corporate monopoly.

The Government of the Republic of Korea owned or operated, either directly or indirectly, corporations other than those established for a special purpose during industrialization. In several cases, the government took over private

---

[1]   Chaebols are large industrial conglomerates run and controlled by an owner or family in the Republic of Korea.

corporations by bailing them out when they ran into serious financial trouble or by offering debt–equity swaps when they incurred a large amount of debt to commercial banks or other creditors. As a result, the government became a major shareholder of various financial institutions engaged to control financial markets toward the country's industrialization.

SOEs in the Republic of Korea are affiliated with their respective competent authorities, who saw SOEs as a means to achieve their goals. The Ministry of Strategy and Finance, which handles budget affairs, controls the number of employees and remuneration of SOEs to ensure that they do not misuse or squander resources. Inevitably, when the private sector lacked capacity, the government used SOEs as the means to industrialize the economy, which also generated positive effects. However, the lack of an effective control system and the government's collusion with the private sector hampered the efficient operation of SOEs. Government control weakened SOEs' competitiveness— rather than focusing on maximizing the efficiency of corporations, government viewed SOEs as a policy tool, thus distorting resource allocation and causing other operational problems. As the biggest shareholder in these corporations, the government wields great influence not only upon corporations but also on the entire economy. There is a growing sentiment that governments should recognize SOEs as private corporations. Yet, from the mid-1990s up to 2002, policies pertaining to commercial SOEs remained the same (Nam 2015). This chapter analyzes the contribution of SOEs to the economic development of the country and examines the lessons to be learned from the SOE policies of the Republic of Korea.

2.2   Definition and Classification of SOEs[2]

The history of SOEs in the Republic of Korea dates back to the founding of the country in 1948. Their definition and purview have since changed numerous times. In 2008, the Ministry of Strategy and Finance classified public institutions into three groups: SOEs, quasi-government institutions, and nonclassified public institutions.

The Minister of Strategy and Finance designated as SOEs or quasi-government institutions those with at least 50 employees. Of these institutions, SOEs have a self-generating revenue amounting to or exceeding half the total revenue, while quasi-government institutions are public institutions that are not classified as SOEs.

---

[2]   This section is based on Jeong et al. (2010).

Furthermore, SOEs can be one of two types: (i) market-type (public corporations with assets amounting to or exceeding W2 trillion, or approximately $1 billion, and a self-generating revenue out of total revenue amounting to or exceeding the criterion prescribed by Presidential Decree); or (ii) quasi-market-type institutions (public corporations other than market-type public corporations). Quasi-government institutions are grouped into fund-management type (quasi-government institutions that are assigned or commissioned to manage a fund pursuant to the National Finance Act) or commissioned-service-type institutions (quasi-government institutions other than fund-management-type quasi-government institutions).

As seen in Table 2.1, market-type and quasi-market-type SOEs fall explicitly within the definition of public corporations. Many institutions exist as nonclassified public institutions in the form of de facto public corporations. As of 2017, there were a total of 338 public institutions in the Republic of Korea, of which 35 were SOEs, 93 were quasi-government institutions, and 210 were nonclassified (Table 2.2).[3] Table 2.3 presents market-type and quasi-market-type SOEs in the Republic of Korea.

Table 2.1: Classification of Public Institutions

Type	Classification Criteria
State-owned enterprises (SOEs)	$\frac{\text{Self-generating revenue}}{\text{Total revenue}} \times 100 \geq 50\%$
• Market type	Agencies with $\frac{\text{Self-generating revenue}}{\text{Total revenue}} \times 100 \geq 85\%$ and assets worth more than W2 trillion
• Quasi-market type	$50\% \leq \frac{\text{Self-generating revenue}}{\text{Total revenue}} \times 100 \leq 85\%$
Quasi-government institutions	$\frac{\text{Self-generating revenue}}{\text{Total revenue}} \times 100 < 50\%$
• Fund-management type	Institutions that handle public funds
• Commissioned-service type	Quasi-government institutions other than fund-management type
Nonclassified	Public institutions that cannot be classified as public corporations or quasi-government institutions

Note: The ratio of self-generating revenue over the total revenue is based on financial statements of the latest 3 years.
Source: Jeong et al. (2010) p. 28.

---

[3] See Ministry of Strategy and Finance (2017). Agencies in nonclassified sections that are practically operating as public corporations are financial SOEs (such as the KDB Financial Group, Industrial Bank of Korea, Korea Development Bank, Export–Import Bank of Korea, Korea Financial Corporation, and Korea Investment Corporation), national university-affiliated hospitals, national hospitals, market-type companies, and quasi-market-type mutual investment companies. Although not classified as public institutions, the Korean Broadcasting System and the Educational Broadcasting System have established and operate under their own management system, but their legal entities are close to if not similar to that of SOEs. As such, these broadcasting companies can be identified as SOEs. The Bank of Korea, on the other hand, which was founded as a noncapital special corporation according to the Bank of Korea Act, is virtually a financial SOE.

Table 2.2: Number of Designated Public Institutions, 2017

Classification	Number of Designated Institutions
State-owned enterprises	35
• Market type	15
• Quasi-market type	20
Quasi-government institutions	93
• Fund-management type	16
• Commissioned-service type	77
Nonclassified	210
Total	**338**

Source: Ministry of Strategy and Finance (2017).

Table 2.3: Market-Type and, Quasi-Market-Type SOEs in 2017

Classification	Institutions
Market-type SOEs (15)	(MOTIE) Korea Gas Corporation, Korea Resources Corporation, Korea National Oil Corporation, Korea Electric Power Corporation, Korea District Heating Corporation, Korea Midland Power Co., Ltd., Korea Hydro and Nuclear Power Co., Ltd., Korea Western Power Co., Ltd., Korea East-West Power Co., Ltd., Korea Southern Power Co., Ltd., Korea South-East Power Co., Ltd., Kangwon Land Co., Ltd. (MOLIT) Incheon International Airport Corporation, Korea Airports Corporation (MOF) Busan Port Authority
Quasi-market-type SOEs (20)	(MOSF) Korea Minting and Security Printing Corporation (MCST) Grand Korea Leisure (MAFRA) Korea Racing Authority (MOTIE) Korea Gas Technology Corporation, Korea Electric Power Corporation Engineering and Construction Company, Inc., KEPCO KDN Co., Ltd., KEPCO KPS Co., Ltd. (MOLIT) Jeju Free International City Development Center, Korea Housing and Urban Guarantee Corporation, Korea Appraisal Board, Korea Expressway Corporation, Korea Water Resources Corporation, Korea Railroad Corporation, Korea Land and Housing Corporation (MOF)Yeosu Gwangyang Port Authority, Ulsan Port Authority, Incheon Port Authority, Korea Marine Environment Management Corporation (KCC) Korea Broadcast Advertising Corporation

KCC = Korea Communications Commission; MAFRA = Ministry of Agriculture, Food and Rural Affairs; MCST = Ministry of Culture, Sports and Tourism; MOF = Ministry of Finance; MOLIT = Ministry of Land, Infrastructure and Transport; MOSF = Ministry of Strategy and Finance; MOTIE = Ministry of Trade, Industry and Energy; SOE = state-owned enterprise.
Source: Ministry of Strategy and Finance (2017).

2.3 Roles, Policies, and Reformation of SOEs in Economic Development

SOEs have played a critical role in the Republic of Korea's economic growth. With no capital, technology, or human resources during the initial phase of industrialization, the state established SOEs and had them take the lead in economic development. But efficient management is essential, particularly as SOEs have considerable influence on the overall economy.

In the 1960s and 1970s, the growth rate of SOEs in the Republic of Korea was 14.5%, higher than the annual gross national product of 9.5% (Figure 2.1). From 1961 until 2017, the annual growth rate of the country's gross domestic product (GDP) averaged 7.41%, reaching an all-time high of 19.60% in the fourth quarter of 1969 and dropping to a record low of –7.40% in the second quarter of 1998.[4] This rapid growth rate even among developing countries is the highest ever recorded during the authoritarian era.

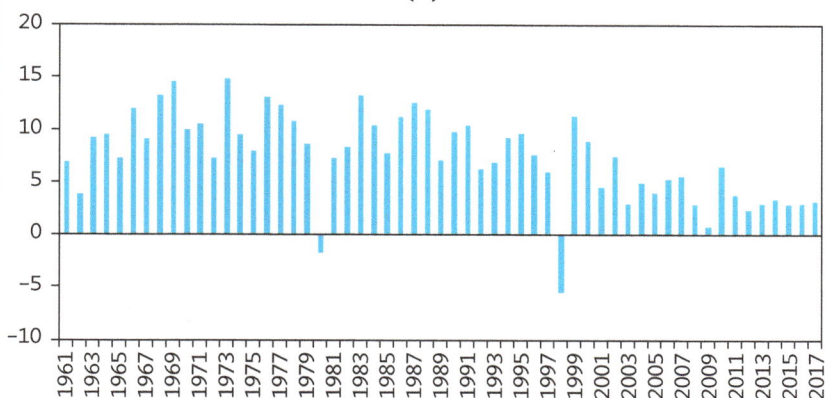

Figure 2.1: Annual Economic Growth Rate of the Republic of Korea, 1961–2017
(%)

Source: Bank of Korea. Economic Statistics System. https://ecos.bok.or.kr/EIndex_en.jsp (accessed 19 September 2018).

---

4   Trading Economics. South Korea GDP Annual Growth Rate. https://tradingeconomics.com/south-korea/gdp-growth-annual (accessed 19 September 2018).

2.3.1   The Role of SOEs in the Industrialization Process

The Government of the Republic of Korea executed the first of its 5-year economic development strategies in 1962. The dynamics of government-led industrialization in the 1960s extended across the government, capital, and finances. SOEs were established and put in charge of investment and production to control the flow of capital in the domestic market. The state's intervention had far-reaching effects in the areas of finance, taxes, labor policies, price control, trade, and customs (Yoon, S.-C 1986).

In the 1960s, the Republic of Korea's industrial policy focused on the export-oriented manufacturing industry. The central government encouraged export-driven plans for several reasons. First, there are limits to growth driven by import substitution policies. The strategic plan to exploit domestic resources did not reap benefits over the short term. Scarce resources and the limited purchasing power of a small domestic market restrained foreign direct investment. Under dire circumstances, the central government turned to export-led industries to acquire foreign currencies.

Additionally, in the wake of the Korean War in 1953, the country had amassed an excessive supply of light industry facilities, some of which had to be rerouted to export industries, taking into account the advantage of having a wealth of highly skilled labor in light industry products. Second, the Republic of Korea was uniquely positioned to attract foreign capital, especially from Japan and the United States (US). The inflow of foreign capital enabled economic growth despite a lower savings rate compared with the economies of Hong Kong, China; Taipei,China; and Singapore, all of which initiated export-driven growth (Sakong and Koh 2010). The authoritarian government might have believed that managing the flow of foreign capital by providing guarantees from state-owned banks or from the state itself and distributing it to corporate behemoths was the ideal economic strategy.

The government exercised control over the economy mainly through the banks. State-managed financial institutions wielded indirect control over the corporations under them (Jones and Sakong 1980). When industrialization burgeoned in the 1960s, the state had under it six government-run banks including the Development Bank and five commercial banks, thus gaining full control over the financial industry. During this period, the state founded other government-run banks such as the Small and Medium Industry Bank, Korea Exchange Bank, Kookin Bank, Korea Housing Bank, and Korea Trust Bank. The other five commercial banks mentioned above—Choheung Bank, Development Bank, Hanil Bank, Korea First Bank, and Seoul Bank—were eventually turned into SOEs (or government-run banks) after the coup of 16 May 1961, in the name of restitution for unjust enrichment. But the state held actual ownership of them only after 1965 when it purchased at least 40% of their shares. Thereafter, the state was able to exercise control over banks and the flow of financial resources (Yoon, S.-G 1986). The Development Bank and the other commercial banks also provided capital for domestic businesses, financing the private sector, managing corporations, and guaranteeing liabilities. The Development Bank served as a credit mobilizer as it provided long-term investment financing and guaranteed long-term foreign exchange loans, which supported the government's economic development strategies. Corporations that were controlled by financial institutions incurred significant loss after introducing foreign capital through the banks, but many of them escaped bankruptcy. Financial institutions under state jurisdiction converted the liabilities of insolvent corporations into corporate bonds or equity investment, in effect taking control of them. By wielding its power through important investment decisions to achieve its aims, the government established what is called a "controlled economy" (Yoon, S.-G 1986).

In addition to (in)direct control of banks and corporations, the government also raised its fiscal and financial investment in SOEs, exercising the type of state ownership that had formed after the May 1961 military coup. Control over domestic financial and loan markets enabled the government to initiate economic growth. The economic circumstances in the aftermath of the Korean War consequently steered the country toward state-led capitalistic growth. With very little capital, Korean industries at the time focused only on perishable goods procured with US aid and managed on a small scale. When financial aid ceased, the country lost its source of capital, forcing the state to intervene. Had multinational corporations invested in the Republic of Korea then, state policies concerning SOEs would have been completely different.

In the 1960s, the country became a major exporter of textiles. As the economy grew rapidly in the 1970s, polyester became the leading textile industry product. In the 1980s, however, export volumes started declining as the People's Republic of China and other developing nations started producing the same products at more reasonable prices. The central government had to consider improving the quality and design of products and develop new technology to remain competitive. It enacted the Industrial Development Act in 1986 to stay competitive globally, create entry barriers for new industries, and provide financing to repair decrepit facilities. It also provided financial assistance to industries to ensure sound management, purchase education materials, and develop new technology and materials (Sakong and Koh 2010).

The central government expanded social overhead capital and constructed oil refineries, steel manufacturing industries, fertilizer industries, and cement plants to support the major export industries. SOEs such as the Korea Electric Power Corporation, the Korea Expressway Corporation, and the Korea Port Authority made enormous contributions to the social overhead capital of these industries, building the infrastructure for industries to grow and advance to the next level.

In the beginning of the 1970s, the Park administration planned to promote the heavy and chemical industries as major export industries by providing massive support. With the domestic market unable to support economies of scale and light industries deterred from expanding into exports, the government had to provide adequate infrastructure for the heavy and chemical industries and through them, develop the defense industry as well. Thus, the authorities developed a strategic defense plan for the country, turning heavy and chemical industries into strategic industries and setting up a comprehensive support scheme.

The President initiated the Committee for Heavy and Chemical Industries in 1973 and introduced the Heavy and Chemical Industries Program to support the committee. He also enacted the National Investment Fund Act to provide financial support. Selecting six strategic industries including nonferrous steel and petrochemical industries, the authorities employed a variety of financial measures such as providing funds to corresponding industries and loans at low interest. Unable to secure large-scale investment funds, the state encouraged large corporations to establish a financial support scheme for industries. Financial assistance to heavy and chemical industries in the 1970s was delivered through development banks that were heavily controlled by the state. Special tax reductions were extended to these industries as well. The central government also gave industries the opportunity to maintain a monopoly. Hence, POSCO or petrochemical industries dominated the domestic market and supplied intermediate goods locally. With the state being the sole shareholder, the profits gained from its monopoly position were not distributed as dividends but used solely for research and development of new technology and for raising productivity. From the early 1970s, the manufacturing industries of the Republic of Korea were already as developed as those in advanced nations (Sakong and Koh 2010).

As political democratization started to bloom in the 1980s, the central government abstained from initiating industry-related policies and started to lay the groundwork for the private sector to flourish by providing needs-based support. This changed industry-related policies significantly. The economic liberalization in the 1980s urged the state to abolish legislations that justified state intervention and enact new laws that stress the role of the market. The 1980 policies restructured the support scheme to subsidize selective major industries and widen the room for competition. State intervention became the exception, requiring clear reasons for the state to intervene and to continue with its intervention. Support schemes were now directed to the labor force and technology development rather than to specific industries. The state replaced its direct intervention strategy to more indirect methods in the 1980s and started to strengthen the independence of SOEs.

In the 1990s, the central government's economic growth strategies were called into question by academia. Industrial restricting had incurred immense social costs, and the central government was allocating resources inefficiently. For instance, the average growth rate of total factor productivity in the heavy and chemical industries was 4.3% from 1966 to 1973, whereas that of light industries was 3.2%. However, light industries exceeded the heavy and chemical industries by 1.44 percentage points between 1975 and 1983 when the government focused its policy on the heavy and chemical industries, indicating inefficiency of government policies (Sakong and Koh 2010).

Before 1990, the Republic of Korea's economic growth can best be described as based off on a factor-driven development strategy.[5] While the heavy and chemical industries required a large amount of capital, automotive and electronics focused on assembly types, and information and technology adopted a catch-up strategy. All three government-initiated strategies required great amounts of energy from the industries and heavily focused on the manufacturing process. As domestic and foreign economic circumstances changed in the 2000s, the government needed to modify its strategy.

The factor-driven development strategy once led by the central government became obsolete, and the private sector transitioned into core technologies, while building environment-friendly and highly efficient structures. The state decentralized its former centrally planned industry-related policies in view

---

[5]   Young (1994) argues that growth factors of East Asia, including the Republic of Korea, are a result of quantitative increase in inputs. Also, Sarel (1997) and Krugman (1994) point out that increase in the amount of inputs was the cause of economic growth of East Asia and its limitation to growth. Young (1994) stressed that the growth rates of total factor productivity in the Republic of Korea; Taipei,China; Hong Kong, China; and Singapore were low during the examination period (1960–1990) and, therefore, their growth was mainly due to capital accumulation. Whereas Sarel (1997) maintained that the total factor productivity indicators of Hong Kong, China and Taipei,China were higher than that of Japan or the United States between 1975 and 1990. Even though capital accumulation and increase of labor force contributed to economic growth, they cannot account for such rapid and precipitous growth rates. Hence, he argues that their rapid growth can be accounted for by the increase in total factor productivity, which incurred technological innovation.

of an autonomous, competitive, and open market at the onset of the 1990s. Investments in heavy and chemical industries expanded with the private sector investing in these industries, consequently reinforcing their growth. In 1989, the state had already established the first 5-year development plan to promote cutting-edge technology and industries in response to rising globalization and competition. The Ministry of Commerce and Industry established the blueprint for an intensive medium-term growth strategy for knowledge and technology.

The emergence of the World Trade Organization (WTO) in 1995 and the Republic of Korea's membership in the Organisation for Economic Co-operation and Development (OECD) in 1996 opened the country's industries and financial market to global competition. The Republic of Korea faced great pressure to opening its market to competition. The central government established a master plan to develop cutting-edge technologies to stay competitive. It enabled private sector investment by enacting relevant laws and established plans to support their investments, giving the private sector opportunities for new investments.

Since 2000, the state has been pushing several policies to seek new momentum for growth. In particular, it initiated a master plan to foster bio- and nanotechnology industries as well as to integrate existing or new technology. The state has committed financial support to corresponding industries under a long-term plan. Pressure to join the global stage and thus fierce competition prompted the transition of the Republic of Korea's growth strategy in the 2000s. Up until then, the entry barriers for new industries and protective measures against competition had impeded industrial productivity and efficiency. The prospect of competing with potential entrants to the market can serve as a threat to domestic industries and give them the incentive to raise productivity and improve the quality of their products. The Republic of Korea lowered its trade barriers in response to the changing global economic environment by signing numerous free trade agreements, pressuring corporations to remain competitive and boost productivity. Along with policies to further encourage an open market, the state retracted its protective measures on industries, thus increasing their overall efficiency.

The majority of SOEs during the industrialization process focused on major national strategic industries (Song 1989). Despite the critical role these corporations played in industrializing the country, their careless management became evident as their structural inefficiencies became prevalent. While major advanced economies started privatizing their public corporations and introducing competition in the 1980s, the government focused on eliminating inefficiency and carrying out reforms in the public sector. The industrial structure into the 1980s became more sophisticated and strategic growth became more qualitative rather than solely quantitative, thus challenging the former SOE policies.

2.3.2 Policies and Reforms, 1948 to 1961

The period from 1948 to 1961 was formative for SOEs in the Republic of Korea. All public corporations in electric power, railway business, and mines that had been operational during the colonization period were transferred to the government after liberation. The government focused on reconstructing the economy, especially reshuffling the exchange rate and enforcing import substitution to protect the country's infant industries. It also restructured some of the existing SOEs and established a few new ones to foster long-term economic growth. Among them was the Korea Coal Corporation, which was established in 1950 to augment the supply of coal during the fuel crisis at the time. Meanwhile, the Korean War waged from 1950 to 1953 and annihilated all industrial sites. In April 1954, the authorities established the Korea Development Bank out of necessity for a government-run bank to take charge of restoring industrial sites and long-term financial policies. With overseas financial aid, the administration also set up several SOEs.

Immediately after the founding of the Republic of Korea in August 1948, control on public institutions relaxed and the government issued no regulations other than an act on the establishment of government-invested institutions. The enactment of the Budget and Accounting Act of Government-Invested Institutions fully entrusted all powers of authority on government-invested institutions upon the ministers of competent agencies, who also exercised supervisory control over their budgets. Auditing was performed by competent agencies and the General Accounting Office, which corresponds to the Board of Audit and Inspection of today.

2.3.3 Policies and Reforms, 1962 to 1984

From 1962 onward, SOEs significantly increased in number as they were seen as a means for economic development. Up until 1965, there were only 36 SOEs.[6] KEPCO was established after the restructuring of other electric power companies in 1961. Other SOEs were reorganized—the Industrial Bank of Korea in 1961; the Korea Oil Corporation, the Korea Housing Corporation,

---

[6] The representative SOE at that time was the Korea Oil Corporation, first established in 1962 and has since continued its development activities.

Kookmin Bank, and Korean Air in 1962; and the Korea Stock Exchange in 1963. The government did not provide capital to the private sector and instead established in 1960 nonfinancial SOEs such as the Korea Trade Promotion Corporation, the Korea Water Resources Development Corporation, the Korea Expressway Corporation, and the Korea Mining Promotion Corporation to sustain the growth of domestic industries and accumulate capital. The initial policies of SOEs in the 1960s aimed to lay the groundwork for the nation's economic development and growth.

Several SOEs in chemical industries were established in the mid-1960s. Chungju Fertilizer was founded in 1964, followed by Yeongnam Chemicals and Jinhae Chemicals in 1965, and Korea Fertilizer in 1967. It is interesting to note that many SOEs in manufacturing industries such as chemicals, fertilizers, steel, and processing agricultural products were established in the 1960s. An example of an SOE that was established to promote a new strategic industry was the Pohang Iron and Steel Company, which is now called POSCO (Appendix A2.1). Founded in 1968, it played a major role in the development of manufacturing industries in the 1970s. It has, since the 1980s, become one of the most competitive steel corporations.

To maintain the efficient management of these public institutions and reinforce its control over them, the Government of the Republic of Korea legislated an act on the establishment of government-invested institutions as well as an act on the management of government-invested institutions. In addition, another act on the establishment of individual government-invested institutions was enacted, allowing government agencies to take control of them based on the Board of Audit and Inspection Act and the Government Procurement Act. This overarching control system is depicted in Figure 2.2. For instance, the Economic Planning Board and the corresponding competent agency controlled the planning and operation of budgets for the government-invested institutions. Personnel management was handled by the respective competent agency. Competent agencies, the Ministry of Finance, the Board of Audit and Inspection, and the Public Procurement Service were responsible for controlling purchase of goods, supervision, and auditing work (Song 1994).

In 1968, the Republic of Korea initiated privatization policies to reform its SOEs. From then on until 1973, 11 SOEs were privatized. At that time, the central government had initiated privatization to promote and encourage sound management of firms, develop technology and certain industries strategically, and resolve instances of reckless management and inefficiency. Most insolvent manufacturing industries became subject to privatization.

Figure 2.2: The Management System before Enactment of the Framework Act on the Management of Government-Invested Institutions

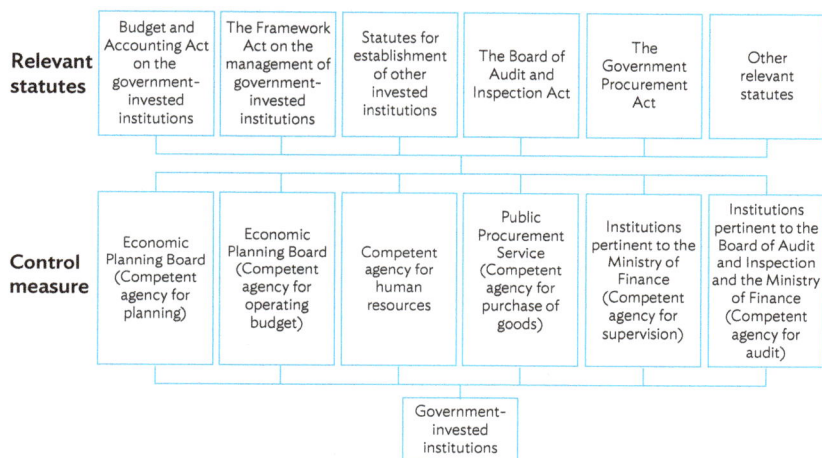

Relevant statutes	Budget and Accounting Act on the government-invested institutions	The Framework Act on the management of government-invested institutions	Statutes for establishment of other invested institutions	The Board of Audit and Inspection Act	The Government Procurement Act	Other relevant statutes
Control measure	Economic Planning Board (Competent agency for planning)	Economic Planning Board (Competent agency for operating budget)	Competent agency for human resources	Public Procurement Service (Competent agency for purchase of goods)	Institutions pertinent to the Ministry of Finance (Competent agency for supervision)	Institutions pertinent to the Board of Audit and Inspection and the Ministry of Finance (Competent agency for audit)

Government-invested institutions

Source: Economic Planning Board. 1988. Gong Ki Up Back Seo. White Paper on State-Owned Enterprises. p. 180 (in Korean).

Incheon Heavy Industries, Korean Airlines, and Mining and Smelting Industries were privatized from 1968 until 1970. The Walkerhill Hotel, a subsidiary of Korea Tourist Service, was privatized into Sunkyung Co., Ltd. (Economic Planning Board 1988). Hanjin Corporation acquired Korean Airlines and has since grown to be one of the top-10 biggest corporations in the country. Other corporations acquired the Korea Shipping Corporation, Korea Shipbuilding Corporation, and Mining and Smelting Industries and have had a great impact on changing the size of corporations.

2.3.4 Policies and Reforms, 1984 to 1997

The Framework Act on the Management of Government-Invested Institutions took effect in March 1984. The government established the act to raise the efficiency of government-invested institutions and to ensure that it can respond quickly and creatively to the institutions under it (Economic Planning Board 1984). Article 3 of the act gives autonomy to manage the institution, Articles 15 and 22 give the head power to appoint and dismiss executive members and compile the budget of government-invested institutions for independent management, Article 27 specifies the procurement of goods and signing of construction contracts, and Articles 28 and 29 reduce the number of audits outside the institution and secure the independent management of goods.

In the early 1980s, the private sector took the lead in developing economic strategies and initiated the privatization of commercial banks, focusing on Hanil Bank, Cheil Bank, Bank of Seoul and Trust Company, and Choheung Bank. The central government amended the Banking Act, allowing it to dominate the financial market. The regulation confined ownership strictly to 8% of a bank's total shares.[7] The firms were privatized through an open and competitive bid and the sale of shares was divided to corporations and individuals at a 50:50 ratio (Kang 1988). The strict regulations on ownership allowed private companies to purchase shares of commercial banks but the banks' management structure was volatile and virtually controlled by the central government. Hence, even after privatization, the prospect of financial independence from the government was remote.[8] The failure to privatize commercial banks seemed to convey a lesson to the Kim Young-sam administration in 1993, when it announced a new privatization plan aiming instead for management with solid ownership.

The Economic Planning Board at the time of the Roh Tae-woo administration in 1987 initiated a large-scale privatization of SOEs to enhance management efficiency (Economic Planning Board 1987). The Committee for Privatization of SOEs developed privatization policies, with its task force reviewing the respective logistics. The task force appointed three prominent figures from academia to occupy advisory positions. After 1987, the committee made major privatization decisions, with the respective competent agencies enforcing the relevant policies.

The 2nd Committee for Privatization of SOEs initiated in May 1987 decided to privatize 30 government-invested institutions and government-funded institutions that were subject to full disposal of government shares, partial disposal of government shares, and undergo changes in their duties. Seven institutions—the Korea Stock Exchange, Kookmin Bank, Industrial Bank of Korea, Korea Exchange Bank, Korea Appraisal Board, Government-Published Textbooks, and Korea Technology Development—belonged to the first group.

---

[7] Following the sell-off of major SOEs, ownership restrictions were applied to almost every enterprise.

[8] The underlying causes can be ascribed to a lack of effort toward deregulation, in addition to structural problems in the management system.

KEPCO, Korea Telecom, and POSCO were regarded as corporations with enormous impact on the national economy and were put in the second group as the central government realized the importance of holding at least 51% of shares to partially manage them (Evaluations Office of Economic Planning Board 1991).

The third privatization plan, in particular the sale of shares, completely ended as the financial recession lingered for a long time after KEPCO and POSCO sold part of their government-owned shares in 1988 and 1989. The sale period was met with backlash from stakeholders, such as employees, the labor union, the board of directors, and relevant agencies who all wanted to preserve their vested interests. As a consequence, the privatization process was never completed for any SOE except the Korea Stock Exchange (Evaluations Office of Economic Planning Board 1991). In addition, since the factors that were to initiate competition (marketization) and deregulation were not formally reviewed, the tendency was to focus instead on changing ownership structure by selling shares. It proved nearly impossible to raise the efficiency of managing SOEs through privatization when these measures were based on incomplete policy designs.

Inaugurated in 1993, the Kim Young-sam administration initiated a new 5-year economic development plan in the same year and publicly announced its plans at the end of the year. The new plan aimed to improve the managerial structure of SOEs. President Kim issued instructions to identify strategies to reengineer the management system of government-invested institutions from an innovative perspective. All SOEs became subject to potential privatization and reorganization and were selected based on the so-called "negative list." Of 133 SOEs on this list comprising government-invested institutions, government-funded institutions, and subsidiaries of government-invested institutions, 58 were selected.

Unlike the privatization plan in 1987, which centered mostly on reforming government-invested institutions, the Kim Young-sam administration targeted all SOEs for privatization, focusing particularly on subsidiaries of government-invested institutions. Above all that, the government decided not to privatize firms by selling government-owned shares; rather, it adopted market principles in order to dissolve any doubt and concern about prerogatives of large corporations to level the playing field and increase transparency. The government also stuck to regulations against monopolistic power in the entire economy.

The outcome of privatization plans based on the detailed plans and committee decisions were not as good as initially expected. While the original plan indicated that 49 SOEs would be completely privatized by the end of 1994, only 13 SOEs completed the process. Eventually, the audacious plan failed with 5 SOEs being merged and shares of 22 SOEs being sold.

In November 1996, the central government announced a new plan to enhance the efficiency of SOEs and privatize them, mainly focusing on reforming the managerial structures of the corporations and abandoning the original plan established in 1993. The new plan was legislated in the Act on Improvement of Managerial Structure and Privatization and took effect in October 1997. All sales of government-owned shares from the Korea Gas Corporation and the Korea Heavy Industries and Construction were postponed until after 2003, as was incorporated in the 1993 privatization plan. In addition, the ceiling of individual ownership was set at a maximum of 7% to prevent a concentration of ownership in a single entity/individual and to establish a new management system operated by professional executives. Unfortunately, the passing of this act conveyed the message that the privatization process would end as sales of stocks were put off, when in fact the intention was actually to continue with the process.

The first privatization policy was successful in fulfilling its initial plans and in separating ownership and management. The second privatization plan succeeded in initiating the plan but failed to transfer management to the private sector and facilitate deregulation. The third and fourth plans were discontinued in the middle of execution and failed to generate any outcome as a consequence. Moreover, privatizing large SOEs was not feasible because of the tension to stabilize the stock market while maintaining control over the economy.

2.3.5 Policies and Reforms, 1998 to Present

Since 1998, the managerial system and structure of SOEs in the Republic of Korea have changed greatly. Reform measures on the managerial structure of public institutions focused on supporting an independent and accountable management system and preventing reckless management and moral hazards. These reforms were pursued even after the Asian financial crisis in 1997. Changing the physical structure, such as privatizing SOEs and shakeouts, was prioritized. At the same time, operating systems such as gratuity, welfare benefits, annual base salary, and team system were improved.

From 1998 onward, the Kim Dae-jung administration[9] executed the most comprehensive and strictest reforms. President Kim Dae-jung was inaugurated in 1998 at the onset of the Asian financial crisis, and he pledged public sector reforms in return for the bailout package offered by advanced economies and international organizations. The financial crisis, which came to be called the "IMF financial crisis" in the Republic of Korea, was a good excuse to compel reform efforts not only in the public sector but also in the entire economy. Aiming for a small government, the Kim administration minimized government intervention and democratized government organizations to revive the market economy. To do this, it had to make strict structural adjustments on SOEs.

The special audit report finalized in June 1998 shows that out of 153 SOEs, 101 were estimated to have incurred losses amounting to W2.5 trillion, including foreign-exchange loss, but excluding all other reserves. In addition, SOE debt more than doubled from W190 trillion to W454 trillion, which indicated that their financial structure had decomposed. In terms of labor costs, the 5-year cumulative pay hike in 38 major SOEs amounted to 68.9%—24 percentage points higher than that of the private sector. The number of employees in SOEs also increased by 18,000 (Board of Audit and Inspection 1998).

The Kim administration presented its major privatization plan twice. The initial plan in 1998 reviewed the status quo of 108 SOEs, of which 26 were parent companies (excluding financial SOEs). Half of these SOEs were government-invested institutions, while the other half were government-financed institutions. Invested institutions had 30 subsidiaries, while financed institutions had 52. Their number of employees totaled 214,000, of which 170,000 were affiliated with parent companies and 44,000 with subsidiaries.[10] Table 2.4 represents the first wave of privatization and management innovation during the Kim administration.

The Kim administration presented three basic principles for privatizing SOEs. First, the privatization of SOEs should be performed rapidly if market conditions and characteristics of corporations were in favor of the process. If this was not possible, privatization should be executed step by step along with structural adjustments. Second, sell-off strategies should be diversified to include the sale of SOEs overseas, and maximizing the sale value by adjusting the timing of sell-offs according to the circumstances at the time. Third, SOEs are principally the property of the public, and therefore public offerings and employee ownership should take place simultaneously with the involvement of the shareholders.

---

[9]   This section rests upon Kwack (1994).

[10] Ministry of Planning and Budget (2002) gives more details on privatization policies during the Kim Dae-jung administration.

Table 2.4: The First Wave of Privatization and Management Innovation of SOEs

Type	Division	Name of Public Enterprise	Number of Subsidiaries	Contents
Full privatization	Financed organization	POSCO	16	The government and the Industrial Bank sell their 26.7% stake to domestic and foreign buyers, up to 3% per individual
		Korea Heavy Industry	3	Promotion of partnerships with overseas leading companies and privatization
		Synthetic Chemistry	1	Sale of assets after the sale of 45% share of Namhae Chemical Corporation
		Comprehensive Technology Finance	1	Sale on competitive bid
		National Textbook		Sale on competitive bid
Gradual privatization	Investment organization	Korea Electric Power Corporation	7	Privatization of the power generation sector by separating power generation from supply and distribution
	Financed organization	Korea Telecom	13	Progressive privatization until the establishment of a competitive system
		Korea Tobacco and Ginseng Corporation	1	Full privatization through the sale of finance shares of government and banks until 2000
		Korea Gas Corporation	5	Step-by-step privatization from 2002, when nationwide pipeline networks were completed
		Korea Pipeline Corporation	2	The sale of government shares in 2000 after integration with its subsidiary, Korea Pipeline Corporation
		District Heating Corporation	3	After dissociating and selling off its Bucheon and Anyang operations with KEPCO's cogeneration power plant, sold more than 51% of its shares in 2001

KEPCO = Korea Electric Power Corporation, POSCO = Pohang Iron and Steel Company, SOE = state-owned enterprise.
Source: Cho (2002).

Established on 3 July 1998, the reformation plan aimed to privatize 26 SOEs (parent companies of government-invested institutions as well as government-financed institutions) based on these principles and undergoing complete or gradual privatization while maintaining the status of an SOE (including merging).

The SOEs to be subject to complete privatization were those that could be privatized without any structural reformation until 1999, such as the Pohang

Iron and Steel Company, Korea Heavy Industry Corporation, Korea Integrated Chemical Inc., Korea Technology Banking Corporation, and National Textbooks and their 21 subsidiaries which were either government-invested or -financed institutions. These five SOEs were privatized between 1998 and 1999.

Next, six government-financed institutions including the Korea Telecom Authority and the Korea Tobacco and Ginseng Corporation were subject to gradual privatization over a period of time. These SOEs were gradually privatized based on their characteristics and market conditions after eliminating any obstacle (Kwack 2000).

The government presented the second policy on privatization of SOEs and managerial reformation in August 1998 to supplement the first policy. Table 2.5 presents an outline of the second wave of privatization and management innovation of SOEs during the Kim administration. The second plan targeted 19 government-financed institutions (parent companies) and their 55 subsidiaries, which excluded financial SOEs,[11] the media, and SOEs subject for complete privatization. It contained intensive structural shakeouts, in which 40 out of 55 subsidiaries were subject to complete or gradual privatization, 6 were to be merged, and 8 were to remain subsidiaries. It also confirmed the managerial reformation plan concerning the organization and employees of 19 parent companies. The workforce was scheduled to be reduced by 20%, from 143,063 (or 28,813 employees), by March 1998 (Ministry of Planning and Budget 1998). This plan set the following key principles regarding privatization of SOEs and promotion of managerial reformation (Ministry of Planning and Budget 2000):

(i)   Reestablish the competencies and role of SOEs in order to cultivate their unique values and serve the public.

(ii) SOEs shall continue to focus on the core competencies for which they were established. The tasks that can be more efficiently undertaken should be outsourced to the private sector; otherwise the corresponding SOE should be privatized.

(iii) Merge all similar and overlapping businesses to ensure no tax revenue is wasted.

(iv) Establish autonomous and responsible management systems by minimizing regulations and interventions.

(v) Fundamentally reform operating systems to improve management efficiency.

---

[11]   The managerial reformation of financial SOEs was handled by the Financial Supervisory Commission.

Table 2.5: Outline of the Second Wave of Privatization and Management Innovation of SOEs

Type	Year	Division	Parent Company	Subsidiary Company
Full privatization (12)	1998	Investment organization	Korea Distribution Corporation	Maeil Dairy, Maeil New Zealand Cheese, Korea Food Service
			Housing Corporation	Korea Construction Resource Management
	1999	Investment organization	Housing Corporation	Hanyang Public, Hanyang Wood, and Hanyang Industry
			Korea Electric Power Corporation (KEPCO)	Saeil Eisic
		Financed organization	Korea Telecom	Korea Telecom Card
			Korea District Heating Corporation	China HuangDao DongHwa Thermoelectric Co., Ltd.
			Pipeline Construction Corporation	G&G Telecom
			Gas Corporation	Cheongyeol
Stepwise privatization (28)	2000	Financed organization	Korea Telecom	Korea Telecom CATV, Korea TRS
			Korea Tobacco Corporation	Korean Tobacco Ginseng Hong Kong Co., Ltd.
	2001	Investment organization	Korea Electric Power Corporation (KEPCO)	Korea Electric Power Technology, KEPCO Technical Industry, KEPCO Industry Development
			Distribution Corporation	Korea Refrigeration, Noryangjin Fisheries Market, Korean Livestock Industry
			Korea Housing, Express Way, Water resource development and earth development corporations	Privatization after integration of Korea Housing, Express Way, Water resource development and earth development corporations
		Financed organization	Korea District Heating Corporation	The Development of the Ansan City, Korea District Heating Technology
	2002	Investment organization	Korea Express Way Corporation	Highway Information and Communication Corporation, Expressway Management Corporation
			Korea Water Resource Development Corporation	Korea Water Resources Technology Corporation
			Korea Earth Development Corporation	Korea Land Trust

Continued on next page

Table 2.5 continued

Stepwise privatization (28)	2002	Financed organization	Korea Telecom	Korea Telecom Technology, Korea Telecom Promotion, Korea Telecom Industry Development, Korea Telecom Americas Corporation (KTAI)
			Korea Gas Corporation	Korea Gas Engineering, Korea LNG Co., Korea Gas Shipping, Korea Gas Technology Industry
Integration and abolishment (6)	1998	Investment organization	Korea Distribution Corporation	Korea Product
			Korea Housing Corporation	Hanyang
		Financed organization	Korea Pipeline Construction Corporation	Korea Pipeline Construction Corporation
			Korea Telecom	ICO Invest Management
			Korea Appraisal Board	Korea Real Estate Trust
	2000	Investment organization	Korea Tourism Organization	Gyeongju Tourism Development Corporation
Restructuring (8)		Investment organization	Korea Electric Power Corporation (KEPCO)	KEPCO Information Network, Korea Nuclear Power Plant
			Petroleum Development Corporation	Korea Captain Oil Field Development (KCCL), Indonesia Oil Field Development (PPSL)
		Financed organization	Korea Telecom	Korea PC Communication, Korea Submarine Communication, Korea Telecom Freetel, Korea Pay Telephone

SOE = state-owned enterprise.
Source: Cho (2002).

The Framework Act on the Management of Government-Affiliated Institutions was legislated in December 2003. From 2005 onward, performance evaluations on the management, reformation, and customer satisfaction of government-affiliated institutions other than SOEs were conducted to boost reforms and instill a favorable attitude toward reforms in public institutions. Nonetheless, reckless management and moral hazards persisted. Some in government have asserted that limits should be set to prevent such instances from recurring, bearing in mind however that public institutions are run by multiple representatives of citizens, the government, and the board of directors, therefore making the lines of responsibility unclear. Inevitably, public institutions needed to completely change their management system and establish clear boundaries of accountability. Fail-safe measures that kick off in the event of malfunction are essential to independent management.

Member states of the Organisation for Economic Co-operation and Development (OECD) and major advanced economies are pursuing reformation of managerial structures in their public institutions. In April 2005, the OECD provided guidelines for establishing managerial structures of SOEs. Following these international movements, reforming the management systems of public institutions in the Republic of Korea became imperative.

Subsequently, the government legislated the Act on the Management of Public Institutions to build independent institutions with transparent operating systems and responsible management systems (Ministry of Planning and Budget 2007). This act integrated the Framework Act on the Management of Government-Invested Institutions and the Framework Act on the Management of Government-Affiliated Institutions. The OECD guidelines recommended that SOEs adopt an autonomous management structure, independent of the competent agencies that were entitled to their ownership and control. However, despite the legislation of new laws, the Broadcasting Act; the Act on the Improvement of Managerial Structure and Privatization; the Act on the Establishment, Operation and Fostering of Government-Funded Research Institutes; and the Act on the Establishment, Operation and Fostering of Government-Funded Science and Technology Research Institutes, remained as they are. Separate management and control systems were created for financial SOEs covered by the Banking Act; government-funded research institutes under the Act on the Establishment, Operation and Fostering of Government-Funded Research Institutes, etc.; and the Act on the Establishment, Operation and Fostering of Government-Funded Science and Technology Research Institutes, etc. (Ministry of Planning and Budget 2007).

Even after the Act on the Management of Public Institutions was legislated, the Act on the Improvement of Managerial Structure and Privatization was still in force. Furthermore, government-funded institutions formed under the former law were reclassified as SOEs, in essence turning the law into a mere piece of paper. The reformation of management systems at public institutions, based on the Act on the Management of Public Institutions, can be summarized as follows:

(i)   The number of public institutions that were in blind spots and due for monitoring has increased significantly.

(ii) Every agency is now obligated to make management information public and to oversee the information to be monitored by the public.

(iii) The various principles for classifying public institutions have been unified into one: the intensity of commerciality, considering international standards. Institutions were first categorized into public corporations and quasi-government institutions and their complicated managerial structure reshaped and standardized according to allocated tasks.

(iv) The responsibility of all executives at public institutions was better defined to curb any excesses on the part of institution heads by eliminating the potential possibility of nonexecutive officers and governors being bound by formality. Consequently, individual nonexecutive officers and governors had to undergo performance and outcome evaluations.

Compared with the administrations from 1998 to present, the Kim Dae-jung administration's privatization policy was highly successful as it privatized 8 parent companies and turned 66 subsidiaries into either private companies or merged some of them. This success is believed to be attributed to the administration's strong will to overcome the economic crisis. In the past, labor unions and groups with vested interests obstructed the state's long-term privatization policies to raise management efficiency and equity in distribution. The Kim administration gained the public's trust for the long-term project, empowering it to overcome the economic crisis and raise sovereign credit rating.

2.4 Contribution of SOEs to the Economy

As mentioned, the Republic of Korea initiated its growth strategies in the 1960s. With no accumulated capital and an inexperienced private sector, it was inevitable for the state to lead the economy. As it engaged in marketing efforts, the state strengthened its control of capital and granted prerogatives such as tax exemptions or financial assistance at low interest rates. The state also established its own enterprises to intervene in major industries. SOEs operated most financial industries, serving as key windows for financing economic development.

SOEs were established mainly to (i) provide public goods and services; (ii) prevent or alleviate the effects of the downside to natural monopoly; (iii) maximize consumer welfare (consumer surplus); (iv) support industries and raise the competitiveness of other firms (e.g., increase in total producer surplus by reducing cost or raising productivity); (v) foster high-risk businesses which the private sector or strategic industries cannot handle; and (vi) create jobs to increase welfare and value added. However, there is a certain limit to evaluating SOEs' competence and role quantitatively. For instance, it is extremely difficult to estimate consumer and producer surplus, and to do so, demand and supply functions would have to be estimated in advance, which is almost impossible. Also, since SOEs are established with the interest of the public in mind, their ramifications on other institutions are therefore their economic contribution, which is extremely difficult to estimate (Ministry of Strategy and Finance 2010).

To measure SOEs' contribution to the overall economy, we estimate how much value added they have created by accounting for GDP and gauging the level of SOEs' contribution. However, this comparative methodology encountered a series of difficulties while conducting a time series analysis.

Obtaining the balance sheets of all SOEs would be difficult, and even then, calculating the final output and intermediate inputs would entail a great deal of time and effort. While a simple comparison of value added would be feasible, this would not verify the efficiency of resource allocation. Nonetheless, it is a meaningful endeavor to compare these proportions as SOEs in the Republic of Korea showed a high degree of contribution to the overall economy with regard to electricity, railroad, and housing, since their prices have an effect on the consumer price index and economic growth rate (Sung 2010a). This study estimates the SOEs' value added in chronological order, which will show the role SOEs played and their contribution to the economy.

Three studies used various methodologies to estimate the value added generated by SOEs: Sakong (1979) reviewed balance sheets during the period 1963 to 1977 and conducted an input–output analysis; Song and Song (1988) analyzed balance sheets from 1970 to 1980; and Sung (2010a) also examined balance sheets. In addition, we looked at the proportion of GDP generated by SOEs against the overall GDP and considered the differences in methodologies of estimation, time, data, stages of economic development, and classification of SOEs, which make the aggregate data a non-balanced set.

First, Sakong (1979) looked at the GDP share of SOEs in the country's GDP from 1963 to 1977, and estimated the share in 1963 at 6.7%. As can be seen in Table 2.6, however, this continued to increase and reached 9.2% in 1970, and dropped slightly to at least 8% during the first half of the 1970s.

On the other hand, Song and Song (1988) compared the share of government-invested institutions (or SOEs as they are now called) in the country's GDP and that of all public institutions. They estimate that the share of all public institutions in GDP then was 9.2%. This slightly decreased in the mid-1970s

Table 2.6: Public Enterprises' Value-Added Share in GDP, 1963–1977
(Current W billion)

	1963	1964	1970	1971	1972	1973	1974	1975	1976	1977
Public enterprises (PE)	31.41	41.57	220.75	254.41	315.37	417.3	537.56	737.52	1,014.58	1,191.06
Gross domestic product (GDP)	469.4	678.05	2,405.05	2,976.55	3,676.22	4,808.64	6,844.21	8,855.53	11,659.1	14,854.04
Nonagricultural GDP	253.45	346.27	1,695.2	2,103.32	2,637.93	3,538.77	5,079.92	6,553.54	8,702.1	11,286.34
PE/GDP (%)	6.7	6.1	9.2	8.6	8.6	8.7	7.9	8.3	8.7	8
PE/Nonagricultural GDP (%)	12.4	12	13	12.1	12	11.8	10.6	11.3	11.7	10.6

Sources: Ministry of Finance. Sae Ip Sae Chul Gyul San Bo Go Suh (Final Budget Report), 1963–1977; Ministry of Finance. Ki Keum Gyul San Bo Go Suh (Final Report of Funds); Ministry of Finance. Jung Bu Tu Ja Gi kwan Gyul San Suh (Government-Invested Enterprise Final Accounts),1963–1977; Ministry of Finance. Ki Up Hoe Gye Gyul San (Official Departmental Agencies Final Accounts), 1963–1977; Various final accounts of public enterprises, 1963–1977; Bank of Korea. National Income in Korea, 1978; and Bank of Korea. Input–Output Tables for 1970 and 1975.

and then increased to 9.1% in the 1980s and reached 9.4% in 1985. The author estimates that the share of government-invested institutions in GDP was 3.2%, which increased steadily to 6.5% until 1986.

Likewise, Sung (2010a) compared the share of SOEs in GDP and that of all public institutions. He estimated the share of all public institutions to GDP at around 4.6% in 2005. This proportion is estimated to have decreased to 3.5% by 2008. Further, he estimated the proportion of SOEs' GDP against total GDP at 2.9% in 2005 and 2.2% in 2008. The downward trend is believed to have been triggered by rapid growth in the private sector and the privatization process that was initiated at the end of 1990s (Sung 2010a).

Figure 2.3 shows the descending trend of the SOEs' GDP shares. This decrease is visible particularly in the 2000s and will most likely last for a significant period. In the next section, we explore how the state raised SOEs systematically and used them as a stepping-stone for economic growth.

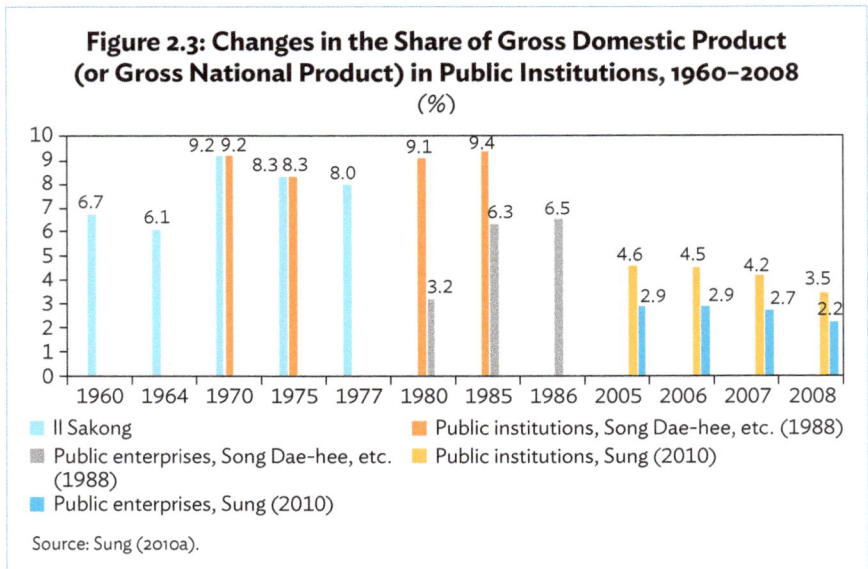

Figure 2.3: Changes in the Share of Gross Domestic Product (or Gross National Product) in Public Institutions, 1960–2008
(%)

Legend:
- Il Sakong
- Public institutions, Song Dae-hee, etc. (1988)
- Public enterprises, Song Dae-hee, etc. (1988)
- Public institutions, Sung (2010)
- Public enterprises, Sung (2010)

Source: Sung (2010a).

Table 2.7 shows the value added produced by each SOE. The data show an increase in the proportion of SOEs in manufacturing industries. In 1963, the value added by SOEs in manufacturing was merely 30.2%, but this increased to 49.7% in 1974, and remained in the 40% range up to the end of the 1970s. It is reasonable to say that SOEs led the growth of the manufacturing industry (and therefore economic growth) in the 1960s and 1970s. The SOEs' growth rate was higher than that of the overall economy and the effect of their growth spread across other areas of industry. Large-scale SOEs were established, such as those in the petrochemical and steel industries, to support private corporations that required substantial investments and bore huge investment risks, which the private sector could not initiate.

Table 2.7: Public Enterprises' Value-Added Share in Industry, 1963–1977
(%)

	1963	1964	1970	1971	1972	1973	1974	1975	1976	1977
Agriculture, hunting, forestry, fishery	1.8	1.9	1.2	1.5	1.3	0.7	0.1	0.1	0.0	0.0
Mining and quarrying	8.8	8.3	3.0	4.2	3.5	2.4	2.4	2.5	3.2	3.2
Manufacturing	30.2	34.5	39.2	38.3	36.0	42.3	49.7	46.6	37.5	39.5
Electricity, gas, water	12.3	11.5	13.9	13.5	13.9	11.8	7.1	12.1	13.1	17.0
Construction	1.8	0.9	2.2	2.5	2.8	2.8	3.3	3.3	4.3	3.9
Wholesale and retail trade	3.0	4.1	1.6	2.0	2.2	2.3	1.8	1.9	0.6	0.9
Transport, storage, and communication	26.5	24.5	21.6	18.6	18.8	16.6	14.6	13.1	13.9	14.9
Finance and insurance	15.4	13.9	16.2	19.0	20.8	20.4	20.1	19.2	23.6	18.1
Community, social, and personal services	0.2	0.4	1.2	0.5	0.7	0.8	1.0	1.2	3.6	2.4
Total	**100**	**100**	**100**	**100**	**100**	**100**	**100**	**100**	**100**	**100**

Sources: Ministry of Finance. Sae Ip Sae Chul Gyul San Bo Go Suh (Final Budget Report), 1963–1977; Ministry of Finance. Ki Keum Gyul San Bo Go Suh (Final Report of Funds); Ministry of Finance. Jung Bu Tu Ja Gi kwan Gyul San Suh (Government-Invested Enterprise Final Accounts), 1963–1977; Ministry of Finance. Ki Up Hoe Gye Gyul San (Official Departmental Agencies Final Accounts), 1963–1977; Various final accounts of public enterprises, 1963–1977; Bank of Korea. National Income in Korea, 1978; and Bank of Korea. Input–Output Tables for 1970 and 1975.

2.5 Assessment of SOE Policies

SOEs in the Republic of Korea have changed over the past 60 years while contributing substantially to the overall economy. The government managed financial industries and steel and chemical industries as SOEs, fostering them into corporate behemoths that execute government projects.

In the 1980s, when political and economic democratization captivated national interest, many attempts were made to make SOEs independent. The Framework Act on the Management of Government-Invested Institutions, which was first introduced in 1983, granted SOEs autonomy in operation. However, SOEs were still considered the means through which the central government executed its policies, rather than an actual corporation. This led to the insolvency of some SOEs. Although the privatization of banks in the 1980s was successful, it failed to establish a business-oriented operating system. In fact, many banks went bankrupt because of political changes even though they were owned by private shareholders (Nam 2012).

Further moves to privatize SOEs had sparked when the two Kim administrations initiated political democratization. Following the Asian financial crisis in 1988, highly business-oriented SOEs were privatized. Competition among SOEs was introduced to enhance efficiency. This development reaped support across the nation, leading many SOEs to be privatized.

However, SOEs and other public institutions were still deemed to be proxies of the central government. During the Roh administration in 2003, the corresponding policies reverted to their original pre-1977 form, and have remained unchanged. SOEs are now focused on following government rules rather than taking commercial initiatives.

SOE-related policies are recognized to have played a big role in the Republic of Korea's economic growth. However, recurring problems such as high wages and retirement packages, inefficient investment, and excess workforce impede SOEs from implementing reforms, although a few have succeeded.

The central government must change its perspective to resolve these issues. As mentioned, SOEs are seen as government agencies rather than private corporations in pursuit of profit. Their organizational structure and operation system remain the same because of the central government's perception that SOEs are the means to an end. The principal solution would be to review all SOE-related policies and reestablish policy targets most efficiently.

SOEs should be classified into two categories: those that provide services on behalf of the government and those that seek profit despite their state ownership. Each group should possess similar properties in terms of the goods and services they produce and the markets they are involved in. Their roles need to be reestablished according to the primary consumers of the goods and services they produce.

SOEs that produce goods and services that closely resemble public goods are no different from the central government and should operate like any other government agency. The best solution would be to incorporate these SOEs into government agencies as separate operating divisions. If this is not feasible, external financing should be increased to minimize the risk of reckless management and enhance management efficiency.

A comprehensive plan containing industry-related policies that aim to raise the competitiveness of SOEs and address their ownership should be developed for business-oriented SOEs. The role of SOEs should be designed according to the respective purposes for which they were established. Business-oriented SOEs need exposure to market competition while SOEs that are by nature monopoly industries should be monitored by independent regulatory bodies.

2.6 Lessons from SOE Policies

This section examines the policy implications which developing nations can derive from the analysis in previous sections.

First, as mentioned earlier, the central government of the Republic of Korea has viewed SOEs as the means through which it can achieve its purposes. At the outset, government intervention was necessary to address market inefficiencies resulting from goods and services and a labor market that was not yet fully shaped. In the 1960s, the central government urged SOEs to develop technologies and pursue economies of scale, particularly when accumulating capital was difficult and allocation of resources was deterred. In the Republic of Korea, particular industries discovered their comparative advantage not by coincidence but through the creation of specific SOE-related policies, substantiating in effect the strategic trade theory. Targeting niche markets and fostering SOEs as well as corporate behemoths with strategic plans and investments was a successful strategy for economic growth. The strategic plans, especially those reinforcing technological development, enabled corporations to enter the global market and stay competitive. The technology developed by a corporation was considered a public good and could be shared by other corporations.

Second, first-hand market intervention by the central government waned in the 1980s, leaving the private sector to develop comparative advantage. The policies of promoting new technology and investment in research and development enabled the private sector's growth, while the national passion for education played a critical role in the success of these policies. The Korean government has acknowledged that the development of new technology is a core strategy to economic growth. POSCO is a prime example of a company that was established initially to meet domestic demand, and then proceeding to invest its monopolistic profits in developing technology and enhancing productivity (see case study in Appendix A2.1). Its case is quite significant, especially as an example of the President setting the target for economic growth and protecting SOEs from exterior political forces or corruption to ensure that profits are used solely for technological development. This indicates that protective policies are as important as providing subsidies or temporary protection measures from a competitive environment. But once industrialization is on track, care should be taken to ensure that these protective measures do not impede competition or generate adverse effects resulting from the monopoly as the industrial policies of the 1980s and the 1990s would attest.

Third, constraining the entry of foreign industries into the domestic market and protecting infant industries are crucial to economic growth. The steel or energy industries, which produce social infrastructure and intermediate goods to build other sophisticated industries, were fostered by SOEs, not by foreign direct investment. These industries later became the foundation for domestic economic growth. Protective measures for infant industries are commonly used to rationalize protectionism. They are based on the argument that production cost is comparatively higher for nations that are in the beginning phase of industrialization; and therefore, it is crucial to ensure low production cost until they reach the same level of efficiency as their counterparts, to grow their industries. Mainstream economists support this idea and new development economists claim that protection for a certain period is necessary for industries to acquire new technologies. For these measures to succeed, the central government should expedite the learning process to help cover the expense of developing these industries.

Fourth, it is essential to improve the governance of SOEs for their efficient management. Privatization is not feasible in most countries for political reasons. In the Republic of Korea, however, privatization of SOEs was feasible because a public consensus had been reached after the 1998 financial crisis. But it was a difficult process after this period. Privatization is not a panacea. Railroads and electricity, with their high initial costs of entry are difficult industries in which to promote competition. Where these two industries are dominated by a natural monopoly, it is best to designate SOEs to take point and consolidate the managerial structure to enhance management efficiency. Prices should be set according to potential consequences of the SOEs' decisions for the overall economy. Electricity and railways have huge ramifications for the economy and therefore prices in both sectors should be set according to conditions within each industry.

A carrot-and-stick approach is useful to raise the efficiency of SOEs. Since 1984, SOEs have been evaluated based on their annual performance.

Employees of SOEs with excellent reviews are provided incentives. The evaluation system has been expanded to every public institution to enhance the efficiency of public agencies. Incentives that are due for delivery should be awarded at a proper time and correspond to excellent performance. Rectifying measures should be taken immediately at any underperforming institution.

Last, the central government established banks for specific industries or owned financial institutions since the early stage of industrialization in the 1960s. The Korea Development Bank and the Export–Import Bank of Korea supported other SOEs and provided financial support to private investors during this time. The state also provided funds to the private sector and enabled the flow of financial support within the boundaries of its policies. It might be necessary for developing nations to establish state-owned financial institutions, as hostile takeovers are prevalent after opening the market. Despite the recent trend toward privatization, state-owned financial institutions are still required, especially considering that they account for 30% of the entire financial system within member states of the European Union.

Appendix A2.1: Case Study – Pohang Iron and Steel Company

The Pohang Iron and Steel Company was privatized in 2000 and renamed POSCO in 2002. It was established as a state-owned enterprise (SOE) in the Republic of Korea as part of a bigger plan to establish integrated iron and steel industries in the 1960s. Starting with almost nothing—no capital, no technology, and no experience—POSCO became the world's leading steel company in 1998 in terms of overall supply of crude steel. The company achieved this through relentless technology development and enhancement of its infrastructure and productivity. The growth model of East Asia and the Park Chung-hee administration was instrumental in POSCO's becoming globally competitive and a cornerstone of the Republic of Korea's economy within 3 decades.

Park's leadership, the efficiency of policies in developing nations, the principle of providing incentives according to economic outcomes, the drastic support of the state, and the distortion of prices and restricted market entry of competitors all played a critical role in POSCO's growth.

Pohang Iron and Steel Company reaped huge economic success—it wielded monopoly power as it was owned by the state. How was it possible that the inefficiency and corruption from the monopolistic power that was backed by the government and the moral hazard of the principal–agent model did not impair the company's competitiveness? With this question in mind, we examine the factors behind POSCO's success.

Factor 1: Strong endorsement from the President (a state within the state)

Clearly, the President's strong endorsement played a critical role in the growth of the Pohang Iron and Steel Company. Former President Park saw steel industries as the key to industrialize the nation and considered them especially to be a significant base for the heavy and defense industries. Speaking at the groundbreaking ceremony on 1 April 1970, President Park presented his strategies and perspective on steel industries: "The steel industry accounts for a great portion of the industrial development of our country. It will be the key industry in terms of fostering machine, ship-building, automotive and other construction industries. Besides this, we are about to promote defense-related industries and the steel industry will play a critical role which should precede raising them" (Pohang Iron and Steel Company 1979).

The first 5-year economic development plan focused on fostering steel industries, and the private sector was originally to lead its implementation. The plan was to encourage heavy industries through an import substitution strategy, rather than an export-oriented one. However, the state failed to mobilize domestic finances, and the United States (US) opposed Park's strategies, creating obstacles in overall economic policies including money supply, fiscal policies, foreign reserves, and inflation (Ryu 2001). President Park had to modify the initial economic development plan to focus on export strategies instead.

Pohang Iron and Steel Company was first established in 1968 as a state-owned corporation. Controlled heavily by the government, it maintained its monopolistic power in the market. The company was placed under the direct control of the President with the cooperation of the Economic Planning Board and the Ministry of Commerce and Industry. This anomaly in jurisdiction enabled the firm to earn privileges and gain autonomy in building its business strategies and operational management.

Factor 2: Technological and managerial innovations

The company thrived sustainably through its technological and managerial innovations. Steel industries of advanced economies were concerned about the backfire that started in 1980 and evaded transfer of technology to Pohang Iron and Steel Company. Competition in technological development among advanced economies and reinforcement of containment against Pohang Iron and Steel Company motivated the company to boost development of its own technology. Consequently, the firm established its own research institute of technology in 1977 and founded Pohang University of Science and Technology (POSTECH) in 1986. It established the Research Institute of Science and Technology in 1987, a joint research development structure between academia and industries, in which it put a large amount of resources into research and development and accumulated new technologies. This increased the company's competitiveness. The research institute of Pohang Iron and Steel Company or POSCO as it is now known, is in charge of steel research and developing technologies to process steel and its by-products. The Research Institute of Science and Technology handles new materials and green energy, which focuses on developing technologies such as lithium and fuel cells, to secure a new growth momentum for POSCO. POSTECH is responsible for conducting groundbreaking scientific research and raising human capital. They seek prodigal talents to educate and focus on advanced research projects that are critical to the future of the steel industry and they collaborate with industries. POSCO continues to invest in research and development to maintain its position as one of the most competitive steel companies in the world. The company constantly searches for distinct technologies that can raise its productivity and secure a higher standard of steel. In surveys conducted by World Steel Dynamics, the global agency for steel industries, POSCO ranked at the top for several years. These achievements are a result of the joint research conducted by academia and the industry, allowing the company to attain high standards of technology. After the 1980s, POSCO was able to finance its own investments and started to minimize state intervention in investment strategies and management of firms. As it acquired autonomy in both finance and technology, it became an enterprise within the state, and no longer a state within the state.

Factor 3: Political network

SOEs are generally thought to represent corruption and inefficiency. In the initial phase of industrialization, the political pressure could have played a bigger role as there was no strict accounting regulations, but Pohang Iron and Steel Company was free from this because of the political bond between President Park and the company's President Park Tae-joon. Their relationship only strengthened the company's autonomy.

The entrepreneurship of the executives and the employees' loyalty to the firm made it possible to lay aside the goal of maximizing profit (Ryu 2001). The company aimed to sever all conflict of interest with the profit-oriented private sector in import substitution industries and raise new investment capital in long-term state projects. The unusually strong ties between the President of the country and the president of the company served as protection from predatory rent-seeking activities and political disputes, a case unlike any in other developing countries. Instead, the chief executive officer's personal network became a communication channel between the company and the state and protected the firm from any type of political pressure, allowing it to maintain its autonomy as a corporation and sever all channels of bribery. President Park granted the firm full autonomy. The company used this autonomy when signing contracts and building investment strategies. The human resources department stuck to its principles as well. It suspended the distribution of dividends in compliance with the national development strategies pursued by the state. Therefore, the firm was able to use its capital to invest consistently in infrastructure as part of its aggressive investment strategy. This political network protected corporate profits, reduced overall production cost, and raised the efficiency of its operations (Ryu 2001).

Factor 4: Aggressive (hostile) and profit-oriented corporate strategies

Despite its status as an SOE, Pohang Iron and Steel Company pursued highly aggressive and profit-oriented strategies as a corporation. It worked closely with the government but at the same time attempted to increase its market share and pursued corporate strategies to reform its managerial system. Not only did it strive to maximize profits in domestic markets, it also tried gaining a competitive advantage in the global market.

Pohang Iron and Steel Company was completely privatized in 2001 and turned into a private corporation pursuing profit-maximizing strategies. Upon complete privatization, the company started to maximize the profits of shareholders instead of following state policies, as its foreign ownership surpassed 60% in September 2001. As it could no longer be a state within the state, the company became an enterprise within the market. Since then, the role of the state has been to supervise the market, promote competition, and prevent monopoly, instead of setting industrial policy.

Factor 5: Cooperation in financial and technological development

Domestic capital and the loans from the US government were neither sufficient to establish Pohang Iron and Steel Company nor drive economic development in the Republic of Korea. At the end of the 1960s, the US government asked the Japanese government to grant a loan to the Republic of Korea. When the administration presented its plan to create the steel company, the US government made its opposition clear, arguing that Korean steel industries were comparatively disadvantaged to those of Japan and that the Republic of Korea should focus particularly on labor-intensive industries instead.

As such, it was highly difficult for the Korean government to obtain overseas financing. The International Bank for Reconstruction and Development (IBRD) at that time was also concerned about the country's capacity to repay and therefore was against financing the establishment of Pohang Iron and Steel Company. Strong opposition from the US and international organizations stemmed from the encroachment of Japanese steel industries on US steel industries, which exposed the risk of oversupply in the steel sector if the Pohang Iron and Steel Company were to be created. Further, it was argued that the Pohang Iron and Steel Company could not expect to have any comparative advantage over its Japanese counterparts and therefore should not cause any turmoil in the world steel market.

Unlike the US government, the Japanese administration at the time wanted the Pohang Iron and Steel Company to be established, since it could then export its plants to the Republic of Korea and achieve division of labor within the steel technology and related industries. Fuji Steel Corporation, Yahata Steel Corporation, and NKK Corporation, the Big Three steel corporations at the time, showed interest in providing financial support to establish the Pohang Iron and Steel Company and cooperating toward technological development.

The three corporations were able to come forward because of the Republic of Korea's property claims against the Japanese government, which secured the construction cost and eliminated any business risk. Japanese corporations competed for contracts to expand their export channels and to take part in establishing the Pohang Iron and Steel Company. Initial financing from Japan and its technologies were crucial to making Pohang Iron and Steel Company the world's leading steel manufacturer. But its projects to develop those technologies further and the assistance of the Republic of Korea government also played an important role in raising the company to the top tier.

The Pohang Iron and Steel Company has enjoyed a monopolistic position since its creation in 1968 and it accumulated a large amount of capital. Its dividends went toward the state budget and were never delivered to shareholders. All revenue went to finance infrastructure expansion. The company invested in infrastructure aggressively, made possible by national tactics to foster steel industries. Despite opposition from the US and international financial institutions, the state promoted policies in favor of heavy and chemical industries to attain national security and expand exports (Ryu 2001).

Factor 6: Corporate culture

There is a cultural aspect to the success of the Pohang Iron and Steel Company. Its employees had a sense of duty to modernize their motherland. Everyone from the president and the chief executive officer to the employee in the lowest chain of command, were dedicated to the company. Both the Republic of Korea's President Park Chung-hee and President Park Tae-joon of the company were patriotic figures trying to found the country's steel industry. Company employees displayed their full sense of entrepreneurship by completing projects ahead of time and demonstrating perfection. Both Parks come from a military background and the resulting authoritarian and totalitarian culture forced employees to complete projects, no matter what. It also reduced construction time and costs, and promoted perfection in work. The poor foundation in 1977 was dismantled publicly and the company became the epitome of perfectionism. This unique culture served as a great boon to a newly industrialized Republic of Korea, enabling it to catch up with advanced economies (Ryu 2001).

References

Bank of Korea. Economic Statistics System. https://ecos.bok.or.kr/EIndex_
     en.jsp.

_____. Input–Output Tables for 1970 and 1975 (in Korean).

_____. National Income in Korea, 1978 (in Korean).

Board of Audit and Inspection. 1998. Various final accounts of public
     enterprises, 1963–1977.

Cho, S. B. 2002. Reform of State-Owned Enterprises and Quasi-
     Governmental Institutions. Korea Economic Research Institute. pp.
     85–136 (in Korean).

Economic Planning Board. 1984, 1987, 1988, 1989, 1991. Gong Ki Up Back Seo. A
     White Paper on State-Owned Enterprises (in Korean).

Evaluations Office of Economic Planning Board. 1991. Trading Economics.
     https://tradingeconomics.com/south-korea/gdp-growth-annual
     (accessed 19 September 2018) (in Korean).

Jeong, H-G., J-w. Kim, H-s. Kim, C-k. Kwak, and J-h. Lee. 2010. Comparative
     Analysis on State-Owned Enterprises in Korea, China, and Japan.
     Korea Institute for International Economic Policy. Policy References
     10–61 (in Korean).

Jones, L. P. and I. Sakong. 1980. Government, Business, and Entrepreneurship
     in Economic Development: The Korean Case. Korea Development
     Institute (in Korean); 1980. Harvard East Asian Monographs. 91.
     Harvard University.

Kang, S-I. 1988. A Study on the Privatization of State-Owned Enterprises.
     Korea Development Institute (in Korean).

Krugman, P. 1994. The Myth of Asia's Miracle. Foreign Affairs. 73 (6). pp. 62–78.

Kwack, C-k. 1994. A Study on the Changes of Government-Business Relations
     through the Public Enterprise Privatization. Seoul National University
     (in Korean).

_____. 2000. Success Factors for SOE Privatization. Gong Gi Up Non Chong.
     12 (1). Korean Society of Public Enterprise (in Korean).

Ministry of Finance. Jung Bu Tu Ja Gi Kwan Gyul San Suh (Government-
     Invested Enterprise Final Accounts), 1963–1977 (in Korean).

_____. Ki Keum Gyul San Bo Go Suh (Final Report of Funds) (in Korean).

_____. Ki Up Hoe Gye Gyul San (Official Departmental Agencies Final
     Accounts), 1963–1977 (in Korean).

_____. Sae Ip Sae Chul Gyul San Bo Go Suh (Final Budget Report), 1963–1977.

Ministry of Planning and Budget. 1998. The Second Wave of Privatization and Management Innovation of SOEs (in Korean).

_____. 2000. 1999 White Book of Government Reform (in Korean).

_____. 2002. White Book of Government Reform. pp. 87–95 (in Korean).

_____. 2007. Korea's Finance. pp. 349–357 (in Korean).

Ministry of Strategy and Finance. 2010. Contribution of SOEs to the Overall Economy and Its Tasks in the Future. pp. 139–140 (in Korean).

_____. 2017. Designation of Public Institutions in 2017 (in Korean).

Nam, I. C. 2012. Governance of SOEs and public institutions in Korea. Korea Development Institute (in Korean).

_____. 2015. Governance of Commercial SOEs in Korea: Main Issues and a Proposal for Reform. Korea Development Institute (in Korean).

Pohang Iron and Steel Company. 1979. A Decade History of Pohang Iron and Steel Company. Supplementary book (in Korean).

Ryu, S-y. 2001. Political Economics of the Growth of Pohang Iron and Steel Company. Korean Political Science Review. 35 (2). pp. 67–87 (in Korean).

Sakong, I. 1979. Macro-Economic Aspects of the Korean Public Enterprises Sector. Working Paper 7906. Korea Development Institute.

Sakong, I. and Y. Koh. 2010. The Korean Economy: Six Decades of Growth and Development. Korea Development Institute. pp. 177–193 (in Korean).

Sarel, M. 1997. Growth in East Asia: What We Can and What We Cannot Infer. IMF Economic Issues. No. 1.

Song, D-h. 1989. Policies of Managing Korean SOEs. Korea Development Institute (in Korean).

_____. 1994. Evaluation on Privatization Performances of the Korean SOEs. Hankook Gae Bal Yon Gu. 16-4. Korea Development Institute (in Korean).

Song, D-h. and M-h. Song. 1988. Analysis on Development Factors of the Korean SOEs: Focusing on KEPCO and KT. Hankook Gae Bal Yon Gu. 10-4. Korea Development Institute. pp. 39–59 (in Korean).

Sung, M-j. 2010a. GDP Share and Economic Roles of State-Owned Enterprises in Korea. The Korean Association of Public Finance (in Korean).

_____. 2010b. SOEs' Contribution to the Korean Economy and Their Roles and Tasks: Focusing on the Estimation of Value Added (in Korean).

Yoon, S-C. 1986. Safe Capital Relation in View of Public Enterprise: Focusing on South Korea in 1962–1979. Seoul National University (in Korean).

Yoon, S-G. 1986. State and Capital Relations in View of Public Enterprise. Seoul National University (in Korean).

Young, A. 1994. Lessons from the East Asian NICs: A Contrarian View. *European Economic Review.* XXXVIII. pp. 964–973.

CHAPTER 3

Enhancing the Development Contribution of Indonesia's State-Owned Enterprises

Yougesh Khatri and Mohamad Ikhsan

3.1 Introduction

The role of the state and state-owned enterprises (SOEs) in economic development has long been controversial and the prevailing wisdom has shifted substantially. Following the Second World War, policy makers assigned SOEs greater roles, involving them in postwar reconstruction and state-led industrialization drives.[1] In the 1980s, against the backdrop of global stagflation followed by the fall of the Berlin Wall, the pendulum swung the other way with the rise of so-called neoliberal thinking (and the associated Washington Consensus) recommending deregulation and privatization (Chang 2003, OECD 2015). In light of events then and in the wake of the global financial crisis, the pendulum had come to rest somewhere in between.

SOEs have played prominent roles in development successes in Asia (the flying geese paradigm)—particularly in Japan and in the newly industrialized economies of Singapore; Hong Kong, China; Taipei,China; and the Republic of Korea; as well as the member economies of the Association of Southeast Asian Nations, and more recently in the dramatic rise of the People's Republic of China (PRC).[2] Undoubtedly, the state and SOEs have played a significant role in Indonesia's development and will continue to do so.

SOEs have a long history in Indonesia, and the Constitution mandates the state's role in key sectors and in natural resources. Indonesia's infrastructure has been identified as one of the main binding constraints on Indonesia's

---

[1] Important developments in the interwar years that laid the foundation for this swing toward state intervention were the birth of the welfare systems (in the wake of the Great Depression), the rise of Keynesian economics, and the consolidation of socialist planning in the former Soviet Union (Chang 2003).

[2] Chang (2003) and OECD (2015) discuss further the role of state capital in Asia's development.

growth (OECD 2016a and 2018; Breuer, Guajardo, and Kinda 2018). SOEs have long been major providers of infrastructure and public services, and this will likely continue until greater private sector involvement can be developed or created.

SOEs account for a relatively small share of output and employment. SOE assets are highly concentrated in finance, energy, power, and other infrastructure.[3] Indonesia's value-added share of SOEs in overall gross domestic product (GDP) is relatively small—at 6% to 8% versus a multiple of this for other major Asian economies—as is the employment share (less than 1% of total employment). The number of SOEs owned by the central government (known as Badan Usaha Milik Negara or BUMN) has declined from 158 in 2002 to 118 in 2018, with some transitioning into government agencies and others being consolidated under holding companies. While there are still more than 100 SOEs (and several hundred subsidiaries), only a few account for the vast majority of SOE assets, revenues, profits, and dividends.

Since 2012, SOE assets as a share of GDP have been increasing, but their financial performance has been deteriorating. After a long period of relative decline, the ratio of SOE assets to GDP began to increase as nominal GDP growth slowed and as infrastructure investment increased. The return on equity (ROE) of Indonesia's SOEs in aggregate, compared with an internationally benchmarked ROE, suggests substantial forgone profits. The increasing role and relative size of Indonesia's SOEs combined with their deteriorating performance highlight the urgency of reinvigorating reforms and building on past progress.

International experience shows that the reform agenda for Indonesia's SOEs will be highly country specific (i.e., not one-size-fits-all). Reforms need to be prioritized depending on the country's level of development and economic, political, and historical context as well as on the specific sectors and the nature of SOEs under consideration. SOE performance across economies differs largely in the way economies are managed and in the strength of complementary governance structures, competition frameworks, and regulatory frameworks (OECD 2015). Clearly, a holistic approach toward getting SOEs to perform their best will require major improvements in economic management and governance as well as in SOE-specific reforms.

---

[3] The vast majority of SOE assets are accounted for by the oil company (Pertamina); state banks (Mandiri, BNI, BRI, BTN); the power company (PLN); telecommunication companies; and other infrastructure. A large number of smaller SOEs are in commercial areas such as manufacturing, construction, professional and technical services, transport and storage, and wholesale and retail trade.

Despite the progress with earlier SOE reforms, an extensive reform agenda will require considerable political resolve. After the Asian financial crisis, the government made notable progress in monitoring, transparency, and governance of major SOEs. Ownership has also evolved substantially as SOEs were privatized and consolidated into holding companies. Nevertheless, the interrelated factors of governance, politics, and vested interest remain major challenges to reform. Absent the catalytic forces of a crisis, a strong political resolve for pushing reforms forward is essential.

3.2   Overview of Indonesia's SOEs

SOEs have a long history in Indonesia with direct links to the 1945 Constitution.[4] Chapter XIV (Article 33, paragraph 2) of the 1945 Constitution states, "Sectors of production which are important for the country and affect the life of the people shall be controlled by the state." While this can be interpreted in various ways, it would seem to compel government or government-controlled entities to provide basic infrastructure services (and indeed a significant portion of overall infrastructure and infrastructure investment relates to SOEs). The Constitution also states in Article 33, paragraph 3, "The land, the waters and the natural resources within shall be under the powers of the State and shall be used to the greatest benefit of the people." This article has been used in general to justify state ownership of natural resource companies (and as a basis for requiring foreign companies to divest majority stakes in Indonesian mines to the government by the end of the 10th year of production under the 2009 Mining Law and its implementing regulations).

Historical, developmental, and political factors also influence the formation and expansion of SOEs. After independence, the nationalization of foreign (mainly Dutch) firms created a number of SOEs such as those in shipping, plantations, and oil and gas. The government also formed SOEs as part of an import substitution strategy for fertilizer, steel, and basic chemicals, among others, and to pioneer development of certain sectors such as toll road and telecommunication. Kim (2018) notes that SOEs are often created with political motives and as a means to supplement the compensation of officials or more generally for political patronage. Governments can also use SOEs

---

4   A variety of SOEs were formed following the nationalization of foreign companies during the Sukarno era (1945–1967), and the SOE sector expanded substantially during the Suharto era (1967–1998). Fitriningrum (2006), Wickasono (2008), Rakhman (2018), ADB (2017a, Box 3.3), and Kim (2018) discuss the history of Indonesia's SOEs in more detail.

to move beyond hard budget constraint and protect or further indigenous interests. Political motivations thus need to be carefully considered when designing SOE reforms.

The Ministry of State-Owned Enterprises (MSOE 2017) defines the purpose of creating SOEs and the SOE objectives as follows:

- Contribute to the development of the national economy in general and state revenue in particular.

- Pursue profit.

- Provide the public with high-quality goods and/or services.

- Pioneer business activities which the private sector and cooperatives have not yet undertaken.

- Guide and assist entrepreneurs of economically weak cooperative and community groups.

An SOE is a business enterprise that is fully owned or majority-owned and controlled by the government (via the MSOE or the Ministry of Finance). SOEs are known in Indonesia as Badan Usaha Milik Negara or BUMN. This chapter does not cover enterprises that are owned and directly controlled by local governments (provinces, regencies, and municipalities) and known by the acronym BUMD or those recently created under the Ministry of Finance for supporting infrastructure development. Law No. 19 adopted in 2003 defines two types of SOEs (MSOE 2017):[5]

i) A **persero** is a limited liability company whose capital is divided into shares of which the Government of Indonesia owns all or at least 51%. Perseros should be highly competitive and provide high-quality goods and/or services to pursue profits and increase business value.

ii) A **perum** is a special purpose entity whose capital is wholly owned by the state and is not divided into shares. Perums conduct business to serve the public by providing quality goods and/or services at affordable prices based on sound business management principles.

---

[5] A third type of company—the *perjan was* funded by government budget, making perjan employees civil servants—ceased to exist in 2005 as they became either a persero or a perum or a government agency.

3.2.1   Portfolio Composition

The number of SOEs declined from 158 in 2002 to 118 in 2017, partly because some SOEs became government agencies and others consolidated in certain sectors under holding companies. In addition to the number of SOEs in 2017, there were 25 companies in which the government owned a minority stake. The large number of SOE subsidiaries—Kim (2018) estimates about 700— constrain effective monitoring by MSOE. As holding companies are created in the different sectors, the number of SOEs can be expected to decline further.

There are 16 SOEs and 12 SOE subsidiaries that are publicly listed, which is about 4% of all listed companies on the Indonesia Stock Exchange. Yet, these listed SOEs accounted for about one quarter of total market capitalization at the end of 2017 (mostly relating to state banks).[6] Of the remaining limited liability companies (perseros), 84 are not publicly listed and 24 are majority or fully owned by the government through the MSOE or the Ministry of Finance. Of the existing 14 perums, the Indonesia Bureau of Logistics (Bulog) deals with food price control and distribution and has by far the largest assets.

Indonesia's SOEs are spread across 13 sectors, with assets mainly in banking and provision of core public infrastructure services (Figure 3.1). The largest number of SOEs are in manufacturing, transport, and financial services, and the largest employers are the agriculture, forestry and fisheries, and financial services sectors. However, the financial services (mainly the state banks) and energy (the power company, PLN; and the oil and gas company, Pertamina) sectors top the list in asset size, equity, and profit. Besides the state banks and Pertamina, the larger SOEs provide basic infrastructure services. Still a large number of SOEs engage in other commercial activities such as manufacturing, agriculture, and wholesale and retail trade; but their share of overall SOE assets is relatively small.[7]

---

[6]   Four SOEs—Telkom, BRI, Bank Mandiri, and BNI—are listed in the top 10 companies according to market capitalization.

[7]   Many manufacturing SOEs are "dying firms." Given the difficulty of closing down loss-making SOEs in Indonesia, they continue to exist or operate but they can be thought of as "zombies."

Figure 3.1: SOE Sectors of Indonesia, 2017

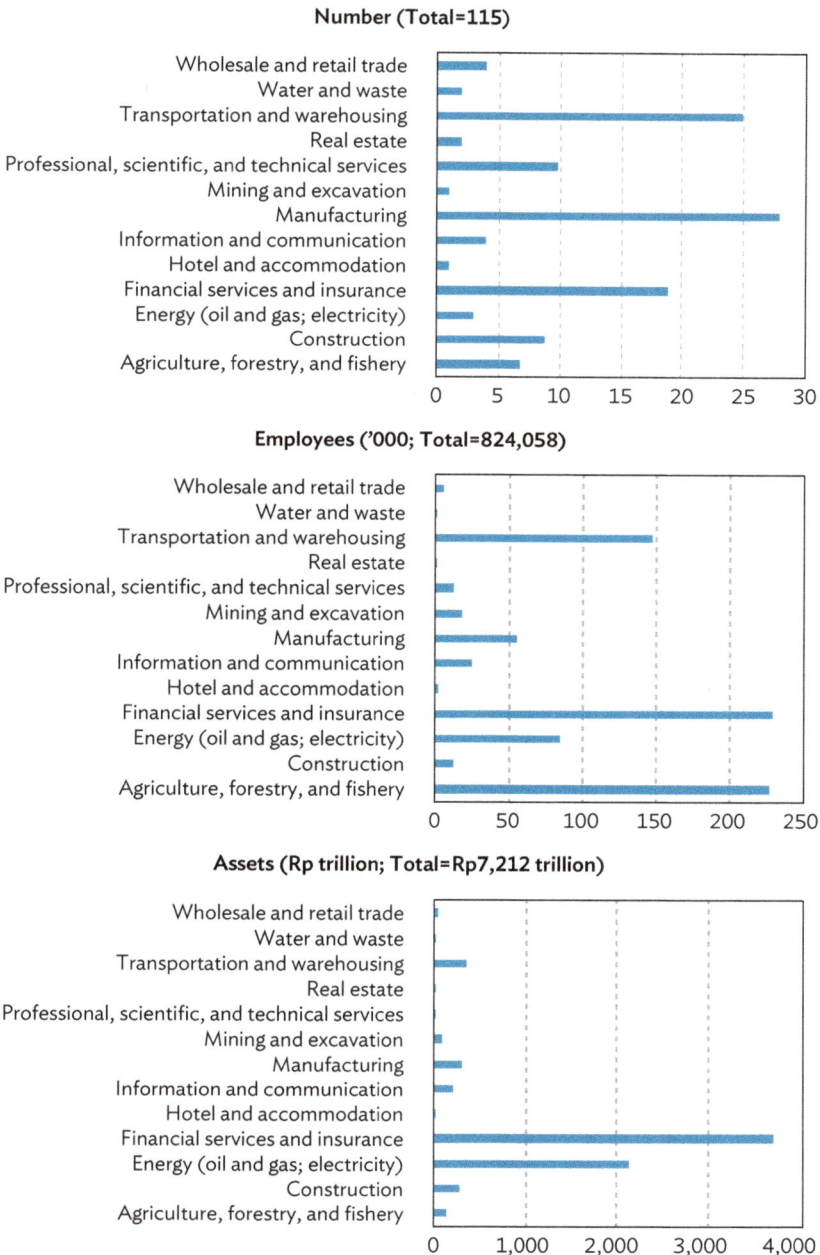

Number (Total=115)

Employees ('000; Total=824,058)

Assets (Rp trillion; Total=Rp7,212 trillion)

Figure 3.1 continued

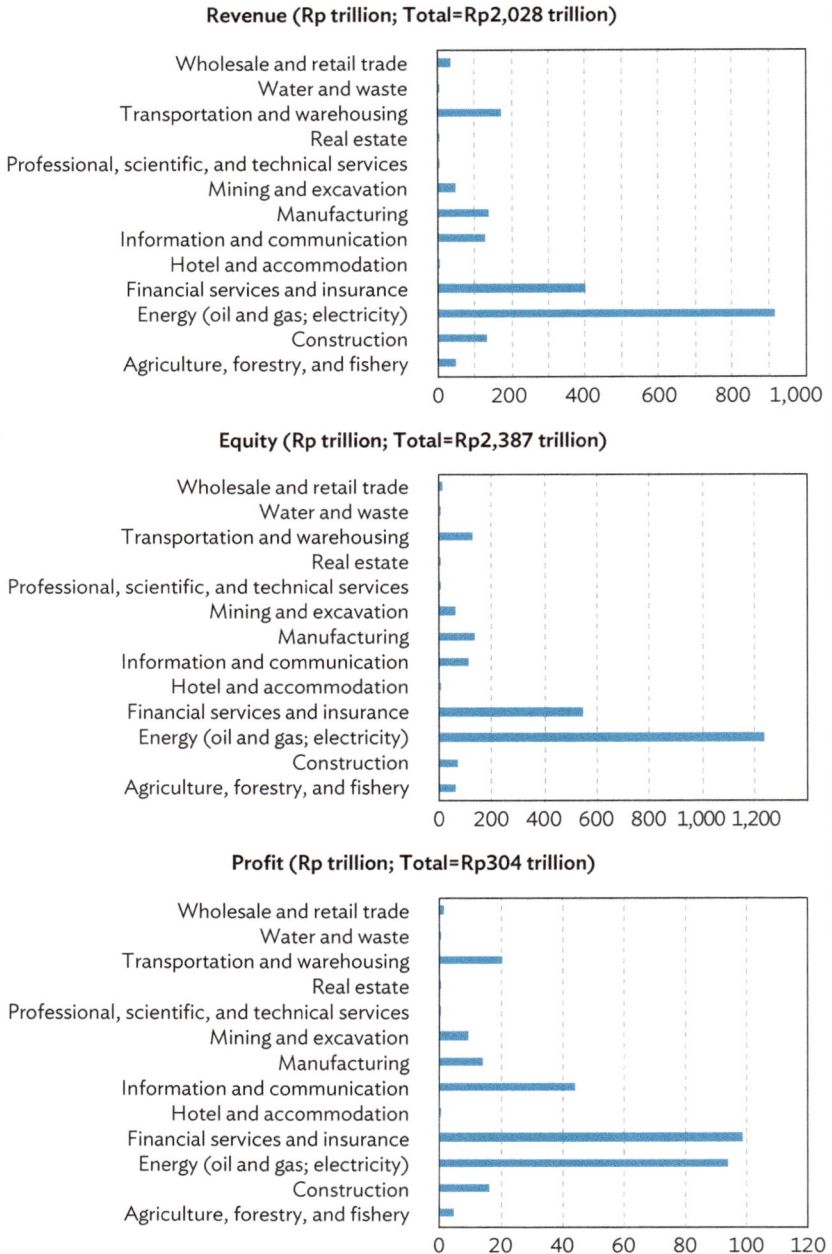

Revenue (Rp trillion; Total=Rp2,028 trillion)

Equity (Rp trillion; Total=Rp2,387 trillion)

Profit (Rp trillion; Total=Rp304 trillion)

SOE = state-owned enterprise.
Source: Authors' calculations using data from the Ministry of State-Owned Enterprises.

In other emerging markets, the concentration of SOE assets depends particularly on whether the country is an exporter of natural resources, but typically network and finance sectors are also important. In the member economies of the Organisation for Economic Co-operation and Development (OECD), around half of the total value of all SOEs are in the network sectors—mostly transportation, power generation, and other energy; financial institutions account for a further quarter of total valuation; and among the partly state-owned listed companies, many are partially privatized telecommunication companies (OECD 2011).

SOE equity, profits, dividends, investment, and employment are also highly concentrated. In 2017, the 20 largest SOEs in asset size accounted for 90% of total SOE assets, while the 10 largest SOEs comprised 80%, and the 5 largest SOEs at 70% (Table 3.1). Also, the top-five SOEs together made up around 70% of liabilities, equity, dividends, and capex; around two-thirds of profits; and half of total SOE employment. Such concentration is also common in both emerging and OECD economies.

Table 3.1: Financial Indicators for Total SOEs versus the Largest 20/10/5 SOEs

Data for 2017	Assets	Liabilities	Equity	Gross Revenue	Gross Profit	EBITDA	Net Profit	Capital Spending	Dividends	Employees '000s
Total for all SOEs (Rp trillion)	7,212	4,825	2,387	2,028	304	389	189	323	41	824
Total for all SOEs ($ billion)	532.0	355.9	176.1	149.6	22.4	28.7	13.9	23.8	3.1	824
Ratio to GDP (% of GDP)	53.1	35.5	17.6	14.9	2.2	2.9	1.4	2.4	0.3	
Top 20 SOEs (% of total)	91	92	91	88	91	90	92	93	99	83
Top 10 SOEs (% of total)	82	84	82	74	80	80	81	84	88	66
Top 5 SOEs (% of total)	69	70	69	61	65	66	69	70	72	49

EBITDA = earnings before interest, tax, depreciation, and amortization; GDP = gross domestic product; SOE = state-owned enterprise.
Note: The top 20/10/5 SOEs are categorized according to each SOE's balance sheet and income statement account item relative to the SOE total for that item.
Source: Authors' calculation based on Ministry of State-Owned Enterprises data.

3.2.2   State-Owned Enterprise Reforms over the Past 2 Decades

Given the central role of SOEs, Indonesia's political landscape has for decades consistently featured plans for reforming SOEs.[8] In the latter part of the Suharto era, the government seemed to acknowledge the need for a concerted strategy to enable SOEs—which have long been viewed as "mismanaged, inefficient, open to corruption, and cash cows for the election chests of political parties" (Cochrane 2007)—to realize their potential. In November 1995, Telkom was partially privatized through an initial public offering (IPO), and the cement holding company had already been partially privatized. After the Asian financial crisis, fiscal pressures, democratization, decentralization, and the need for better transparency and governance pressed the need for SOE reforms, while at the same time reforms became more complicated as relevant stakeholders (including political parties and levels of government) proliferated.

The government introduced privatization and reforms in performance and governance as part of its programs with the International Monetary Fund (IMF) during 1997–2003. As a consequence, several letters of intent were issued:

- In the program's first letter of intent (LOI) dated 31 October 1997, SOE reforms pushed for domestic competition and promoted privatization, expanded private provision of infrastructure, reviewed public expenditure, and shifted SOE oversight from line ministries to the Ministry of Finance. The program also developed a framework for managing and privatizing SOEs, notably for closing nonviable SOEs and setting clear performance targets.

- Subsequent LOIs set targets for privatization, established plans for closing nonviable enterprises, and introduced special audits of the largest SOEs, particularly on their efficiency, capital budgeting, and financing, and identifying possible fraudulent and corrupt practices. In the March 1999 LOI, the government committed to restructuring the power sector.[9]

---

[8]   In the run-up to the 2019 Presidential election, the role of SOEs and the need for private participation in infrastructure provision were featured among the main topics of a dialogue between the two camps (Gorbiano 2018).

[9]   Restructuring consisted of (i) establishing a legal and regulatory framework for a competitive electricity market; (ii) restructuring and reorganizing PLN; (iii) adjusting electricity tariffs; and (iv) rationalizing purchases from the private sector power producers.

- In the January 2000 LOI, the government committed to not establishing holding companies for public enterprises "as such arrangements would dampen competition and slow privatization." Steps were also taken to ensure that SOEs adhere to the same corporate governance standards required of listed companies, including having to lodge annual reports with the company registrar.

The structure of SOE ownership thus changed significantly—privatizations (partial equity sales) and consolidation under holding companies prevailed in the post-program era, leading to the following series of events:

- Privatization had long been a prominent feature in all administrations, but it increasingly lost steam. The government planned to "privatize all but a few selected enterprises within the next decade" (IMF 1998). In practice, full privatization and sales of majority stakes have rarely occurred, waning instead in the face of strong political opposition and with the crises increasingly in the rearview mirror (Kim 2018). Big bang privatization in the immediate aftermath of the Asian financial crisis was followed by partial privatization of state banks and other SOEs during 2001–2004 and then, what was termed rightsizing (continued partial privatization through IPOs) until 2014. Increasingly, privatization also seemed to be carried out to meet fiscal needs. Privatization has not been a prominent policy feature under the current administration, and SOEs have taken over some private sector companies.[10]

- Plans to consolidate SOEs into holding companies date back to 2007 but the process had been slow until the Widodo administration. In 2007, MSOE announced a plan to reduce the number of SOEs from 139 in 2006 by around half, to 69 by 2009, and to 25 by 2015, through merger, divestment, and liquidation (Wicaksono 2008). Statements by the President and the minister of state-owned enterprises (around the April 2019 general elections) suggest an intention to establish a super holding company structure—similar to Singapore's Temasek Holdings or Malaysia's Khazanah Nasional.

Under President Joko Widodo (Jokowi), SOEs were used to ramp up the provision of infrastructure, and privatization basically halted. This pragmatic approach (of using SOEs to develop infrastructure) was used to address Indonesia's fiscal constraints (e.g., the 3% deficit ceiling imposed by the fiscal rules), the lack of private sector participation, and the difficult political

---

[10] For example, Semen Indonesia bought Holcim Indonesia, and Bank Mandiri has injected capital into various local fintech startups.

environment for privatization. Since privatization ceased in 2014, the role of SOEs in building infrastructure has heightened as the government made infrastructure a priority. The administration has been using a multipronged approach of boosting SOE balance sheets through capital injections, accepting lower dividend payments, and developing the financing framework (IMF 2018).

Initially, the current government injected a large amount of capital into strategic infrastructure-related SOEs[11] (see Figure 3.14) with a view to those SOEs being able to leverage the capital injections to ramp up infrastructure investment. However, fiscal and political constraints limited the scope for further capital injections.[12]

To promote private and non-budget infrastructure investments, the government set up the Committee for Acceleration of Priority Infrastructure Delivery and established several financing initiatives. Key among these recent financing initiatives are the following:[13]

- Establishing in 2017 a nongovernment investment financing initiative (PINA) at the National Development Planning Agency (BAPPENAS) to promote private and other non-budget investments in selected projects;[14]

- Permitting direct lending from bilateral and multilateral agencies to SOEs for infrastructure investment under a sovereign guarantee;

- Establishing various equity, debt, and credit enhancement facilities through PT SMI (an infrastructure financing SOE established in 2009 which may become an infrastructure bank) and PT Infrastructure Financing Facility; project development facilities at the Ministry of Finance; risk guarantees through the Indonesia Infrastructure Guarantee Fund; and fiscal support through the Viability Gap Fund; and

- Developing the regulatory framework for new financing instruments, including structured products (e.g., asset-backed securities) and infrastructure bonds.

---

[11] The capital injections included PLN, two construction SOEs (Hutama Karya and Waskita Karya), and air and rail transport SOEs (Angkaa Pura and Kereta Api). Earlier capital injections supported ailing SOEs and were used to stimulate private infrastructure investment (Kim 2018).

[12] For example, disbursement of the 2016 capital injection was frozen for half the year as a consequence of opposing policy arguments that social spending should be prioritized over capital injection (Kim 2018).

[13] The government also established the Committee for Acceleration of Priority Infrastructure Delivery (KPPIP) to address coordination problems leading to delays in the rollout of infrastructure projects.

[14] These projects include 19 toll roads, 4 airports, 10 power projects, and 1 tourism project with a total value of $25.8 million. PINA Center for Private Investment. http://pina.bappenas.go.id/.

Reform is now focused on consolidating SOEs into sectoral holding companies. SOE sectoral consolidation maintains the end goal of moving from sector holding companies to a super holding company. Kim (2018) and Wicaksono (2008) discuss in detail privatization and the shift to holding companies—Indonesia's historical background and model of SOE ownership is different from many countries (in Indonesia, ownership is under the MSOE rather than either a line ministry or a company-type structure with a separate legal entity which is more common elsewhere).

The motivations for consolidating SOEs into sector-based holding companies were as follows:

(i)   to strengthen SOEs' development contribution through synergies, scale economies, reduced duplication (e.g., pipelines and networks), and increased ability to leverage larger balance sheets;

(ii) professionalize management and reduce political influence;

(iii) relieve the government from the burden of managing individual companies; and

(iv) create world-class (Fortune 500) companies.

Consolidation into six holding companies was achieved initially in the following sectors:

(i)   fertilizer (PT Pupuk Indonesia) in April 2012 as a strategic holding company (following consolidation initiated in 1997 under the operating holding scheme);

(ii) cement (Semen Indonesia) in January 2013 as strategic holding company (following consolidation in 1995 under an operating holding company);

(iii) forestry (Perum Perhutani) in September 2014;

(iv) plantations (PT Perkebunan Nusantara III) in October 2014;

(v) mining (under PT Indonesia Asahan Aluminium or Inalum) in November 2017; and

(vi) oil and gas (under Pertamina) in April 2018.

In addition, the consolidation process is either being planned or ongoing in the following sectors:[15]

---

15   Based on information from the Ministry of State-Owned Enterprises, 26 November 2018.

(i)   banking and financial services (under Danareksa);

(ii) insurance;

(iii) housing-related construction;

(iv) infrastructure-related construction;

(v)   pharmaceutical;

(vi) testing, inspection, and certification; and

(vii) restructuring company (to manage nonperforming state assets).

As mentioned above, there may be a second phase of consolidation to create a super holding company along the lines of Temasek in Singapore or Khazanah in Malaysia.

3.3   SOEs and the Overall Economy

SOE assets are increasing relative to gross domestic product (GDP) with increased leverage and investment. While SOE value added to overall GDP is relatively smaller than others in the region (despite increases in recent years), SOEs dominate the large listed companies in Indonesia. SOEs employ less than 1% of the labor force but account for around 6% of GDP, suggesting relatively much higher labor productivity than the average firm. SOEs contribute around 7.5% of total investment and now around one-third of infrastructure investment. SOEs are involved increasingly in providing infrastructure, which underscores the importance of reforms.

3.3.1   Assets, Profits, and Dividend Trends of SOEs

SOE assets, relative to GDP, began increasing in 2012 after a long period of relative decline (Figure 3.2). While these assets have grown by over 16% on average since the Asian financial crisis, they were already on a downward trend relative to a rapidly growing nominal GDP until 2012. This growth of SOE assets reflects several factors. First, nominal GDP growth since 2012 slowed to around 10% compared with over 15% during the decade to 2012, reflecting a lower trend in growth and inflation. SOE leverage has increased in the course of low interest rates and long-standing efforts to boost infrastructure spending while facing increasingly binding fiscal constraints. Also, in line with the government's more concerted push toward infrastructure, capital injections into SOEs during 2015 and 2016 totaled around 1% of GDP. In 2015, many SOEs conducted asset revaluations, generating a rise in asset values and bumping up profits, equity, and tax payments.

Figure 3.2: Assets, Liabilities, and Equity, 1992–2017

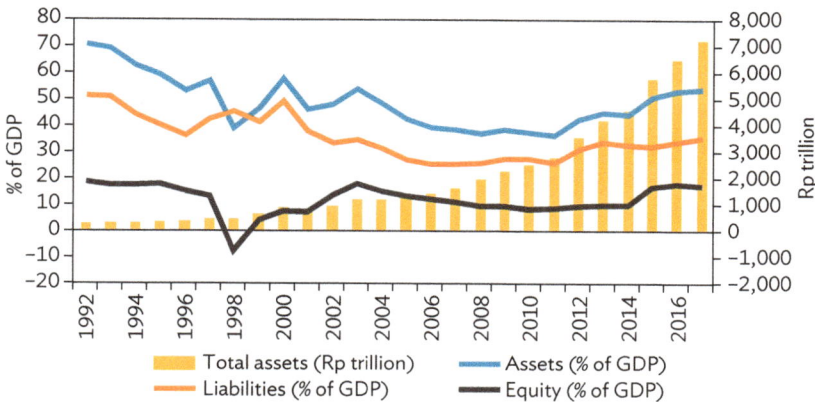

Total assets (Rp trillion)   Assets (% of GDP)
Liabilities (% of GDP)   Equity (% of GDP)

GDP = gross domestic product.
Source: Authors' calculations based on data provided by the Ministry of State-Owned Enterprises.

Relative to GDP, SOE profits have been increasing since 2003 while dividends paid to the government (as a share of GDP) have been declining (Figure 3.3). SOE profits have grown by nearly 13% (compounded annual growth rate) over the past decade while dividends paid to the government grew by less than 5% over the same period. Pertamina, Telkom, the state banks, and PLN contributed major dividends, accounting for three-quarters of total SOE dividends. Dividends are not being distributed in line with profit growth as part of government efforts to build SOE balance sheets in support of infrastructure spending (IMF 2018; and see Figure 3.3).

Figure 3.3: Profits and Dividends to Government, 1992–2017
(% of GDP)

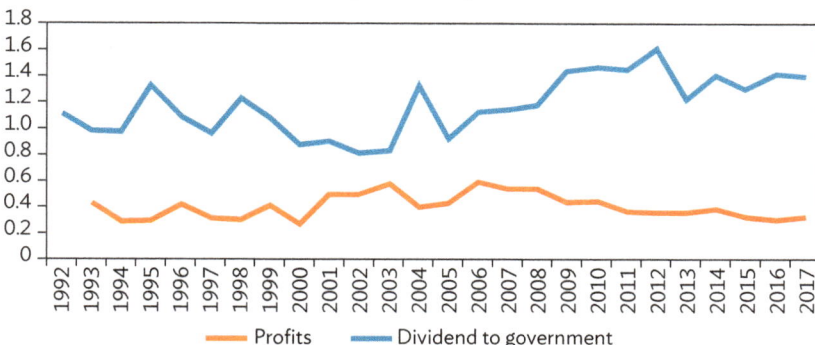

Profits   Dividend to government

GDP = gross domestic product.
Source: Authors' calculations using data from the Ministry of State-Owned Enterprises.

3.3.2   SOE Contributions to Gross Domestic Product and Employment

SOEs have contributed between 6% and 8% to overall GDP (Figure 3.4). Since there is no officially published figure for SOEs' total contribution to GDP, we use estimates compiled by PROSPERA (unpublished). Using company data, they calculate each SOE's value added (relevant to understanding each SOE's contribution to GDP) as follows:

Value Added = Revenue – Indirect Taxes – Cost of Intermediate Goods[16]

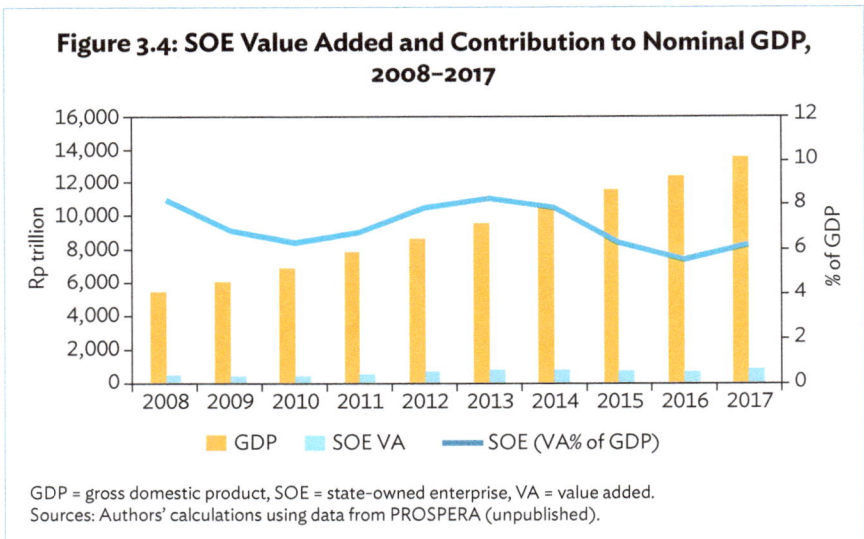

Figure 3.4: SOE Value Added and Contribution to Nominal GDP, 2008–2017

GDP = gross domestic product, SOE = state-owned enterprise, VA = value added.
Sources: Authors' calculations using data from PROSPERA (unpublished).

Companies have their revenue and indirect taxes available, but only some have reported the cost of intermediate goods. For large companies that reported cost of intermediate goods (which accounted for 72% of overall SOE revenue), the share of "cost of intermediate goods" relative to the cost of goods sold was derived (the average ratio was 62.5%). This ratio was then applied to the cost of goods sold for the remaining companies to approximate their cost of intermediate goods and thus derive their value added.[17]

---

[16] A cross-check on the contributions to GDP using the "value-added approach" was done for two large SOEs (Pertamina and Telkom) using the "income approach," which produced similar contributions.

[17] We estimate the 2017 aggregate SOE value added by taking the ratio of total SOE value added to total SOE revenues for 2014–2016 (42%) and applied that to 2017 revenues to yield a total value added of Rp847 trillion or 6.2% of 2017 GDP.

Even though SOE contribution to GDP is smaller than that of other major emerging markets in the region, SOEs dominate the top 10 listed firms in Indonesia (Figure 3.5). SOEs account for about 30% of overall GDP in the People's Republic of China (PRC), 38% in Viet Nam, and 25% in India and Thailand (see section 3.1 for regional comparisons). Indonesian SOEs' dominance over the largest listed companies in emerging markets tends to be higher than in developed markets, with Norway being an obvious exception (the Government of Norway plays a relatively large role for state capital directly, such as through ownership of Statoil, and indirectly, via stakes of the sovereign wealth fund in the local stock market).[18]

Figure 3.5: Dominant SOEs in Top 10 Listed Companies
(% of top-listed firms)

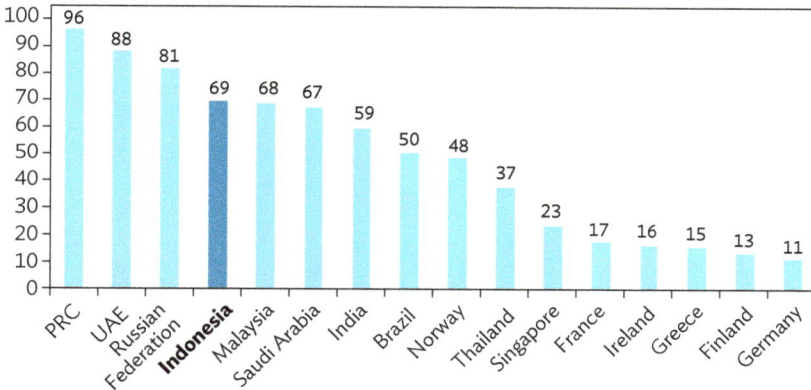

PRC = People's Republic of China, SOE = state-owned enterprise, UAE = United Arab Emirates.
Source: Kowalski et al. (2013).

SOEs in the mining and finance sectors have contributed the highest shares in Indonesia's GDP, but the contribution and share of mining has been shrinking over time while financials have been increasing over time (Figure 3.6). In 2016, the mining sector accounted for one-third (5.5% of GDP) of the total value added of Rp685 trillion, and the finance sector accounted for one-quarter of total SOE value added. In 2008, SOE mining companies contributed more than 4% of GDP, which fell to around 1.3% by 2016. In the electricity and gas

---

[18]   To determine which countries have the highest state-owned enterprise presence among their top firms, Kowalski et al. (2013) use the average shares of SOEs in sales, assets, and market value of the country's top 10 firms.

sector, SOEs' contribution also declined from around 1.3% of GDP in 2008 to around 0.25% in 2016. With its 1.8% increase in share to GDP in 2016, financial SOEs (state banks) are now the largest contributing SOE sector.[19]

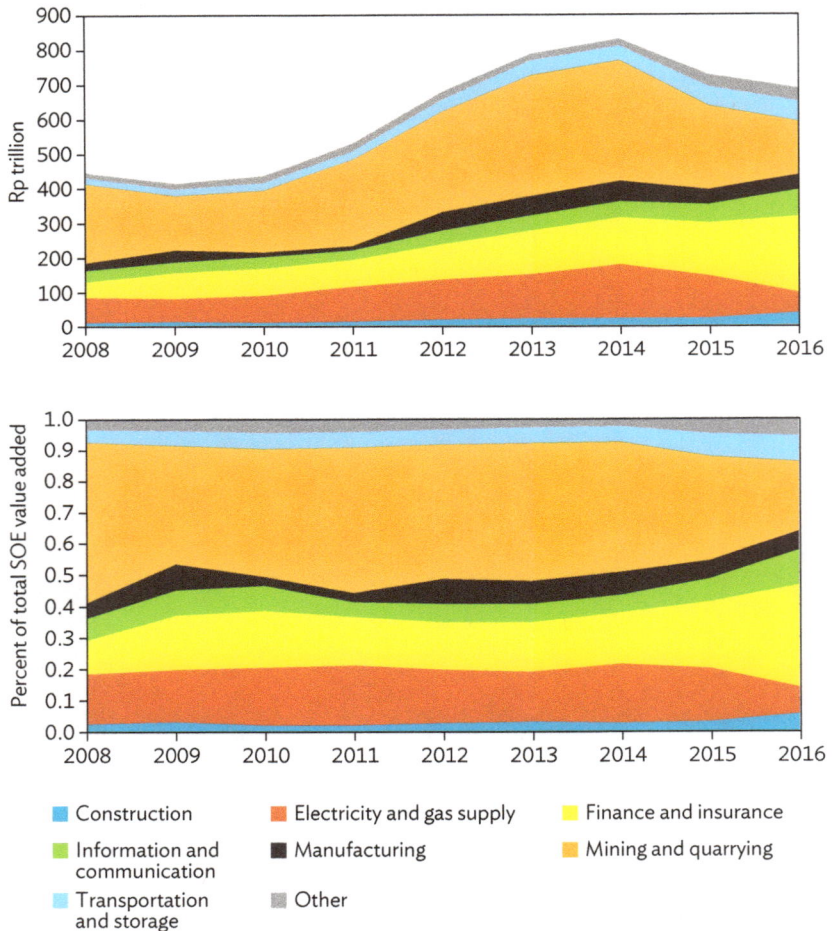

Figure 3.6: SOE Value Added by Sector, 2008–2016

SOE = state-owned enterprise.
Sources: Authors' calculations using data from PROSPERA (unpublished).

---

[19] The sectoral shares of SOEs are relative to sectoral GDP estimates from Statistics Indonesia (BPS). As some SOEs straddle multiple sectors, the sum of the sectoral shares exceeds the overall value added of SOEs in total GDP.

SOEs contribute to less than 1% of overall employment. In 2017, SOEs employed around 824,000 people, which was around 0.7% of total employment or 0.6% of Indonesia's labor force (128 million in 2017). The PRC's SOEs in contrast account for over half of overall employment. Given that Indonesia's SOE sector is estimated to contribute 6%–8% of GDP with less than 1% of employment, SOEs in aggregate must have a notably higher level of labor productivity than the average firms.

3.3.3   SOE Contributions to Overall Investment

Capital expenditure by SOEs accounts for around 7.5% of Indonesia's overall investment (gross fixed capital formation) (Figure 3.7). In recent years, the share of SOE investment in total investment has increased, which is consistent with their role of boosting infrastructure spending. Figure 3.8 shows Indonesia's infrastructure spending from 1995 to 2017, broken down by central government, subnational government, SOEs, and the private sector (based on a database compiled and maintained by PROSPERA). During and after the Asian financial crisis, SOEs accounted for half of total infrastructure spending as private sector infrastructure (and overall) investment fell sharply. With decentralization, the share of subnational government spending on infrastructure continued to increase. After the government's big push to raise overall infrastructure investment, the real overall infrastructure investment level finally exceeded the peak before the Asian financial crisis. However, relative to GDP, total infrastructure spending of around 5% of GDP is still only half the precrisis peak of 10% of GDP.

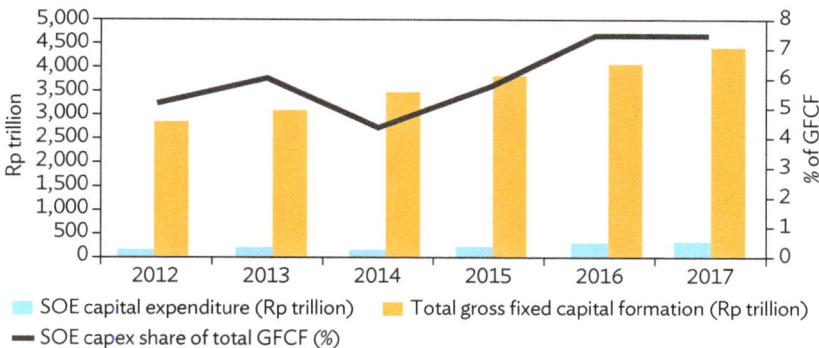

Figure 3.7: SOE Capital Expenditure and Overall Investment, 2012–2017

GFCF = gross fixed capital formation, SOE = state-owned enterprise.
Sources: Authors' calculations using data from the Ministry of State-Owned Enterprises and Indonesia Statistics (BPS).

Figure 3.8: Infrastructure Spending by Government, SOEs, and the Private Sector, 1995–2017

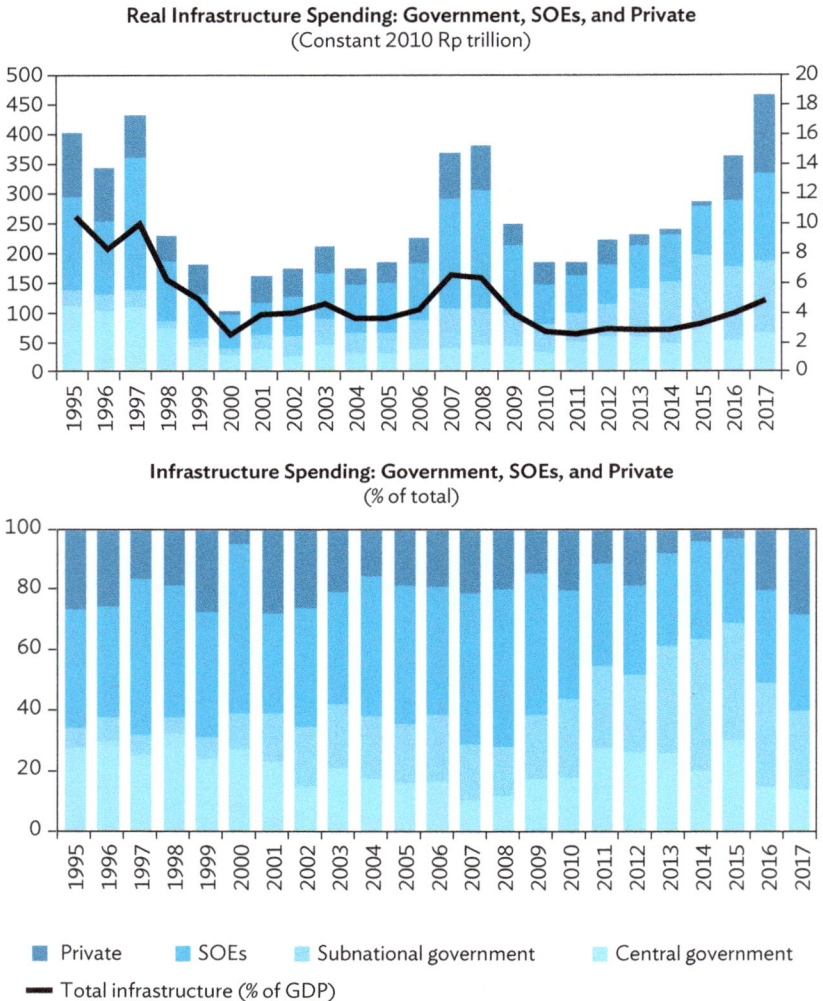

Real Infrastructure Spending: Government, SOEs, and Private
(Constant 2010 Rp trillion)

Infrastructure Spending: Government, SOEs, and Private
(% of total)

■ Private   ■ SOEs   ■ Subnational government   ■ Central government
━━ Total infrastructure (% of GDP)

GDP = gross domestic product, SOE = state-owned enterprise.
Sources: Authors' calculations based on data provided by PROSPERA.

3.4   Financial Performance of SOEs

Indicators of profitability, performance, and solvency for SOEs have deteriorated quite broadly across sectors since 2012. This deterioration was preceded by a period of improving SOE profitability beginning in the aftermath of the Asian financial crisis and continuing during the upswing in commodity prices ahead of the global financial crisis. Returns on equity (ROEs) were well above peers in the region or international benchmark in 2009. The period of the rapid decline in financial performance corresponds to the period infrastructure build-out and a weakening of Indonesia's terms of trade (i.e., softer commodity prices). According to S&P Global (2018), SOE credit metrics are likely to continue to deteriorate through 2019.

Evaluating the financial performance of SOEs is fraught with difficulties and it is often taken as an article of faith that SOEs will underperform their private counterparts. SOEs are typically characterized as being prone to mismanagement and captured by political interest. The greater chance of political interference affecting their operations and governance (Chang 2003) could manifest in many ways. They could, for example, be compelled to employ excess labor and hire those that are politically connected rather than best qualified. Often, SOEs are subject to administered prices and compliance to public service requirements, which might not be fully compensated through subsidies or be quantifiable and deductible before financial ratios are derived. The stakes of unlisted SOEs are not readily transferable, which affects incentives to monitor the performance of managers and firms.

Nevertheless, SOEs often enjoy several advantages over their private counterparts. Government policies may favor them by granting subsidies, capital injections, implicit or explicit government guarantees on debt, favorable loan terms from state banks, favorable terms on inputs from other SOEs (e.g., a below-market coal price for state power companies), and monopolies (Rakhman 2018). SOEs may also enjoy privileged access to information (via government interactions or public officials on their boards). On the other hand, private firms face agency problems (e.g., managers with little or no equity have scope to pursue different objectives from that of owners, especially given the costs of monitoring managers).

From the vast literature on SOE performance, we cannot conclude that SOE returns systematically underperform their private counterparts, but we might deduce that SOEs might be operationally less efficient. Compared with SOEs operating internationally, domestic SOEs tend to be particularly less efficient and flexible than private counterparts, for example, within the bounds of no hard budget constraint or low shareholder pressures for returns (OECD 2016b). OECD research found little or no evidence of systematically lower rates or return in SOEs and inferred that the advantages conferred upon the SOEs were probably sufficient to compensate for the lower operational efficiency they are generally assumed to have (OECD 2016b). In Indonesia's case, Rakhman (2018) finds that partially privatized Indonesian SOEs performed as well as their private counterparts for 13 consecutive years during the sample period of the study in 2000–2012.

3.4.1   Indicators of Profitability

Financial ratios are a useful starting point for assessing trends in SOE performance.[20] ROE and return on assets (ROA) are common measures of financial performance.[21]

- ROE (calculated as net income in year t/average equity during year t) indicates how effectively company management has used investor (or government in the case of SOEs) funds.

- ROA (calculated as net income in year t/average total assets during year t) accounts for leverage and thus considers how well management is using both equity and debt.

The trend in these financial ratios shows improvement through to 2012 and subsequent deterioration in both ROE and ROA. Figure 3.2 showed increasing SOE assets to GDP in relation to the buildup in investment and leverage. However, SOE revenues and profits (as a share of GDP) have declined since 2012, and hence, ROA and ROE have declined as well (Figure 3.9). Post-1998, aggregate SOE ROE/ROA increased in the course of a strong run-up in commodity prices, improved governance and monitoring of SOEs, and sustained period of corporatization and privatization. The decline in overall ROEs and ROAs is driven by various sectors but notably by the finance sector (as banks increased capital ratios and reduced leverage over the period), the natural resource sectors and energy (as a result of the secular decline in oil production and the uncertainty associated with the mining law), and manufacturing.

---

[20] Working through the many and sometimes unclear adjustments needed for a "clean" financial assessment and comparison with private firms is beyond the scope of this study but would provide valuable insights. Micro and industry case studies are usually needed to better understand what is going on and the adjustments required.

[21] Investopedia at www.investopedia.com discusses in detail financial ratio and alternative indicators of profitability, productivity, and solvency.

Figure 3.9: Return on Assets and Return on Equity, 1992–2017

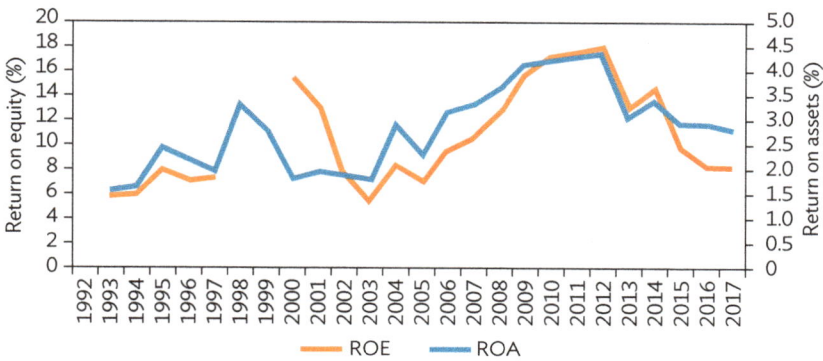

ROA = return on assets, ROE = return on equity.
Note: We exclude the Asian financial crisis period-related negative and positive spikes in the ROE series as these distort the chart.
Source: Authors' calculations using data from the Ministry of State-Owned Enterprises.

Financial SOEs, which are dominated by state banks, account for about 50% of SOE assets. The banks' balance sheets are asset (mainly loans) and liability (mainly deposits) heavy and their ROAs are lower than nonfinancial SOEs. Conversely, financial SOEs enjoy a substantially higher ROE than nonfinancial SOEs, but as banks delivered and built up risk-weighted capital ratios, their ROE declined, pulling down the overall ROEs of SOEs (Figure 3.10).

Figure 3.10: Nonfinancial SOEs and Overall SOE Return on Assets and Return on Equity, 2013–2017

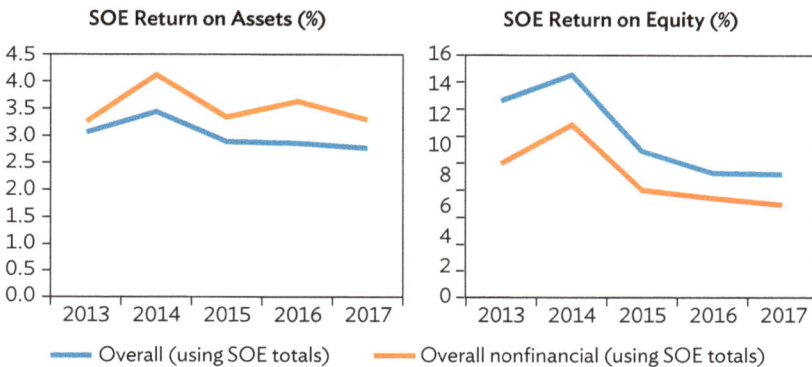

SOE = state-owned enterprise.
Source: Authors' calculations using data from the Ministry of State-Owned Enterprises.

Overall ROEs for Indonesia's listed SOEs were high in 2009 but these have converged downward to the market ROE and toward or below international benchmarks. The left-hand panel of Figure 3.11 shows a substantially higher ROE for Indonesia's listed SOEs than the overall ROE for Indonesia's SOEs and the ROE of the aggregate Indonesia Stock Exchange (IDX) stock market. SOEs account for about one quarter of Indonesia's stock market, and SOE bank, power, and energy stocks dominate the SOE market capitalization. Thus, the decline in ROEs in these sectors as discussed above help explain much of the convergence of the ROEs of listed SOEs toward the ROEs of overall SOEs.[22] On the right-hand panel of Figure 3.11, we see that Indonesia was an outlier in terms of the ROE of its listed SOEs but this has declined below the average ROE of emerging markets and the ROE for the overall United States (US) market. By 2017, the overall ROE for Indonesia's listed SOEs was 10.8% and for overall SOEs it dropped to 8.1%—but still above the IDX overall ROE of 5.7% in 2017, but below the overall market ROE in the US of 13.6% and the emerging markets ROE of 11.4% (as reported in the Damodaran database in January 2018).

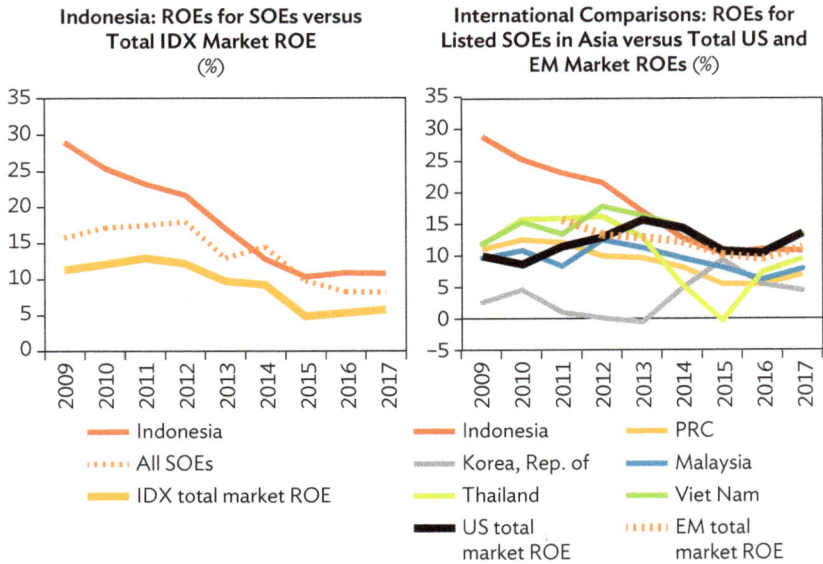

Figure 3.11: Return on Equity of Indonesia's SOEs:
Market and International Comparisons, 2009–2017

EM = emerging market, PRC = People's Republic of China, ROE = return on equity, US = United States.
Source: Authors' calculations using data from the Ministry of State-Owned Enterprises, Damodaran Online, and Orbis database.

---

[22] State-owned banks in Indonesia seem to have usually high ROEs (over 15% in 2017 and averaging almost 19% over the past 5 years) compared with say around 9% in the US.

3.4.2   Indicators of Productive Efficiency

The asset turnover ratio, a simple indicator of productive efficiency, almost halved between 2013 and 2017. The asset turnover ratio (= revenues/assets) indicates how effectively assets are being used to generate revenue (proxying the economic concept of capital intensity of output). The ratio for nonfinancial SOEs dropped to almost half, from nearly 80% in 2013 to 42% in 2017, suggesting a substantial and rapid decline in the effectiveness with which SOEs were converting assets into revenue. The decline can be seen across many sectors, but it is large in the energy sector which accounts for three-fifths of nonfinancial SOE assets. Commodity prices and administered price settings therefore are likely important drivers.

3.4.3   Indicators of Solvency

Various indicators of SOE indebtedness and leverage have been increasing rapidly. The debt-to-equity ratio in Table 3.2 is somewhat distorted by asset revaluations and equity injections which contribute to a discreet drop in the 2015 ratio. Yet, in Figure 3.2, overall SOE liabilities relative to GDP had started to trend upward and the debt-to-equity ratio in Table 3.2 increased sharply as SOEs increased infrastructure investment. S&P Global (2018) ratings find that "for each dollar of EBITDA generated in 2011, listed and rated Indonesian SOEs invested about 30 cents on average. We estimate that by now, SOEs are investing 1.1 dollar for every dollar they generate."

S&P sees no sign of spending slowing down and notes that credit-metric deterioration is already widespread, with leverage increasing and cash flow adequacy ratios weakening for 16 out of 20 listed SOEs (particularly across commodities, infrastructure, and construction sectors). They estimate that the median debt-to-earnings before interest, tax, depreciation, and amortization (EBIDTA) ratio—an indicator of debt servicing capacity—deteriorated (increased) from around 1x in 2011 to around 4.5x in 2017; and they forecast that it will continue to increase toward 5.5x through 2019. (While S&P ratings are stable for now, they note that the headroom under the ratings for some SOEs has reduced.)

Table 3.2: Financial Ratios for SOEs in Aggregate and by Sector, 2013–2017

	Return on Assets (%)					Return on Equity (%)				
	2013	2014	2015	2016	2017	2013	2014	2015	2016	2017
Overall (using SOE totals)	3.1	3.5	2.9	2.9	2.8	13.0	14.7	9.7	8.3	8.1
Overall nonfinancial (using SOE totals)	3.3	4.1	3.4	3.6	3.3	8.9	11.4	7.1	6.6	6.1
Overall (unweighted average of SOEs)	4.8	3.0	2.2	2.3	3.9	24.5	9.2	3.2	(3.7)	1.8
Median from all SOEs	4.1	3.5	3.4	3.3	3.0	16.3	14.0	12.1	9.0	9.3
Sector Averages										
Agriculture, forestry, and fishery	(1.6)	0.9	(0.5)	(1.2)	1.6	(4.3)	2.8	(1.3)	(2.6)	3.5
Construction	4.3	4.2	4.2	3.4	4.1	20.7	19.6	14.9	10.8	14.7
Energy (oil and gas and electricity)	1.1	3.0	2.5	2.9	2.0	3.4	9.8	5.1	4.8	3.3
Financial services and insurance	2.9	2.9	2.5	2.1	2.3	22.9	22.3	18.4	14.8	15.3
Hotel and accommodation	(5.2)	9.1	(9.0)	(1.6)	0.0	(48.0)	82.3	(120.0)	(2.1)	0.0
Information and communication	16.7	15.5	14.8	16.5	17.1	27.9	25.8	25.6	28.9	30.0
Manufacturing	6.9	5.8	2.5	2.6	2.1	16.0	13.8	6.0v	5.6	4.4
Mining and excavation	7.0	6.0	2.7	4.2	7.9	9.9	9.1	4.1	6.3	11.2
Professional, scientific, and technical services	13.9	12.9	10.3	5.2	7.6	24.6	22.0	16.1	7.7	11.8
Real estate	6.9	8.1	9.0	8.1	7.9	8.0	9.5	10.4	9.4	9.5
Transportation and warehousing	4.8	2.6	3.8	4.1	3.6	9.8	5.7	9.2	9.9	9.1
Water and waste	15.1	14.0	10.9	20.8	17.2	19.1	17.5	14.0	27.9	22.4
Wholesale and retail trade	(0.9)	(2.0)	4.9	3.5	2.8	(4.0)	(8.2)	17.8	11.1	7.5

( ) = negative, SOE = state-owned enterprise.
Source: Authors' calculations using data from the Ministry of State-Owned Enterprises.

Continued on next page

Table 3.2 continued

	Assets Turnover Ratio (%)					Debt–Equity Ratio (%)				
	2013	2014	2015	2016	2017	2013	2014	2015	2016	2017
Overall (using SOE totals)	43	43	30	26	28	328	320	189	185	202
Overall nonfinancial (using SOE totals)	79	82	47	42	46	183	172	83	79	91
Overall (unweighted average of SOEs)	67	63	53	51	50	199	198	112	417	301
Median from all SOEs	58	55	44	41	44	104	107	98	114	131
Sector Averages										
Agriculture, forestry, and fishery	68	65	38	34	35	197	236	116	124	123
Construction	96	83	59	46	48	385	355	215	213	291
Energy (oil and gas and electricity)	83	90	42	37	43	237	207	68	64	71
Financial services and insurance	10	11	12	11	11	681	657	631	579	578
Hotel and accommodation	30	28	32	6	6	1,273	608	9,936	15	15
Information and communication	67	64	61	65	65	67	65	79	71	79
Manufacturing	79	76	59	49	47	133	145	138	103	115
Mining and excavation	63	59	52	45	51	46	57	52	45	41
Professional, scientific, and technical service	136	124	85	78	75	71	71	48	50	61
Real estate	26	28	26	26	27	18	17	14	18	23
Transportation and warehousing	58	58	50	47	49	113	130	149	138	170
Water and waste	83	77	80	82	72	27	22	37	33	28
Wholesale and retail trade	105	119	103	97	103	337	287	252	189	140

( ) = negative, SOE = state-owned enterprise.
Source: Authors' calculations using data from the Ministry of State-Owned Enterprises.

3.5   SOE-Related Revenues, Subsidies, Costs, and Risks

SOEs make substantive fiscal and broader contributions to Indonesia's economy. They receive direct compensation from users for services through levies and fees and various forms of explicit (budgetary) and implicit subsidies from government—which may or may not fully compensate for public service obligation or below-market administered prices. Implicit subsidies are large, difficult to quantify, and not transparent and, thus, not subject to the same budgetary rigor as budget expenditure items. While the important role of SOEs in supporting Indonesia's development and growth objectives is well acknowledged, the risks associated with their increasing role—such as competition issues, crowding out, and contingent fiscal liabilities—need to be carefully considered and monitored.

3.5.1   Fiscal and Other Contributions of SOEs

Total fiscal contributions, through SOE tax payments, nontax payments, and dividends, ranged from $20 billion to $25 billion per annum during 2015–2017 or around 2.5% of GDP (Figure 3.12). This represents a substantial share of overall general government revenues (which totaled only 14% of GDP in 2017). Yet, while overall profitability of SOEs as a share of GDP has been increasing, dividends as a share of GDP have been trending down from a peak of 0.6% of GDP in 2006 to around 0.3% of GDP during 2015–2017 (Figure 3.3).

Figure 3.12: Fiscal Contribution of SOEs, 2015–2017
($ billion)

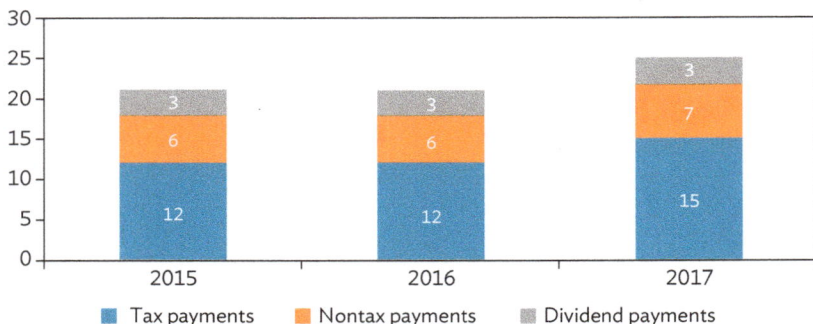

SOE = state-owned enterprise.
Source: Ministry of State-Owned Enterprises.

SOEs have also substantially contributed to Indonesia's economic development, but these contributions have been difficult to quantify. SOEs' contribution to GDP, employment, and investment as discussed in section 3.3 may be relatively smaller in Indonesia than in other major economies in Asia. But they have built much-needed infrastructure (for which the fiscal multipliers can be large); deepened capital and financial markets; accessed foreign exchange; and helped in the "formalization" of the economy. Breuer, Guajardo, and Kinda (2018) have most likely included some of these benefits in their *reform scenario*.

3.5.2   Budget Subsidies Associated with SOEs

On-budget subsidies paid to SOEs dropped from a peak of around 5% of GDP in 2008 to around 1% of GDP in 2017 (Figure 3.13). However, these on-budget subsidies are not usually intended to support SOE operations per se but to compensate for government policy on administered prices (mainly for fuel, power, and fertilizer) or counterparts to public service obligations. As discussed earlier, a detailed case study may be the best approach to assess financial performance (and untangle the state-imposed factors from the company's performance). The government's move toward market pricing, lower subsidies, and some offsetting to target direct cash transfers to the vulnerable is a very welcome and much-needed direction. It should help better determine

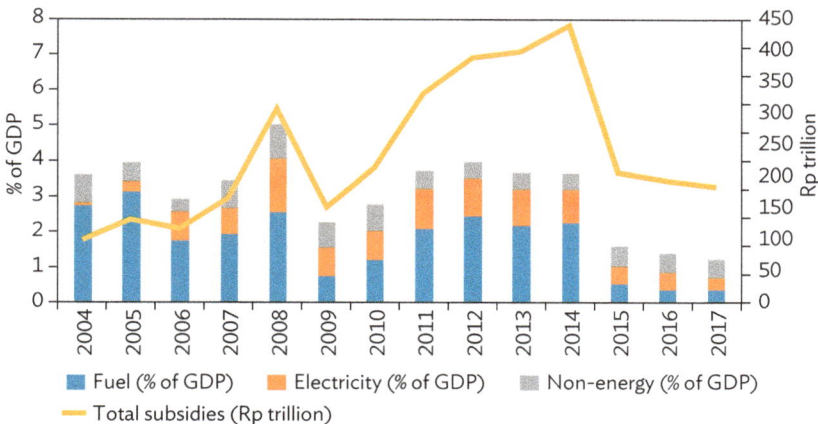

Figure 3.13: On-Budget Subsidies, 2004–2017

Fuel (% of GDP)   Electricity (% of GDP)   Non-energy (% of GDP)
Total subsidies (Rp trillion)

GDP = gross domestic product.
Source: Authors' calculations using data from the Ministry of State-Owned Enterprises.

the underlying performance of the SOE and reduce economic distortions associated with the administered pricing. Yet with on-budget subsidies still around 1% of GDP—which is almost the amount spent by general government on health expenditure (1.3% of GDP in 2017)—there is scope to continue this process.

3.5.3   Implicit Subsidies Associated with SOEs

In addition to on-budget subsidies, various implicit subsidies and support contribute to "soft budget constraint" for SOEs, such as equity injections, forgone dividends, and debt guarantees.

- Government equity injections totaled around 1.5% of GDP during 2009–2018 (Figure 3.14). These equity injections are treated as financing (or "below the line") in the budget, unlike the subsidies that appear under expenditure. Capital injections into SOEs have been regular, including those that support ailing SOEs.[23] These amounts were particularly large in 2015 and in 2016 (totaling around 1% of GDP) in an effort to leverage the capital injection toward building infrastructure. Breuer, Guajardo, and Kinda (2018) present mixed evidence of whether this strategy worked.

- Forgone dividends are another form of implicit subsidy. The government also made lower dividend transfers as part of its effort to support SOE balance sheets and push infrastructure. SOE profits (in nominal rupiah terms) grew annually by over 13% (compound annual growth rate) on average during 2008–2017, while dividend growth has been a more modest 5%. The forgone dividends might be considered as another form of implicit subsidy. The average annual dividend transfer from all SOEs during the decade to 2009 was 0.5% of GDP versus around 0.3% of GDP since 2015, suggesting at least 0.2% of GDP in dividends forgone annually.

- SOEs enjoy implicit and explicit government guarantees for borrowing and are likely to receive preferential terms from state banks. This is another implicit subsidy, which should ideally be accounted for both in terms of the implied benefits and the contingent liability implications.

---

[23] In 2017, 9 SOEs had negative equity and 27 SOEs incurred an overall loss (aggregating profits and losses) during 2012–2017.

Figure 3.14: Government Equity Injections into SOEs, 2005–2018

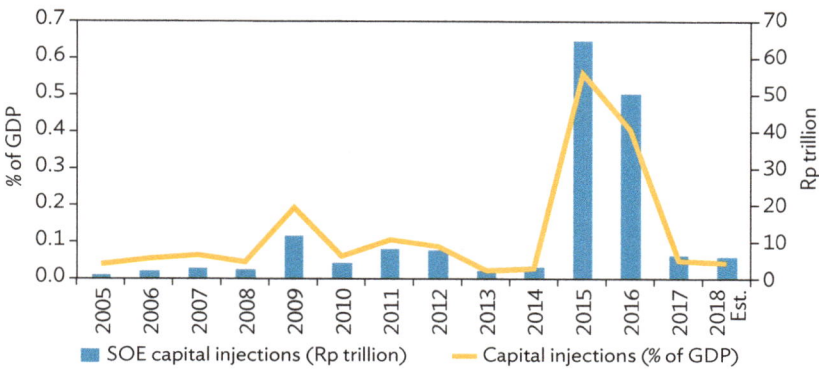

GDP = gross domestic product, SOE = state-owned enterprise.
Source: Authors' calculations using data from the Ministry of State-Owned Enterprises.

To assess the implicit subsidy to SOEs in aggregate, one approach is to consider their combined financial "underperformance" relative to an appropriate benchmark. The Australia Indonesia Partnership for Economic Development (PROSPERA) developed a simple implicit subsidy measure, which measures factors in some of the above issues by considering actual profit versus profits SOEs would have achieved in receiving the "efficient" ROE.[24] Thus, we might consider an overall measure of the implicit subsidy as follows:

$$Implicit\ Subsidy = Profit - Equity \times ROE^*$$

where ROE* is the efficient risk-weighted cost of equity for SOEs. As shown earlier, the ROE can vary substantially between industries and over time. Also discussed were the distortionary effects of implicit benefits enjoyed by SOEs (such as below-cost inputs from other SOEs, implicit government guarantees, and favorable credit from a state bank). By considering SOEs *in aggregate,* some of the intra-SOE issues are at least dealt with (and some of the other factors could be built into a customized efficient ROE for that SOE, which we do not pursue).

The implicit subsidy estimate indicates a substantial annual forgone SOE profit nearing Rp100 trillion (or more than 0.7% of 2017 GDP). Figure 3.15 shows the estimated implicit subsidy based on an assumed ROE* of 12%—which

---

[24] John Cheong-Holdaway proposed the implicit subsidy methodology while at the Australia Indonesia Partnership for Economic Governance (AIPEG), the Department of Foreign Affairs and Trade-funded program that was the precursor to PROSPERA.

is the 10-year average of the ROE on the US stock market (through 2017) and approximately the long-term average ROE for overall emerging markets (12.2%). This approach suggests that implicit subsidies associated with SOE underperformance in aggregate have been in the region of more than 1% of GDP in the past and have averaged around 0.5% of GDP over this long period. Cumulatively, since 1992 (excluding the Asian financial crisis period) the implicit subsidies, using the same ROE* of 12%, have totaled more than 10% of GDP—in addition to the much larger explicit fuel, electricity, and fertilizer subsidies and some of the unquantified costs and risks discussed in the next section.

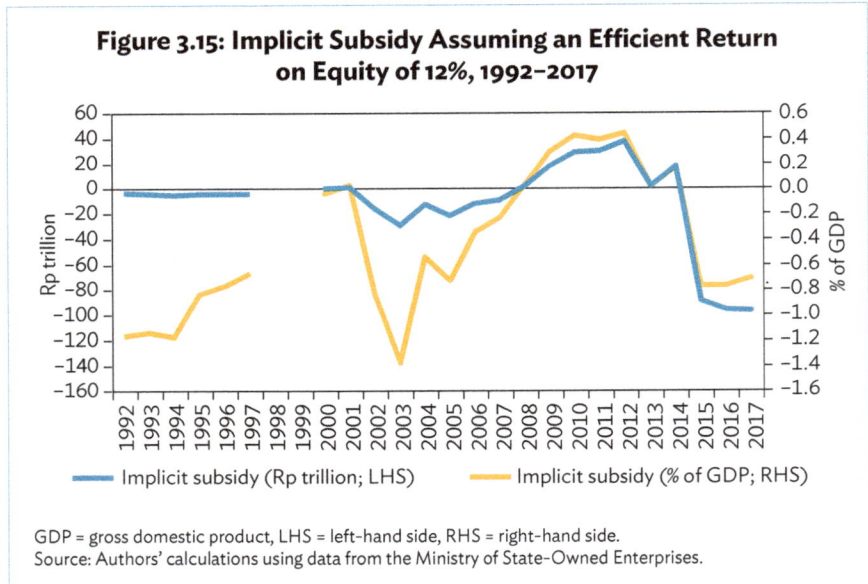

Figure 3.15: Implicit Subsidy Assuming an Efficient Return on Equity of 12%, 1992–2017

GDP = gross domestic product, LHS = left-hand side, RHS = right-hand side.
Source: Authors' calculations using data from the Ministry of State-Owned Enterprises.

3.5.4   Risks and Costs Associated with SOEs

As the role of SOEs expands, the risks they face and the costs they incur will require greater attention and monitoring. These include contingent fiscal risks and the consequences for competition and crowding-out of the private sector.[25]

---

[25]   There are other dimensions through which a large and growing SOE sector could distort the economy or reforms. For example, could SOEs operating in sectors with high levels of trade protection impede trade liberalization? If an appointment to SOE boards is an important means of salary supplementation for civil servants, do SOEs complicate the bureaucratic reform agenda?

Contingent liabilities of the public sector are rising as SOEs leverage up, and there are corresponding risks to having state banks as major counterparts to this increased leverage. The government will need to assess and monitor the contingent fiscal risk SOEs pose to the budget—particularly in light of the 1998 financial crisis in Indonesia, where much of the cost was related to SOEs (and state banks in particular). For example, a recent Asian Development Bank working paper by Ferrarini and Hinojales (2018) suggests a simple risk-assessment framework based on considering SOE interest coverage ratios under various stress scenarios in which part of SOE debt becomes an explicit government liability. SOE debt directly guaranteed by the government was expected to grow to around 1.2% of GDP in 2019 (IMF 2018) and thus risks seem moderate for now. However, the amount of SOE guaranteed debt is trending upward and unguaranteed SOE debt is also a likely contingent liability for the government, and thus the overall debt of SOEs warrants close monitoring. Associated risks relate to the concentration of SOE loans in certain state banks and the general duration mismatch (as long-term infrastructure loans are funded by banks which rely largely on short-term deposits). With these risks in mind, Indonesia's Ministry of Finance has created an SOE fiscal risk monitoring framework around SOEs and associated bank exposures.

The lack of a level playing field in some areas may impede private sector growth and, therefore, overall economic development. Any aspiration to support and boost growth will require a substantial increase in private participation in infrastructure (given limits to funding and financing of public investment discussed in the next section). Thus, it will be essential to address competition and crowding-out issues as SOEs enjoy various competitive advantages such as preferred access to government contracts, direct assignment of projects, subsidized and preferred access to finance, and effective monopoly in some sectors.

- PLN accounts for 70% of installed generation capacity and it dominates transmission and distribution; airports and ports are generally SOE owned and/or operated; SOEs control most toll roads (e.g., Jasa Marga operates around 60% of Indonesia's toll roads) and often receive contracts to build these toll roads; and state-owned banks dominate the finance sector. The private sector can and should be operating effectively and competing in these important sectors. IMF (2018) argues that the dominance of SOEs needs to be reduced and that "SOEs should be subject to the competition law and proper bidding procedures, and they should refrain from exercising dominant power."

- Public investment is likely already crowding out private investment given Indonesia's relatively shallow and bank-centric financial system. Moreover, the share of the private sector in total infrastructure has trended down (Figure 3.8). In addition to ensuring equal treatment between SOEs and private companies, Indonesia needs to deepen its financial markets.

3.6   Recommendations

Reforming SOEs will require strong political will and a calibrated approach to (i) implement politically feasible priorities in the near term such as corporatization, listing, and improving corporate governance; and (ii) build awareness and consensus over the long term as the government adheres to the politically difficult requirements of the SOE Law, particularly in privatization, governance, and competition.

The role of SOEs and reform priorities will need to be shaped according to the needs of the country and the sectors and/or SOEs under consideration. The performance of SOEs depend largely on the way the economy is managed and the strength of the country's complementary governance structure, competition framework, and regulatory framework (OECD 2015). Thus, gradual improvement in operational efficiency and service delivery focusing on making markets contestable, reforming SOE regulation and governance, and improving macroeconomic conditions, rather than emphasizing SOE ownership, would be the most likely and politically feasible approach in Indonesia.

3.6.1   Reform Challenges

The government will require substantial political will to overcome the interrelated challenges stemming from governance shortfalls, political incentives, and vested interests. Rakhman (2018) states, "SOEs in Indonesia have a long history of inefficiency, poor governance, and corruption. Many were used as cash cows by certain political interests... especially prior to the political reforms in 1998, leading to poor financial performance...." While Indonesia has made notable progress with SOE reforms following the Asian financial crisis, it has regressed slightly. Substantive progress with broader SOE reforms will likely have the following attributes:

- **SOE reforms are politically desirable.** Reform benefits outweigh the costs to leadership and its constituencies. This is a potentially high hurdle that is difficult to assess as the most effective SOE reforms would narrow scope for political "use" of SOEs immediately while in fact the benefits would manifest over a longer period of time.

- **SOE reforms are politically feasible.** The leadership is able to enact reforms and overcome opposition. It is encouraging to observe that SOE reforms are always featured in presidential campaigns and political documents. Yet, as argued below, a key SOE reform element would be divestment, which has become a politically taboo topic; also, the global political pendulum (post global financial crisis) has swung toward a greater role for the state.

- **SOE reforms are credible.** The government keeps its promises, such as for example, when it promises to compensate losers or deliver faster growth and more efficient public services. Experience from the fuel subsidy reductions and associated cash transfers and increase in infrastructure spending provide some support for reform credibility.

Given these hurdles to SOE reforms, we suggest a gradual two-pronged approach. In the near term, the government should focus on the politically feasible reforms and low-hanging fruit to nurture credibility and demonstrate a positive effect. In the longer term, the government could pursue more politically difficult and substantive structural measures by invoking the requirements under the SOE Law, while working to create awareness, cross-party support, and social consensus on the need for these reforms (again drawing lessons from earlier rounds of fuel subsidy reforms).

3.6.2   Near-Term Measures

Reform measures in the near term could focus on the following actions:

- Improve governance, corporatization, and public listing to increase independence, transparency, and overall market discipline, thus enhance performance (as a precursor to asset sales and recycling).[26] IMF (2018) notes, "The governance of SOEs also needs to be improved for proper risk management, including through public listing on the Indonesia Stock Exchange, which would enhance public scrutiny and the transparency of financial information." Currently, there are only 20 listed SOEs (plus some listed subsidiaries), with a large majority (84) remaining unlisted (and around 24 corporations with a minority government holding).

---

[26] We use the term "corporatization" in the broader sense of not just transforming a state asset or government agency into a corporate entity but also providing greater autonomy and better governance, and applying financial and operational standards to improve efficiency.

- Open SOEs to market competition as this has been associated with better service and performance. Ensuring equal treatment, where appropriate, is essential to improving efficiency and raising private sector participation in key sectors. SOE dominance in network industries (such as railways and power) and the finance sector could be rationalized to crowd in much-needed private and foreign investment, but creating competition between SOEs could be an initial step (although this might be inconsistent with the move toward sectoral holding companies for SOEs). Indonesia's experience with the effects of increased competition on SOE performance and service quality is compelling. Examples, which have all been largely (if anecdotally) attributed to a higher level of competition, include Garuda's turnaround in the airline industry; Pertamina's retail fuel distribution following downstream liberalization; and Telkom Indonesia's success in the competitive telecommunication sector.

- Consolidate and continue to carry out the IPOs of SOE subsidiaries as planned. Consolidation of the large (and seemingly uncertain) number of SOE subsidiaries would enable the Ministry of State-Owned Enterprises to more effectively monitor and manage them (subject to the caveat of not undermining market contestability and competition). The IPOs of SOE subsidiaries have continued in recent years (with plans for further sales being reported by the press in 2018). These tend to go unnoticed whereas IPOs or asset sales of the parent or major SOEs would seem too difficult politically. The IPOs of SOE subsidiaries help to raise much-needed fiscal revenue, capital for infrastructure spending, deepen capital markets, and "crowd in" the private sector.

- Close or reform "zombie" SOEs through hard budget constraint. "Zombie" SOEs drain public funds and therefore need to be resolved so that tied-up resources can be used for more productive activities.

In monitoring and evaluating the performance of SOEs, indicators need to be tailored to supplement those presented in section 3.4 or other standard indicators of efficiency. For example, for SOEs like PLN, a combined financial performance and economic rate of return could be considered. For "pioneers" like BRI, the evaluation criteria could include elements such as penetration. In the banking sector, indicators of oligopolistic competition could be considered.

3.6.3   Long-Term Focus on Reforms as Required by the SOE Law

Indonesia's SOE Law No. 19 (2003) articulates very well the long-term aims of SOE reforms.[27] The law <u>requires</u> some of the following reform guidance relating to privatization, governance, and competition:

- "Improved efficiency and productivity of SOEs must be undertaken through restructuring and privatization steps."

- "Privatization of SOEs does not mean the state control or sovereignty of SOEs is tempered or lost accordingly, but the state continues to perform the function of control through sectoral regulation upon which the privatized SOEs perform their business activities."

- "SOEs, the business of which is not engaged in the public interest but in competitive sector are encouraged to be privatized."

- Article 74: "Privatization shall be conducted with the aim of improvement of corporate performance and added value and improvement of public participation in the share ownership in the SOE." (Elucidation of Article 74: Through privatization, it is expected that a change in the corporate culture occurs following the entry of new shareholders.)

- Article 77: negative list (unprivatizable) including—"were law forbids, were defence/security related, were special assignments by government to perform certain activities that concern public interest, and natural resource sectors where law expressly forbids."

Similarly, the SOE reforms required under SOE Law No. 19 of 2003 relating to competition, restructuring, and governance are also still relevant and include the following:

Article 72:

- Restructuring shall be conducted with the aim of maintaining an SOE solvent in order to operate efficiently, transparently, and professionally.

---

[27] The translation of the SOE Law No. 19 (2003) used in this study can be found at https://www.scribd.com/doc/30876080/Law-No-19-of-2003-Indonesia-State-Owned-Entities-BUMN-Wishnu-Basuki.

- The purposes of restructuring shall be to

    (i)   improve the corporate performance and value;

    (ii) give benefit through dividends and taxes to the state;

    (iii) produce outputs and services at competitive prices to consumers; and

    (iv) facilitate the implementation of privatization.

Article 73:

- "Restructuring of a company or cooperative including

    - Improvement of intensity of business competition, especially in sectors where monopoly occurs, both deregulated and natural monopoly;

- "SOEs need to grow corporate culture and professionalism through, inter alia, the reorganization of their management and supervision... conducted under the principles of good corporate governance."

Article 25:

"At no time shall a member of the Board of Directors hold concurrent office as

    (i)   a member of the board of directors of a state-owned entity (MSOE), region-owned entity, private-owned entity, and other office that may result in a conflict of interest;

    (ii) part of another structural and functional office in agency/central and regional government;"

Elucidation of Article 73:

- "Sectoral restructuring is intended to create a sound business climate for fair competition, efficiency, and optimal service."

3.6.4   Overall Framework for Reforming SOEs

The IMF proposed a top-down, systematic framework for reforming SOEs and illustrates how it might be applied. The IMF (2016) report, *How to Improve the Financial Oversight of Public Corporations*, provides a framework (Figure 3.16), which is compelling in its logic and recommendations once criteria for the two axes are appropriately defined.

Figure 3.16: International Monetary Fund Framework for Reviewing the Status of SOEs

| | | Policy or Strategic Relevance | |
		Low	High
Commercial Viability	Low	Close	Convert into noncommercial government entity
	High	Privatize	Retain as public corporation, monitor closely operations and finances

SOE = state-owned enterprise.
Source: IMF (2016).

To illustrate how this framework might be employed, the following criteria are used:

- For assessing *commercial viability* (the vertical axis), we consider SOEs with ROEs above 6% on average for the past 5 years as commercially viable (this return on equity [ROE] is arbitrarily half of the assumed ROE* above and so a generous definition of viability—sector-specific thresholds would be formulated ideally by policy makers).

- For assessing the *policy or strategic relevance* of each SOE (the horizontal axis), we consider the Constitution and knowledge of Indonesia to come up with a list of seemingly "unavoidable" SOEs—the oil, gas, and mining companies; and the water and waste companies, Taspen and Bulog.

Figure 3.17: Illustrative Example of a Criteria-Based SOE Classification for Reform

| | | "Unavoidable" SOEs | |
		Low	High
Commercial Viability	Low	34 SOEs	3 SOEs: PLN, Aneka Tambang, Bulog
	High	73 SOEs	8 SOEs: 2 water/waste, 3 mining, PGN, Pertamina, and Taspen

SOE = state-owned enterprise.
Source: Authors' calculations.

The illustrative application in Figure 3.17 demonstrates how well-defined criteria can be used to design an effective and objective framework for classifying SOEs and identifying the required actions:

- The 73 SOEs that are deemed financially viable (based on the ROE criteria above) and with no compelling case to be publicly owned (bottom left-hand quadrant) have equity totaling 7% of GDP (i.e., releasing or recycling those assets could raise a substantial amount toward infrastructure financing over the coming few years).

- Of the three SOEs in the top right-hand quadrant (seemingly "unavoidable" SOEs that are not financially viable), PLN is largely about getting the price setting and regulatory framework right (see below); Aneka, the mining company, will fall under the new holding company, possibly masking its losses; while Bulog might best become a government agency or department funded directly and transparently on budget rather than run as an SOE.

- On the top left-hand corner (again stressing this is just an illustrative exercise), a likely large number of enterprises would be classified as not financially viable and with no compelling case for public ownership. We suggest below a systematic approach to determine what to do with the worst-performing of those SOEs.

- The bottom right-hand quadrant (seemingly "unavoidable" SOEs that are financially viable) is about continuing to improve governance and performance of SOEs rather than immediately about the mode of ownership (although even for these, asset recycling would particularly help with funding needs and crowding in the private sector).

A number of outright "zombie" SOEs should be reformed or shut down as a priority. In 2017, nine SOEs had negative equity (in previous years this number was larger, but some have been consolidated within holding companies). In addition, 27 SOEs incurred overall losses (aggregating profits and losses) during 2012–2017 amounting to Rp29.3 trillion (or 0.2% of GDP). A simple decision tree approach could be used to determine what to do with these zombies:

If there is market failure in the industry, and
    If the market failure is best addressed via an SOE, and
        If reforming the SOE is more cost-effective than starting from scratch,
Then reinvest and reform the SOE;

Else, the most appropriate path would (by definition) be to close the SOE and address the market failure another way.

Ultimately it boils down to political will and determination in dealing with the three more difficult quadrants above. Politics and political sensitivities around SOEs in Indonesia are important (like elsewhere) for the usual reasons—SOEs contribute to development goals and are a means of off-budget control and patronage. The challenge is how to depoliticize and change the "story." The example of cutting fuel subsidies illustrates the possibility of implementing politically difficult reforms in Indonesia when (i) the messaging is right (e.g., "we need to reallocate wasteful fuel subsidies toward much-needed infrastructure investment"); (ii) social protection is in place for the most vulnerable and affected by the reform; and (iii) cross-party support is nurtured. Other examples of successful reforms in Indonesia involved "tying political hands to the mast" through the adoption of central bank independence and fiscal rules (which have been important elements of the macro stability enjoyed by Indonesia).

3.6.5   SOE-Wide and Sector-Specific Issues

To complement the above framework, some SOE-wide reforms should form part of the long-term agenda, while considering the substantial political challenges. The issues these reforms must address are covered extensively in other literature[28] and are therefore only outlined below.

In some sectors, pricing and tariffs are too low to cover operating costs let alone support investment. Pricing right (and appropriate compensation for public service requirements) and generating sufficient and sustainable revenues for investment needs is a central issue in some of the largest SOEs/sectors.

- For example, the Electricity Cost of Service and Tariff Review in 2017 reported that the average electricity tariff of PLN, the electricity utility company, was below the cost recovery level (World Bank 2018). PLN's tariffs should be set to balance cost recovery and investment coverage with affordability. PLN should set tariffs to incentivize efficiency rather than use the current cost-plus formula.

- Tariffs in a variety of other sectors, such as in water and ports, also need to be adjusted.

- Fuel prices should return to being set by an automatic price adjustment mechanism which would help cap future fuel subsidies and depoliticize fuel price adjustments.

- Tariff setting for toll roads needs to be stable and predictable if there was to be any hope of increasing private investment.

---

[28] See for example ADB (2017a, 2017b); Kim and Ali (2017); World Bank (2017, 2018); Breuer, Guajardo, and Kinda (2018); and OECD (2018).

Appropriate regulatory frameworks need to support competition and investment.

- In the oil and gas sector, regulation has been in a state of flux or uncertainty since the Asian financial crisis. There has also been a secular decline in oil output, which has been plateauing in recent years; exploration investment (particularly foreign participation in the sector); and a massive decline in the relative contribution of the sector to the economy and fiscal revenue.[29] An independent regulator is needed to reduce political influence, improve governance in the sector, among others, and serve as basis for raising much-needed private and foreign investment in the sector.

- In the mining sector, a long period of uncertainty followed the passage of the Mining Law in 2009 and its implementation; and mining exploration declined (foreign investors dominated earlier exploration investment). Regulatory certainty is needed to boost domestic value added and environmental sustainability and bring in foreign direct investment and higher public revenue.

- In the power sector, regulation and policy should target more effective competition and private participation in generation and distribution.

- In infrastructure, best practice suggests separate roles for infrastructure providers and regulators.

- In the finance sector, policy and regulation need to ensure that (i) the current bank-dominated finance sector effectively delivers financial intermediation and is able to support Indonesia's development objectives (see below); and (ii) the (oligopolistic) dominance of state banks is addressed through regulation, competition policy, and divestment.

Deciding how best to manage SOEs—particularly if further consolidation under a super holding company is being considered—should only proceed after a detailed study of international experience and Indonesia's specific circumstances. OECD (2015) considers the experiences of Singapore, Brazil, India, the People's Republic of China, and South Africa, and finds in common the following criteria for successful SOE-based development strategies: (i) competence of the state bureaucracy; (ii) SOEs operate in areas free from concentration of commercial, financial, and other powers; and (iii) developmental objectives are clearly spelled out and not combined with

---

[29]   The fiscal contribution of oil and gas has declined from over 20% a decade ago to less than 5% in recent years.

social policy objectives.[30] Within Asia, Singapore is often considered to have effectively managed its SOEs within the context of leadership continuity, public listing, exposure to international markets and competition, and robust corporate governance practices (ADB 2016). This chapter does not include a review of international experience on the different forms of SOE management, including holding companies, but offers some broad lessons (including Singapore's experience with Temasek)[31] on effective SOE management:

- Sufficient autonomy and competence of SOE boards (by appointing professional board members and management) are essential.
- Ownership must be clearly separate from regulation of SOEs.
- Policy objectives for SOEs must be clearly defined, with explicit, realistic, time-bound, and quantifiable outcomes to better guide and evaluate SOE performance.
- SOE ownership entities undergo regular monitoring and evaluation.
- Practical guidelines on how to get from where we are toward the "best" frontier need to be developed (e.g., building broad political consensus, depoliticization, some "changing of hearts and minds").

Clearly, a reform agenda will need to be carefully tailored for each major SOE and/or sector. A case study approach would be most suitable (but beyond the scope of this study). Yet, the needed reforms are well understood and well documented, and involve getting pricing right, making policy predictable, establishing appropriate (best practice) regulatory frameworks, continuing to improve governance and transparency, increasing competition, and reducing public stakes—to recycle assets to finance public investment and crowd in private participation.

3.6.6 Economy-Wide Reforms to Complement and Support the Development Role of SOEs

Indonesia will need to intensify its private as well as public infrastructure investment to achieve its development plans and growth aspirations. The postcrisis decline in infrastructure spending relative to GDP has resulted in a downward trend in Indonesia's capital stock (Figure 3.18) and has thus been a

---

[30] "A strong conclusion ... regards path dependency: a faulty design of an SOE sector and the surrounding legislation, regulation and political environment in the early stages of the development process can be almost impossible to correct later on" (OECD 2015, 30).

[31] Temasek was formed in 1974 as the holding company for 35 SOEs. Singapore has had an active privatization program and Temasek now has less than 30% of its assets domiciled in Singapore.

headwind to potential growth.[32] Expansion of public (government and SOE) infrastructure spending has helped arrest the capital stock decline in recent years but is reaching limits in the fiscal rule and SOE leverage. The investment ecosystem needs to be rebalanced toward sustainable and effective infrastructure delivery across government, SOEs, and the private sector. Indonesia's development strategy, as articulated in the National Medium-Term Development Plan (RPJMN), 2015–2019, had an infrastructure spending target of Rp5.5 trillion (over $400 billion) over the 5 years to 2019 (or over $80 billion a year). Indonesia's future infrastructure needs are also estimated to be in the range of $74 billion–$82 billion annually in 2015 prices (or around 5% of GDP annually for the period 2016–2030) by ADB (2017a), with an overall infrastructure "gap" of around $1.5 trillion according to the World Bank (2018). Thus, Indonesia will need to substantially expand (i) government funding, (ii) private investment for infrastructure, and (iii) the financing capacity of the finance sector.

Figure 3.18: Infrastructure Investment and Capital Stock, 1995–2017

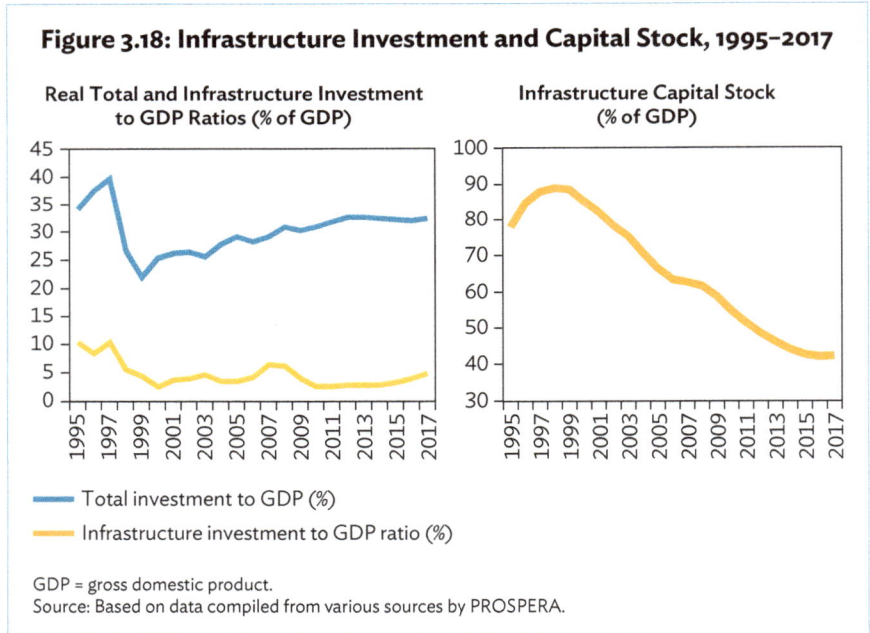

Real Total and Infrastructure Investment to GDP Ratios (% of GDP)

Infrastructure Capital Stock (% of GDP)

━━━ Total investment to GDP (%)

━━━ Infrastructure investment to GDP ratio (%)

GDP = gross domestic product.
Source: Based on data compiled from various sources by PROSPERA.

---

[32] The capital stock series is constructed using a perpetual inventory method and a depreciation rate of 6%. The downward trend in capital stock is robust to the usual range of depreciation assumptions for infrastructure.

(i) Higher government revenue to support more and better public expenditure

The fiscal imperative is to boost revenue substantially, increase expenditure efficiency, and redeploy public assets to create fiscal space for much-needed public investment. Indonesia's general government revenue-to-GDP and public expenditure-to-GDP ratios—at 14% and 16.5% in 2017, respectively—are among the lowest in the G20, well below the level typically associated with Indonesia's development. Khatri (2016) finds a large and growing medium-term fiscal "policy gap," considering the medium-term expenditure needs, commitments, and the associated projections of revenue to GDP. Either expenditure will continue to be pulled down by available revenue (given the fiscal rule constraining the deficit to 3% of GDP) or revenue will need to increase dramatically. International benchmarks suggest that Indonesia should be able to comfortably boost its revenue ratio by 3% of GDP over the medium term. If this additional revenue was allocated to infrastructure investment and targeted transfers to education, health, and social expenditures, Breuer, Guajardo, and Kinda (2018) forecast a growth boost of around 1% by 2022. Furthermore, Indonesia's public expenditure could be around one-third more effective (Khatri 2016). Realizing even a slight improvement in expenditure efficiency, together with asset sales, would free up substantial resources for infrastructure investment.

(ii) Much greater private participation in infrastructure provision

The private sector will need to play a much larger role in Indonesia's infrastructure investment.[33] The RPJMN, 2015–2019 targeted an increase in private infrastructure investment from 9% of the total during 2011–2015 to 37% during 2015–2019. Figure 3.19 shows that the actual share of the private sector over 5 years is likely to be much smaller. Some of the core issues constraining private investment have already been covered such as tariff setting, the regulatory and competition environment, and crowding out. Other core impediments will likely include land acquisition issues (somewhat improved by the 2012 law and implementing regulations); dealing with the multiple levels of government and bureaucracy; and more general "investment climate" issues. ADB (2017b); World Bank (2018); and Breuer, Guajardo, and Kinda (2018) discuss in detail the reforms needed for a major upscaling of private participation in infrastructure.

---

[33] Public–private partnerships (PPPs) in Indonesia date back to toll road and energy projects in the early 1990s. A formal PPP modality was introduced in 2005, and PPPs continue to be promoted and an institutional framework created, including the establishment of the PPP unit at the Ministry of Finance, the Project Development Fund, and setting up guarantee facilities as discussed earlier, enacting new pieces of enabling regulation, and a land acquisition mechanism. ADB (2017b) provides a more detailed discussion.

Figure 3.19: Shares in Core Infrastructure Investment, 2011–2019
(% of total)

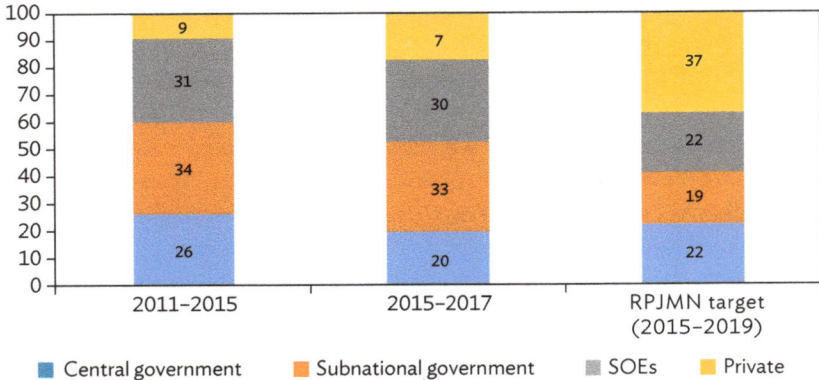

RPJMN = National Medium-Term Development Plan, SOE = state-owned enterprise.
Sources: PROSPERA; RPJMN (2015–2019).

Indonesia's public investment framework is currently not designed to systematically leverage private financing. World Bank (2018) notes that the project identification process first asks which projects should be publicly funded, then which should be funded by SOEs, and last, which should be implemented as public–private partnerships (PPPs)—the reverse of best practice. A framework is needed to better prioritize private financing and leverage existing public assets. This framework includes reformulating the project identification process; addressing capacity constraints in project planning, appraisal, and selection; reforming SOE incentives (through key performance indicators and bonuses) to incentivize private sector involvement; and developing a comprehensive asset-recycling framework (asset recycling has been limited, such as Jasa Marga issuing debt securities backed by future cash flows from its operating assets).

(iii) Indonesia's finance sector needs to develop and expand substantially

Indonesia's finance sector, on its current trajectory, is unlikely to meet the future needs for public and private sector financing. Khatri and Rowter (2016) estimate the total investment needed to achieve a 5.5% potential growth rate in the medium term (from a simple incremental capital output ratio approach and a production function) and find that the baseline projections for growth in financing (from banks, capital markets, and other sources) implies a growing "financing gap."[34] While Indonesia's overall savings and investment rates are not low, savings are not well intermediated to productive long-term investments. Infrastructure financing is bank-centric and thus the maturity profiles of infrastructure financing and assets are not well matched. "Long-money" (pension and insurance funds) is growing but from a very low base in Indonesia. A concerted effort is needed to develop Indonesia's finance sector to avoid it constraining growth further. Priorities include increasing the pools of "long money" and available long-term assets (such as infrastructure bonds) and better matching these (by removing regulatory and tax distortions) and attracting more foreign direct investment. World Bank (2018); Breuer, Guajardo, and Kinda (2018); and IMF (2018) provide a more detailed reform agenda for the finance sector.

3.7   Conclusions

SOEs will continue to play an important and likely expanding role in Indonesia's development. Since Indonesia's independence, SOEs have been used to nurture key industries and develop core infrastructure; and SOEs have a firm foundation in the Constitution. Given the large infrastructure needs ahead and the government's infrastructure push—both on budget and through SOEs—SOE assets and contributions relative to the overall economy have been expanding in recent years.

In light of the increasing role of SOEs, it is imperative to improve their performance and contain associated risks. The financial performance of listed SOEs has been better than private listed companies in Indonesia (and for a while, better than international listed counterparts), suggesting overall net advantages (PLN is an obvious outlier given its tariff setting). However, SOE performance has deteriorated, and fiscal risks—while seemingly manageable—are growing and warrant close monitoring. Furthermore, implicit and explicit subsidies associated with Indonesia's SOEs are similar in magnitude to central government infrastructure spending, suggesting much room to redirect overall subsidies toward more productive infrastructure investment.

We propose a pragmatic two-tiered reform strategy, given major political hurdles and the need for substantial political will:

---

[34] World Bank (2018) similarly finds that the cumulative capacity in the banking sector (at most $20 billion) and institutional investors (optimistically, $10 billion) falls short of the $49 billion in private financing need annually.

- In the near term, politically feasible measures could yield quick gains and positive demonstration effects such as corporatization, public listing, improved SOE governance, closing "zombies," and IPOs and/or consolidation of SOE subsidiaries.

- For the longer term, focus on meeting the requirements already stipulated under the SOE law with regard to privatization, governance, and competition. A gradual approach to some of the main SOE-wide and SOE-specific issues will be required and will need to link closely to the requirements of the SOE law (such as setting appropriate tariffs and developing best-practice regulatory frameworks to support better governance and effective competition).

Important and urgent economy-wide reforms are needed. Future infrastructure needs extend well beyond the capacity of the public sector. A more balanced and sustainable approach will entail the following:

- A boost in public funding. A large increase in government revenue, improved efficiency in public expenditure, and asset sales or recycling to create fiscal space for on-budget infrastructure investment where this is the best mode of delivery (for example, the public sector is better placed to deal with land acquisition issues and coordination between different levels of government).

- Massive increase in the role of the private sector in infrastructure investment, including through PPPs and crowding in private sector financing.

- Substantial expansion in the capacity of the finance sector to provide long-term financing and minimize crowding out.

The SOE and broader economic reforms will require substantial political will. The phased approach should help—with near-term reforms providing demonstration effects and reform credibility, and long-term reforms invoking the requirements of the SOE Law. Developing the political capital to move forward will also require "changing the story" (e.g., existing public assets will need to be redeployed more effectively); careful insulation and compensation of the most vulnerable; and building cross-party support (which are lessons learned from past difficult but ultimately successful fuel subsidy reforms).

The potential development gains from these reforms are difficult to quantify but are likely to be significant. World Bank (2017) reports that on average, increasing a country's infrastructure capital stock by 1 standard deviation can raise growth by 3 percentage points. Breuer, Guajardo, and Kinda (2018) find that in a reform scenario with higher revenue and higher infrastructure and social spending, potential growth could be raised by around 1% by 2022. Given Indonesia's rather low starting point for infrastructure capital stock, it is conceivable that the growth benefits (fiscal multipliers) could be even larger than average. Failure to make progress with this reform agenda will constrain growth and development, and ultimately the political and social consequences of a rapidly increasing young and highly aspiring workforce frustrated by diminishing opportunities.

References

ADB. 2016. *Finding Balance: Benchmarking the Performance of State-Owned Enterprises in Island Countries.* Manila.

_____. 2017a. *Meeting Asia's Infrastructure Needs.* Manila.

_____. 2017b. *Public–Private Partnership Monitor.* Manila.

Australia Indonesia Partnership for Economic Governance (AIPEG). 2017. Implicit Subsidies' to Indonesia's SOEs Cost Over IDR 100 Trillion per Year and Are Creating Significant Risks to Indonesia's Economy. May.

Breuer, L., J. Guajardo, and T. Kinda, eds. 2018. *Realizing Indonesia's Economic Potential.* Washington, DC: IMF.

Bureau van Dijk. Orbis. https://www.bvdinfo.com/en-gb/our-products/data/international/orbis.

Chang, H.-J. 2003. *Globalization, Economic Development and the Role of the State.* London: Zed Books Ltd.

Cochrane, J. 2007. Indonesia Relaunches Privatisation Drive. *Financial Times.* 8 June. https://www.ft.com/content/45392978-1515-11dc-b48a-000b5df10621.

Damodaran Online. http://www.stern.nyu.edu/~adamodar/New_Home_Page/data.html.

Ferrarini, B. and M. Hinojales. 2018. State-Owned Enterprises Leverage as a Contingency in Public Debt Sustainability: The Case of the People's Republic of China. *ADB Economics Working Paper Series.* January 2018.

Fitriningrum, A. 2006. Indonesia Experiences in Managing the State Companies. Presentation at the OECD–Asian Roundtable on Corporate Governance, Network on Corporate Governance of SOEs. Singapore. 15 May.

Gorbiano, M. I. 2018. Two Camps Pitch Top Economic Priorities. *The Jakarta Post.* 13 November. Jakarta.

Government of Indonesia. Law of The Republic Of Indonesia No. 19 of 2003 Concerning State-Owned Entities (English Translation). https://www.scribd.com/doc/30876080/Law-No-19-of-2003-Indonesia-State-Owned-Entities-BUMN-Wishnu-Basuki.

International Monetary Fund (IMF). 1998. Letter of Intent of the Government of Indonesia. 19 October. https://www.imf.org/external/np/loi/101998.htm.

_____. 2014. Is It Time for an Infrastructure Push? The Macroeconomic Effects of Public Investment. Chapter 3 in *World Economic Outlook: Legacies, Clouds, Uncertainties*. Washington, DC.

_____. 2016. Fiscal Policy: How to Improve the Financial Oversight of Public Corporations. How To Notes. November 2016. Washington, DC.

_____. 2018. Indonesia: Financial Sector Assessment Program – Detailed Assessment of Observance—Insurance Core Principles. https://www. imf.org/en/Publications/CR/Issues/2018/03/12/Indonesia-Financial-Sector-Assessment-Program-Detailed-Assessment-of-Observance-Insurance-45712.

Investopedia. www.investopedia.com.

Khatri, Y. 2016. Indonesia's Macro-Fiscal Challenges and Opportunities in International Perspective. MOF/BKF-AIPEG Workshop on Medium Term Macro-Fiscal Revenue Strategies. Borobudur Hotel, Jakarta, Indonesia. 4–5 August.

Khatri, Y. and K. Rowter. 2016. Can Indonesia's Financial Sector Meet the Long-term Financing Needs?. International Forum on Economic Development and Public Policy. BKF (Ministry of Finance), Bali, Indonesia. 8–9 December.

Kim, C. J. and Z. Ali. 2017. Efficient Management of State-Owned Enterprises: Challenges and Opportunities. ADB Institute Policy Brief. No. 2017-4 (December). Tokyo: ADB Institute. https://www.adb.org/sites/default/files/publication/390251/adbi-pb2017-4.pdf.

Kim K. 2018. Matchmaking: Establishment of State-Owned Holding Companies in Indonesia. *Asia & the Pacific Policy Studies*. 5. pp. 313–330.

Kowalski, P. et al. 2013. State-Owned Enterprises: Trade Effects and Policy Implications. *OECD Trade Policy Papers*. No. 147. Paris: OECD Publishing. http://dx.doi.org/10.1787/5k4869ckqk7l-en.

Ministry of State-Owned Enterprises (MSOE). 2017. *Profile of State-Owned Enterprises in Indonesia, 2017 Edition*. Jakarta.

Organisation for Economic Co-operation and Development (OECD). 2011. The Size and Composition of the SOE Sector in OECD Countries. *OECD Corporate Governance Working Papers*. No. 5. Paris.

_____. 2015. *State-Owned Enterprises in the Development Process*. Paris. http://dx.doi.org/10.1787/9789264229617-en.

_____. 2016a. *State-Owned Enterprises in Asia: National Practices for Performance Evaluation and Management*. OECD and Korea Institute of Public Finance.

_____. 2016b. *State-Owned Enterprises as Global Competitors: A Challenge or Opportunity?*. http://dx.doi.org/10.1787/9789264262096-en.

_____. 2018. *OECD Economic Surveys: Indonesia 2018.* Paris.

PROSPERA. Has the Private Sector Shrunk? Unpublished paper led by A. Suputro and D. Nellor.

Rakhman, F. 2018. Can Partially Privatized SOEs Outperform Fully Private Firms? Evidence from Indonesia. *Research in International Business and Finance.* 45 (October). pp. 285–292. http://dx.doi.org/10.1016/j.ribaf.2017.07.160.

S&P Global. 2018. Is Indonesia's Infrastructure Buildout Weakening SOE Balance Sheets? Short Answer: Yes. 12 March.

Wicaksono, A. 2008. Indonesian State-Owned Enterprises: The Challenge of Reform. *Southeast Asian Affairs.* (2008). pp. 146–16.

World Bank. 2017. Closing the Infrastructure Gap. *Indonesia Economic Quarterly.* October.

_____. 2018. *Infrastructure Sector Assessment Program.* Washington, DC.

CHAPTER 4

Performance of State-Owned Enterprises in Kazakhstan

*Kaukab Naqvi**

4.1   Background

The transition of Kazakhstan from a centrally planned economy to a market-oriented one coincided with its independence and the downfall of the Soviet Union in 1991. However, economic turmoil and disruptions in the production network during the early transition stage led to the virtual collapse of the domestic economy. In 1992–1995, decline in industrial production derailed economic activity, causing gross domestic product (GDP) to fall by 31% and wiping out 1.6 million jobs (OECD 2015). Kazakhstan faced enormous challenges not only in reforming the economy but also in state building in a much broader sense.

To revive the economy and attain macroeconomic stability, the government introduced reforms to dismantle the command economy and create a market economy. Although growth resumed in 1996, recovery was short-lived because of the economic crises in Asia and in the Russian Federation in 1997–1998.

Although the government succeeded in managing initial setbacks, economic growth was largely driven by resource-based sectors. From 2000 to 2007, rising oil prices and production helped maintain high GDP growth. Oil production increased from 25.6 million tons in 1998 to 47.3 million tons in 2002 and further to 67.5 million tons in 2007. At the same time, the price of a barrel of oil rose from $13.10 in 1998, to $24.90 in 2002, and finally to $72.70 in 2007.

With the rise in oil prices in 2000, growth accelerated sharply and GDP growth during 2000–2017 averaged around 6.0% per annum. Per capita income at

*   Rica Cynthia Maddawin provided support in compiling data and performing DuPont and data envelopment analyses. The chapter has also benefited from a background report prepared by Aigul Kosherbayeva.

current prices rose from $1,229 in 2000 to $8,837 in 2017, while poverty incidence declined from 46.1% in 2001 to 2.6% in 2016.

While the oil boom supported high economic growth, it made the economy vulnerable to external demand shocks. Additionally, the speculative boom in construction which was supported by private investments created an array of nonperforming loans, and instead of strengthening the industrial base, caused the financial crisis of 2007–2008, even before the start of the global financial crisis. As such, Kazakhstan needed to resolve the economy's vulnerability to external shocks and maintain macroeconomic stability to sustain and attain inclusive growth.

Kazakhstan has made tremendous progress, but many of its challenges during transition remain relevant today. Without a vibrant private sector, private investment remained low and with continuous reliance on extractive industry, state-owned enterprises (SOEs) became the main instrument to propel economic development.

SOEs are prevalent in virtually all sectors, but public sector delivery, corporate governance, areas of planning, financial management, and project management are inefficient. Additionally, the presence of state ownership in economic affairs has not created the equal treatment necessary in developing a competitive private sector. The global financial crisis in 2009 along with the downturn of oil and commodity prices in 2014 further exposed the economy's weaknesses. Economic growth during the postcrisis period of 2010–2017 declined to 1.1% per annum and wiped out some of the earlier gains in poverty reduction. GDP growth swayed as the price and production of crude oil changed, in 1999–2006 averaging around 8.5% as oil prices and production rose, and slackening in 2013–2014 to 2.8% as oil prices plummeted. Although the recent oil price hike was expected to raise GDP growth to an estimated 4% in 2017, these movements highlight the vulnerability of resource-based sectors (Figure 4.1).

In 2000–2017, the services sector provided the major impetus to growth, contributing an average of 52.9%, followed by industry at 38.1%, and agriculture at 9.0% (Figure 4.2). Within the subsectors of services, wholesale and retail trade, construction, and transport and communication were major contributors.

The state's presence in economic activities is much higher in Kazakhstan than in other resource-intensive countries. Such a high presence of state ownership poses considerable challenges in managing natural resources toward developing the non-oil sector and improving the quality of public services.

Figure 4.1: Growth Rates of GDP, Prices and Production of Oil, 1997–2017

(5-year moving average, %)

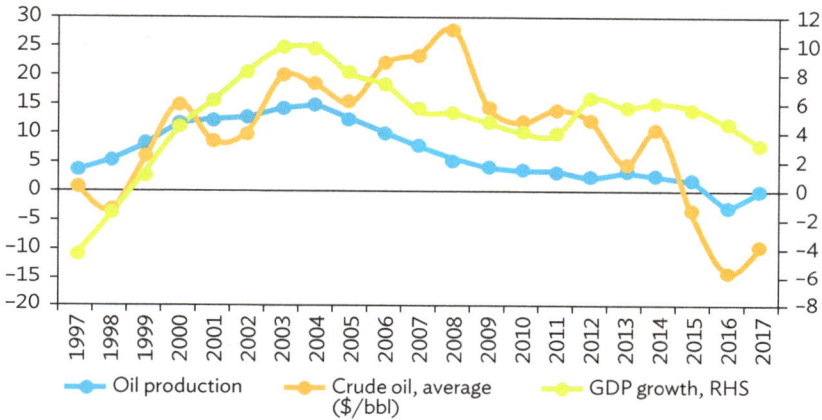

bbl = barrel, GDP = gross domestic product, RHS = right-hand side.
Sources: World Bank. World Development Indicators. https://datacatalog.worldbank.org/dataset/world-development-indicators; and World Bank. World Bank Commodity Markets. http://www.worldbank.org/en/research/commodity-markets (both accessed 26 November 2018).

Figure 4.2: Sector Contribution to GDP Growth Rate, 2001–2017

(%)

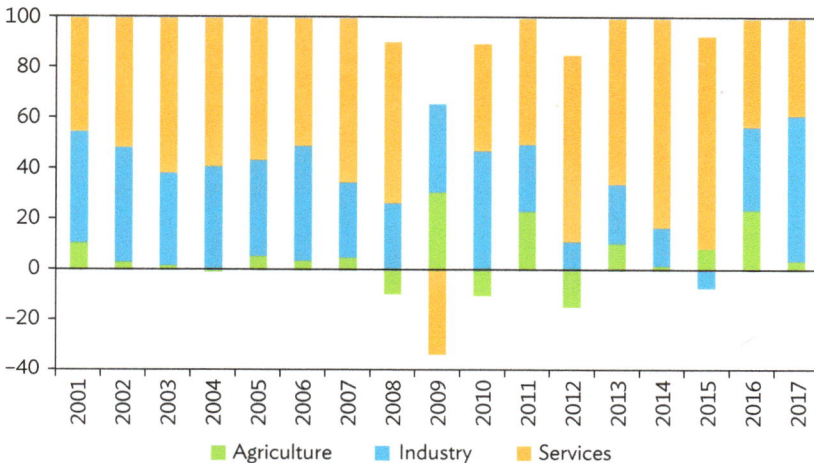

GDP = gross domestic product.
Source: Author's estimates based on ADB (2018).

Kazakhstan Strategy 2050 seeks to achieve an open and efficient economy and list the country among the top 30 economies in the world by 2050. High economic growth during the first half of the 2000s gave some hope for achieving the ambitious goal. However, the collapse of oil and commodity prices in 2014, derailing economic growth from its upward trajectory and exposing the country's vulnerability to external demand shocks, suggests that such optimism is of guarded nature. To achieve Strategy 2050 goals, Kazakhstan needs to rely less on the oil sector, diversify its economic base, and make the non-oil sector more competitive.

4.2   The Role and Structure of SOEs

The government's system of state institutions classifies them into sovereign wealth funds, state shareholding companies, and state banks and development institutions, through which it promotes industrial upgrading and socioeconomic welfare. SOEs are active in key economic sectors such as oil and gas, mining, transportation, energy, and telecommunication and finance, providing vital infrastructure services. Since economic growth is largely driven by extractive industry, the large presence of state in economic affairs is not that surprising; however, SOEs also dominate in sectors and market segments which other countries typically open to private entrepreneurs. The strong presence of SOEs generates significant spillovers on firms downstream with important implications for economy-wide productivity and growth (World Bank 2015).

The government regulates economic activities by controlling a large number of SOEs through national managing holdings. In compliance with the Law on State Property, it participates in

(i)   state legal entities (including SOEs and public institutions),

(ii) joint-stock companies, and

(iii) limited liabilities partnerships.

SOEs are defined broadly as entities in which the state owns more than 50% of voting shares of joint-stock companies (JSCs), or more than 50% of shares in the authorized capital of limited liability partnerships, including national managing holdings, national holdings, and national companies, in which the state is a participant or shareholder, as well as subsidiaries and affiliated organizations that are part of their corporate structure, except for nonresidents.

The Register of State Property as of 1 January 2018 reported a total of 25,111 state enterprises and institutions, and legal entities with state participation.[1] Of these, 18,403 (or 73.3%) were state institutions providing public services at the regional and central levels, and 6,708 were state enterprises (26.7%) operating commercially. Gross value added of SOEs was estimated to be $46.8 billion (21.1% of GDP) in 2014, which gradually declined to $28.1 billion (17.3% of GDP) by 2017. Although SOEs' share in GDP has declined, they nevertheless continued to dominate the Kazakhstan economy (Figure 4.3).

Figure 4.3: Share of SOEs in GDP, 2014–2017

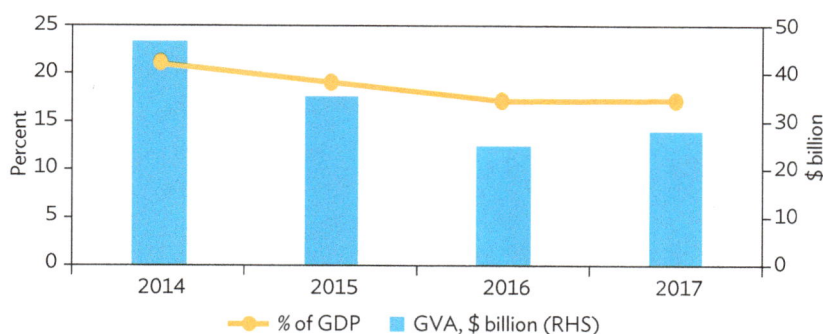

GDP = gross domestic product, GVA = gross value added, RHS = right-hand side, SOEs = state-owned enterprises.
Source: Statistical Committee of the Ministry of National Economy of the Republic of Kazakhstan. Accounts Committee for Control over Execution of the Republican Budget (in Russian). http://esep.kz/rus/showin/article/3105.

The state has full ownership and control of the network sectors which include gas; transport; the post; mobile services; and electricity distribution, supply, and generation. The presence of state is much higher compared with the average of Organisation for Economic Co-operation and Development (OECD) countries and other resource-intensive economies (Figure 4.4). Even otherwise, price controls are more prevalent, and state ownership has barely created incentives to modernize and innovate the economy. Majority of the SOEs have easy access to finance and receive preferential treatment from the government, rendering private entrepreneurs uncompetitive. Based on the

---

[1] Ministry of National Economy of the Republic of Kazakhstan. Committee on Statistics (in Russian). http://stat.gov.kz/faces/wcnav_externalId/homeNumbersBusinessRegisters?_afrLoop=38939551586814#%40%3F_afrLoop%3D38939551586814%26_adf.ctrl-state%3D18awdae4qb_50 (accessed 14 November 2018).

OECD Product Market Regulation State Control Index,[2] which is only available for 2013, the state's presence in Kazakhstan is considerably larger than other resource-intensive countries. India and Indonesia—which have even more restrictive regimes than Kazakhstan—are the only exceptions (World Bank 2018).

Figure 4.4: State Presence in Kazakhstan

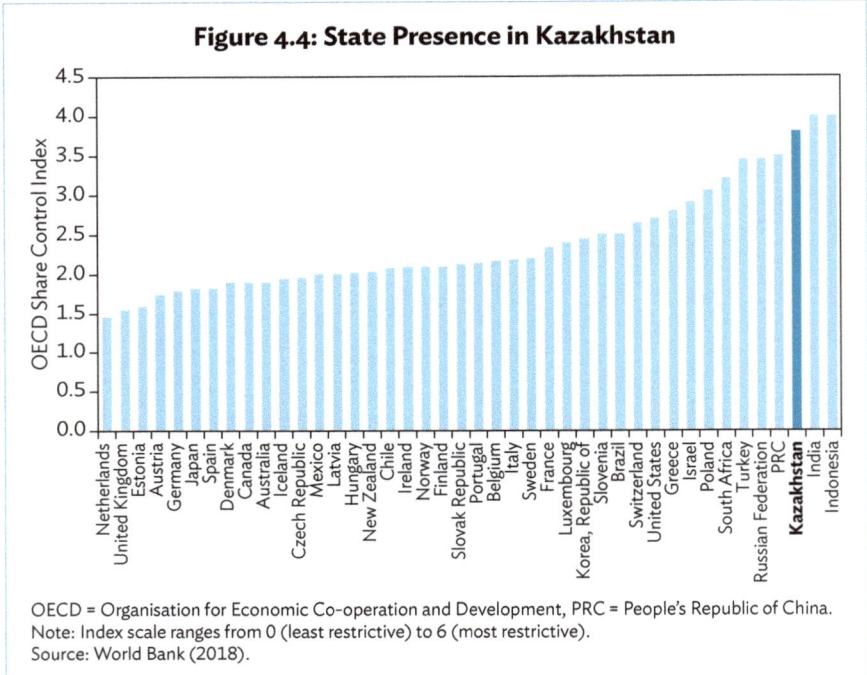

OECD = Organisation for Economic Co-operation and Development, PRC = People's Republic of China.
Note: Index scale ranges from 0 (least restrictive) to 6 (most restrictive).
Source: World Bank (2018).

While SOEs dominate the economy, the weak finance sector constrains private sector growth. The government continues to diversify the economy, paying particular attention to agribusiness, financial services, and transportation. In the early 1990s, SOEs employed 87% of the workforce. The government has since then introduced several reforms to redefine the role of the state in the economy and to develop the private sector. In 1991–1995, the government privatized some state properties which formed many of the existing large private companies. Despite these reforms, SOEs remain dominant in Kazakhstan's economy.

---

[2]   The Product Market Regulation State Control Index assesses the extent and design of regulation in product markets. It summarizes the various dimensions of the state's presence in the observed sectors according to whether an SOE is active in the sector, as well as what proportion of the most important enterprises in each sector is owned by the state. State control measures the nature of the relationship between the state and SOEs by observing the form of regulation applied, constraints on the sale of the firms, governance of the firms, degree to which they are insulated from market discipline, and political interference in management. The index ranges from 0 (least restrictive) to 6 (most restrictive) (OECD 2017).

Kazakhstan has a long way to go to become a competitive market-oriented economy. Although the state's share in industry declined from 69.7% in 2014 to 45.3% in 2016, its presence in economic activities is still prevalent. In the transport sector, the state's share in 2016 was 18.2% followed by health and social services at 15.4%, trade at 5.9%, and construction at 6.9% (Figure 4.5).

Figure 4.5: Share of State in Gross Value Added, 2014–2017 (%)

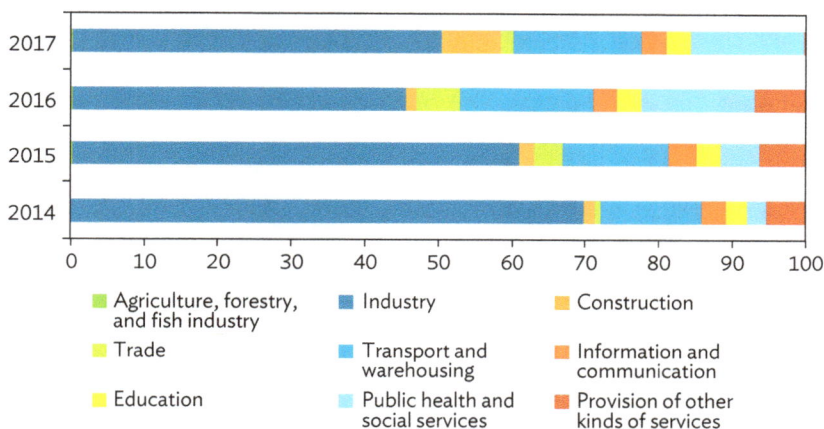

Source: Statistical Committee of the Ministry of National Economy of the Republic of Kazakhstan. Accounts Committee for Control over Execution of the Republican Budget (in Russian). http://esep.kz/rus/showin/article/3105.

Given their large presence in economic activities, SOEs have the potential to influence policy and competition in individual sectors, not only through the direct presence of government representatives in SOEs' board of directors, but also through privileged access to government. In key product markets, SOEs are able to easily access subsidized loans, undermining the competition and thus crowding out the private sector.

Legal Framework of SOEs

The Ministry of National Economy and the Ministry of Finance are responsible primarily for the ownership and governance of SOEs. The Department of State Assets Management Policy designs regulation policy, while the Committee of State Property and Privatization under the Ministry of Finance guides governance and privatization of state assets. The committee is authorized to account for all state assets—it is the central coordinating body and legal owner of entities through whom the government delegates ownership rights to other sector ministries (OECD 2017).

The Ministry of National Economy, the Ministry of Finance, and the Ministry of Agriculture are responsible for regulating several sectors affecting SOE operations such as taxation, general industrial policy, competition policy, and general procurement. The same applies to sector ministries that have ownership rights such as the Ministry of Agriculture. Large groups of companies under national managing holdings are detached enough to warrant the segregation of regulation and ownership. However, the presence of relevant ministries, such as the Ministry of Finance and the Ministry of National Economy, as members of the board of many companies under national managing holdings, in fact, involves the state in actual decision-making (OECD 2017).

Managing Holding Companies

The government controls a large number of state enterprises through national managing holding companies.[3] These state holdings are established to improve and manage national companies and state assets effectively, improve corporate governance and coordination between SOEs, implement major economic projects, and develop the stock market. The three largest holding companies—Samruk-Kazyna, KazAgro, and Baiterek, along with their more than 600 subsidiaries—virtually control important economic sectors such as energy, transport, public utilities, small and medium-sized enterprise finance, agriculture finance, and product development (World Bank 2018). The total assets of KazAgro, Baiterek, and Samruk-Kazyna combined increased from $77.3 billion in 2009 to $90 billion in 2017. Despite the decline in their share of assets to GDP from 66.3% in 2009 to 50% of GDP, these public holdings remain dominant (Figure 4.6).

---

[3]   A national company is a joint-stock company (JSC) that operates in fundamental industries or those facilitating regional economic development. It is controlled by the state through majority ownership or otherwise, directly or through a national managing holding company. A national holding company is likewise a government-created entity that owns shares in national companies. A national managing company manages the interests of the government in national holding companies, national companies, development institutes, and other entities.

Figure 4.6: Total Assets of Samruk-Kazyna, Baiterek, and KazAgro, 2009–2017

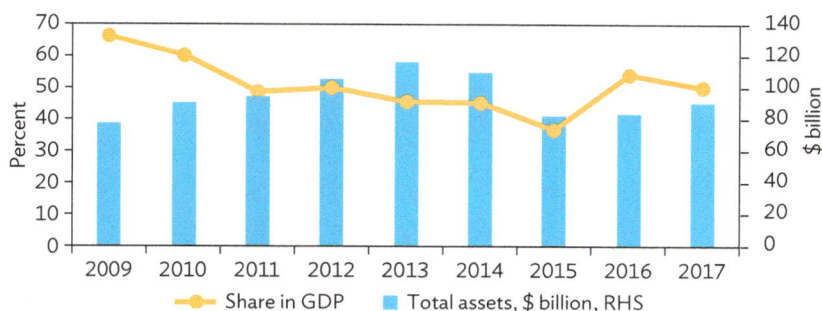

GDP = gross domestic product, RHS = right-hand side.
Source: Computations based on Bureau van Dijk. Orbis Database. https://www.bvdinfo.com/en-apac/our-products/company-information/international-products/orbis.

Kazakhstan has a hybrid-ownership model, with the government authority acting as a shareholder in the sovereign wealth fund, Samruk-Kazyna JSC (the fund). Samruk-Kazyna in turn holds shares in several large SOEs. The fund is under the purview of the Committee of State Property and Privatization under the Ministry of Finance. Companies owned by Kazakhstan's national holding, Samruk-Kazyna (SK Holding) in particular retain a significant and often dominant role in many important sectors, such as mining and quarrying (60% of the sector by assets); electricity, gas steam, and air-conditioning supply (42%); transportation and storage (31%); and information and telecommunication (30%). The agriculture sector also has a strong state presence, with the Food Contract Corporation fully owned by the state through the national holding KazAgro, the largest trader and exporter of grain.

SK Holding companies and other SOEs play a critical role in creating a framework for private sector development by shaping the competitive landscape and investors' perceptions, providing infrastructure and public services, and procuring goods and services. At the same time, authorities have implemented ambitious state support and industrialization programs amounting to more than $97 billion since 1997. The government acknowledges the critical need to improve the state's effectiveness and lessen its involvement in the economy by privatizing SOEs.

To channel and allocate efficiently the inflow of foreign exchange, the government has created a system of state asset management and development institutions, including two domestic sovereign wealth funds: the

National Fund of Kazakhstan and the Sovereign Wealth Fund Samruk-Kazyna (Box 4.1), through which the government achieves economic diversification, provides socioeconomic stability, and retains political control. They serve to accumulate and preserve wealth, diminish resource dependence, and achieve industrialization.

Box 4.1: National Fund of the Republic of Kazakhstan

Sovereign wealth funds (SWFs) are often created to help governments deal with problems emerging from variable revenues mainly in energy or other commodity sectors. The Kazakhstan government established the National Fund of the Republic of Kazakhstan (NFRK) in 2000 when oil prices were soaring and funds had accumulated. SWFs serve both as a stabilization and a savings fund, which the Kazakhstan government used to mitigate the effects of the 2007–2009 financial crisis.

An examination of resource-rich countries suggests that governments often face the challenge of devising policies to channel foreign exchange from foreign investments to the government. SWFs are designed for this purpose and have become popular in the face of high and volatile oil prices and new discoveries of hydrocarbon deposits. While they offer opportunities for economic development, unpredictable resource revenues, volatile and ultimately exhaustible by nature, are challenging to manage and can be problematic for policy makers, and sometimes turning out to be an economic curse rather than a blessing (Sachs and Warner 1995). The creation of SWFs is broadly justified to (i) address volatility in public spending, (ii) alleviate concerns particularly when resources are depleted, and (iii) minimize the impact of real exchange rate appreciation in the context of resource inflow from the export of resources (Paldam 1997). These three justifications can be grouped under the SWFs' two major roles of savings and stabilization. In Kazakhstan, the government is making an effort to combine these three functions in one institutional setup.

Fund Performance

The NFRK was established based on the Norwegian government's Petroleum Fund, in which the government maintains an account with the national bank, to serve as both savings and stabilization fund. The NFRK accumulates funds when the price of oil exceeds $19 per barrel (bbl) and diminishes when the price drops below $19/bbl. From the accumulated funds, 10% is paid quarterly into the savings account, and 90% is allocated for the budget. Initially, the NFRK had a long-term savings portfolio of 75% and a stabilization portfolio of 25%, which later increased to 80% and 20%, respectively. To mitigate the effects of exchange rate

Continued on next page

Box 4.1 continued

appreciation, the government invested both portfolios entirely overseas, while the stabilization portfolio had no equity assets and was held in short-term liquid assets. Along with rising oil prices in 2000–2005, the NFRK accumulated funds and made extra payments to Kazakhstan's budget from the oil and gas sector. By 2008, the fund's reserves exceeded $27.4 billion. However, as oil prices dropped during the financial crisis, tax revenues from oil companies declined, slackening NFRK growth. Since the NFRK was also used to stabilize the economy, its assets in 2009 reduced to $26 billion. Before the financial crisis, the government, as it pursued a conservative fiscal policy, kept large reserves overseas. During that period, credit growth of private banks escalated, resulting in asset bubbles.

The financial crisis also caused Kazakhstan's banking sector to borrow heavily from international and capital markets. As banks faced considerable liquidity-related problems and poor quality of their assets, the government introduced a bailout program which was financed partially with NFRK assets. External debt repayments in 2009 amounted to $11 billion. Since the financial crisis also hit other economic sectors, the government withdrew $10 billion (9.5% of gross domestic product) from the NFRK to stabilize the financial system and support the housing program, small and medium-sized enterprises, and industrial development. As a result, toward the end of the first quarter of 2009, NFRK assets declined by 20% to $26.6 billion. Overall, the NFRK did help ease the detrimental effects of the financial crisis. However, the banking and financial crisis in Kazakhstan and other oil-rich countries raised doubts over the effectiveness of the stabilization mechanism in resource-rich countries, thus calling for a fresh look at domestic investment to finance economic diversification (Heuty and Aristi 2009). Postcrisis, the NFRK shifted its focus from performance issues of firms to portfolio strategy and investment horizon.

Source: Kalyuzhnova (2011).

4.3   Performance of SOEs

In this section, we analyze the performance and contribution of SOEs during 2009–2017. To ensure consistent empirical analysis, we confine data to SOEs in the Orbis database from 2009 to 2017. A total of 250 SOEs, in which the state's share is more than 50% were selected. The data suggest that the total assets of these SOEs increased from $132.1 billion in 2009 to $220.3 billion in 2017. Included were 28 SOEs in the financial and insurance sector with a share of 65% in total assets in 2017, followed by mining and quarrying with a share of 23.8%, accommodation and food services at 6.0%, wholesale and retail trade at 1.6%, and electricity and gas with a share of 1.2% (Table 4.1).

Table 4.1: Total Assets of SOEs, by Sector, 2009–2017
($ billion)

Sector	No. of SOEs	2009	2010	2011	2012	2013	2014	2015	2016	2017
Finance and insurance	28	77.1	91.4	99.4	113.2	163.5	174.9	124.4	134.3	143.1
Mining and quarrying	15	43.2	51.6	55.3	63.5	69.2	63.1	41.5	46.4	52.5
Accommodation and food services	11	8.6	12.8	14.7	15.7	18.6	20.4	12.3	13.7	13.3
Wholesale and retail trade	7	0.5	1.3	1.7	2.1	2.4	3.1	2.1	2.9	3.4
Electricity, gas, steam and air-conditioning supply	13	0.5	0.7	0.9	2.5	3.3	3.9	2.3	2.4	2.6
All others	176	2.2	3.4	4.3	5.8	7.6	8.4	5.1	5.9	5.4
Total	**250**	**132.1**	**161.2**	**176.3**	**202.8**	**264.6**	**273.8**	**187.7**	**205.6**	**220.3**

SOE = state-owned enterprise.
Source: Author's computation based on the Orbis database.

To have an idea of the corporate health of SOEs, we use the concepts of return on equity (ROE) and return on assets (ROA). ROE is defined as the ratio of net income to equity, while ROA is the ratio of net income to assets. These ratios provide useful insights into a company's ability to generate earnings from its investments. For example, ROE measures how effectively a company's management uses investors' money and shows whether management is growing the company's value at an acceptable rate. On the other hand, ROA basically provides information on management's effectiveness and reveals how much profit a company earns for every dollar of its assets.

A comparison of SOEs and private companies in Figure 4.7 shows that the ROE and ROA for private companies have always remained higher than SOEs except in 2015. The average ROE for private companies during 2009–2017 was 26.9% compared with 8.5% for SOEs. Similarly, the average ROA for private listed companies during the same period was 16.8%, still higher than the 3.0% for SOEs, which suggests that private listed companies have outperformed SOEs in profitability and productivity.

Detailed analysis reveals that during the 2009 financial crisis, ROE and ROA were negative, while between 2010 and 2017, both ratios had declined over time, implying that SOE performance had deteriorated. However, ROE remained higher than ROA throughout the period, suggesting that SOEs continued to receive financial leverage from the government. The decline in ROE indicates that the majority of SOEs have not managed their invested capital efficiently. In a way, the ROE sets the pace for a firm's growth rate. During 2010–2013, ROE averaged around 15.4% and reduced subsequently to 4.7% in 2014–2017, indicating that SOEs cannot increase their earnings any more rapidly without borrowing from the government or selling shares. As ROE declined gradually, SOEs relied increasingly on government funding to finance their operations. Figure 4.7 shows that SOE productivity also deteriorated—ROA dropped from 6.4% in 2010 to 0.9% by 2017, reflecting the poor productivity of these companies.

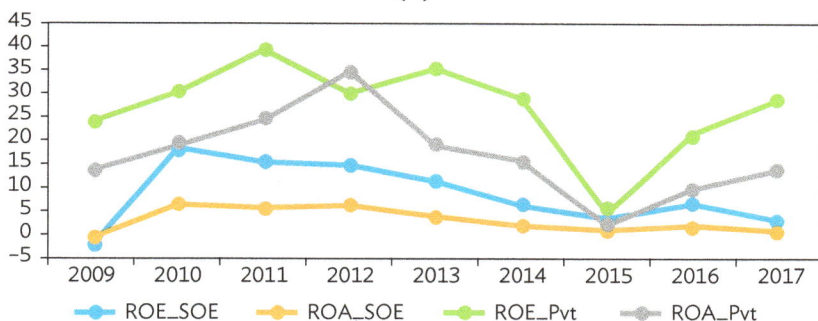

Figure 4.7: Trends in Return on Equity and Return on Assets, 2009–2017
(%)

ROE_SOE = SOEs' return on equity, ROA_SOE = SOEs' return on assets, ROE_Pvt = return on equity of private listed companies, ROA_Pvt = return on assets of private listed companies.
Source: Author's computation based on the Orbis database.

Disaggregated data covering major sectors reveal that the ROE in the mining sector had declined from 17.5% in 2009 to –0.3% in 2017 (Table 4.2). More specifically, during 2013–2017, ROE remained negative, except in 2015 when it marginally improved to 1.5%. The ROE for mining support services also dropped from 24.3% in 2009 to 8.8% in 2017. A similar trend was observed for land transport-related services, where ROE fell from 30.4% in 2010 to 8.4% in 2017. Average ROE for all sectors also declined from 20.7% in 2009 to 8.4% by 2017, reflecting a generally diminishing profitability among major SOEs. More importantly, in the absence of a competitive environment along with a weak finance sector, resources have not been allocated efficiently. And poor governance and preferential treatment of SOEs have given rise to unequal treatment, rendering the private sector uncompetitive.

Table 4.2: Return on Equity, by Sector, 2009–2017
(%)

	2009	2010	2011	2012	2013	2014	2015	2016	2017
Overall	**(2.4)**	**18.3**	**15.4**	**14.7**	**11.4**	**6.1**	**3.5**	**6.5**	**2.9**
Mining of metal ores	17.5	22.6	23.9	13.4	(30.1)	(11.0)	1.5	(0.9)	(0.3)
Mining support services	13.9	19.0	14.2	10.8	10.8	4.4	8.1	5.3	7.2
Electricity, gas, steam, and air-conditioning supply	24.3	26.8	10.6	6.4	0.3	3.8	0.1	7.6	8.8
Land transport and transport via pipelines	0.0	30.4	20.9	13.6	22.2	10.1	9.5	7.6	8.4
Financial services, except insurance and pension funds	0.0	0.0	0.0	14.4	5.4	0.0	0.0	0.0	0.0
Insurance, reinsurance, and pension funds, except compulsory social security	0.0	0.0	10.6	11.3	0.0	0.0	0.0	0.0	0.0

( ) = negative.
Source: Author's computation based on the Orbis database.

Determinants of Return on Equity

To examine the factors underlying the decline in ROE, we disaggregate data into three components: profit margin, asset turnover, and financial leverage. This analysis provides useful insights about the major factors affecting return on equity (Botika 2012). Profit margin is a measure of profitability and hence an indicator of a company's pricing strategies and how well the company controls costs. As a company's profit margin increases, so does ROE. Asset turnover, on the other hand, is a financial ratio that measures how efficiently assets are being used to generate sales revenue. Companies with low profit margins tend to have high turnover of assets, while turnover of assets for those with high profit margins is likely to be low. Therefore, if asset turnover increases, a company generates more sales per asset owned and its ROE also increases. Financial leverage, on the other hand, provides information on the amount of debt a company utilizes to finance its operations. An increase in financial leverage also results in higher ROE. Accordingly, ROE can be disaggregated into its three components:[4]

---

[4]   The analysis is based on the DuPont equation which originated in 1920 and developed by the management of DuPont Corporation for the purpose of detailed assessment of the company's profitability. It basically breaks down the ROE ratio into three components: operating efficiency, asset efficiency, and financial leverage.

$$ROE = \frac{Net\ Income\ (NI)}{Shareholder\ Equity\ (E)} \tag{i}$$

$$ROE = \frac{Net\ Income}{Sales} \times \frac{Sales}{Total\ Assets} \times \frac{Total\ Assets}{Shareholder\ Equity} \tag{ii}$$

$$ROE = NPM \times AT \times EM \tag{iii}$$
ROE = Net Profit Margin x Asset Turnover x Equity Multiplier

Equation (iii) provides useful insights about a company's profitability, asset turnover, and financial leverage. The first two components assess the operations of the business. For example, net profit margin of a company reflects management's pricing strategy and shows how much earnings they can generate from a single monetary unit. Asset turnover describes how effectively management is using assets to make sales, whereas equity multiplier provides information on financial leverage. A higher equity multiplier ratio would imply that the company has largely financed its operations through debts. The more leverage the company takes, the higher the risk of default. The decomposition, therefore, integrates the three attributes of productivity, profitability, and leverage, and highlighting that ROE is influenced by these three aspects. Next, we investigate these three attributes by analyzing the ROE for Kazakhstan's SOE sector as a whole and also by examining the three largest national holding companies. The analysis results show that the major factors responsible for reducing the ROE have been the decline in net profit margin and assets turnover (Figure 4.8).

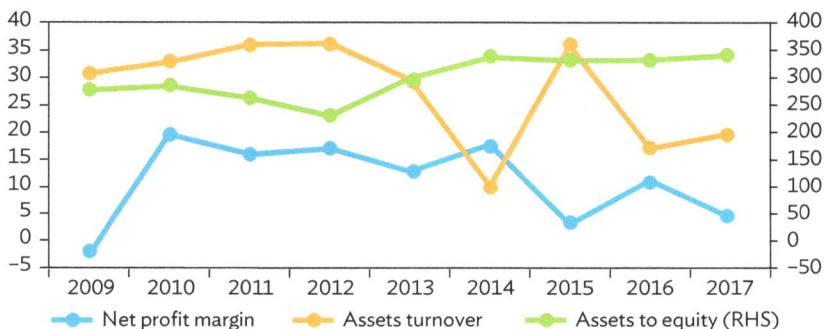

Figure 4.8: Determinants of Return on Equity
in Kazakhstan's SOEs, 2009–2017
(%)

RHS = right-hand side, SOE = state-owned enterprise.
Source: Author's computation based on the Orbis database.

The analysis shows that net profit margin declined from 19.6% in 2010 to 4.3% in 2017, while assets turnover dropped from 30.8% to 19.7% (Table 4.3). In 2009–2017, net profit margin remained on average at 11%, while assets turnover averaged around 27.6%. To finance their operations, SOEs continued to rely on debt as reflected in the higher value of financial leverage, which increased from 279.1% in 2009 to 342% in 2017. The proportion of debt financing surged from 64.2% in 2009 to 70.8% in 2017. SOE productivity as measured by the ROA also declined from 6.4% in 2010 to 0.9% by 2017.

Table 4.3: Decomposition of Return on Equity for SOEs in Kazakhstan, 2009–2017

	2009	2010	2011	2012	2013	2014	2015	2016	2017
				($ billion)					
Net income	(1.1)	10.4	10.2	12.6	10.1	4.9	1.9	3.9	1.9
Total assets	132.1	161.2	176.3	202.8	264.6	273.8	187.7	205.6	220.3
Total equity	47.3	56.4	66.2	85.5	88.3	80.7	56.3	60.5	64.4
Total sales	40.7	52.9	63.8	73.6	78.5	27.7	67.5	35.2	43.5
				(%)					
Return on equity	(2.4)	18.3	15.4	14.7	11.4	6.1	3.5	6.5	2.9
Net profit margin	(2.8)	19.6	16.0	17.1	12.8	17.8	2.9	11.2	4.3
Assets turnover	30.8	32.8	36.2	36.3	29.7	10.1	36.0	17.1	19.7
Assets to equity	279.1	285.6	266.3	237.2	299.6	339.5	333.7	339.7	342.0
Debt financing	64.2	65.0	62.5	57.8	66.6	70.5	70.0	70.6	70.8
Productivity	(0.9)	6.4	5.8	6.2	3.8	1.8	1.0	1.9	0.9

( ) = negative, SOE = state-owned enterprise.
Source: Author's computation based on the Orbis database.

Next, a detailed examination of the factors behind the decline in productivity indicates that ROA for mining of metal ores dipped from 10.7% in 2009 to 7.6% by 2012 (Table 4.4). In 2015, it recovered to 1.3%, but continued dropping for all other years and remained negative. Likewise, ROA for mining support services fell from 6.2% in 2009 to 4% by 2017. ROA for electricity, gas supply, and land transport also declined substantially.

Table 4.4: Return on Assets, 2009–2017
(%)

	2009	2010	2011	2012	2013	2014	2015	2016	2017
Overall	**(0.9)**	**6.4**	**5.8**	**6.2**	**3.8**	**1.8**	**1.0**	**1.9**	**0.9**
Mining of metal ores	10.7	11.4	13.0	7.6	(27.4)	(7.8)	1.3	(0.9)	(0.3)
Mining support services	6.2	8.8	8.2	6.4	6.4	2.5	5.0	3.1	4.0
Electricity and gas supply	13.4	15.3	6.3	3.7	0.2	2.5	0.1	4.4	5.2
Land transport	0.0	24.6	17.3	10.8	17.6	7.9	7.2	6.0	6.6
Financial service activities	0.0	0.0	0.0	7.0	2.7	0.0	0.0	0.0	0.0
Insurance and pension funding	0.0	0.0	10.1	10.9	0.0	0.0	0.0	0.0	0.0

( ) = negative.
Source: Author's computation based on the Orbis database.

As discussed, SOEs often enjoy implicit and explicit government guarantees for borrowing and preferential treatment to sustain their operations. Generally, these companies tend to have easy access to credit and capital injections, as well as various types of subsidies, which put them at a clear advantage over private sector firms which generally do not have such privileges. To perform a quantitative assessment of these preferential treatments, we compare the SOEs' actual profits vis-à-vis the profits had these companies attained the "efficient" ROE* (PROSPERA unpublished). In this way, implicit subsidy/ surplus can be calculated using the following equation:

Implicit subsidy/Surplus = Profit – [Equity x ROE*]

where ROE* is the efficient risk-weighted cost of equity. A largely positive (a surplus) difference between actual and potential profits, based on ROE*, reflects unfair advantages such as state monopoly or cheap financing. On the other hand, a largely negative difference reflects the amount of forgone profits and implies that SOEs are underperforming. The forgone profits could be treated like an implicit subsidy. The above relationship can be used to compare the actual profits of SOEs versus the potential profits that would have accrued had these companies achieved a rate of return equal to international peers and private listed companies.

We have used two proxies for ROE*. First, to compare with international companies, ROE* is defined as the return on equity in United States (US) firms. Second, to compare the performance of SOEs with private listed companies in Kazakhstan, ROE* is used as a proxy for the average ROE of these companies. Since ROE can vary substantially between industries, we have used time-varying ROE*, proxied by average ROE for the US and private listed companies in Kazakhstan during 2009–2017.

Comparing SOEs with US companies during the 2009 financial crisis, forgone profits reached a total $6.9 billion or 6.0% of GDP. To stabilize the economy, the government financially assisted the largest holding companies and injected $10 billion (10% of GDP) from the National Fund of the Republic of Kazakhstan (NFRK) in 2009. As a result, actual profits of SOEs during 2010–2012 exceeded even the potential profits. In the following years, however, SOE performance again deteriorated as the cumulative amount of forgone profits amounted to $2.9 billion or 1.6% of GDP in 2013–2017 (Figure 4.9 left). A similar comparison with private listed companies reveals that the wedge between actual and potential profits was even higher partly because of the higher profits of private listed companies and the collapse of oil prices, which lowered the performance of SOEs and reduced their profits substantially. Accordingly, implicit subsidies surged sharply from 1.8% of GDP in 2009 to 6.8% of GDP in 2015. Forgone profits during 2012–2017 amounted to $7.6 billion or 3.9% of GDP (Figure 4.9 right).

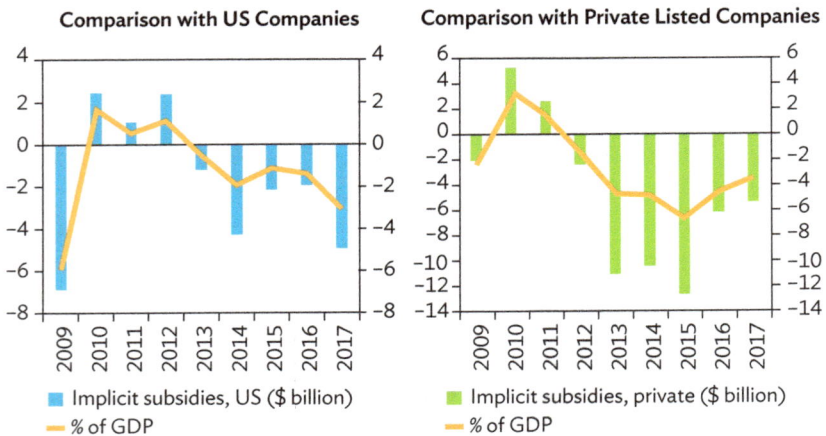

Figure 4.9: Implicit Subsidy to SOEs in Kazakhstan, 2009–2017

GDP = gross domestic product, SOE = state-owned enterprise, US = United States.
Source: Author's computation based on the Orbis database.

As government continued to inject capital despite the SOEs' deteriorating performance and SOEs continued to finance their operation through debts, actual profits remained lower than comparator organizations, thus implying a substantial amount of forgone profits, which basically reflects the underperformance of SOEs vis-à-vis international and private listed companies in Kazakhstan.

Operating Efficiency of SOEs

In this section, we examine the operating efficiency of SOEs and evaluate their net operating profits, i.e., earnings before interest and taxes (EBIT) and return on capital employed (ROCE). EBIT is a measure of a firm's profit including all income and expenses (operating and nonoperating) except interest expenses and income tax expenses. The data of the 250 SOEs listed in the Orbis database reveal that overall net operating profits declined substantially between 2009 and 2017. In fact, against the reduction in oil prices, SOEs' net operating profits declined by 64.5% in 2014 (Figure 4.10).

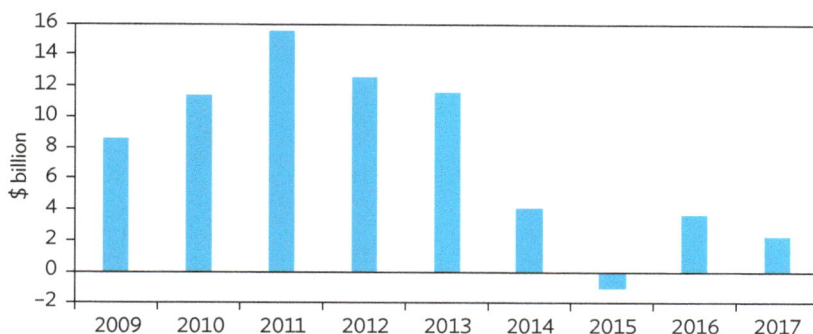

Figure 4.10: Net Operating Income and Earnings Before Interest and Taxes of SOEs, 2009–2017
($ billion)

SOE = state-owned enterprise.
Source: Author's computation based on the Orbis database.

Next, we analyze ROCE between 2009 and 2017 to evaluate the allocative efficiency of capital employed by SOEs. ROCE is a ratio of profitability that measures how efficiently a company can use its capital to generate profits. Again, we examine data on the 250 SOEs listed in the Orbis database and organize them into major sectors. Table 4.5 summarizes the ROCE statistics by major sectors.

Table 4.5: Allocative Efficiency of Capital, 2009–2017

(%)

SOEs Major Sectors	Number of SOEs (out of 250)	Return on Capital Employed (ROCE), %								
		2009	2010	2011	2012	2013	2014	2015	2016	2017
Mining and quarrying	15	8.3	15.2	15.3	14.0	8.9	1.4	(3.5)	3.0	0.1
Manufacturing	8	4.6	7.3	8.4	9.9	7.1	8.7	10.5	13.5	8.5
Electricity, gas, steam, and air-conditioning supply	13	3.5	11.9	10.3	6.1	5.4	4.4	5.8	7.0	8.9
Water supply, sewerage, waste management, and remediation	2	9.1	(4.5)	0.0	(6.4)	(13.0)	(4.9)	(1.6)	7.0	1.8
Construction	5	(19.4)	0.0	10.2	(27.7)	(640.8)	81.8	4.7	1.6	(25.3)
Wholesale and retail trade	7	(35.1)	18.5	14.4	9.5	13.7	5.4	3.8	5.5	2.9
Accommodation and food services	11	8.0	10.5	10.0	7.6	8.7	6.8	4.9	4.6	4.0
Transportation and storage	1				(133.4)	0.2	0.0	(1.6)	(0.9)	(0.3)
Information and communication	12	10.0	5.8	1.6	1.8	1.4	(0.3)	0.1	(2.3)	(0.3)
Finance and insurance	28	8.5	4.6	8.2	4.1	2.9	1.2	(0.3)	1.3	1.1
Professional, scientific, and technical services	22	(2.9)	(3.0)	(41.9)	(4.5)	(6.0)	(9.8)	(36.3)	(3.2)	(2.1)
Administrative and support services	7	9.7	23.2	23.4	(1.9)	0.7	0.1	(25.4)	3.4	2.6
Public administration and defense, compulsory social security	3	42.7	42.8	29.7	39.0	52.8	38.4	31.2	30.5	4.5
Education	10	(0.1)	(0.2)	0.5	1.0	0.3	0.2	(1.7)	(0.8)	(1.8)
Human health and social work	8	47.5	(2.7)	(4.1)	(1.2)	0.2	(0.1)	(2.8)	0.9	(0.5)
Arts, entertainment, and recreation	2			90.0	0.4	(6.7)	(7.6)	(1.9)	(1.3)	(2.1)
Other services	96				(2.6)	(4.9)	(0.2)	0.8	(0.2)	
Total	**250**	**8.4**	**8.7**	**10.5**	**7.6**	**5.0**	**1.7**	**(0.6)**	**2.0**	**1.2**

( ) = negative, SOE = state-owned enterprise.
Source: Author's computation based on the Orbis database.

Table 4.5 indicates that ROCE for total SOEs dropped from 8.4% in 2009 to 1.2% by 2017. More importantly, as oil prices plummeted in 2014, ROCE continued to fall between 2014 and 2017, reflecting the companies' inability to reinvest capital and obtain a higher rate of return. Hence, the declining ROCE can be an indicator of these enterprises' poor performance.

Contribution to Employment and Productivity

SOEs have contributed significantly toward creating jobs in the country. In 2009–2016, SOEs created about 86,000 jobs, although the majority were concentrated in low-productivity nontradable services sectors. Employment in total SOEs increased from 151,000 in 2009 to 237,000 by 2017, an increase of 5.8% per annum (Table 4.6). During 2009–2017, accommodation and food services alone provided about 50,000 jobs. Mining and quarrying created 16,000 jobs while the health sector opened another 3,000 jobs.

The major sectors that contributed to employment growth during 2009–2016 were mining and quarrying (30.1%) and health and social work (13.7%). Accommodation and food services contributed 5.3%, while education's share was 2.8%.

On the other hand, employment in manufacturing declined by 3.6%. Most of the 13 SOEs in this sector remained concentrated in resource-based industry and were capital intensive in nature. Thus, despite high economic growth during 2009–2016, manufacturing did not contribute significantly to employment. Likewise, employment growth in wholesale and retail trade registered a decline of 1.4%, and information and communication fell by 1%.

To gain deeper insight into the dynamics of employment and output of different SOEs, we next examine trends in labor productivity. In SOE sectors as a whole, labor productivity declined by 8.6% during 2009–2017 (Figure 4.11). The major sectors contributing to the decline in labor productivity were administrative and support services (–12.5%); mining and quarrying (–11.9%); accommodation and food services (–10.2%); health (–6.0%); education (–4.5%); and electricity and gas (–4.3%). On the other hand, professional, scientific, and technical services and wholesale and trade saw an increase in labor productivity by 19.7% and 7.1%, respectively.

Table 4.6: Contribution of SOEs to Employment, 2009–2017

| SOEs by Sector | No. of SOEs | Number of Employees ('000) | | | | | | | | | ACGR (%) |
		2009	2010	2011	2012	2013	2014	2015	2016	2017	2009–2017
Mining and quarrying	15	2.2	2.3	1.9	17.4	17.4	17.6	8.1	17.9	17.7	30.1
Manufacturing	8	8.1	5.9	6.3	6.1	6.5	6.4	2.6	2.4	6.0	(3.6)
Electricity and gas	13	4.0	4.0	4.0	4.0	4.0	4.0	4.0	0.7	4.1	0.5
Wholesale and retail trade	7	4.7	16.7	16.7	16.6	5.9	5.9	4.5	2.4	4.2	(1.4)
Accommodation and food services	11	96.7	95.9	94.8	95.1	93.6	92.1	91.5	151.3	146.1	5.3
Information and communication	12	7.8	6.2	6.0	7.1	7.5	7.5	7.7	7.4	7.3	(0.9)
Education	10	3.1	4.9	6.2	6.1	6.6	6.7	4.8	3.0	3.9	2.8
Health and social work	8	1.6	3.5	4.3	4.4	4.4	4.5	3.3	4.3	4.3	13.7
Other services	166	23.0	18.7	19.0	21.9	27.4	23.3	23.4	43.6	43.2	8.2
Total	**250**	**151.1**	**158.0**	**159.2**	**178.7**	**173.3**	**168.1**	**150.0**	**233.0**	**236.9**	**5.8**

( ) = negative, ACGR = annual compound growth rate, SOE = state-owned enterprise.
Source: Author's computation based on the Orbis database.

Figure 4.11: Labor Productivity Growth in Major SOE Sectors, 2009–2017
(%)

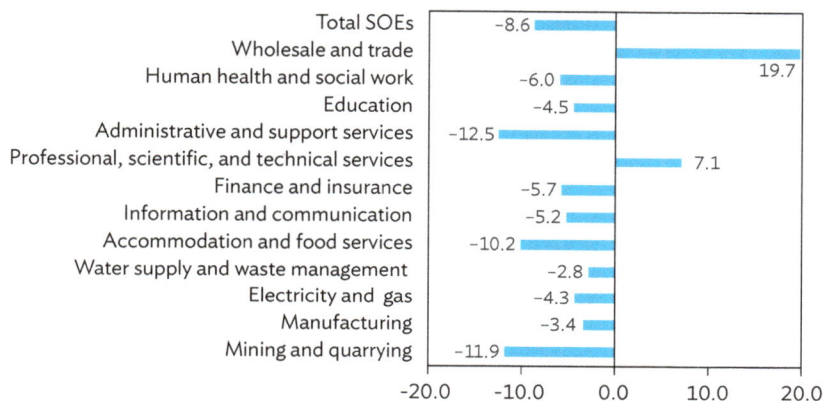

Sector	Value
Total SOEs	−8.6
Wholesale and trade	19.7
Human health and social work	−6.0
Education	−4.5
Administrative and support services	−12.5
Professional, scientific, and technical services	7.1
Finance and insurance	−5.7
Information and communication	−5.2
Accommodation and food services	−10.2
Water supply and waste management	−2.8
Electricity and gas	−4.3
Manufacturing	−3.4
Mining and quarrying	−11.9

SOE = state-owned enterprise.
Note: Figures in parentheses are the growth rate of labor productivity.
Source: Author's computation based on the Orbis database for 250 SOEs classified into major sectors.

Decline in labor productivity is disaggregated into productivity changes within industries and productivity changes resulting from reallocating labor to different industries. This process helps us understand the underlying dynamics of productivity and how it is linked to structural change in the economy. It will also highlight Kazakhstan's ability to shift resources from low to high productivity sectors.

We use the method of shift–share analysis (Chapter 1, Appendix A1.1) to capture changes in labor productivity in Kazakhstan, the decline resulting from productivity changes within an industry is measured through what is called "within shift effect," while productivity changes caused by reallocating labor to different industries are measured through the "static shift effect." On the other hand, "dynamic shift effect," which is measured by combining these pieces of information, provides insight on productivity growth and employment share of the different economic sectors. The results of the shift–share analysis show that decline in Kazakhstan SOEs' labor productivity stems mainly from the reallocation of labor to low productivity sectors, which is reflected in the negative value of "dynamic shift effect." In addition, the analysis reveals that labor productivity within sectors also decreased mainly because both output and employment declined and that SOE employment remains concentrated in low productivity sectors (Table 4.7).

Table 4.7: Decomposition of Labor Productivity Growth, 2009–2017
(%)

	Static Shift Effects	Within Shift Effects	Dynamic Shift Effects	Sum
Mining and quarrying	19.82	(4.43)	(18.83)	19.82
Manufacturing	(0.02)	(0.01)	0.01	(0.02)
Electricity, gas, and air conditioning supply	(0.05)	(0.05)	0.02	(0.05)
Construction	0.00	(0.00)	0.00	0.00
Wholesale and retail trade	(0.05)	0.19	(0.08)	(0.05)
Accommodation and food services	(0.05)	(1.05)	0.04	(0.05)
Information and communication	(0.02)	(0.02)	0.01	(0.02)
Finance and insurance	(2.34)	(2.77)	1.07	(2.34)
Professional, scientific, and technical services	(0.00)	0.00	(0.00)	(0.00)
Administrative and support services	(0.00)	(0.00)	0.00	(0.00)
Education	(0.00)	(0.00)	0.00	(0.00)
Human health and social work	0.01	(0.01)	(0.00)	0.01
Others	0.04	(0.02)	(0.01)	0.04
Total	**17.30**	**(8.20)**	**(17.80)**	**(8.60)**

( ) = negative, SOE = state-owned enterprise.
Source: Author's computation based on the Orbis database for the selected 250 SOEs.

4.4   Measuring the Efficiency of SOEs

In this section, we examine the relative efficiency of SOEs during 2009–2017 by using data envelopment analysis (DEA), a popular method used widely for estimating relative efficiency of decision-making units. DEA compares the efficiency of different organizational units such as SOEs and identifies units that operate relatively efficiently and those that do not. It not only identifies inefficient units but also estimates inefficiency empirically and shows how much inefficient units need to reduce their input or increase their output to become efficient (Chapter 1, Appendix A1.2). First, we analyze the trends in overall efficiency of SOEs from 2009 to 2017 which is shown in Figure 4.12.

In Figure 4.12, the horizontal line reflects the "efficient frontier," which denotes the maximum efficiency score an SOE can attain by utilizing available resources—this value is equal to 1. The vertical bars on the other hand show the estimated efficiency scores of 250 SOEs from 2009 to 2017. For example, the efficiency score for SOEs in 2009 was 0.80, implying an efficiency rating of

Figure 4.12: Efficient Frontier of SOEs, 2009–2017
(Index 0–1)

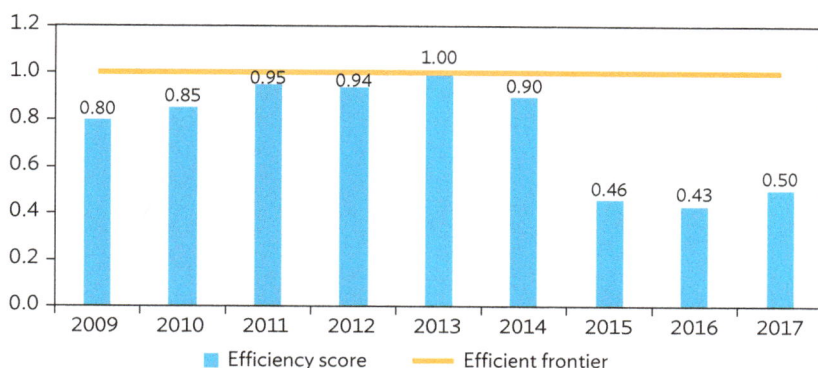

SOE = state-owned enterprise.
Source: Author's computation based on the Orbis database.

80%, which means that SOEs in 2009 were using about 20% excess resources compared with the efficiency threshold of 100%. Hence, by adopting modern technology and improving corporate governance, these companies can produce at least an additional 20% output with the same level of input. It is important to note that the SOEs' efficiency has remained particularly low after the decline in oil prices in 2014. The efficiency score started to decline from 0.9 in 2014 to 0.5 by 2017.

Next, to have an idea of efficiency at a more disaggregated level, we analyze the SOEs in different sectors and focus on the year 2017. Once again, we use the DEA, the results of which are shown in Figure 4.13.

The yellow circle in Figure 4.13 signifies the "efficient frontier" with a maximum score of 1, while the blue circle inside the efficient frontier indicates the estimated efficiency scores for different sectors in 2017. The analysis suggests that efficiency scores for most of the companies operating in different sectors lie inside the efficient frontier, implying various degrees of inefficiency. The efficiency scores of various sectors range from 0.19 to 1.0, while the average efficiency score of all sectors turns out to be 0.53. Once again, our analysis points to considerable room for improvement in efficiency and quality of public service delivery. Majority of the sectors scored less than 1, suggesting that proper management and improvement in corporate governance can substantially increase the overall level of output.

Figure 4.13: Efficient Frontier Sector-Wise, 2017
(efficiency scores, 0–1)

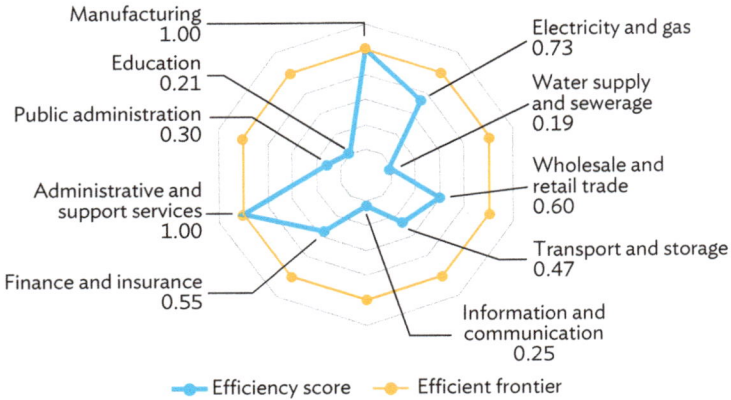

Source: Author's computation based on the Orbis database.

As discussed earlier, while SOEs dominate economic activity and have created about 86,000 jobs in the public sector, the majority of these jobs are in low-productivity sectors. Between 2009 and 2017, productivity declined by 20.2% per annum and Kazakhstan had not experienced a structural shift in its resources. This carries negative implications for sustainable growth in non-oil sectors and in providing decent jobs to the growing labor force. Similarly, the results of the efficiency analysis reveal that on average SOEs are using about 26% excess resources, which indicates therefore that through the right policies and practices and better corporate governance, output can be increased at least by this margin.

4.5   Performance of Joint-Stock Companies

Next, we focus on the performance of the three largest joint-stock companies (JSCs) in Kazakhstan: Samruk-Kazyna, Baiterek, and KazAgro. Once again for consistency, we use data from the Orbis database.

1.   Samruk-Kazyna Joint Stock Company

The Samruk-Kazyna Joint Stock Company (SK JSC)[5] was created in 2008 through the merger of two large state conglomerates: Sustainable

---

5   Samruk-Kazyna Joint Stock Company (SK JSC) was incorporated in accordance with Presidential Decree No. 668 of 13 October 2008 and Government Resolution No. 962 of 17 October 2008.

Development Fund Kazyna and Kazakhstan's Holding for the Management of State Assets Samruk.[6] The fund was established to

(i)   facilitate modernization and diversification of the economy,

(ii) participate in the process of stabilizing the economy, and

(iii) enhance the efficiency of companies.

The SK JSC aims to strengthen financial performance, increase investment returns, and improve portfolio development on a par with leading sovereign wealth funds. It is mandated to manage effectively its portfolio of companies by aligning performance indicators with those of the world's leading peer companies, raising corporate governance at the highest level, and sustaining the development of the fund and its portfolio. As one of its primary objectives is to improve profitability, it focuses on strengthening financial stability and operational efficiency of companies by making their investments attractive.

The SK Fund fulfills its objectives through the efficient management of its portfolio. Given the importance of SK JSC in the economy, we look at its financial performance and evaluate it against its long-term objectives. SK JSC controls almost all of Kazakhstan's strategic corporate assets amounting to approximately 40% of gross domestic product (GDP) in 2017. In 2015, the government announced plans to privatize some of its assets, including those in the energy, mining, and transport sectors, to attract foreign direct investment and stimulate economic growth. The privatization list features some 215 entities owned and operated by SK JSC. The largest of its subsidiaries—AirAstana, Kazatomprom, Kazakhtelecom, KazMunayGas, KTZ, Samruk-Energy, and Kazpost—are targeted for initial public offering. The government plans to float a 15%–25% share of these companies on the Astana stock exchange by 2020.

Performance of Samruk-Kazyna

Next, we examine return on equity (ROE) trends by disaggregating ROE into profit margin, assets turnover, and assets-to-equity ratios. During 2009, ROE was −16.5%, and between 2010 and 2017 it declined from 12% to 6.3% and peaked at 14.4% in 2012 (Table 4.8). With the collapse of oil prices in 2014, net profit margin also started declining and dropped to as low as 3.4% in 2015. Disaggregated analysis reveals that the decline in ROE between 2010 and 2017 resulted in reduction in the profit margin.

---

[6]   Samruk-Kazyna. https://www.sk.kz/about-fund/history-of-the-fund/.

Table 4.8: Decomposition of Return on Equity for Samruk-Kazyna, 2009–2017

	2009	2010	2011	2012	2013	2014	2015	2016	2017
	($ billion)								
Net income	(4.6)	3.8	2.2	7.1	2.6	1.5	0.5	1.4	2.2
Total assets	74.5	86.9	90.4	101.3	99.3	91.2	61.4	67.4	72.7
Total equity	27.9	31.5	33.5	49.2	48.7	44.6	30.6	33.0	35.1
Total sales	19.7	24.6	29.8	31.3	32.5	28.2	13.8	17.5	22.6
	(%)								
ROE	(16.5)	12.0	6.6	14.4	5.4	3.3	1.6	4.1	6.3
Net profit margin	(23.4)	15.4	7.5	22.6	8.1	5.3	3.4	7.8	9.8
Assets turnover	26.5	28.3	33.0	30.9	32.7	30.9	22.5	25.9	31.1
Assets to equity	267.1	275.4	269.9	206.0	203.7	204.6	200.8	204.3	207.2
Debt financing	62.6	63.7	62.9	51.5	50.9	51.1	50.2	51.1	51.7
Productivity	(6.2)	4.4	2.5	7.0	2.7	1.6	0.8	2.0	3.0

( ) = negative, ROE = return on equity.
Source: Author's computation based on the Orbis database.

Return on equity deteriorated mainly because net profit margin dropped from 15.4% in 2010 to 9.8% by 2017. Profit margins declined substantially as crude oil prices in the international market plummeted in 2014. Assets turnover, on the other hand, increased from 26.5% in 2009 and to 33% by 2011. Thereafter, it declined to 25.9% by 2016, until it rose again to 31% in 2017. To finance its operations and assets, SK JSC continued to rely on debt financing, as reflected in the higher asset-to-equity ratio. The analysis suggests that during 2009–2017 about 55% of the assets were financed through debt. Meanwhile, productivity dropped from 4.4% in 2010 to 3.0% by 2017.

As discussed, the net profit margin of SK JSC declined substantially between 2009 and 2017, but it continued to receive the government's preferential treatment to finance its operations. Using the methodology discussed, the cumulative amount of forgone profits against United States (US) companies turned out to be $22 billion or 1.6% of GDP during 2009–2017 (Figure 4.14 left). Similar computations in comparison to private listed companies in Kazakhstan suggest that the amount of forgone profits during the same year was $36.3 billion or 2.26% of GDP (Figure 4.14 right). Such a high amount of forgone profits basically reflects underperformance of SK JSC vis-à-vis US and private listed companies in Kazakhstan, even while it continues to rely on capital injections from the government. During 2008–2016, SK JSC received about $14 billion from national fund to finance its operations.

Figure 4.14: Implicit Subsidy to Samruk-Kazyna, 2009–2017

Comparison with US Companies

Comparison with Private Companies

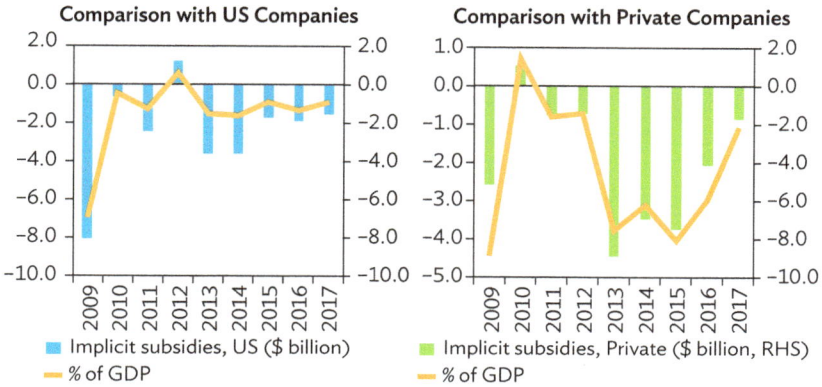

Implicit subsidies, US ($ billion)
— % of GDP

Implicit subsidies, Private ($ billion, RHS)
— % of GDP

GDP = gross domestic product, RHS = right-hand side, US = United States.
Source: Author's computation based on the Orbis database.

An examination of the operational and allocative efficiency of SK JSC indicates that both the EBIT margin and ROCE declined substantially between 2009 and 2017, implying that the allocative efficiency of the capital employed had deteriorated during the period (Figure 4.15).

Figure 4.15: Earnings Before Interest and Taxes Margin and Allocative Efficiency, 2009–2017

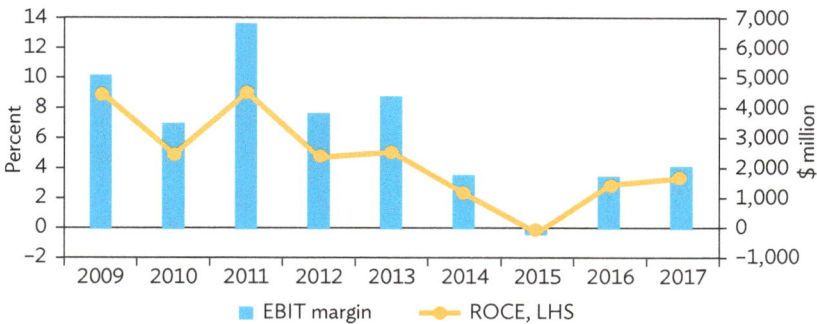

EBIT margin   ROCE, LHS

EBIT = earnings before interest and taxes, LHS = left-hand side, ROCE = return on capital employed.
Source: Author's computations based on the Orbis database.

The discussion suggests that the overall financial performance of the fund remains dismal. Return on equity and fund productivity had deteriorated over time, while reliance on debt financing increased. Poor financial performance of companies under the fund will make it difficult to put Kazakhstan on the list of the top 30 economies in the world by 2050. Hence, SK JSC needs to focus on improving productivity of companies and promote private investments in the country to sustain high economic growth in the non-oil sector.

2. Baiterek Joint Stock Company

Next, we evaluate the performance of Baiterek JSC,[7] which was established in 2013 to provide financial and investment support to the non-commodity sector and to ensure sustainable economic development and diversification. The Holding also attracts foreign investments, helps develop clusters, and improves corporate governance in its subsidiaries. It aims to implement public policies and achieve 2050 Strategy goals. Baiterek JSC's vision is to be the foremost government institution complying with best practice standards in corporate governance and ensuring that sustainable development of Kazakhstan's economy is achieved through diversification, support for innovations, exports promotion, and increase in productivity. The main objectives of the Holding are to

(i)   introduce an efficient risk management system;

(ii) increase transparency and people's confidence level;

(iii) develop synergy in working collaboratively with subsidiaries;

(iv) increase economic efficiency of subsidiaries and/or applying the breakeven principle;

(v)   attract additional investments; and

(vi) interact with the private sector.

Baiterek JSC abides by state policy in developing industry and innovation, promoting exports, and developing small and medium-sized enterprises. The Holding is also involved in the residential and construction sector, improving people's welfare and meeting other targets set by the President and the Government of Kazakhstan. In particular, it helps to diversify and modernize the economy by enhancing competitiveness, developing infrastructure, making housing affordable, and expanding export potential.

---

[7]   Baiterek JSC was established by Presidential Decree on 22 May 2013 to optimize the management system of development institutions, financial organizations, and national economic development.

Performance of Baiterek

Total assets of Baiterek JSC in 2017 amounted to $13.6 billion or 7.8% of GDP. The bulk of Baiterek's corporate loan portfolio goes to financing state-owned companies and the commodity sector. To finance its operations, Baiterek JSC takes out loans and credit from the government at low interest rates. Analysis based on the Orbis database reveals that the ROE of Baiterek JSC remained relatively stable and marginally declined from 4.4% in 2013 to 4.1% in 2017 (Table 4.9). Since Baiterek is not a profit-maximizing institution, net profit remains low while sales turnover is quite high. Assets-to-equity ratio surged from 276.3% in 2013 to 421.4% in 2017. On average, financial leverage during 2013–2017 remained around 365%, implying that reliance on debt increased from 63.8% in 2013 to 76.3% in 2017. Meanwhile, productivity declined from 1.6% in 2013 to around 1% in 2017.

Table 4.9: Decomposition of Return on Equity for Baiterek JSC, 2013–2017

	2013	2014	2015	2016	2017
	($ billion)				
Net income	0.19	0.23	0.22	0.14	0.13
Total assets	12.3	13.0	15.6	12.0	13.6
Total equity	4.4	4.5	3.9	2.8	3.2
Total sales	433.3	445.3	518.2	380.3	347.4
	(%)				
ROE	4.4	5.2	5.7	5.2	4.1
Net profit margin	0.04	0.05	0.04	0.04	0.04
Assets turnover	3,534.2	3,432.1	3,320.5	3,171.4	2,555.3
Assets to equity	276.3	290.7	400.9	434.9	421.4
Debt financing	63.8	65.6	75.1	77.0	76.3
Productivity	1.6	1.8	1.4	1.2	1.0

ROE = return on equity.
Source: Author's computation based on the Orbis database.

A comparison of Baiterek with US companies and private listed companies in Kazakhstan show that Baiterek's performance was not that impressive. Cumulative amount of forgone profits during 2013–2017 ranged from $1.9 billion to $2.8 billion or 0.2% of GDP, reflecting underperformance of SOEs, emanating from a combination of lower profits and poor corporate governance. However, the amount of forgone profits declined considerably between 2013 and 2017 (Figure 4.16).

Figure 4.16: Implicit Subsidy to Baiterik JSC, 2013–2017

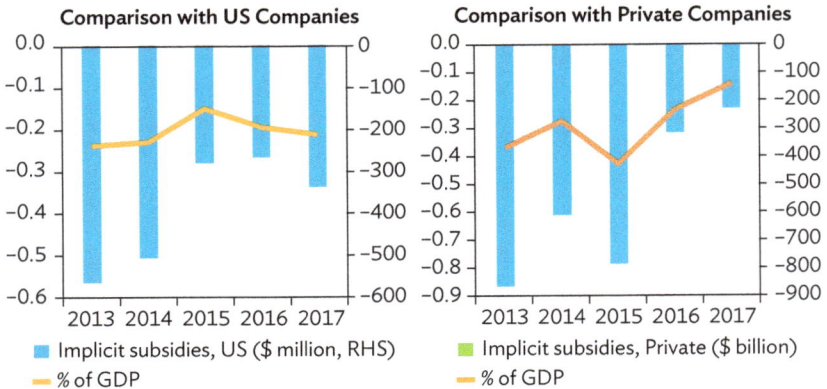

GDP = gross domestic product, RHS = right-hand side, US = United States.
Source: Author's computation based on Orbis the database.

With regard to operational efficiency, which is measured through the EBIT margin, Baiterek's performance was not that impressive either. Its net operating income which rose from $30 million in 2013 to $68 million in 2015, had declined to $19 million during 2016, though it again increased to $39 million in 2017. Meanwhile, ROCE, a measure of the allocative efficiency of the capital employed, improved only marginally from 0.4% in 2013 to about 1% by 2017 (Figure 4.17).

Figure 4.17: Earnings Before Interest and Taxes Margin and Allocative Efficiency, 2013–2017

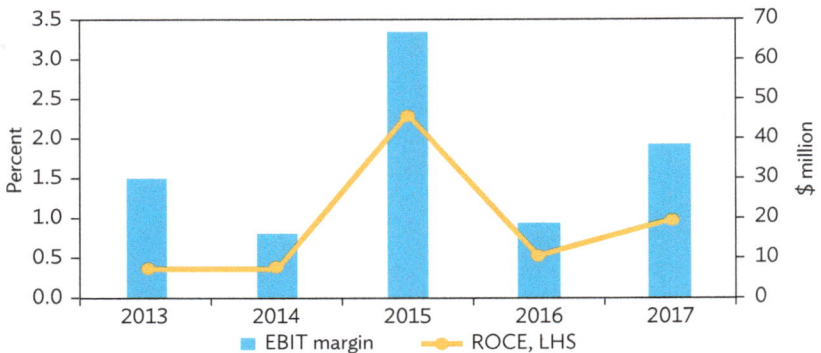

EBIT = earnings before interest and taxes, LHS = left-hand side, ROCE = return on capital employed.
Source: Author's computation based on the Orbis database.

Standard & Poor's (S&P) in its 2016 report, points out that although the number of problematic loans had decreased from 9.3% in 2015 to 7.2% in 2016, the level of restructured loans for the same period surged from 2.7% to 13.5%. This suggests that the apparent improvement in problematic loans is most likely a reflection of the restructured bad loans.

3. KazAgro Joint Stock Company

National Managing Holding KazAgro JSC holds and leads several groups of agribusiness companies in Kazakhstan. It aims to increase the availability of financing and sales markets, make corporate management efficient, and develop human capital in agribusiness entities. The group comprises 53 companies which help implement state policy on stimulating industrial development of the agro-industrial complex through transparent and effective corporate management. It has five strategic goals:

(i)   Stimulate labor production growth by financing highly technological (innovative) projects with the use of modern agro-technologies.

(ii) Participate in ensuring food security in Kazakhstan.

(iii) Facilitate the development of the agribusiness complex's export potential.

(iv) Increase availability of services to support agribusiness entities.

(v)   Increase quality of corporate governance and transparency of the Holding's activities.

Performance of KazAgro

The goal of KazAgro JSC is comprehensive development and increased competitiveness of Kazakhstan's agro-industrial complex. An evaluation of its performance during 2009–2017 reveals that it did not manage its funds well and its ROE remained quite dismal. For example, ROE was –5.9% in 2009, and barely averaged around 1.5% between 2010 and 2014 (Table 4.10). In 2015, ROE once again dropped to –34.4%. In 2016, ROE jumped to 4.9% and fell to –49.2% in 2017. Likewise, assets turnover also declined from 14.0% in 2009 to 1.5% by 2017. With a declining ROE and assets turnover, KazAgro relied mainly on debt financing, as reflected in the higher ratio of financial leverage which averaged around 270% during 2009–2017. The implied debt-to-finance ratio increased from 50.7% in 2009 to 78.6% by 2017. Furthermore, productivity trend was also weak, declining from 0.9% in 2009 to –10.5% in 2017.

Table 4.10: Decomposition of Return on Equity, 2009–2017
(%)

	2009	2010	2011	2012	2013	2014	2015	2016	2017
	($ million)								
Net income	(81.6)	27.3	27.8	15.3	11.1	31.4	(448.0)	54.2	(386.6)
Total assets	2,802	2,974	3,588	3,676	4,567	5,277	4,990	3,708	3,675
Total equity	1,383	1,621	1,964	1,996	2,070	1,918	1,301	1,110	785
Total sales	394	550	438	500	338	336	218	93	56
EBIT margin	(5.7)	(10.3)	2.8	(5.9)	(14.9)	0.4	(393.8)	4.8	(495.5)
	(%)								
ROE	(5.9)	1.7	1.4	0.8	0.5	1.6	(34.4)	4.9	(49.2)
NPM	(20.7)	5.0	6.3	3.1	3.3	9.4	(205.4)	58.2	(695.4)
AT	14.0	18.5	12.2	13.6	7.4	6.4	4.4	2.5	1.5
EM	202.7	183.5	182.7	184.2	220.6	275.1	383.5	333.9	468.0
Debt financing	50.7	45.5	45.3	45.7	54.7	63.7	73.9	70.1	78.6
Productivity	(2.9)	0.9	0.8	0.4	0.2	0.6	(9.0)	1.5	(10.5)
ROCE	(0.3)	(0.5)	0.1	(0.2)	(0.4)	0.0	(13.1)	0.1	(16.2)

( ) = negative, AT = asset turnover, EBIT = earnings before interest and taxes, EM = equity multiplier, NPM = net profit margin, ROCE = return on capital employed, ROE = return on equity.
Source: Author's computation based on the Orbis database.

The analysis suggests that decline in net profit margin and assets turnover were the main factors behind the weakening ROE during 2009–2017. KazAgro relied on debt financing, but then it also continued to receive easy access to credit and capital injections, which have given it an edge over the private companies in the country. The cumulative amount of forgone profits during 2009–2017 is estimated to range from $2.5 billion to $2.9 billion, reflecting underperformance of SOEs because of lower profits combined with poor corporate governance (Figure 4.18).

The ROCE and EBIT margin as shown in Table 4.10 points out that KazAgro's performance in terms of operational and allocative efficiency also remained dismal. In 2009, EBIT margin was –$5.7 million, but it reduced further to –$495.5 million in 2017. Likewise, ROCE also declined from –0.3% in 2009 to –16.2% in 2017.

Figure 4.18: Implicit Subsidy to KazAgro, 2009–2017

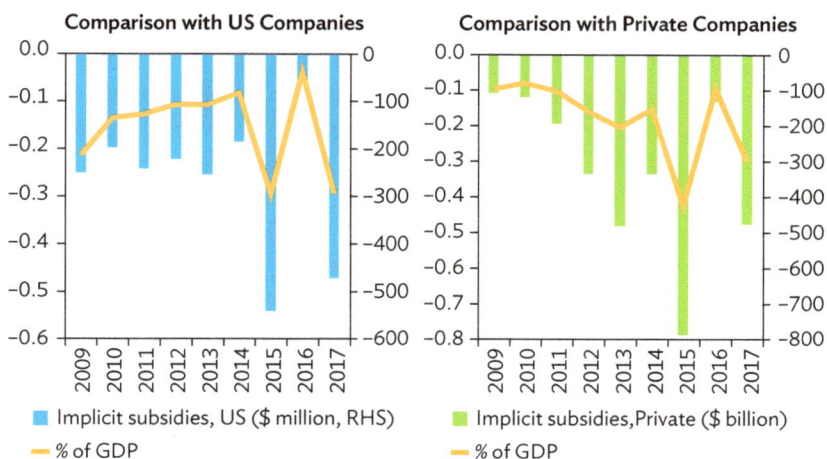

GDP = gross domestic product, RHS = right-hand side, US = United States.
Source: Author's computation based on the Orbis database.

The analysis of the three largest JSCs indicates that overall performance of these companies was not up to the mark. Nonetheless, SOEs continued to receive preferential treatment from the government which is reflected in the high amount of forgone profits. Since these JSCs have a larger share in GDP with respect to assets and contribution to employment, their poor performance implies a disadvantage for sustaining economic growth in the medium to long term.

4.6 Macroeconomic Risks and Poor Performance of SOEs

Kazakhstan faces various macroeconomic risks stemming mainly from volatility in oil prices, a weak finance sector, and poor performance of SOEs. Over the last 2 decades, volatility in oil prices and large swings in exchange rates exposed the economy's weaknesses and vulnerability to external demand shocks. As oil prices collapsed in 2008–2009 and in 2014–2015, revenues and export receipts declined. The government had to bail out highly dollarized banks in 2009 and 2016. It also provided financial assistance in 2015 to KazMunaiGas to ensure the company's timely debt service payments (IMF 2018). The rise in contingent liabilities and government bailout of large banks and poorly performing SOEs can potentially undermine macroeconomic stability.

As already mentioned, despite the poor performance of the three largest holding companies—SK JSC, Baiterek, and KazAgro—they continued receiving capital injections from the government. Since they are therefore benefiting from the "soft budget constraint syndrome," a further rise in contingent liabilities of SOEs and continuous borrowing from the banking sector can destabilize the finance sector. It is worthwhile to note that with SOEs dominating economic activity, their performance in turn will have significant spillovers to economy-wide productivity and growth.

In this context, we analyze some macroeconomic implications of SOEs' poor performance on Kazakhstan's economy:

Fiscal risk and contingent liabilities. Contingent liabilities are obligations triggered by discrete but uncertain events. These liabilities may also rise with weaknesses in the macroeconomic framework, in the finance sector and in regulatory and supervisory systems. The drop in oil prices in 2014 and the resulting rise in contingent liabilities proved to be a wake-up call for Kazakhstan to extend fiscal management beyond the budgeted fiscal risks. For example, when oil prices soared, SOEs spent huge amounts of money on infrastructure projects, the purchase of foreign assets, and social projects. To finance these costs, state companies aggressively borrowed from external sources as well. Consequently, foreign debt of the quasi-public sector grew to $55.5 billion by 2017. When oil prices dropped, many of the largest SOEs were unable to repay foreign debt and turned to the state for help. To stabilize the economy, the government between 2014 and 2017 provided a fiscal stimulus of 10% of GDP which was largely financed through the NFRK. To meet the contingent liabilities of SOEs and the banking system, a result of macroeconomic shocks, the government also provided additional support of about 4% of GDP. Because of these quasi-fiscal activities, which were not part of the budgetary framework, contingent liabilities of SOEs surged sharply from around 0.2% of GDP in 2010 to 4.8% of GDP and amounted to $7.6 billion in 2017 (Figure 4.19). Since the fiscal cost of contingent liabilities is invisible until they are triggered, they represent a hidden subsidy, blur fiscal analysis, and drain government finances only later. To minimize these associated risks, the government must control and manage risk exposure. If left unchecked, further rise in contingent liabilities will only aggravate the risk profile and undermine fiscal sustainability.

Figure 4.19: Contingent Liabilities of SOEs, 2007–2017

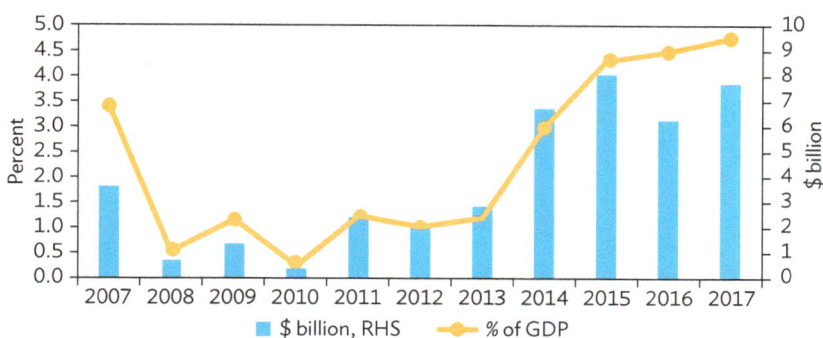

GDP = gross domestic product, RHS = right-hand side, SOE = state-owned enterprise.
Source: International Monetary Fund. International Reserves and Foreign Currency Liquidity Data (extracted 26 November 2018).

Rise in nonperforming loans. Kazakhstan's banking system is relatively small and highly concentrated. The banking sector has not yet recovered fully from the 2008–2009 global financial crisis and the 2014–2015 oil price collapse. Credit growth has remained stagnant because of the rise in nonperforming loans (NPLs). Although the government has taken various steps such as recapitalization and closed some of the problematic banks, it has not addressed completely the problem of NPLs. According to the National Bank of Kazakhstan, around 25% of total outstanding loans as of 2016 were classified as NPLs, while international agencies estimate it in the range of 35%–45%. In 2017, the government provided about $10 billion or 6% of GDP to support troubled banks, which included the bailout of the largest debtor, BTA Bank, whose NPL ratio reached close to 100% (IMF 2018). Most banks prefer to secure their lending for large private companies and SOEs rather than for private entrepreneurs. Meanwhile, NPLs in the banking sector rose sharply from 7.1% in 2008 to 20.9% in 2010 and remained at around 20% until 2013 (Figure 4.20). NPLs have thereafter started declining, reaching 6.7% in 2016, but surging again to 12.7% in 2017.

Figure 4.20: Nonperforming Loans in Kazakhstan, 2008–2017 (%)

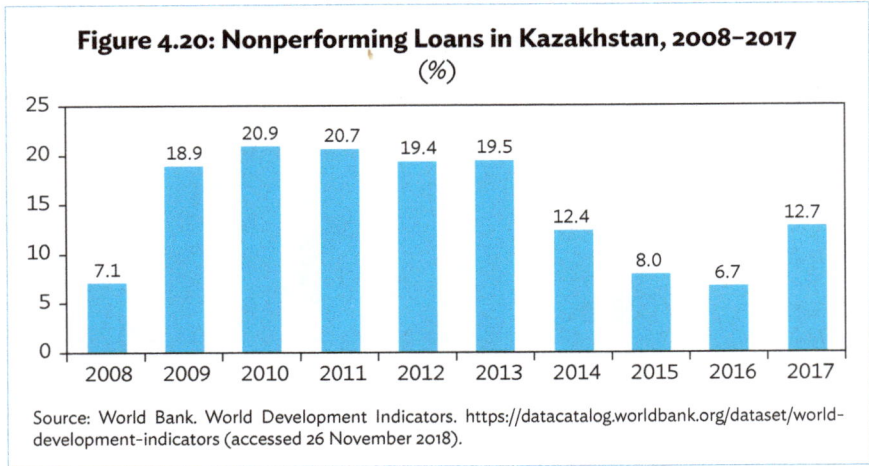

Source: World Bank. World Development Indicators. https://datacatalog.worldbank.org/dataset/world-development-indicators (accessed 26 November 2018).

While NPLs and contingent liabilities of the banking sector increased, the return on banks' assets declined from 7.5% in 1996 to 0.6% in 2015, implying that while banks continue to finance SOE operations, they have not utilized their assets effectively, which could also indicate decline in productivity (Figure 4.21).

Figure 4.21: Return on Assets of Kazakhstan Banks, 1996–2015 (%)

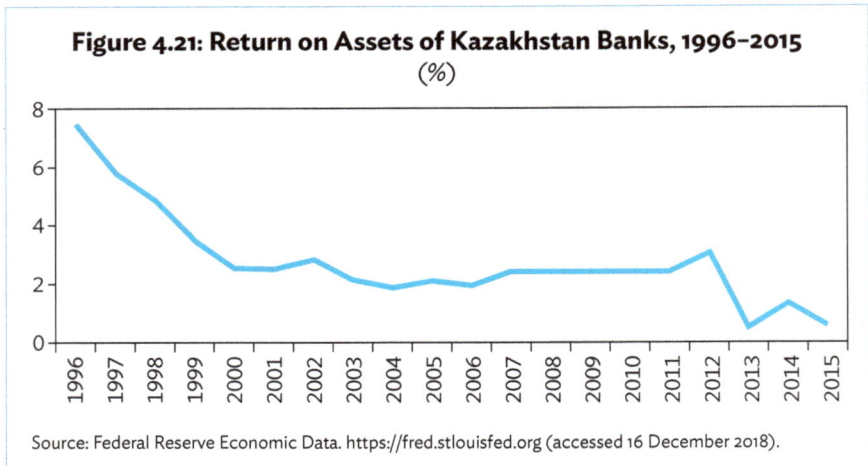

Source: Federal Reserve Economic Data. https://fred.stlouisfed.org (accessed 16 December 2018).

Rise in non-oil fiscal deficit. The large and protracted budget deficit could undermine fiscal sustainability and indirectly affect financial stability through elevated country risk, rating downgrades, and higher borrowing costs. With the 60% collapse of oil prices in 2014 combined with external demand shocks from the Russian Federation and the People's Republic of China (PRC), the government enforced a countercyclical fiscal policy, which resulted in overall fiscal balance deteriorating from a surplus of 5% of GDP in 2013 to a deficit of 6% of GDP in 2016. Similarly, non-oil fiscal deficit which was 8.8% of GDP in 2013 before the decline in oil prices, surged sharply to 11.9% in 2014 and further to 15.6% in 2015. The latest estimates put it at around 11.8% of GDP in 2018 (Figure 4.22).

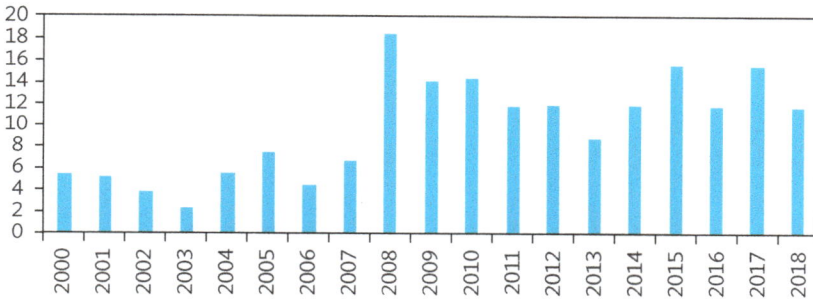

Figure 4.22: Fiscal Deficit of the Non-Oil Sector, 2000–2018 (%)

Source: Federal Reserve Economic Data. https://fred.stlouisfed.org (accessed 15 December 2018).

The rise in fiscal deficit increased the government's liabilities by a cumulative 31 percentage points of GDP between 2013 and 2016 mainly because of high borrowing and an increased drawdown in NFRK reserves. Thus, the government should pay attention to fiscal buffers and monitor the trends in the overall deficit as well as in non-oil deficit. To this end, fiscal consolidation measures would require not only to raise non-oil revenues but also reduce liabilities of SOEs and the banking sector. So far, Kazakhstan has financed fiscal deficits through the Oil Fund and through external and domestic borrowings. However, given the vulnerability of the Oil Fund to decline in oil prices, it is important to have a more diversified economic structure and to increase non-oil revenues.

Sustainability of non-oil fiscal deficit would require rebuilding of the non-oil tax base and keeping the public sector's debt and contingent liabilities in order. This becomes even more important as further rise in corporate debt and contingent liabilities of SOEs would exert pressure on the Oil Fund reserves which may deplete at an increasing rate. According to World Bank estimates, to achieve fiscal sustainability, Kazakhstan needs to reduce non-oil deficit by about 7–8 percentage points (World Bank 2018).

External debt of state-owned enterprises. Total government and foreign debt of the quasi-public sector in 2017 reached $55.5 billion, which was 96.2% of the National Wealth Fund's foreign exchange assets ($57.7 billion). Given the poor performance of the largest Holdings, further rise in external debt can threaten financial stability (Figure 4.23).

Figure 4.23: External Debt of Joint-Stock Companies, 2017
($ billion)

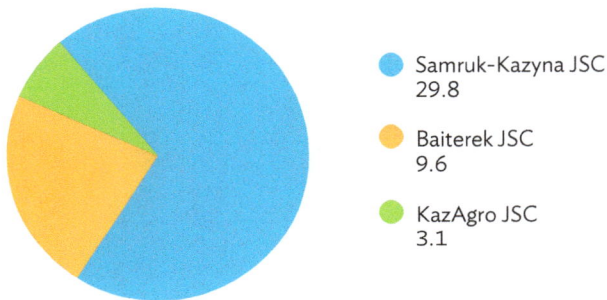

- Samruk-Kazyna JSC 29.8
- Baiterek JSC 9.6
- KazAgro JSC 3.1

Source: Forbes. Accounting Committee report (in Russian). https://forbes.kz/process/expertise/schetnyiy_komitet_istochniki_dohoda_sokraschayutsya_a_gosdolg_rastet/.

The external debt of state-owned companies has grown rapidly since 2008. In response to the 2007 financial crisis, the government nationalized some troubled banks and provided funding—directly (to commercial banks) and indirectly (low-interest loans for state-owned companies and debt refinancing for mortgage holders). To sustain a high level of spending, the government also borrowed aggressively. As a result, public and publicly guaranteed external debt stock increased 13 times from $1.7 billion in 2007 to $21.4 billion in 2017. To attain financial stability without compromising macroeconomic stability, the government needs to monitor the trends in external debt. If left unchecked, SOE-related external debt can have adverse effects on the rest of the economy.

Poor quality of infrastructure. A plethora of literature suggests that poor or lack of infrastructure can impede economic development. According to available information and cross-country comparisons, Kazakhstan ranks low in infrastructure development. Despite the various government-initiated programs to improve infrastructure, Kazakhstan still lags behind, ranking 57th of 137 countries in the Global Competitiveness Index. Table 4.11 shows Kazakhstan with lower infrastructure quality for roads, ports, and air transport than other countries. With SOEs involved in providing the necessary infrastructure to the economy, the poor quality of infrastructure could severely constrain private investment and derail efforts to diversify the non-oil sector. Therefore, the government needs to focus on enhancing infrastructure development. The poor quality of infrastructure creates disincentives to attract upscale private investments and ultimately may retard economic growth in the long run.

Table 4.11: Quality of Infrastructure

	Overall	Roads	Railroad	Ports	Air Transport	Electricity Supply
Azerbaijan	26	36	20	40	24	50
People's Republic of China	47	42	17	49	45	65
India	46	55	28	47	61	80
Indonesia	68	64	30	72	51	86
Kazakhstan	**77**	**115**	**32**	**105**	**90**	**82**
Republic of Korea	14	12	7	23	13	21
Poland	61	65	45	64	66	48
Russian Federation	74	114	23	66	59	59
Sri Lanka	79	61	55	57	75	96
Sweden	15	18	21	15	15	15
Tajikistan	64	70	41	132	70	100
Viet Nam	89	92	59	82	103	90

Note: Ranking is from 1 (highest) to 137 (lowest).
Source: World Economic Forum (2017).

Risk to Productivity and Growth. SOEs have the potential to influence the rest of the economy through their performance. State enterprises are not only involved in network industry but also in production of goods, and these companies are capable of making a significant impact on the productivity of other firms engaged in manufacturing and downstream services. For example, World Bank (2015) research based on Bulgarian firm-level data indicates that improvement in network services can enhance the productivity of electricity and transport firms downstream. Opening these sectors to private and foreign entrepreneurs and thus promoting competition can improve the quality of services substantially. Increased competition also raises firm-level total factor productivity in downstream firms. The evidence suggests that the performance of SOE-dominated services generates both positive or negative spillovers on the productivity of firms downstream. More specifically, while poor performance of SOEs threaten economy-wide productivity and growth, improved SOE performance, on the other hand, can boost productivity across the economy as a whole. To transition from middle-income to a high-income country and achieve the Strategy 2050 goals, higher productivity is essential. Hence, the government needs to strengthen corporate governance and introduce measures to enhance SOEs' productivity and public service delivery.

4.7   Evaluation of Reforms

Kazakhstan initiated economic reforms soon after its independence in 1991. The main objectives of the reforms at that time was to revive the economy and attain macroeconomic stability. These reforms also entailed restructuring various elements of SOEs. As part of the initial reforms, the government privatized some of the large public sector organizations and transferred government-owned assets and services to the private sector. At that time, wholly state-owned enterprises numbered 21,000, while industry including energy accounted for 73% of SOEs and employed 1,320 workers. Overall, SOEs accounted for about 90% of industrial output and employed about 83% of the workforce (Jermakowicz, Kozarzewski, and Pańków 1996).

The government's reform agenda planned initially a three-stage program to commercialize and privatize all state enterprises. During the initial phase of reforms in 1991–1992, the government aimed to privatize 50% of small and medium-sized industrial and agricultural units. The second phase was designed to complete the process during 1993–1996, however, it was shortened and lasted only until the end of 1995. In the second quarter of 1992, the government created a legal framework to incorporate medium-sized and large state enterprises as joint-stock companies (JSCs). By the end of August 1992, about 205 SOEs were transformed into JSCs. But despite the corporatization of SOEs, the state continued to hold the majority of shares through the State Property Committee (or the GKI). Technically, these JSCs were still state-owned.

In April 1992, the government enhanced the scope of privatization further, aiming to privatize 70%–80% of small enterprises in retail trade, restaurants, and services; 50% of all SOEs; and most of the SOEs in the housing sector. However, most of these schemes did not achieve the expected results. The State Property Committee (GKI), which was responsible for reforming the SOEs, could only transfer one-third of the ownership of all business units from state to the private sector, much lower than the targeted 50%. Many of the privatized units were only parts of larger enterprises, and 68.3% were engaged in trade, catering, and services. Agriculture accounted for about 10%, industry 9%, and construction 5% of the transformed units. Because of these initial reforms, about 35.4% of the mostly small SOEs were transferred to the private sector. The first episode of reforms focused mainly on small enterprises and did not consider privatizing large enterprises.

The second phase of reforms started during 1993–1995 and included small-scale privatization, a mass privatization program (MPP), case-by-case privatization, and agricultural privatization. Small-scale privatization applied to firms with fewer than 200 employees, while case-by-case privatization was reserved for large enterprises with more than 5,000 employees. By the end of phase 2, about 63% of all small firms were sold, still lower than the goal set by the government. The MPP, on the other hand, aimed for corporatization of enterprises and the subsequent sale of shares through specialized auctions. All SOEs with 200–5,000 employees were included in the MPP, and about 3,473 companies were privatized. Each privatized and corporatized firm assumed the JSC status and issued shares.

The MPP program resulted in 16 million shareholders of private investment funds, but the state retained effective control over the firms. Hence, despite the reforms introduced in phase 2, restructuring and SOE-related issues persisted with considerable state presence and control of companies. In the case-by-case approach, large firms with more than 5,000 employees were considered, of which 142 firms were designated. Of these firms, 5 were completely sold, 32 were sold partially, and 44 were given in management, while up to 10% of the shares of 7 firms were designated for coupon auctions. In each company, about 10% of shares were given to employees. However, the state still owned approximately 85% of shares in large enterprises. In 1993, the government also gave farmers the right to own agricultural land based on an inheritable 99-year lease. Likewise, in 1995, another 395 agro farms were privatized.

The third phase occurred in 1996–1999, during which the government through various legislative works, created the legal basis for the private economy to function. The government introduced various new laws covering property, corporate governance, and antitrust. Civil and contract codes were also introduced. To improve the labor market and promote foreign investment, the government enacted in 1993 a new law on foreign investment. Since 1996, the government has privatized state property through auctions and tenders which improved the work of several enterprises. The state believed that foreign companies would bring not only investment, but also advanced technology and management experience to the economy. Major companies that were privatized during 1996–1998 included several enterprises from the fuel and energy complex, particularly the oil-producing companies

Mangistaumunaigas, Aktobe-munaigas, and 22 enterprises from the gas sector. Numerous social facilities, including health, education, and culture were also privatized. In October 1999, the new government established a socioeconomic development plan for Kazakhstan, targeting the creation of a competitive national economy and achievement of at least a twofold increase in GDP. These measures were implemented to achieve sustainable economic growth by promoting key sectors, stimulating development of the agriculture sector, maintaining low inflation, and strengthening the financial and credit market.

From 2000 onward, reforms shifted focus to effective management of the economy and SOE assets. During 2001–2003, the government adopted a program to improve the efficiency of state property management and privatization. The program was valid until 2005 and its main thrust was to lay the foundation for a competitive economy in the long term. State properties that were privatized in the early 1990s formed many of the large private companies today. The state delegated the governance of privatized entities to a newly formed group of managers. Many of those enterprises survived and succeeded. However, the lack of professional knowledge and experience in corporate and risk management, and the absence of contract enforcement and proper commitment devices resulted in many failures.

The reforms introduced during 2007–2012 focused mainly on improving the efficiency of large SOEs through better corporate governance. The emphasis during this period was to develop state corporate entrepreneurship and promote public–private partnerships (PPPs). In 2012, the President of Kazakhstan promulgated Strategy 2050, which provides priority actions and strategic direction for the next 40 years. The strategy adopts "economic pragmatism" as its motto and is oriented toward results. Strategy 2050 has a strong modernizing thrust toward private sector-led growth and economic diversification. The strategy also accords government the responsibility for developing an efficient, market-supportive framework and designing specific policies to accelerate productivity gains through technology upgrade, innovation, and greening of the economy. To improve overall performance of SOEs, the government in 2014 further defined the role of state participation in economic activities. The government introduced new laws on promoting private sector development and limiting the creation of new SOEs.

Reforms in 2013–2017 emphasized the Strategic Development Plan 2025 and the new tax and customs codes, which focus on improving business environment and promoting competition. In this regard, budget legislation and regulations pertaining to PPPs were amended.

Promoting Public-Private Partnership

One way to improve the performance of SOEs is to introduce private sector discipline and expose these institutions to competitive market pressures. This is particularly important in reducing the costs of doing business and improving the quality of the basic services. Recognizing the complementary roles of the public and private sectors in promoting economic development, the government has introduced reforms to promote PPPs. In particular, during 2015–2018, the state adopted the Law on PPP which broadened the opportunities for PPP implementation in economic sectors (Box 4.2).

Box 4.2: Public-Private Partnerships

The Government of Kazakhstan enacted major reforms during two distinguishable periods: in 2007–2012 and in 2015–2018. From 2008 to 2010, the state established legal norms on concession agreements based on its experience of implementing concession projects in 2006. Among those projects, the Construction and Operation of Aktau City Airport and the Construction and Operation of the Interregional Line of Electric Transmission in North Kazakhstan—Aktobe Region projects stood as the main case for adopting new measures to promote public–private partnership (PPP). The sequence of events underscored the need to create a special agency to take charge of the policy relating to PPP projects. Thereafter, the Ministry of National Economy through a joint-stock company (JSC) formed the Kazakhstan Public–Private Partnership Center. The formation of the center resulted in the adoption in 2011 of the first PPP development program in Kazakhstan for 2011–2015.

In 2015–2018, the state adopted the Law on PPP and related regulations, which broadened the opportunities for PPP implementation in economic sectors. Under the PPP law, two types of agreements were established: contractual PPP and institutional PPP. Both types of agreement are currently in force.

(1)   The contractual PPP covers the following contracts:
   - Concession agreement: construction and operation of facilities (for large infrastructure projects)
   - Management contract: trust management of state property (for existing social facilities)
   - Lease contract: long-term lease of private property
   - Service contract: provision of services and maintenance
   - Rent contract: rent of state or private property
   - Life cycle contract: contract terms from design to maintenance
   - Research and development (R&D) contract: new technology and scientific research
   - Mixed contracts: mixed contracts corresponding to PPP features

Continued on next page

Box 4.2 continued

(2) The institutional PPP is a partnership between public and private parties formed by establishing a special purpose vehicle (joint venture). As an alternative to state entrepreneurship, private and public partners set up equity for lenders. This form of partnership has greater potential to attract a state budget for the purposes of creating equity.

The number of operating private enterprises with state participation had decreased from 685 in 2018 to 651 or by 5% at the end of May 2019, compared with a decrease of 6.7% between 2017 and 2018 and the start of the descent in 2016 of 16.6% from 2015.

Even though the state refrains from direct participation in business, it uses another mechanism to support various PPP projects. Thus, the number of completed PPP projects has been increasing every year. Kazakhstan now actively uses PPP tools. At the end of 2018, 302 project contracts were signed—61.5% more than the 187 projects signed in 2017.

About 80.8% of all PPP projects are predominantly found in three sectors: 49.6% in education (271 projects); 20.5% in health (112 projects); and 10.6% in energy and utilities (58 projects). Under the policy of separate ministries, the government designates relevant ministries to PPP projects. For instance, the Ministry of Health adopted the implementation of the regional perspective plan for health care infrastructure up to 2025, which considers the construction of new facilities worth more than T700 billion by using the PPP scheme.

In general, the number of state projects has increased sharply compared with private sector projects for several reasons: (i) the state provides financial stability and non-sequestration of the PPP budget for signed contracts; (ii) the state requires innovative resources and methods for facility management; and (iii) the state encourages direct participation in PPP projects.

To expand the policy and encourage direct participation of subcontractors in PPP projects, the state included in the PPP law a provision for direct agreements to protect creditors' rights.

The direct agreement includes terms and conditions pertaining to

- the obligation of public partners to inform creditors about any breach of agreement by private partners;
- the pledge of rights under the PPP contract and/or assignment of claims, or transfer of a private partner's debt;
- step-in right, or the right of a creditor to replace a private partner; and
- the procedure for replacing a private partner.

Continued on next page

Box 4.2 continued

State-owned enterprises (SOEs) can increase their participation in PPP projects in a variety of ways. Since SOEs have a significant impact on public policy, an SOE can act as a guarantor for private investors in PPP projects. By implementing the institutional PPP agreement, an SOE can participate as a shareholder in the authorized capital of a PPP company established jointly with the private sector.

Kazakhstan legislation does not restrict SOEs from initiating a specific project or project pipeline. For example, developing economies stand to face economic development constraints and risks related to political instability. Under such circumstances, an SOE can be an active market player that can mitigate potential risks for investors better than government authorities.

In the course of its economic development, Kazakhstan has had to address the effects of economic instability after the collapse of the former Soviet Union. In the effort to provide much-needed services, companies with full and/or partial participation of the government have gained entry and became major players. Before the crisis of 2007, Kazakhstan had since independence showed significant economic growth. State policy focused mainly on PPPs and foreign direct investment to develop a market-based economy, paying more attention to the private sector even as the business community set up small and medium-sized enterprises to develop a competitive market.

To reduce the share of state participation in its economy, Kazakhstan must now provide opportunities for the widespread use of PPP mechanisms to encourage and expand the growth of small and medium-sized enterprises in different sectors of the economy toward sustainable business development.

Source: Author, based on input from government representatives.

Recognizing the weaknesses of Kazakhstan's private sector, Strategy 2050 focuses on providing an incentive framework for upscale private investments. The strategy stresses that the government should move from its role of selecting sectors, activities, or companies for public support toward fostering innovation, upgrading technology, and developing new products. Similarly, the strategy puts emphasis on promoting competition in the economy and shifting industrial policies from heavy industry to services. The new model for economic growth builds a new economy through technology, develops human capital, and expands exports. The strategy recognizes that private sector development and promotion of small and medium-sized entrepreneurs are essential to achieving sustained and inclusive growth.

Corporate Governance and SOEs

Corporate governance can be viewed as both the structure and relationship that determine corporate direction and performance of SOEs. As discussed, improved performance of SOEs can spill over substantial positive impacts on the rest of the economy. Hence, well-designed corporate governance policies and structure carry important implications in the performance and public service delivery of SOEs. To compare and highlight the weaknesses and challenges associated with Kazakhstan's governance structure, we first describe the OECD guidelines on SOE governance, which provide an international benchmark of best practices. The OECD guidelines can be summarized as follows:

1. **Rationale for state ownership:** The state exercises ownership of SOEs in the interest of the public. It should carefully evaluate and disclose the objectives that justify state ownership and review these regularly.

2. **The state's role as an owner:** The state should act as an informed and active owner, ensuring transparent, professional, effective, and accountable governance of SOEs.

3. **State-owned enterprises in the marketplace:** Consistent with the rationale for state ownership, the legal and regulatory framework for SOEs should ensure equal opportunity for all and fair competition in the marketplace.

4. **Equitable treatment of shareholders:** Where SOEs are listed as owners or where SOE owners include non-state investors, the state and the enterprises should recognize equally the rights of all shareholders and ensure they have equal access to corporate information.

5. **Stakeholder relationships and responsible business:** The state ownership policy should recognize SOEs' responsibilities toward stakeholders and request that SOEs report on their relations with stakeholders. The policy should explain clearly any expectations of the state with regard to responsible business conduct of SOEs.

6. **Disclosure and transparency:** SOEs should observe high standards of transparency and be subject to the same high-quality accounting, disclosure, compliance, and auditing standards as listed companies.

7. **Responsibilities of the board of directors of state-owned enterprises:** SOE board of directors should have the necessary authority, competencies, and objectivity to perform functions of

strategic guidance and monitoring of management. They should act with integrity and be held accountable for their actions.

Corporate Governance in Kazakhstan

Kazakhstan has a general policy of striving for better corporate governance in the public and private sectors. Corporate governance legislation in Kazakhstan is based on the Law on Joint Stock Companies, the Law on Banks and Banking Activity, the Law on Accounting and Financial Reporting, and the Law on Securities Market. The government adopted a formal code on corporate governance in 2005 which it later amended in 2007. Although the code is voluntary and applies to listed companies, implementation of its principles remains weak. The European Bank for Reconstruction and Development (EBRD) examined the top 10 companies in Kazakhstan to assess the corporate sector's performance. The EBRD assessment divided the corporate governance framework and practices into the following five key areas, rating them on a scale of 1 (very weak) to 5 (very strong): (i) structure and functioning of the board, (ii) transparency and disclosure of company information, (iii) internal control, (iv) rights of shareholders, and (v) stakeholders and institutions (Cigna, Kobel, and Sigheartau 2017). The report's major findings are as follows:

1. Neither the law nor the Corporate Governance Code requires that listed companies' committees make up a majority of independent directors.

2. Most of the companies do not have auditors with proper qualifications for audit risk or accounting education or experience.

3. Corporate governance laws in Kazakhstan do not clearly assign to the board all of its key functions such as management oversight, budget approval, and risk management.

4. The majority of companies do not disclose their compliance with the Corporate Governance Code, and only half of the largest listed companies disclose their compliance with the code, which is a legal requirement.

5. It appears that not much monitoring is being carried out by the exchange and the regulator on the quality of nonfinancial disclosure.

6. The periodic review of the effectiveness of the internal audit system is not an established practice. While auditors are required to be independent, it is not clear who is in charge of this "independence

test" and why the law does not assign such responsibility to the internal audit committee, which should be renamed "audit committee."

7.   There seems to be limited monitoring of corporate governance practices by the exchange and the regulator.

8.   The stock exchange website is relatively informative, but incomplete, and judicial practice on many corporate governance issues is inadequate.

9.   There are inconsistencies in the law and regulations, and some key corporate governance issues are not regulated, such as the composition and responsibilities of committees.

The report's findings suggest that Kazakhstan's performance in all five categories of corporate governance is below par. In Figure 4.24, the outermost boundary with a score of 5 signifies the ideal score corresponding to the standards set forth in OECD best practices and international standards. Kazakhstan's score in all spheres is much lower than the ideal.

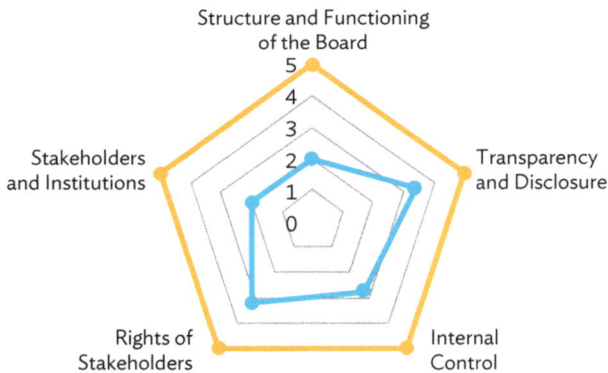

Figure 4.24: Corporate Legislation and Practices in Kazakhstan

OECD = Organisation for Economic Co-operation and Development.
Note: The extremity of each axis represents an ideal score, i.e., corresponding to the standards set forth in best practices and international standards (e.g., OECD Corporate Governance Principles). The fuller the "web," the closer the corporate governance legislation and practices of the country approximate best practices.
Source: Cigna, Kobel, and Sigheartau (2017).

An evaluation of corporate governance in Kazakhstan further reveals that the capacity of the regulator and other aspects of regulation in natural monopoly sectors, such as electricity transmission and distribution and water and wastewater, remain underdeveloped. Although steps have been taken to enhance the regulation (for example, adoption of the new utility tariff methodology, which is now being piloted), power sector development continues to face challenges, such as

(i)   the lack of an effectively functioning wholesale electricity market that could provide sufficient investment signals for new generation;

(ii) problems ensuring effective and independent regulation; and

(iii) distortions due to cross-subsidies and tariffs for consumers that do not ensure cost recovery.

The limited capacity of the civil service appears to be a major constraint on enacting effective legislation and regulations, and in designing and executing government policies and projects. Improving the capacity of the civil service is critical to ensuring the state plays a positive role in creating an effective platform for private sector development. On a more micro level, the inability of authorities to manage projects effectively is an issue to address when participating in the tenders for projects under state support and industrialization programs and those carried out by SOEs.

Procurement practices at SK Holding companies and other SOEs remain problematic (EBRD 2017). Although precise data are not available, interviews with enterprises and other stakeholders suggest that negative perceptions of the private sector toward SK Holding procurement practices are caused by artificial entry barriers. Measures, such as overly stringent technical specification criteria, and sometimes significant financial pledges required from tender participants, could potentially restrict private sector development. Likewise, weaknesses in decision-making caused mainly by lack of transparency, subjectivity, favoritism, and unbalanced contracts have discouraged private investors from coming forward with new investments.

Kazakhstan has embarked on the process of negotiating accession to the World Trade Organization's General Agreement on Procurement and has made improvements in the procurement framework such as introducing mandatory e-procurement in July 2012; but practical implementation has not been effective. SK Holding approved new procurement rules for its holding companies in September 2015, but again their ultimate impact will depend on implementation. Transparency and the use of e-platforms and open tenders need to be promoted further to increase competition and streamline procedures.

4.8   Conclusions and Way Forward

Since its independence in 1991, Kazakhstan has made significant progress, however, most of the challenges it faced during transition remain relevant today. SOEs continue to dominate the economy. Their privileged access to resources, markets, licenses, and finance leaves private firms at a disadvantage and undermines efforts to diversify the economy. Without a vibrant private sector, the government has used SOEs as its main instrument to achieve development objectives. But public sector delivery, corporate governance, areas of planning, financial management, and project management have been inefficient. Consequently, productivity and public service delivery of SOEs remain poor.

To achieve its ambitious goal of being among the top 30 economies in the world by 2050, Kazakhstan must face and surmount the challenges of raising the productivity of SOEs, drawing upscale private investments, and promoting economic diversification. Its experience of high economic growth in the past decade offers some hope for success, but such optimism can only be guarded as decline in oil and commodity prices has consequently derailed the economy from its long-term growth trajectory.

Its transition from a middle-income to high-income country hinges specifically upon enhancing productivity-related growth. Kazakhstan needs to modernize its public sector management to improve SOEs' productivity and make them efficient driver of growth. In light of declining SOE productivity between 2009 and 2017, the government needs to induce professionalism and improve corporate governance of SOEs. It should also provide equal opportunity to all and expand private sector development to expedite the process of structural transformation and enhance economy-wide labor productivity.

Kazakhstan must concentrate on enhancing governance and strengthen the capacity of the public sector particularly in prioritizing expenditure and credit allocation to public and private organizations. Modernized and transformed SOEs and public sector institutions will be crucial to improving delivery of public services. Kazakhstan would have to strengthen its institutions and expand the capabilities of its human capital to support a more productive and adaptable workforce. The government and policy makers must improve governance, develop the finance sector, help build a vibrant private sector, and restructure and ultimately reduce the presence of SOEs in the economy.

Restructuring and resizing SOEs and public institutions would also require diversifying the production structure which currently relies heavily on resource-based products. Measures such as exercising hard budget constraint, improving the performance of the banking sector, reforming the finance sector, and rationalizing subsidies to SOEs will be necessary. Kazakhstan's economic growth will depend on the quality of its public sector and whether it can attract upscale private investments in an environment free of major macro-fiscal and finance sector distortions. To this end, it needs to develop a more competitive and diversified private sector. The government needs to act as facilitator and create equal opportunities for private entrepreneurs. To mitigate the disadvantageous impacts of external demand shocks, it needs to diversify and upgrade production structure.

Poor SOE performance creates risks to fiscal, financial, and macro stability. Improving corporate governance is imperative. The government needs to engender professionalism and infuse a sense of dynamism in managing state enterprises. Transparent ownership structures and clear privatization strategies, particularly for the banking sector can propel financial stability. A regular review of state ownership should make the case for divesting SOEs if deemed no longer aligned with state-ownership objectives. To improve corporate governance, the roles and responsibilities of various government bodies should be clear and locked-in to avoid inconsistency and overlaps. SOEs' ownership rights should be managed by one dedicated, accountable entity within the government. And government should strive to devise and implement policies and rules in accordance with the OECD guidelines for improved corporate governance.

References

Asian Development Bank (ADB). 2018. *Key Indicators for Asia and the Pacific 2018*. Manila. https://www.adb.org/publications/key-indicators-asia-and-pacific-2018.

Botika, M. 2012. The Use of DuPont Analysis in Abnormal Returns Evaluation: Empirical Study of Romanian Market. *Procedia – Social and Behavioral Sciences*. 62. pp. 1179–1183.

Charnes, A., W. W. Cooper, and E. L. Rhodes. 1978. Measuring the Efficiency of Decision Making Units. *European Journal of Operational Research*. 2 (6). pp. 429–444.

Cigna, G. P., Y. Kobel, and A. Sigheartau. 2017. *Corporate Governance in Transition Economies: Kazakhstan Country Report*. London: European Bank for Reconstruction and Development (EBRD).

EBRD. 2017. *Kazakhstan Diagnostic Paper: Assessing Progress and Challenges in Developing Sustainable Market Economy*. London.

Farrell, M. J. 1957. The Measurement of Productive Efficiency. *Journal of the Royal Statistical Society*. Series A (120). pp. 253–281.

Farrell, M. J. and M. Fieldhouse. 1962. Estimating Efficient Production Functions under Increasing Returns to Scale. *Journal of the Royal Statistical Society*. Series A (125). pp. 252–267.

Heuty, A. and J. Aristi. 2009. Fool's Gold: Assessing the Performance of Alternative Fiscal Instruments During the Commodities Boom and the Global Crisis. Revenue Watch Institute. https://resourcegovernance.org/sites/default/files/RWI_Fools_Gold_Heuty_Aristi_FINAL.pdf

Huguenin, J-M. 2012. Data Envelopment Analysis (DEA): A Pedagogical Guide for Decision Makers in the Public Sector. Lausanne: IDHEAP.

Ichihashi, M. et al. 2013. Structural Change, Labor Productivity Growth, and Convergence of BRIC Countries. *Development Discussion Policy Paper*. 3 (5). Japan: Graduate School for International Development and Cooperation, Hiroshima University.

International Monetary Fund (IMF). 2018. *IMF Country Report No. 18/278: Republic of Kazakhstan*. Selected Issues. Washington, DC.

Jermakowicz, W., P. Kozarzewski, and J. Pańków. 1996. *Privatization in the Republic of Kazakhstan*. Warsaw.

Kalyuzhnova, Y. 2011. The National Fund of the Republic of Kazakhstan (NFRK): From Accumulation to Stress-Test to Global Future. *Energy Policy*. 39 (10). pp. 6650–6657.

Organisation for Economic Co-operation and Development (OECD). 2015. *OECD Guidelines on Corporate Governance of State-Owned Enterprises.* Paris.

_____. 2017. Multi-Dimensional Review of Kazakhstan: Volume 2. In Depth Analysis and Recommendations. *OECD Development Pathways.* Paris: OECD Publishing. http://dx.doi.org/10.1787/9789264269200-en.

Paldam, M. 1997. Dutch Disease and Rent Seeking: The Greenland Model. *European Journal of Political Economy.* 13 (3). pp. 591–614.

PROSPERA. Has the Private Sector Shrunk? Unpublished paper led by Adhi Suputro and David Nellor.

Sachs, J. and A. Warner. 1995. Natural Resource Abundance and Economic Growth. *NBER Working Paper.* No. 5398.

World Bank. 2015. *Productivity in Bulgaria: Trends and Options.* Washington, DC.

_____. 2018. A New Growth Model for Building a Secure Middle Class. *Kazakhstan Systematic Country Diagnostic.* Washington, DC.

World Economic Forum. 2017. *The Global Competitiveness Report 2017–2018.* Geneva.

CHAPTER 5

State-Owned Enterprises in the People's Republic of China

*Minsoo Lee and Kaukab Naqvi**

5.1 Introduction

State-owned enterprises (SOEs) have played an important role in the economic development of the People's Republic of China (PRC) since the 1980s. The PRC's rapid and unprecedented economic growth since then has altered the structure of its output and employment, turning the country into a global economic powerhouse. Although SOE reforms have been a core element of policy during the transition from a centrally planned to a market-oriented economy, state ownership remains prevalent in different sectors.

SOEs contribute about 30% of gross domestic product (GDP). They are a significant source of employment, particularly in industries where they provide new sources of energy, telecommunication and information technology, automation, transport equipment, space technology, construction materials, and infrastructure development. The government also uses SOEs to promote economic development and to achieve goals to develop high-end manufacturing industries.

This chapter gives an overview of the evolving role of SOEs and highlights the importance of SOE reforms for economic development in the PRC. It analyzes state-owned units and facilities, such as government administrative departments and their immediate extended offices, and universities. SOEs in the PRC are categorized according to the government institution assigned to manage them:[1]

---

* The ideas expressed in this chapter have also benefited from comments and discussions with Jeffery Liang, Principal Economist at Asian Development Bank, and from a background paper prepared by Carsten A. Holz.

[1] OECD (2015: 14) defines SOEs as "any corporate entity recognised by national law as an enterprise, and in which the state exercises ownership."

- The National Bureau of Statistics (NBS) classifies state enterprises according to their mode of registration.
- Ministry of Finance (MOF) statistics cover only SOEs that fall under its control.
- State Asset Supervision and Administration Commission (SASAC) statistics cover the SOEs it supervises and manages, as well as those supervised by provincial governments, i.e., the majority of nonfinancial state enterprises that are, in theory, a subset of the MOF.

The NBS and MOF statistics vary in the number of SOEs they cover, as some state enterprises are not formally registered and others are deemed to be outside the MOF's remit. While MOF statistics account for SOEs in all economic sectors, the NBS collects detailed data only for industry SOEs (and for a few other sectors).

The NBS statistics on industry SOEs are used widely in research literature. The NBS definition for industrial SOEs has evolved over time, starting from when the Company Law was passed in 1993. In 1998, industrial SOEs included (i) all traditional or unreformed SOEs; (ii) joint enterprises formed between an SOE and another SOE, and between an SOE and a collectively owned enterprise; and (iii) state-owned limited liability companies.

Since 1998, the NBS has used the term industrial "state-owned and state-controlled enterprises" (SOSCEs) to refer to the agglomeration of (i) the pre-1998 definition of SOEs, comprising the three categories just mentioned; and (ii) all other shareholding companies, such as limited liability companies and stock companies, in which the state has a controlling share.[2]

SOEs, as defined in the NBS statistics, refer only to traditional (or unreformed) SOEs; they exclude joint enterprises comprising an SOE and solely state-owned limited liability companies.[3]

---

[2]   State-controlled companies come in two forms: absolute state control implies the state holds more than 50% of total capital; relative state control implies that although the state holds less than 50% of total capital, the state's share is (i) relatively large compared with the shares of other ownership categories (i.e., "relative state control" in its narrow meaning); or (ii) even though one or more other ownership categories have a larger capital share than the state, the state in effect holds the control rights by agreement. Both forms of state-controlled companies are included in the definition.

[3]   The NBS uses similar classifications and transitions in its definition of SOEs for other economic sectors. The 2013 economic census covered registration-based data on all legal persons in the PRC, but the census statistics do not provide the aggregate SOSCE measure. The registration-based classification includes a stock company category, which, however, does not come with a state versus non-state breakdown.

This chapter uses "SOEs" generally to capture both the pre-1998 definition of SOEs and the SOSCE definition since 1998. Where a distinction gives more clarity, the accurate terms of "traditional (or unreformed) SOEs," and "SOSCEs" are used.

5.2 SOE Overview

This section presents basic statistics on SOEs; these differ significantly depending on the data source (Table 5.1). For example, MOF data report the total number of enterprises at 173,996, while SASAC has 132,948. The number of SOEs in industry and services also diverge. Overall, the share of services SOEs ranges 62%–65%, and 31%–35% for industry SOEs.

Although employment statistics also show a discrepancy, both sources indicate that industry SOEs employ about 20 million workers, and services SOEs about 10 million–14 million (Table 5.1). In 2016, SOEs accounted for about 4.7% of economy-wide employment.[4]

Table 5.1: Number of Enterprises and Employment, 2016

	Enterprises		Employment ('000)	
	MOF	**SASAC**	**MOF**	**SASAC**
National total	**173,996**	**132,948**	**36,114**	**30,489**
Agriculture	6,939	3,120	2,461	512
Industry[a]	54,397	46,779	19,387	19,357
Services	112,660	83,049	14,266	10,620

MOF = Ministry of Finance, SASAC = State Asset Supervision and Administration Commission.
[a] Industry also includes data on construction activities.
Sources: Ministry of Finance. 2018. China Finance Yearbook 2018. Beijing; SASAC. 2017. *SASAC Yearbook 2017.* Beijing.

The industrial distribution of SOEs reported by SASAC suggests that nearly one-third of them are involved in secondary industry, including electric power and the coal, chemical, and machinery industries, highlighting the importance of these sectors in the economy (Figure 5.1).

The total assets of SOEs in 2016 are estimated at $22 trillion–$23 trillion, about double the GDP in that year, and total equity at $7 trillion–$8 trillion (Table 5.2). Total liabilities in the same year were about $15 trillion, which puts the ratio of SOE assets to liabilities in a range of 65%–69%.

---

[4]   This percentage is obtained by comparing the MOF employment figure of 36.1 million to the nationwide employment figure of 776.0 million in the China Statistical Yearbook 2017.

Figure 5.1: Industrial Distribution of SOEs, 2016

(%)

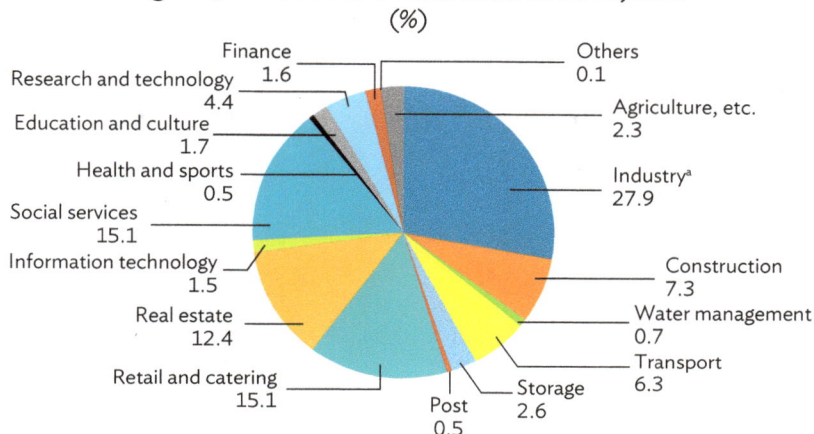

Finance 1.6
Others 0.1
Research and technology 4.4
Education and culture 1.7
Health and sports 0.5
Social services 15.1
Information technology 1.5
Real estate 12.4
Retail and catering 15.1
Post 0.5
Storage 2.6
Transport 6.3
Water management 0.7
Construction 7.3
Industry[a] 27.9
Agriculture, etc. 2.3

[a] Industry includes coal, petroleum, metallurgy, building materials, chemistry, forest, food, tobacco, textile, pharmaceutical, machinery, automobile, electronic power, and municipal industries.
SOE = state-owned enterprise.
Source: SASAC Yearbook 2017.

Table 5.2: SOE Financial Statistics, 2016

($ billion)

	Assets		Equity		Liabilities	
	MOF	SASAC	MOF	SASAC	MOF	SASAC
National total	23,323	22,064	8,039	6,958	15,285	15,105

MOF = Ministry of Finance, SASAC = State Asset Supervision and Administration Commission, SOE = state-owned enterprise.
Sources: Ministry of Finance. 2018. China Finance Yearbook 2018. Beijing; SASAC. 2017. SASAC Yearbook 2017. Beijing.

The rest of this section is a descriptive analysis of SOE statistics across various sectors using the Orbis database from 2009 to 2017. This analysis gives particularly useful insights into the importance and prevalence of SOEs in different sectors. The sectoral distribution of output suggests the contribution of SOEs in manufacturing during the review period was 31.5%, followed by SOEs in trade and transport (18.5%), energy and water (15.4%), construction (8.6%), and finance and insurance (8.3%) (Figure 5.2).

In terms of the distribution of assets across sectors during 2009–2017, SOEs in financial and insurance services had the largest share, at 66.5% (Figure 5.3). Other sectors with relatively large shares were manufacturing (10.5%), energy and water (6.8%), and trade and transport (5.8%). The shares of other sectors were not significant.

Figure 5.2: Distribution of Output by Sectors, Average 2009–2017
(%)

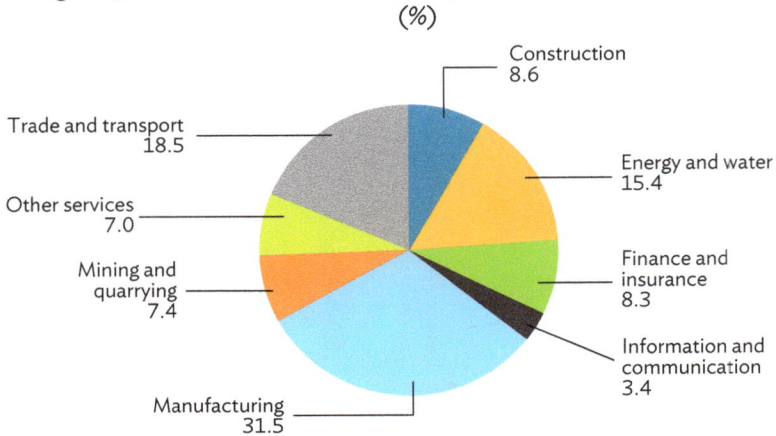

Construction 8.6
Energy and water 15.4
Finance and insurance 8.3
Information and communication 3.4
Manufacturing 31.5
Mining and quarrying 7.4
Other services 7.0
Trade and transport 18.5

Source: Authors' calculations based on the Orbis database.

Figure 5.3: Distribution of Assets by Sectors, Average 2009–2017
(%)

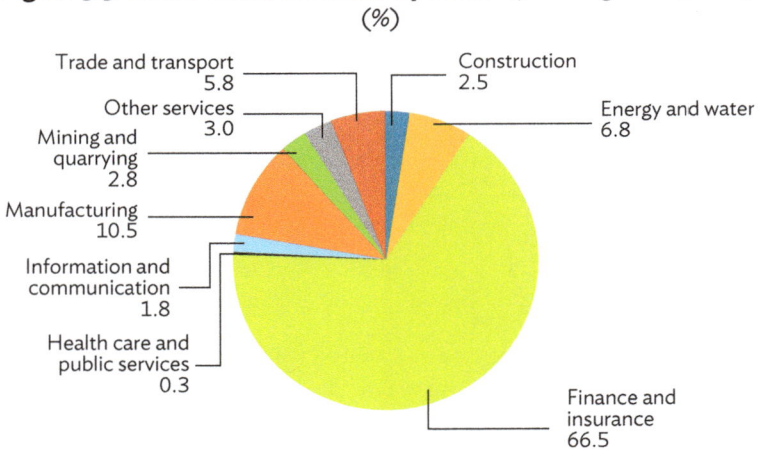

Trade and transport 5.8
Construction 2.5
Other services 3.0
Energy and water 6.8
Mining and quarrying 2.8
Manufacturing 10.5
Information and communication 1.8
Health care and public services 0.3
Finance and insurance 66.5

Source: Authors' calculations based on the Orbis database.

In terms of the distribution of the total equity of SOEs across sectors, mining and quarrying sectors had the largest share during 2009–2017, at 23.9% (Figure 5.4). SOEs in manufacturing, energy and water, and information and communication also had substantial shares.

Figure 5.4: Distribution of Equity, Average 2009–2017
(%)

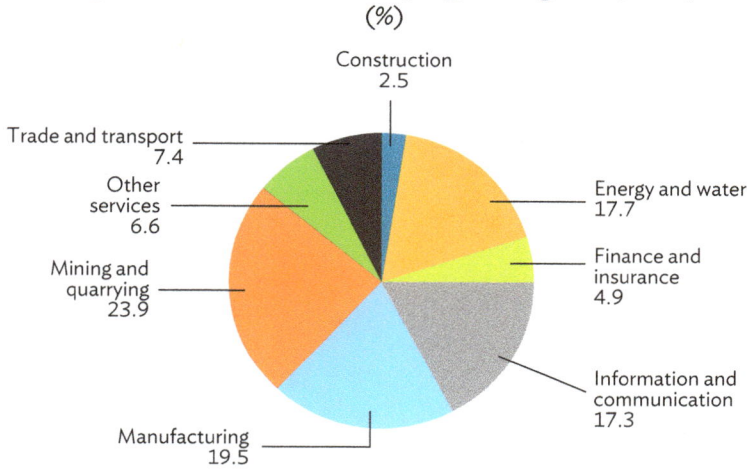

Construction
2.5

Trade and transport
7.4

Other
services
6.6

Mining and
quarrying
23.9

Manufacturing
19.5

Energy and water
17.7

Finance and
insurance
4.9

Information and
communication
17.3

Source: Authors' calculations based on the Orbis database.

By sector, SOEs in financial and insurance services were the most profitable, with their share of total net income during 2009–2017 estimated at 31.6% (Figure 5.5). SOEs in manufacturing and energy and water also contributed significantly to total net income.

Figure 5.5: Distribution of Net Income, Average 2009–2017
(%)

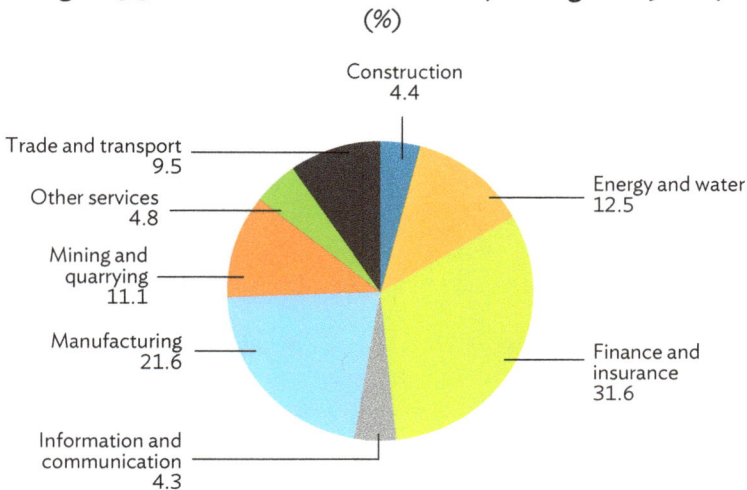

Construction
4.4

Trade and transport
9.5

Other services
4.8

Mining and
quarrying
11.1

Manufacturing
21.6

Information and
communication
4.3

Energy and water
12.5

Finance and
insurance
31.6

Source: Authors' calculations based on the Orbis database.

Figure 5.6 shows a positive correlation between the number of local SOEs and provincial GDP data, highlighting the role and importance of their contribution to promoting regional growth.

Figure 5.6: GDP per Capita and Number of SOEs by Region, 2017

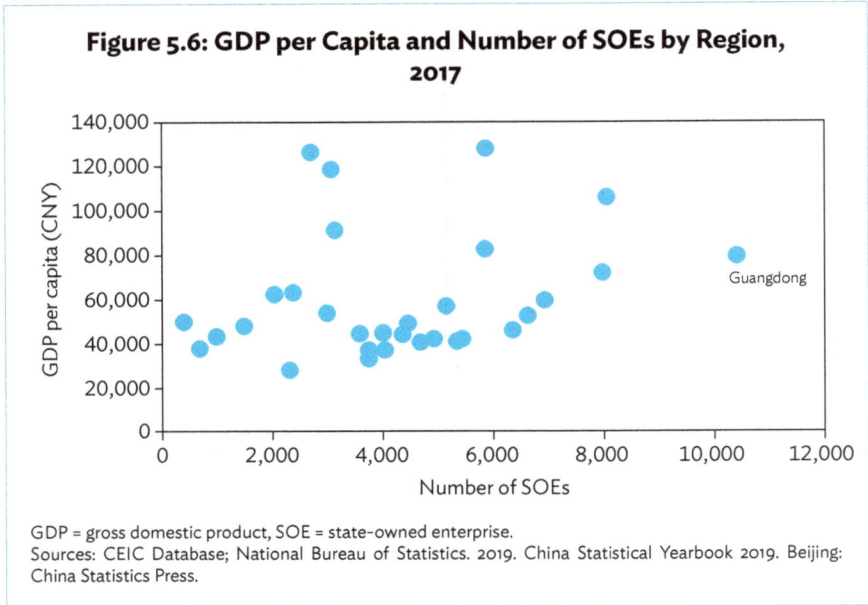

GDP = gross domestic product, SOE = state-owned enterprise.
Sources: CEIC Database; National Bureau of Statistics. 2019. China Statistical Yearbook 2019. Beijing: China Statistics Press.

5.3   Comparison of SOEs and Private Counterparts

This section examines central and local SOEs by industry and region, and compares them with private firms to show their significance and impact in the domestic market. It is important to note that in comparing the financial performance of SOEs in relation to private firms, the differences between them must be considered. For example, while private firms aim to maximize profits, SOEs aim to maximize social welfare in economic activity. SOEs face political constraints, and governments use them as tools to promote economic development. Thus, their relatively lower profitability and efficiency compared with private firms does not necessarily signify intrinsic weakness (Holz 2003).

Figure 5.7 shows the dramatic reallocation of employment from the state sector to the private sector in the PRC since 1990. In that year, only 3.5% of the labor force was employed by the private sector—by 2017, this had surged to 44%. Over this period, the share of SOEs in total employment fell from 16% to 8%. This reallocation contributed to growth because the average rate of productivity growth of the state sector was 1.5% in the period, compared with 4.5% for the private firms.

Figure 5.7: Employment Share of SOEs versus Private Enterprises, 1990–2017
(%)

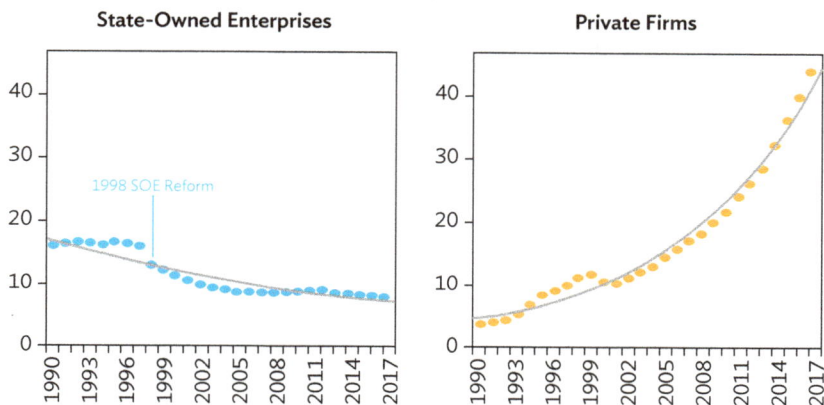

SOE = state-owned enterprise.
Source: Ministry of Human Resources and Social Security of the People's Republic of China.

Figure 5.8 shows the return on assets of SOEs compared with private firms during 2001–2018. While this increased from 1.0% to 2.8% over the period for industrial SOEs, the 2018 level was still only about a third of the return on assets of private firms.

Figure 5.8: Return on Assets of Industrial SOEs and Private Firms, 2001–2018
(%)

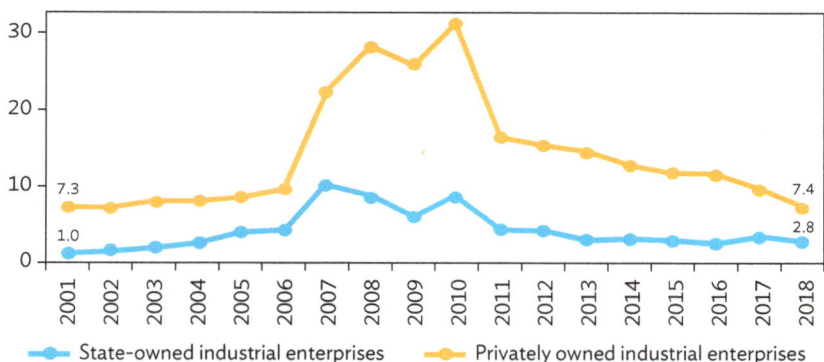

Sources: National Bureau of Statistics (based on http://www.stats.gov.cn/english/) and Asian Development Bank calculations.

This inefficiency is further confirmed by the large share of loss-making SOEs. Over 30% of industrial SOEs made a loss during 2001–2018 (except in 2011), compared with only 13% of private firms (Figure 5.9).

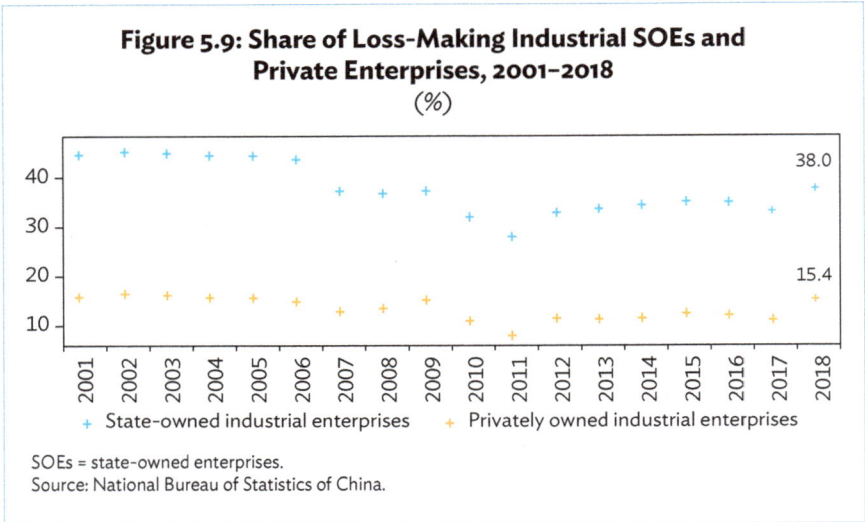

Figure 5.9: Share of Loss-Making Industrial SOEs and Private Enterprises, 2001–2018
(%)

SOEs = state-owned enterprises.
Source: National Bureau of Statistics of China.

It is, however, important to note that despite the low return on equity and the high losses of industrial SOEs, their workers still receive high salaries. From 2013 to 2017, SOE wages totaled more than 120% of the national average, and the salaries of central management was over 170% (Figure 5.10). Private industrial firms paid about 80% of the average national wage.

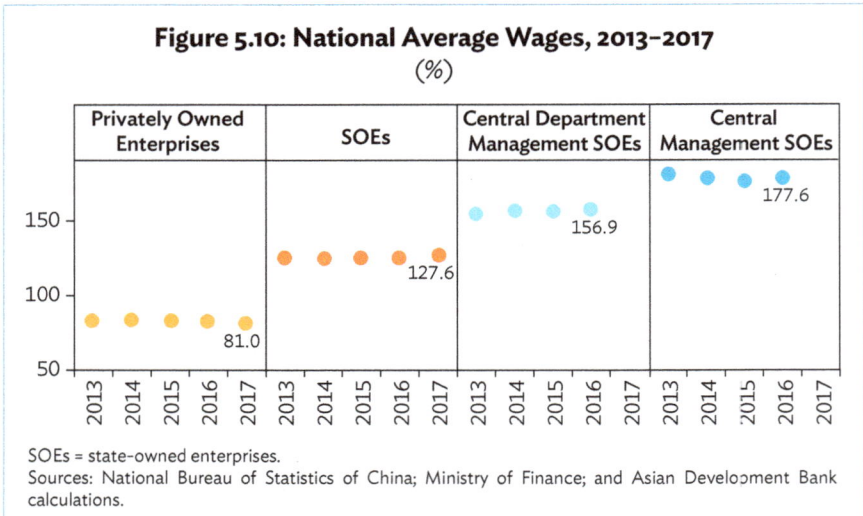

Figure 5.10: National Average Wages, 2013–2017
(%)

SOEs = state-owned enterprises.
Sources: National Bureau of Statistics of China; Ministry of Finance; and Asian Development Bank calculations.

With increasing globalization, the PRC's SOEs are competing in international markets, but private firms are much more export-oriented, which can deliver productivity and efficiency gains. In general, the export performance of SOEs has been lower than that of private firms. As Figure 5.11 shows, private firms exported at least four times more than SOEs in 2018. Future reforms should be geared toward encouraging SOEs to be more competitive, especially in the global market.

Figure 5.11: Industrial SOE and Private Firm Exports, 2013–2018
($ trillion)

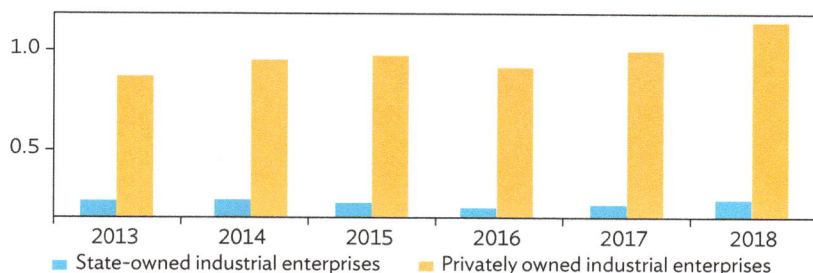

SOE = state-owned enterprise.
Source: General Administration of Customs.

Although the private sector in the PRC creates most jobs and contributes more to growth, banks still allocate more loans to SOEs. In fact, loans to private firms have declined since 2014. In 2016, they were only 20.7% of total loans, indicating an inefficient allocation of capital (Figure 5.12).

Figure 5.12: Bank Loans to SOEs and Private Firms, 2010–2016
(%)

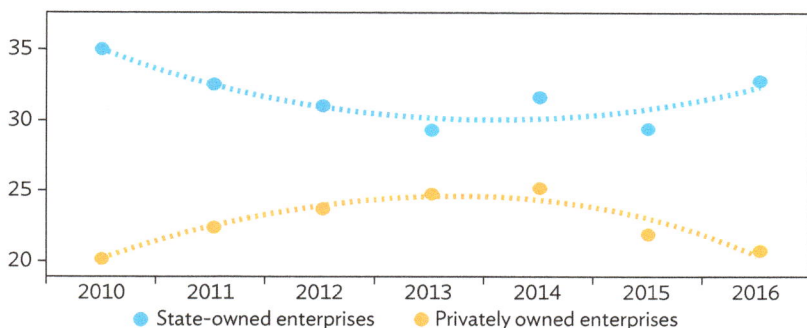

SOEs = state-owned enterprises.
Source: The People's Bank of China.

Access to credit is another entry point for productivity and efficiency gains for SOEs—and these gains are expected to be larger if financing is for investment purposes. According to the World Bank's 2012 Enterprise Survey, 70.9% of SOEs owned most of the land they occupied, compared with 46.1% of private firms, and 14.3% of SOEs experienced considerable obstacles to getting finance, compared with 19.9% of private firms (Figure 5.13). Both examples highlight the inefficiency of capital allocation by SOEs.

Figure 5.13: PRC – Land and Financial Access

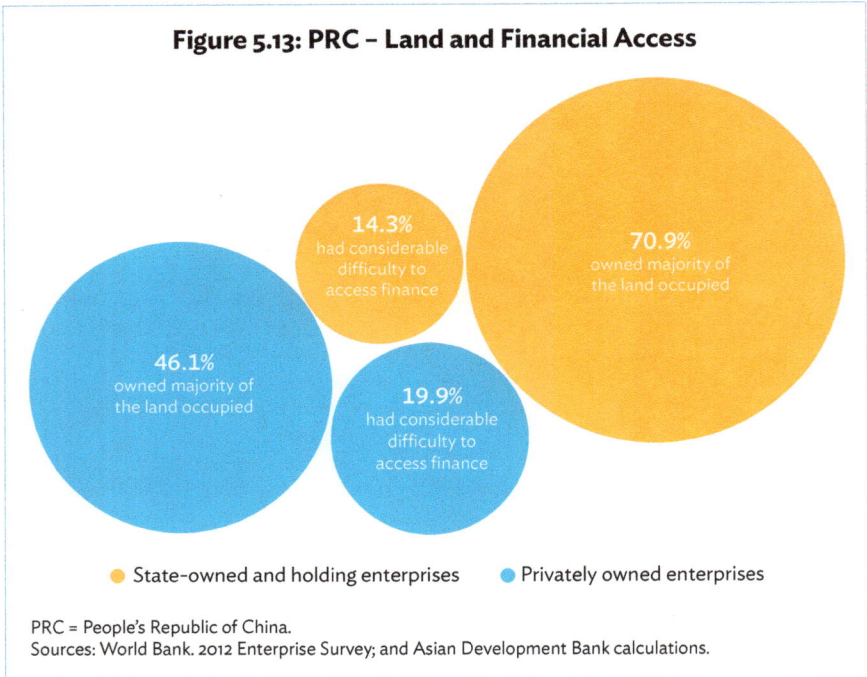

14.3%
had considerable
difficulty to
access finance

70.9%
owned majority of
the land occupied

46.1%
owned majority of
the land occupied

19.9%
had considerable
difficulty to
access finance

● State-owned and holding enterprises   ● Privately owned enterprises

PRC = People's Republic of China.
Sources: World Bank. 2012 Enterprise Survey; and Asian Development Bank calculations.

Although SOEs are prevalent in many important sectors of the economy, there is a marked difference in their value added compared with private firms. From 2007 to 2016, the growth rate of industrial value added for SOEs was consistently lower than for private firms (Figure 5.14).

The analysis in this section supports the viewpoint that generally the productivity of SOEs is lower than their private counterparts (Dewenter and Malatesta 2001). Empirical evidence based on PRC steel firms shows private firms are on average 7.4% more productive than central SOEs and 1.1% more productive than provincial SOEs (Box 5.1).

Figure 5.14: Real Percent Change in Industrial Value Added, 2007–2018
(%)

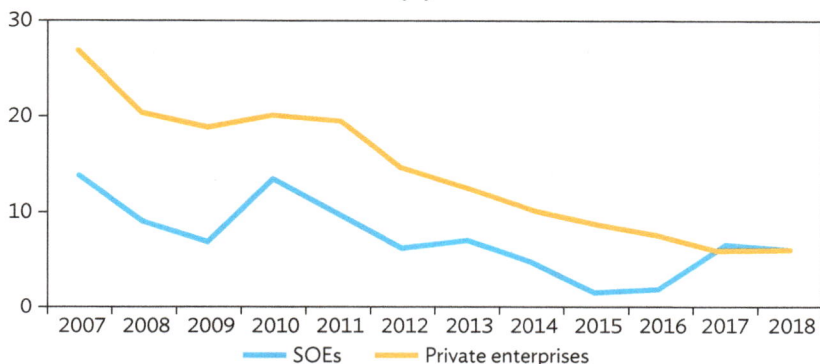

SOEs = state-owned enterprises.
Source: National Bureau of Statistics.

Box 5.1: Ownership and Productivity in Vertically Integrated Steel Firms

In 2015, the People's Republic of China (PRC) produced 803.8 million metric tons of crude steel, accounting for 49.6% of the world's total production. Brandt et al. (2019) investigate the source of productivity differences between production facilities through the lens of their internal structure, and find that

- private firms are on average 7.4% more productive than central state-owned enterprises (SOEs), and 1.1% more productive than provincial SOEs;

- central state-owned facilities outperform in sintering most likely because of their use of high-quality raw materials;

- the productivity premium of private firms declines with facility size; and

- these patterns are linked with how private firms internally configure their production facilities when they build larger integrated plants.

The decline in the productivity premium of private firms in the steel sector in relation to SOEs can partly be attributed to the better resource management of state firms and the investments they have made in improving the skills of their workers, which allows them to reap the benefits of economies of scale. Private firms, however, appear to be more productive in smaller-scale production.

Continued on next page

Box 5.1 continued

Another factor that explains the falling productivity premium of private firms is that when they build plants with larger capacity, they install furnaces and sintering machines. But this requires better human capital both on the shop floor and management—exactly the areas in which private firms face constraints. Larger furnaces and sintering machines have newer technologies that are highly complementary with the human capital endowments of SOEs—for example, more talented and experienced managers, and more highly skilled workers. Moreover, the larger number of units at larger private steel plants spread their scarce human capital more thinly to the detriment of productivity.

The analysis suggests that improved human resources and better quality of inputs can be instrumental in enhancing productivity. Supporting evidence comes from the significantly larger productivity premium of privatized SOEs, which are likely less constrained than newly established private firms. Privatized SOEs, for example, may be able to leverage the network of former SOEs to help access raw materials, finance, and human capital.

Source: Authors, based on Brandt et al. (2019).

5.4 Empirical Analysis of Efficiency and Productivity

Economic policies around the world stress the importance of productivity and efficiency for the delivery of SOE services. Every government tries to optimize the delivery of services through the cost-effective and efficient use of available resources. And against the backdrop of growing financial and economic concerns around the world, the need to enhance the productivity and the quality of public services is getting a lot of attention. Because of the PRC's large SOE sector, the performance of state firms, good or poor bad, will have spillover effects on downstream firms, which will affect economy-wide productivity. This section analyzes the efficiency and productivity of SOEs in the PRC and compares them with private firms (Box 5.2). Appendix A5.1 has the detailed results of the estimated model.

The major findings of the analysis are as follows:

- Of the chosen productivity and efficiency measures, labor productivity and labor input efficiency are consistent (in both estimation methods) where SOEs tend to perform weaker than their private counterpart firms. This could be because of the overemployment observed in most SOEs.

Box 5.2: Efficiency and Productivity of SOEs versus Private Firms

The following model is used to empirically analyze the efficiency and productivity of state-owned enterprises (SOE) and private firms in the People's Republic of China:

$$y_i = \alpha + \beta Firm_i + \gamma(Firm_i \times Channel_i) + \delta X_i + \varepsilon_i.$$

Efficiency and productivity measures in y_i include (i) labor productivity (sales/ number of employed); (ii) research and development efficiency (sales/research and development expenses); (iii) capacity utilization (reflecting efficiency in using relevant assets); (iv) labor input efficiency (sales per labor input cost); (v) raw materials and intermediate inputs efficiency (sales per raw materials and intermediate inputs cost); and (vi) fixed assets efficiency (sales per land and building cost).

$Firm_i$ is a binary variable with value equals 1 if an SOE and 0 otherwise. The coefficient β measures the difference in productivity and efficiency between the two types of firms. To identify the factors causing such differences or gaps, $Firm_i$ is interacted with select channels. These include (i) export-orientation; (ii) ease of access to finance—to highlight the role of state-owned banks; (iii) part of multinational firm to capture mergers and acquisitions; (iv) bank borrowing to finance working capital or fixed-asset purchases; (v) the source of the credit or loan; and (vi) government ties or connection.

X_i represents control variables to isolate firm ownership and channel impact. These include the sector in which each firm is classified (manufacturing, retail services, and other services); age of the firm; location; size of firm (small, medium-sized, large); and legal status (sole proprietorship, partnership, corporation, among other things).

Source: Authors.

- Export-orientation may drive productivity and efficiency gains for SOEs, indicating that reforms should be geared toward encouraging them to be more competitive, especially in the global market.

- The difficulty in getting credit to finance operations is generally seen to weaken a firm's productivity. Interestingly, this is where the productivity and efficiency gap between SOEs and private firms tends to narrow. In general, SOEs tend to have better access to credit, particularly from state-owned and state-controlled banks.

- Consistent with the findings in the previous four points, the availability of private and state-owned bank financing to support working capital and fixed-asset purchases are significant channels through which SOE labor productivity and efficiency can improve.

- For loan sources, closing the efficiency gap is more pronounced because SOEs can get credit from state-owned banks or government agencies.

- Mergers of SOEs as a reform mechanism seem to work out fairly in improving labor productivity and efficiency when they use labor, raw materials, and intermediate inputs of SOEs.

The total productivity of SOEs in the PRC during 2009–2017 increased by 10.2% a year, mainly as a result of productivity growth in information and communication, and water supply services (Figure 5.15). In all other sectors, labor productivity declined.

Figure 5.15: Productivity Growth in Major SOEs, 2009–2017
(%)

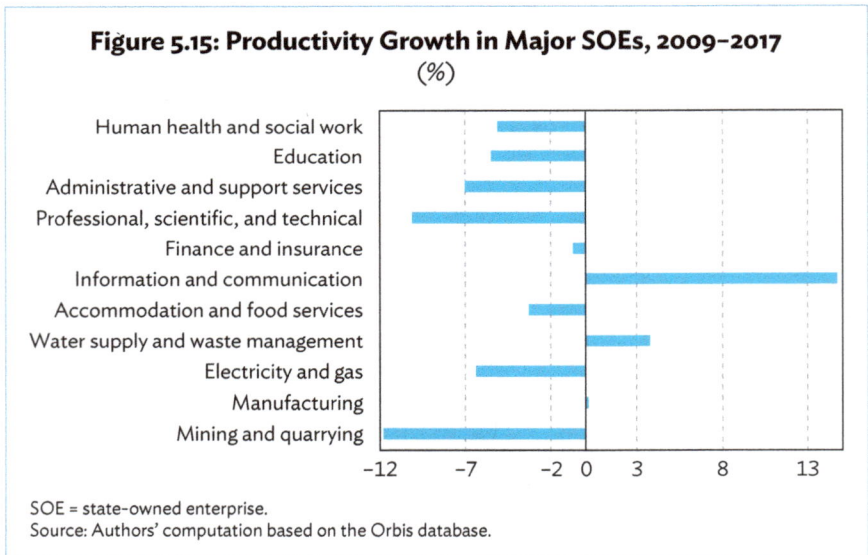

SOE = state-owned enterprise.
Source: Authors' computation based on the Orbis database.

Shift–share analysis and the productivity decomposition of growth during 2009–2017 is used to gain insights on the underlying causes of changes in productivity (Chapter 1, Appendix A1.1). Figure 5.16 shows the results of the productivity decomposition analysis.

The analysis shows that the increased productivity of individual sectors contributed significantly to total productivity, as shown by the orange bars in Figure 5.16, which represent the within-shift effects. But despite overall productivity growth, labor barely moved from low to higher-productivity sectors. Consequently, the contribution of structural change was rather low, implying that most of the labor force continues to work in low-productivity sectors. This has important implications for the sustainability of high economic

Figure 5.16: Productivity Decomposition, 2009–2017
(%)

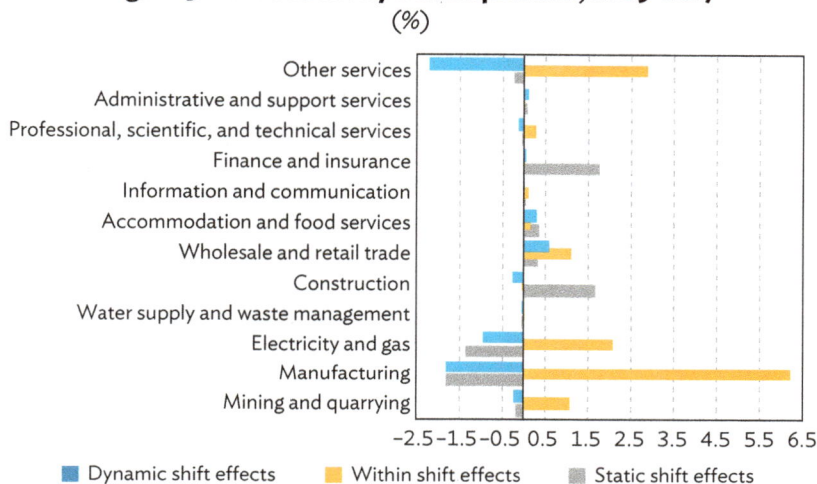

Source: Authors' computation based on shift–share analysis using the Orbis database.

growth in the long term. And while labor continues to concentrate in economic activities with low productivity, the move from low- to high-productivity sectors slowed, impeding the process of structural transformation.

The efficiency of SOEs operating in different sectors, using data envelopment analysis, is now examined. Appendix A1.2 in Chapter 1 gives details of the data envelopment analysis. The "efficient frontier"—the maximum efficiency score of 1.0—is represented by the outermost polygon in Figure 5.17, while the estimated efficiency scores of SOEs engaged in various sectors are shown by the vertex of the inner polygon. The results indicate that efficiency scores, except for trade and transport, range from 0.42 to 0.73, implying various degrees of inefficiency. For example, SOEs in the construction sector with an efficiency score of 0.43 suggest that by using same level on inputs, output can be increased by at least 57%. Similarly, with optimal use of resources in other sectors, output can also be increased substantially.

The findings suggest that with proper allocation of resources and improved corporate governance of SOEs, the degree of inefficiency in different sectors can be reduced—and this will improve the overall quality of public services. Hence, it will be crucial for policy makers to induce reforms and measures that aim to improve the productivity of SOEs and make them efficient drivers of growth. This becomes particularly important as the PRC transitions from middle- to high-income status, and from high-growth to high-quality development.

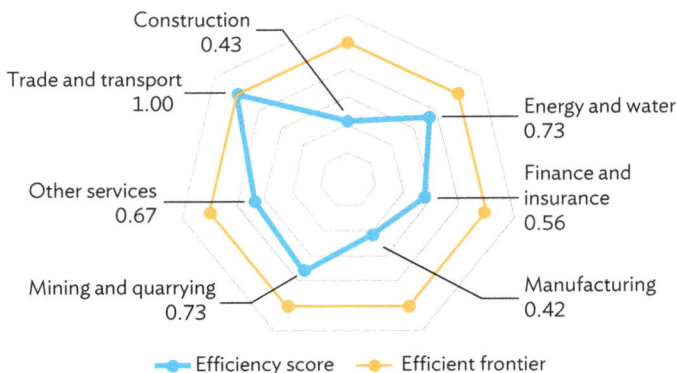

Figure 5.17: Efficient Frontier and Relative Efficiency, Average 2009–2017

Construction 0.43
Trade and transport 1.00
Energy and water 0.73
Finance and insurance 0.56
Other services 0.67
Manufacturing 0.42
Mining and quarrying 0.73

Efficiency score   Efficient frontier

Source: Authors' estimates derived from data envelopment analysis based on the Orbis database.

5.5   Public Sector Management and Fiscal Risks

As discussed in Chapter 1, the quality of public asset management is one of the crucial building blocks that distinguish well-run countries from failed states. It is worth noting that better management of public assets—such as SOEs—is not simply about maximizing financial returns but also accomplishing other important social objectives. IMF (2018) suggests that better management of public assets can lead to substantial gains. Empirical evidence also supports the view that countries with strong fiscal space are in a better position to mitigate adverse shocks and are quick to recover.

The availability of ample fiscal space and better management of public assets can provide a comfort zone to governments to mitigate the impact of external shocks. Since fiscal space enhances the sustainability of budgetary resources to stimulate economic activity and promote growth, having that space is equally important in developing and advanced economies. Although there is no single definition of fiscal space, it can be visualized as the budgetary room to create and allocate funding for various purposes.

Compared with the six other countries in Table 5.3, the PRC had relatively limited fiscal space during 2008–2017, which may have constrained the government's ability to allocate resources to priority sectors. The Republic of Korea, which had sounder macroeconomic fundamentals and higher fiscal space than the other countries, managed its SOEs effectively. It had a surplus of 1.2% of GDP on its fiscal and cyclically adjusted balances in the review period. All other countries except resource-rich Azerbaijan and Kazakhstan experienced higher deficits on primary, cyclically adjusted fiscal balances.

Table 5.3: Fiscal Space in Selected Asian Countries, Average 2008–2017
(% of GDP)

Country	General Government Debt	Primary Balance	Cyclically Adjusted Balance	Fiscal Balance	5-Year Sovereign CDS Spreads[a]
Emerging economies	45.6	(1.2)	(2.7)	(2.4)	739.4
Advanced economies	66.5	(1.2)	(2.1)	(1.9)	346.5
PRC	**37.2**	**(0.9)**	**(1.7)**	**(1.5)**	**94.5**
Republic of Korea	34.6	0.4	1.2	1.2	99.9
Azerbaijan	22.4	5.0	3.2	4.8	
Indonesia	26.1	(0.3)	(1.7)	(1.7)	205.0
Kazakhstan	13.9	0.1	0.1	0.1	254.0
Sri Lanka	74.0	(1.4)	(6.4)	(6.3)	
Viet Nam	50.9	(3.1)	(4.3)	(4.6)	266.0

( ) = negative values, CDS = credit default swap, GDP = gross domestic product, PRC = People's Republic of China.
[a] Basis points.
Source: Kose et al. (2017).

The fact that the Republic of Korea and developed economies have dealt with external crises generally better than developing economies—and still have ample fiscal space—suggests more effective economic management. The large number of loss-making SOEs in the PRC, coupled with the country's limited fiscal space, has negative implications for macroeconomic stability. An evaluation of the financial performance of SOEs indicates that the share of state firms making a loss increased from 2010 to 2017 (Figure 5.18).

The return-on-equity for loss-making SOEs declined in this period. This substantially deteriorated the government's net financial worth, indicating that it had at that time limited options to mitigate the adverse impacts of external shocks. It is important to note that the decline in net financial worth was driven mainly by rising local government debt and underperforming SOEs. This again suggests the limited availability of fiscal space to mitigate the impact of external shocks. IMF (2018) suggests that in the PRC, the net financial worth of the general government declined from 16% of GDP in 2010 to about 8% by 2017 (Figure 5.19).

Figure 5.18: Financial Performance of SOEs, 2010–2017

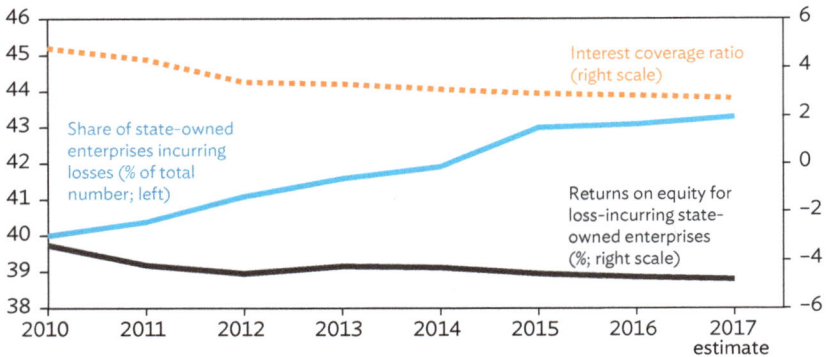

Interest coverage ratio (right scale)

Share of state-owned enterprises incurring losses (% of total number; left)

Returns on equity for loss-incurring state-owned enterprises (%; right scale)

ROE = return on equity, SOE = state-owned enterprise.
Source: IMF (2018).

Figure 5.19: Net Financial Worth of the PRC Government, 2010-2017 (% of GDP)

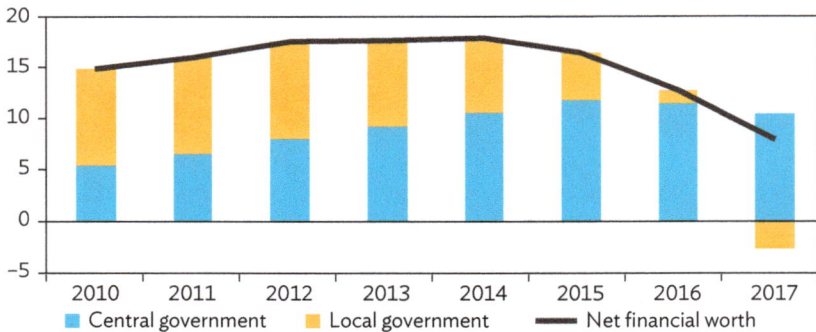

■ Central government   ■ Local government   ━ Net financial worth

GDP = gross domestic product, PRC = People's Republic of China.
Source: IMF (2018).

The rising share of loss-making SOEs, combined with off-budget debt and the weak performance of state firms, should be seen as warnings of substantial risks for the future. To maintain macroeconomic stability, the government should consider the effect of policies on assets and nondebt liabilities in addition to debt. This also applies to risk management, where valuation changes can have large effects on wealth. Because considerable fiscal activity takes place outside the central government, the government should monitor the fiscal situation and use long-term fiscal projections to compare current levels of public wealth. Adopting this strategy may provide more fiscal room in the long term, and help mitigate the adverse effects of external shocks to the economy (IMF 2018).

Empirical evidence corroborates the view that the rising contingent liabilities of the SOEs and subnational government debt pose a substantial fiscal risk that could destabilize macroeconomic stability. For example, IMF (2016) suggests that, among various type of contingent liabilities, government bailouts and SOE support were major factors for fiscal crises. Table 5.4 shows that the average fiscal costs of contingent liabilities emanating from SOEs amount to 3% of GDP. However, the maximum fiscal costs are high as just over 15% of GDP (Bova et al. 2016).

Table 5.4: Fiscal Cost of Contingent Liabilities, Average 1990–2014

Type of Contingent Liability	Number of Episodes	Number of Episodes with Identified Fiscal Costs	Average Fiscal Cost (% GDP)	Maximum Fiscal Costs (% of GDP)
Finance sector	91	82	9.7	56.8
Legal	9	9	7.9	15.3
Subnational government	13	9	3.7	12.0
SOEs	32	31	3.0	15.1
Natural disaster(s)	65	29	1.6	6.0
Private nonfinance sector	7	6	1.7	4.5
PPPs	8	5	1.2	2.0
Other	5	3	1.4	2.5
Total	**230**	**174**	**6.1**	**56.8**

GDP = gross domestic product, PPP = public–private partnership, SOE = state-owned enterprise.
Source: Bova (2016).

It is evident that on average SOEs in the PRC are structurally less efficient than their counterparts in the private sector, and that the public sector's stagnating growth has shrunk SOE asset holdings. Although SOEs continue to get preferential treatment from the government, it is now widely argued that they would not survive in an innovation-driven market without the perks they currently enjoy. Experience in successful transitions from upper-middle-income to high-income status suggests the government will have to improve the efficiency and productivity of public sector institutions. It is particularly important that the government moves away from its current growth model, which heavily relies on an investment-driven approach, and   move toward a productivity-induced, high-quality growth model. This approach will require restructuring SOEs to make them efficient drivers of high-quality development.

The government should also provide equal treatment for private sector development and promote the competition necessary for better public services. The success of the private sector is worth noting in this regard. For example, Huawei Technologies Company Ltd. is leading global 5G, and the company is eager to spread its innovation globally (Guluzade 2019).

In sum, effective asset management is vital for maintaining macroeconomic stability and mitigating the impacts of crises. SASAC is making great strides in carrying out the government's agenda to "grasp the big, release the small," and to reduce the number of SOEs through privatization, asset sales, and mergers and acquisitions.

5.6 SOE Reforms

This section gives a brief overview of SOE reforms in the PRC from the 1980s to 2018. These have created the necessary conditions for increasing private investments and providing equal treatment with the private sector. These reforms have been particularly instrumental in improving the efficiency and competitiveness of SOEs and have helped sustain economic growth. These reforms have, importantly, created a new generation of SOEs with diversified types of ownership and a significant level of internationalization. Although reforms have led to substantial improvements in the financial performance of many SOEs, the sector's overall performance still lags behind private firms (Song 2018).

The reforms began in the 1980s, with the World Bank working closely with the government by providing analytical and advisory services. The reforms focused on giving SOE managers the power they needed to do their jobs effectively and strengthening incentives for managers through profit sharing. Performance contracts were instituted between SOE managers and their government supervisors to specify the decision-making rights to be delegated and the terms of profit sharing in relation to performance.

The reforms were contingent on two conditions: a competitive market environment and internal profit motives. The belief back then was that SOEs were reformable and systemic—and therefore widespread privatization was not the only path to success. The World Bank stressed the main challenge was to build a proper relationship between the state and the enterprise. To this end, reforms regarded SOEs within the framework of state ownership alongside creating an environment to promote private enterprise (World Bank 1985).

Further reforms in 1989 were premised on the newly created State Property Management Board functioning as a policy-making and monitoring body.

These reforms also devised a set of regulations governing the valuation of assets, enterprises, and ownership rights to facilitate the transfer of SOE ownership (Zhang 2019).

One of the key messages of these reforms was the introduction of a corporatization strategy for SOEs, which policy makers widely recognized as an important step in SOE reform. The government stayed focused on introducing market-oriented reforms and, in 1992, introduced second-generation reforms to transform SOEs into modern corporations.

The government acknowledged that the traditional SOE model introduced in the 1980s had reached its limit, and that this model needed reforming to move forward. A new company law was passed in 1994. Following the "grasp the big, release the small" policy a large number of financially distressed SOEs were corporatized and merged into industrial groups under the control of the state, while small SOEs were privatized or closed.

The fundamental goal of the "grasp the big" strategy was to transform large SOEs into profit-maximizing firms while retaining state control. In the steel industry from the 1990s to the early 2000s, five large industrial groups were created to which the ownership of SOEs was transferred. The closure of inefficient and loss-making SOEs released resources to private firms, which used them more efficiently than had they stayed with these SOEs. Despite these restructuring and privatization efforts, the largest firms in the PRC remained under state control. In Fortune Magazine's 2014 list of the world's 500 largest companies, 67 of the 69 PRC companies in this list were state-owned (Hsieh and Song 2015).

One of the major challenges policy makers faced in the PRC in the 1990s was how to establish agencies to represent the owner of state-owned assets in SOEs, and to efficiently exercise the rights of state ownership. In 1995, the State Economic and Trade Commission was tasked to lead SOE reforms. The World Bank was brought in it to advise the government on strengthening the state's ownership rights by simplifying SOE structures, eliminating layers, and reorienting public institutions toward improving financial management.

The World Bank also expanded its engagement into areas related to the financial performance and restructuring of SOEs. It recommended measures to improve profitability and to transfer SOEs to non-state sectors through mergers and other ways. The government started restructuring SOEs, which proved helpful in containing their nonperforming loans. These had the potential to drag state-owned commercial banks into crisis that would have destabilized public finances. The World Bank worked with the government in this area, providing technical advice on SOE bankruptcy and helping to formulate a new bankruptcy law (World Bank 1985).

To supervise SOE assets and ownership, the government, in 2002, created a centralized ownership agency, SASAC. To improve SOE performance, the World Bank advised the government to (i) focus on large SOEs and make efficient use of state capital a central objective, (ii) stress the importance of the "economic value added" concept, and (iii) specify SOE performance goals in the statement of SOEs.

The World Bank emphasized the importance of SASAC being a professional and commercially focused organization. Setting up SASAC marked the end of second-generation SOE reforms. From then on, the focus shifted to improving the efficiency of state capital. In 2005, the World Bank advised the government to implement a dividend policy for SOEs—advice that was in line with international SOE practice.

The SASAC model was a major step in the SOE reform agenda in that it advanced the restructuring of SOEs and improved their efficiency. Recognizing that state ownership of SOEs was widespread across sectors, the government during the next phase of reforms started, in 2013, work on setting up state capital operation and state capital investment companies. By 2017, 142 of both types of companies were set up at the provincial level and 11 at the national level. To improve SASAC's performance, a reform plan was introduced in 2017 to limit the commission's intervention in SOEs to certain specific areas.

Meeting today's development challenges calls for a new generation of SOE reform. The thrust should not only be improving performance but also redefining the role of the SOE sector in the economy in relation to non-SOE sectors, and creating equal treatment for both sectors—the latter being particularly important to promote competition and to enhance the quality of public services. World Bank (1985) urged the government to ensure equal treatment with private firms and remove implicit guarantees to SOEs.

The government is aware of the importance of promoting fair competition. The central government has been trying to formulate new competition policies and strengthen existing ones since 2016. Considerable progress has been made on this, including a more powerful administrative body and safeguards to ensure that new policies are based on fair competition. Following the principle of competitive neutrality, the State Council, in 2018, required businesses of all sizes and types of ownership to be given equal treatment in tendering, land use, and other aspects of enterprise (Zhang 2019).

Despite the SOE reforms taken since 1985, this is still a work in progress. For example, state ownership will play a big role in the successful transition from middle- to high-income status. With the PRC's growing importance in the global market, reforming SOEs and improving their performance becomes increasingly vital, and may have significant implications for the country's trading partners.

5.7 Evolution of the Corporate Governance Structure

Economic reforms have fueled rapid economic growth since the late 1970s and significantly transformed the PRC's economic structure. The corporate governance policies and measures introduced by policy makers have been instrumental in improving the overall governance framework. These reforms can broadly be classified into four phases.

Phase 1 (1978–1984). The main emphasis of reforms was decentralization. In 1979, the State Council promulgated rules and regulations for enterprise reforms that redefined the relationship between the state and enterprises. These reforms provided more autonomy and freedom to SOE managers in making decisions on business matters.

Phase 2 (1984–1992). Reforms brought changes to the profit distribution of SOEs, allowing after-tax profits to be shared by the state and enterprises (before this all SOEs' profits went to the state). From the 1990s, the government introduced reforms to create a modern corporate governance structure by establishing the Shanghai and Shenzhen stock exchanges (in 1990 and 1991). To regulate the stock market, it created a new government agency, the China Securities Regulatory Commission, which took measures to improve corporate governance (Xu and Wang 1999).

The Shanghai and Shenzhen stock exchanges helped develop the market for equities and played a role in modernizing the economy. Listed companies rose from 1,088 in 2000 to 3,485 by 2017, with their market capitalization surging from $581 billion to $8.4 trillion in this period (Figure 5.20). The formulation and implementation of various measures for listed companies identified by the China Securities Regulatory Commission greatly promoted the reform process for corporate governance and facilitated better corporate governance in these companies.

Figure 5.20: Market Capitalization and Turnover, 2000-2017
($ billion)

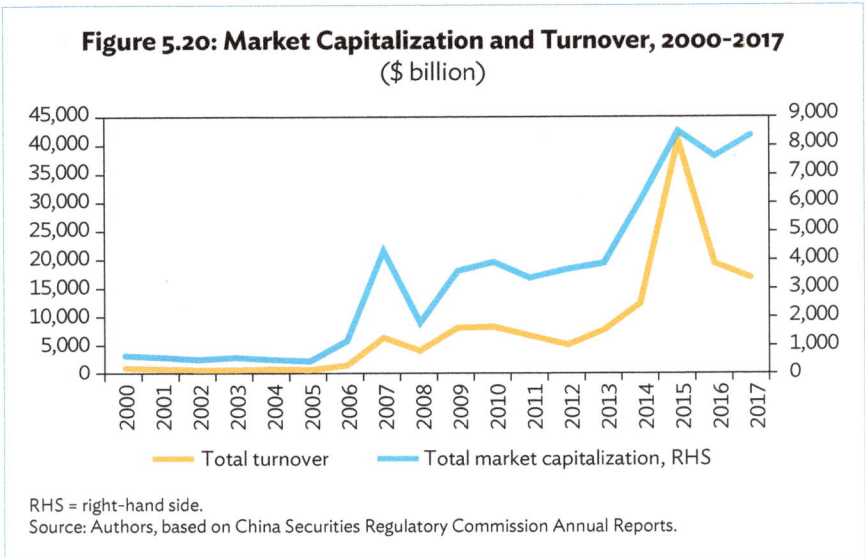

RHS = right-hand side.
Source: Authors, based on China Securities Regulatory Commission Annual Reports.

Reforms introduced during this phase set out the roles and responsibilities of SOE managers, and put in place an SOE manager accountability mechanism. The ownership and management of SOEs was separated, giving managers more autonomy and incentives to expand businesses (OECD 2011).

Phase 3 (1993–2003). The main feature of this phase was establishing a modern enterprise system suitable for a market economy. Reforms aimed to transform the SOE management mechanism to fit this goal. The Company Law, passed in 1993, provided the legal foundation for establishing a modern enterprise system and corporate governance structure. In 2001, the PRC joined the World Trade Organization and adopted the Principles of Corporate Governance of the Organisation for Economic Co-operation and Development (OECD) for listed companies. The China Securities Regulatory Commission and the OECD agreed to cooperate on a joint corporate governance assessment program. In 2002, the securities commission and the National Economic and Trade Commission drew up a code of corporate governance for the listed companies based on the OECD's corporate governance principles (OECD 2011).

Phase 4 (2004 to present). This phase focused on addressing the remaining constraints to good corporate governance in the public sector. Because of the importance of capital markets in the PRC's economic development, the State Council, in 2004, issued the Opinions on Promoting the Reform, Opening and Steady Growth of Capital Markets. In 2005, the China Securities Regulatory Commission, under the guidance of the State Council, introduced new measures to address the nontradability of certain classes of shares held by shareholders. These measures solved the problem of dividing interests and prices among different shareholders. A 2006 amendment to the 1998 Securities Law opened the door for trading shares other than using spot trading. These reforms laid the foundation for a modern corporate governance system. The next 10 years saw the emergence of a modern enterprise structure. In 2007, the China Securities Regulatory Commission launched a 3-year campaign to create awareness among listed companies on the standard operations and level of governance. As a result, investments in the PRC stock markets surged (Kang, Shi, and Brown 2008).

The revised laws helped to improve corporate governance, put in place mechanisms to protect the rights of shareholders and the public, and enhanced the financing and financial accounting systems of listed companies.

The development of corporate governance in the PRC also provides valuable insights for other countries to follow. In general, these reforms were successful in transforming the economic structure of large SOEs, paving the way for a smooth transition from a centrally planned economy to a market-oriented one. Measures allowing citizens to invest in overseas stock markets will help in aligning listed companies with international standards of governance. As the market economy matures further, the PRC will need to ensure that SOE managers have the requisite skills and take steps to ensure that they can acquire these skills (Kang, Shi, and Brown 2008).

While reforms have been helpful, state ownership and the large presence of SOEs will require the corporate structure to be enhanced further. The government recognizes the need to expedite reforms. In this context, public–private partnership (PPP) is one of the modes identified in the first types of SOE reform. The government has, in particular, encouraged the sharing of research capacities to accelerate the development of PPPs, leading many private companies, including Baidu Inc., Alibaba Group Holding Ltd., and Tencent Holdings Ltd., to share their operations with the government. These companies have joint labs for research and development with state entities. As a co-owner in these companies, the government is responsible for advancing the interests of public shareholders. The government is also responsible for protecting the interests of local private firms against foreign competition, and provides equal treatment for promoting the domestic private sector.

The government is adopting measures to improve the efficiency and productivity of SOEs. It has, for example, introduced mixed ownership in China United Network Communications Group Co. Ltd., selling $11 billion of the telecom company's shares to 14 private investors. This was an important step in making companies more accountable and focused on generating returns on equity, while still retaining state control (Guluzade 2019).

The government is making noteworthy progress in improving its corporate governance system. In addition to promoting PPPs, it has taken measures to make SOEs more competitive and allowing the market to be the ultimate resource allocator. Despite a stronger governance structure, the legal and regulatory system is still not mature enough to regulate large, strategically significant SOEs. Because of this, the government has chosen to retain control over final decision-making, and it is keeping a close eye on market forces so that it can, if necessary, intervene in SOEs' operations in critical situations (Guluzade 2019).

Improving SOE corporate governance will be vital for enhancing the quality of public services. Although no one-size-fits-all approach exists for this, measures for better corporate governance could include limiting structural overlaps between the SOE boards of directors and the government, increasing transparency, and deepening collaboration with international and private sector entities to gain further governance experience.

The case study on oil industry reforms in Appendix A5.2 illustrates a successful transformation resulting from the measures the government took to improve the corporate governance of some of its large SOEs in the industry.

Better corporate governance will be critical for other reforms to succeed. To create a more competitive business environment, financial, fiscal, and competition policy reforms are needed. For them to succeed, corporate governance framework must be well-structured and transparent. Viewed in this context, it is essential for this framework to be in place before starting on these reforms so that SOEs can make responsible choices after consultation with all stakeholders.

Economies that have successfully transitioned from middle- to high-income status have achieved innovation- and productivity-induced growth. Given the PRC's large SOE sector and the country's rising importance in the global economy, a better-performing and reformed SOE sector can play a significant role in its transition from middle-income to high-income status. But for this to happen, the government needs to continue to improve the corporate governance and economic performance of SOEs.

5.8 Conclusions and Way Forward

The reform journey of the PRC's SOEs has been a long one and much has been achieved. Reforms have been taken at the central, provincial, and local levels, and large numbers of SOEs have been privatized. The authority on decision-making for SOEs has increasingly been devolved from central government to lower levels. Reforms put a heavy emphasis on corporate governance, management practices, and decision-making arrangements—and as a result, SOEs have, overall, shifted toward greater commercial orientation based on market forces. SOEs, for their part, have adopted professional management systems and standards more akin to internationally accepted practices.

Despite the reforms and the economy's structural transformation, SOEs and state ownership continue to be prevalent in key sectors of the economy, including petroleum extraction, telecommunication, capital construction, and finance. The government continues to use SOEs as instruments to promote economic development. Because of this, SOEs continue to benefit from government-sponsored regulatory and preferential policies. Even so, the large presence of SOEs in certain sectors presents both opportunities and challenges for business development. And because of reforms, SOEs are under pressure to improve their corporate governance and service delivery.

Because of the changing global landscape and to meet the challenges of transitioning to high-income status, the PRC needs to improve the structure and corporate governance of its SOEs. To meet these transition challenges, the government needs to pay greater attention to enhancing the quality of public services. It needs to realign the economy's structure to make this transition smooth. The government should devise ways and introduce reforms to move the economy from its current investment-driven growth model to a productivity-induced and innovation-driven model. Greater competition in the public sector will increase productivity across the economy.

Appendix A5.1: SOE Efficiency and Various Channels

Variables	Weighted OLS Regression						Ordered Logistic Regression					
	Labor Productivity (log)	R&D Efficiency (log)	Capacity Utilization	Labor Input Efficiency (log)	Raw Materials and Intermediate Inputs Efficiency (log)	Fixed Assets Efficiency (log)	Labor Productivity (quartile)	R&D Efficiency (quartile)	Capacity Utilization (quartile)	Labor Input Efficiency (quartile)	Raw Materials and Intermediate Inputs Efficiency (quartile)	Fixed Assets Efficiency (quartile)
Export Orientation SOE (1 if SOE, 0 otherwise)	-0.164*** (0.027)	0.435*** (0.136)	0.746 (0.595)	-0.277*** (0.023)	0.236*** (0.061)	1.366*** (0.178)	-0.578*** (0.042)	-0.239 (0.219)	0.085 (0.140)	-0.551*** (0.044)	-0.046 (0.170)	3.103*** (0.426)
Loan/Credit Access SOE (1 if SOE, 0 otherwise)	-0.375*** (0.031)	0.499*** (0.111)	5.614*** (0.597)	-0.480*** (0.027)	1.046*** (0.066)	-0.539*** (0.100)	-1.026*** (0.056)	-1.371*** (0.224)	0.304 (0.190)	-0.914*** (0.059)	2.603*** (0.226)	-1.039*** (0.314)
Bank borrowings to finance working capital SOE (1 if SOE, 0 otherwise)	-0.118*** (0.027)	0.402*** (0.132)	-0.000 (0.605)	-0.299*** (0.024)	0.343*** (0.063)	1.343*** (0.179)	-0.448*** (0.045)	-0.504** (0.222)	0.301** (0.147)	-0.493*** (0.047)	0.106 (0.173)	2.955*** (0.424)
Bank borrowings to finance fixed assets purchases SOE (1 if SOE, 0 otherwise)	-0.118*** (0.027)	0.402*** (0.132)	-0.000 (0.605)	-0.299*** (0.024)	0.343*** (0.063)	1.343*** (0.179)	-0.448*** (0.045)	-0.504** (0.222)	0.301** (0.147)	-0.493*** (0.047)	0.106 (0.173)	2.955*** (0.424)

Continued on next page

Appendix A5.1 continued

	(1)	(2)	(3)	(4)	(5)	(6)	(1)	(2)	(3)	(4)	(5)	(6)
	(0.027)	(0.132)	(0.605)	(0.024)	(0.063)	(0.179)	(0.045)	(0.222)	(0.147)	(0.047)	(0.173)	(0.424)
Source of loan/credit SOE (1 if SOE, 0 otherwise)	-0.128	-0.412***	2.875***	-1.178***	0.227***	-1.893***						
	(0.400)	(0.141)	(0.795)	(0.372)	(0.060)	(0.166)						
Forming part within larger firm SOE (1 if SOE, 0 otherwise)	-0.146***	-0.362***	1.444**	-0.274***	0.477***	-1.157***	-0.434***	-0.199	-0.522***	-0.382***	1.074***	-2.203***
	(0.030)	(0.119)	(0.578)	(0.027)	(0.059)	(0.116)	(0.049)	(0.173)	(0.143)	(0.052)	(0.167)	(0.313)
Government ties/connection (Access to finance) SOE (1 if SOE, 0 otherwise)	-0.405***	0.462***	3.778***	-0.491***	0.850***	-0.927***	-0.735***	-0.218	-0.456***	-0.646***	1.758***	-1.667***
	(0.034)	(0.110)	(0.649)	(0.029)	(0.068)	(0.112)	(0.055)	(0.178)	(0.173)	(0.058)	(0.240)	(0.284)
Government ties/connection (Tax administration) SOE (1 if SOE, 0 otherwise)	0.056	0.541***	-0.375	-0.064**	0.435***	1.715***	-0.468***	-1.157***	-0.045	-0.107*	0.543***	2.850***
	(0.036)	(0.172)	(0.651)	(0.032)	(0.066)	(0.179)	(0.059)	(0.281)	(0.155)	(0.060)	(0.184)	(0.424)

Continued on next page

Appendix A5.1 continued

Government ties/connection (Business and licensing permits) SOE (1 if SOE, 0 otherwise)	-0.115***	0.222**	2.237***	-0.210***	0.423***	-1.056***	-0.513***	-0.327**	-0.058	-0.429***	0.904***	-2.018***
	(0.027)	(0.110)	(0.539)	(0.023)	(0.054)	(0.112)	(0.043)	(0.161)	(0.129)	(0.044)	(0.150)	(0.284)
Government ties/connection (Political instability) SOE (1 if SOE, 0 otherwise)	-0.170***	0.253**	2.777***	-0.266***	0.364***	-1.068***	-0.597***	-0.184	-0.034	-0.518***	0.714***	-2.032***
	(0.026)	(0.105)	(0.544)	(0.023)	(0.053)	(0.111)	(0.042)	(0.164)	(0.129)	(0.044)	(0.146)	(0.284)
Government ties/connection (Corruption) SOE (1 if SOE, 0 otherwise)	-0.086***	0.278**	2.875***	-0.203***	0.404***	-1.066***	-0.537***	-0.334**	-0.054	-0.460***	0.662***	-2.049***
	(0.028)	(0.110)	(0.569)	(0.024)	(0.057)	(0.111)	(0.045)	(0.162)	(0.139)	(0.047)	(0.160)	(0.285)

R&D = research and development, SOE = state-owned enterprise.
Notes: Standard errors in parentheses; ***$p < 0.01$, **$p < 0.05$, *$p < 0.1$.
Source: Authors.

Appendix A5.2: Case Study – Oil Industry Reforms

Reforms in the oil industry were carried out in two stages. In the first phase during the 1980s, line ministries were gradually abolished and their tasks shifted to holding companies. In the second phase during the mid-1990s, reforms typically involved the transfer of personnel who retained their positions in the previous bureaucratic ranks.

In the first phase, China National Offshore Oil Corporation (CNOOC) was created in 1982 to manage all offshore upstream activities, such as offshore exploration, extraction, production, and offshore cooperation with other foreign oil companies. In 1983, China National Petrochemical Corporation (Sinopec) was set up and put under the State Council's direct control. Sinopec's main objective is to develop oil industry development plans, price oil products, and allocate crude oil to its subsidiaries. In 1988, the Ministry of Petroleum Industry was reorganized into the China National Petroleum Corporation (CNPC). This holds ministerial rank and took on many of the former ministry's functions. Its main responsibilities are onshore upstream oil exploration, extraction, and production.

Despite these reforms and the oil industry's restructuring, the sale and purchase of crude oil stayed under the administrative control of the government and the holding companies. By the mid-1990s, it became obvious that this arrangement was counterproductive for developing and expanding national oil companies. In 1998, the government restructured CNPC and made them operationally independent so that they could pursue profit as their sole aim, and they were encouraged to compete with each other.

In April 2000, oil and gas company PetroChina Company Ltd. was floated on the stock exchanges of New York and Hong Kong, China as the listed arm of CNPC. In October 2000, Sinopec was listed on both stock exchanges, followed by CNOOC in February 2001.

In 2003, all three national oil companies were put under the control of the newly created State Asset Supervision and Administration Commission (SASAC). The outcome was a multitier holding structure comprising the State Council; SASAC; individual group companies (CNPC, Sinopec, CNOOC); listed companies (PetroChina, Sinopec, CNOOC); and their subsidiaries (some of which may be independently listed).

The subsequent discussion provides a snapshot of the key reforms in the area of pricing policies, governance, profitability, and ownership of oil industry.

Pricing. Until the mid-1990s, the state controlled the prices of oil products. Initial reforms liberalized upstream oil prices, but downstream prices remained tightly controlled. Government subsidies were given on a discretionary basis, resulting in the profits of CNPC and Sinopec being the residual of government decisions. In 1998, domestic crude oil prices were closely linked to international prices. Prices were set once per month in line with changes in the international price. Despite these reforms, CNPC and Sinopec continued to set domestic wholesale and retail prices at the provincial level and below.

The current practice is to adjust domestic oil prices every 10 days in accordance with changes in international market prices. The government, however, still reserves the right to temporarily impose specific price controls for oil products. An elaborate system of subsidies is still in place that benefit many different types of users, including agricultural users. The three national oil companies are required to smooth out price fluctuations internally.

Governance. The government introduced various measures to improve the industry's corporate governance structure. In 1998, it abolished the Ministry of Petroleum Industry. The surplus workers were then absorbed by the CNPC and bureaucrats were transferred from the government to the national oil companies.

Profitability and profit sharing. By 2017, Sinopec and PetroChina had become the world's two largest oil companies by revenue (Table A5.2.1). Spending on research and development at CNPC surged and exceeded those of Royal Dutch Shell PLC, previously the biggest research and development spender.

Mixed-ownership reform. The government undertaken mixed-ownership reforms to develop the nonpublic oil industry. Sinopec was one of the first companies to respond to this initiative, opening its wholly owned subsidiary Sinopec Sales Co. Ltd. to 29.99% outside ownership via a capital increase in a share valued at CNY107.1 billion. And Sinopec Sales Co. Ltd. signed agreements with 10 of its investors, enabling them to expand their businesses.

The CNPC also instituted mixed-ownership reform. In April 2014, it sold six oil refining, pipeline construction, financing, and other units to private interests. In May 2014, it announced a plan to raise private funds to develop oilfields in the Xinjiang Uyghur Autonomous Region.

Table A5.2.1: Fortune Global 500 List 2018

	Rank	$ million Revenues	Profits	Assets	ROA (%)	Employees Number ('000)	Profit per Employee ($)	Assets per Employee ($)
Sinopec	3	326,953	1,538	346,545	0.4	668	2	519
China National Petroleum	4	326,008	-691	629,411	(0.1)	1,470	(0.5)	428
Royal Dutch Shell	5	311,870	12,977	407,097	3.2	84	154	4,846
British Petroleum	8	244,582	3,389	276,515	1.2	74	46	3,737
Exxon Mobil	9	244,363	19,710	348,691	5.7	71	278	4,911

( ) = negative, ROA = return on assets.
Note: Data presumably are for 2017.
Source: Fortune Global 500. http://fortune.com/global500/ (accessed 21 September 2018).

References

Bova, E., M. Ruiz-Arranz, F. Toscana, and H. Elif Ture. 2016. The Fiscal Costs of Contingent Liabilities: A New Dataset. *IMF Working Paper*. No. 16/14. Washington, DC: International Monetary Fund.

Brandt, L., F. Jiang, L. Yao Luo, and Y. Su. 2019. Ownership and Productivity in Vertically-Integrated Firms: Evidence from the Chinese Steel Industry. *Department of Economics Working Papers*. July. Toronto: University of Toronto.

Dewenter, K. L. and P. H. Malatesta. 2001. State-Owned and Privately Owned Firms: An Empirical Analysis of Profitability, Leverage, and Labor Intensity. *American Economic Review*. 91 (1). pp. 320–34.

Guluzade, A. 2019. Explained, the Role of China's State-Owned Companies. https://www.weforum.org/agenda/2019/05/why-chinas-state-owned-companies-still-have-a-key-role-to-play/.

Holz, C. A. 2003. *China's State-Owned Enterprises between Profitability and Bankruptcy*. Singapore: World Scientific.

Hsieh, C.-T. and Z. Song. 2015. Grasp the Large, Let Go of the Small: The Transformation of the State Sector in China. *Brookings Papers on Economic Activity*. Washington, DC.

International Monetary Fund (IMF). 2016. How to Improve the Financial Oversight of Public Corporations. *Fiscal Affairs Department Fiscal Policy Paper*. Washington, DC.

————. 2018. Fiscal Monitor: Managing Public Wealth. Washington, DC.

Kang, Y., L. Shi, and E. D. Brown. 2008. *Chinese Corporate Governance: History and Institutional Framework*. Santa Monica, CA: RAND Corporation. https://www.rand.org/pubs/technical_reports/TR618.html.

Kose, A., S. Kurlat, F. Obnsorge, and N. Sugawara. 2017. A Cross-Country Database of Fiscal Space. *Policy Research Working Paper*. 8157. Washington, DC: World Bank.

Ministry of Finance of China. 2018. *China Finance Yearbook 2018*. Beijing.

National Bureau of Statistics. 2019. *China Statistical Yearbook 2019*. Beijing: China Statistics Press.

Organisation for Economic Co-operation and Development (OECD). 2011. *Corporate Governance of Listed Companies in China: Self- Assessment by the China Securities Regulatory Commission*. Paris. http://dx.doi.org/10.1787/9789264119208-en.

_____. 2015. *OECD Guidelines on Corporate Governance of State-Owned Enterprises, 2015 Edition,* OECD Publishing, Paris. http://dx.doi.org/10.1787/9789264244160-en

Song, L. 2018. The Past, Present and Future of SOE Reform in China. *East Asia Forum.* https://www.eastasiaforum.org/2018/10/25/the-past-present-and-future-of-soe-reform-in-china/.

State Asset Supervision and Administration Commission (SASAC). 2017. SASAC Yearbook 2017. Beijing.

World Bank. 1985. China: Long-Term Development Issues and Options. *Country Economic Report.* Washington, DC: org/ curated/en/993081468746712782/pdf/multi-page.pdf.

_____. 2012. 2012 World Bank Enterprise Survey. Washington, DC. https://microdata.worldbank.org/index.php/catalog/1086.

Xu, X. and Y. Wang. 1999. Ownership Structure and Corporate Governance in Chinese Stock Companies. *China Economic Review.* 10 (1). pp. 75–98.

Zhang, C. 2019. *The World Bank in China's State-Owned Enterprise Reform Since the 1980s.* Washington, DC: World Bank.

CHAPTER 6

State-Owned Enterprise Reforms in Azerbaijan

Michael Schur and Aziz Haydarov

6.1 Introduction

State-owned enterprises (SOEs) play an important role in the economic development of Azerbaijan. SOEs have dominant positions in various sectors such as power generation, transmission, and distribution; production and distribution of oil and gas; water supply and sanitation; air and road transport; railway and freight services; and telecommunication. A large amount of economic output and employment contributions arise from SOEs within Azerbaijan's social services, communication, and transport sectors.

The sharp fall in oil prices in mid-2014 and subsequent economic crisis forced Azerbaijan to rethink its economic policy direction and shift its focus to accelerating development of the non-oil sector to facilitate sustainable, diversified economic growth. The country's still heavy dependence on hydrocarbon revenues (as much as 60% of the state budget revenues came from hydrocarbon exports) and the round of manat devaluations exposed financial and governance weaknesses of major SOEs and their heavy interdependence. The State Oil Company of the Azerbaijan Republic (SOCAR), a government holding with a specific regulatory framework, was unable to generate a profit in 2015, and the International Bank of Azerbaijan (IBAR) and Azerbaijan Railways (ADY) both required the Government of Azerbaijan to provide financial assistance of $3.3 billion and $600 million, respectively, placing a significant burden on the budget.

Acknowledging that global oil prices may not return to their historic peak, and that SOCAR profits could no longer be relied upon to counterbalance the non-oil sectors, the government deployed measures to coordinate short-, medium-, and long-term strategies. On 16 March 2016, the President of Azerbaijan signed Decree No. 1897 on the "Primary Directions of Strategic Roadmaps for National Economy and Main Sectors of Economy" and 11 sectoral strategic road maps that define the country's economic development strategy.

The Strategic Roadmaps for National Economy can be distilled into four strategic targets: (1) strengthen fiscal sustainability and ensure a robust monetary policy, (2) facilitate privatization and state-owned enterprise reforms, (3) develop human capital, and (4) improve the business climate.

Target 2 aims to transform SOEs into the country's development agent. To this extent, the government has set two targets to improve SOE development and productivity within the economy: (i) coordinate the overall approach to improve the efficiency of the public sector, which includes identifying sectors that should remain in government hands and those that could function more efficiently under a private model, and conducting SOE reform to improve governance and efficiency; and (ii) develop a privatization agenda in priority sectors and implement it.

The sharp manat devaluation in 2015 followed by sluggish economic growth, quasi-fiscal activity, and poor governance weakened the financial position of most SOEs, which required increased budget support. The weak operational results of SOEs in Azerbaijan were exacerbated by two policy choices of the government: to shield consumers from cost-recovery tariffs and to keep surplus labor in SOEs from unemployment. Addressing these constraints will require fiscal, sectoral, and social protection reforms, such as the use of public service obligation contracts with SOEs to provide below-cost recovery, stronger employment programs, and expansion of unemployment insurance.

6.2   Importance of SOEs in the Economy

SOEs have played a significant role in the development of Azerbaijan. They are active across major sectors and hold monopoly status in the oil and gas, power, water, and transport sectors. As of 2017, SOEs accounted for 8.9% (10,565) of all registered enterprises in Azerbaijan. Of these registered SOEs, 25% of taxes to state budget were paid by 14 large SOEs, including SOCAR (19%), and the remaining by 13 SOEs (6%).

SOEs predominate in the oil, gas, and power generation and distribution; water supply and sanitation; railway, roads, air passenger transportation; and telecommunication sectors. During the oil boom period from 2004 to 2014, the Government of Azerbaijan invested heavily in infrastructure services at roughly 32% of gross domestic product (GDP).[1]

Given the nature of public goods and the systemic role of the infrastructure service sectors to the rest of the economy, inefficiencies and underperformance in public utility and infrastructure SOEs' service delivery affect a wide range of private sector activities.

---

[1] Asian Development Bank (ADB). Azerbaijan: Railway Sector Development Program. https://www.adb.org/projects/48386-001/main.

Before the external shocks of 2015–2016, management and pricing of infrastructure services were generally not guided by (i) cost-recovery principles (or explicitly subsidized policy purposes, such as in public service obligation contracts, for example); or (ii) financial sustainability and performance targets. As a result, operational losses and significant distortions in service provision recurred over the years. Fiscally inefficient support to SOE operations in key sectors remained the rule.[2]

By having to operate under tariff policies and surplus labor circumstances that did not allow for cost recovery, SOEs became, de facto, an integral part of the Government of Azerbaijan's employment and social policies implementation arm.[3] When the sharp currency devaluation dealt a severe financial shock to currency-risk vulnerable SOEs in 2014–2015, the systemic role of SOEs to the economy implied that the government had to step in with direct fiscal support or guarantees to keep key SOEs going. Government intervention averted disruptions in the provision of key infrastructure services and worse consequences to the economy and population. But it also revealed clearly at the highest policy levels that private sector development will require modern and sustainable infrastructure services and policy reforms that prioritize ways to address the system-wide inefficiency and mismanagement of SOEs in the country.

Corporatization reforms to modernize SOE management and legal ledgers and improvement of management control practices were identified as priorities, as well as the establishment of centralized financial management control and monitoring of SOEs. SOEs incurred recurrent operational losses largely because of ineffective sector policy setups and decisions. Hence, sector-specific reforms are key to lifting financial results and improving the autonomy of SOEs. These reforms over the medium term will actually require a fiscally paced[4] and well-sequenced approach to properly address the multitude of legacy issues in the SOE sector.[5]

---

[2]   The consequent fiscal risks, and the periodic, ex post, outright fiscal outlays that were necessary were mostly provided in incentive-incompatible ways (e.g., not ex ante or contractualized, and not performance-based). This perpetuated corporate management decisions that were inefficient (and ultimately more costly fiscally).

[3]   SOEs did not, however, benefit from any formalization of that role, at least one that could enable fiscal outlays to be performance-based and duly reflected as operational revenues rather than as ex post and sporadic balance sheet support (equity injections or subordinated lending) immediately meant in most cases to address cash emergencies.

[4]   In terms of the pace of specific reforms, it is also important for the government to reignite job growth in the private sector and to establish more effective social safety net functions, so that labor restructuring possibilities across many major SOEs remain fiscally affordable and socially feasible at the same time. This was a key challenge from the outset, which called for a more phased and paced approach. Informal assessments of Azerbaijan's major SOEs often highlight nonnegligible labor surpluses, which the non-oil private sector would need to absorb quickly if SOE labor restructuring were to progress rapidly across the board.

[5]   Issues include (i) high level of foreign debt and exchange rate vulnerability; (ii) poor financial performance and dependency on cost-inefficient and performance-incompatible solutions to fiscal support; (iii) low accountability, transparency, and reporting; (iv) the government's fragmented and incomplete discharge of the ownership function; and (v) lack of autonomous and capable utility regulators to govern tariffs and oversee customer service.

Table 6.1 provides a breakdown of the quantity of SOEs by sector and identifies monopolies within each sector by either their position as a commercial monopoly, or natural monopoly that benefits from economies of scale.

Table 6.1: Number of SOEs by Sector

Sector	Number	Percentage of Total Enterprises in Sector (%)	Dominant SOEs
Agriculture, forestry, and fishing	545	5.16	
Mining and quarrying	35	0.33	SOCAR – Commercial monopoly
Manufacturing	251	2.38	
Electricity, gas and steam production, distribution, and supply	258	2.44	Azerishiq and Azerenerji – Natural monopolies
Water supply; waste treatment and disposal	210	1.99	Azersu – Natural monopoly
Construction	498	4.71	
Trade; repair of transport modes	715	6.77	Port of Baku, Azerbaijan Caspian Shipping – Monopolies
Transportation and storage	254	2.40	Baku Metropolitan and Azerbaijan Natural Railways – Natural monopolies
Accommodation and food services	46	0.44	
Information and communication	213	2.02	Aztelekom – Natural monopoly
Finance and insurance	142	1.34	International Bank of Azerbaijan – Market sharer
Real estate	100	0.95	
Professional, scientific, and technical	619	5.86	Azercosmos – Monopoly
Administrative and support services	261	2.47	
Public administration and defense; social security	3,232	30.59	
Education	2,164	20.48	
Human health and social work	431	4.08	
Arts, entertainment, and recreation	462	4.37	
Other services	129	1.21	Azerpost – Monopoly
Total	**10,565**	**100.00**	

SOCAR = State Oil Company of the Azerbaijan Republic, SOE = state-owned enterprise.
Source: State Statistical Committee of Azerbaijan, Azerbaijan Fact of Facts 2017.

6.3 SOEs' Contribution to GDP

After independence from the former Soviet Union, Azerbaijan's share of public sector involvement in both GDP and employment declined because of significant increase in private sector participation, economic reform, and the shift toward a market-based economy. In 1995, the state accounted for 69.7% of GDP; but, as reform evolved and private sector investment picked up, the state's share of economic output fell to 16.2% in 2016 (Figure 6.1).

Figure 6.1: Declining Role of Azerbaijan's SOE Sector in the Economy, 1995 and 2016
(%)

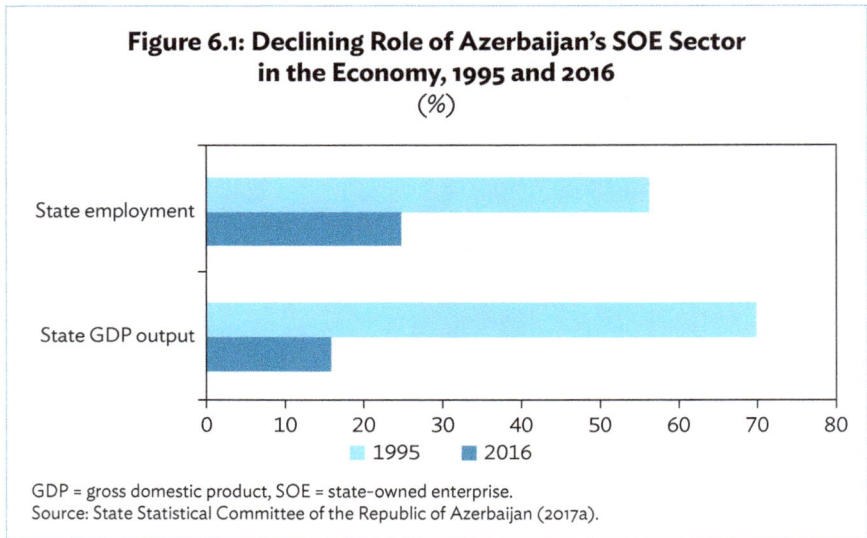

GDP = gross domestic product, SOE = state-owned enterprise.
Source: State Statistical Committee of the Republic of Azerbaijan (2017a).

The state's share of employment likewise declined from 56.1% of total employment in 1995 to only 24.6% as of 2016 (with a proportional increase in private sector employment to 75.4% of total employment) (State Statistical Committee of the Republic of Azerbaijan 2017a).

Figure 6.2 corroborates the overall declining trend of the SOEs' role in economic output across sectors. We note that SOEs remain important in value addition within the social and other services, communication, and transport sectors. These sectors include monopoly status SOEs such as the state-owned SOCAR (oil and gas), Azersu (water), Azerishiq (electricity distribution), and Azerenerji (electricity generation and transmission).

Figure 6.2: Share of the State Sector in GDP, 1995, 2005, and 2017
(Percent of sector GDP output)

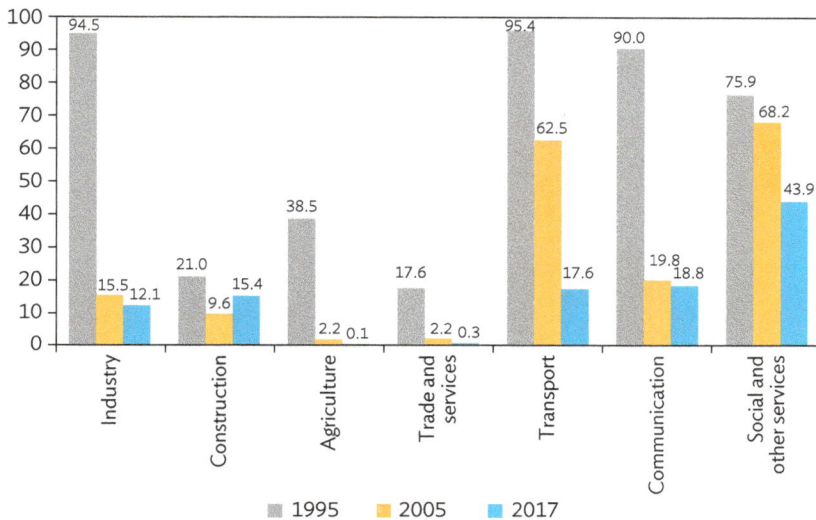

GDP = gross domestic product.
Notes: Industry includes crude oil and gas; social and other services include tourism, forestry, catering, sport, electricity and steam production, distribution and supply, water supply, manufacturing, and information and communication.
Source: State Statistical Committee of the Republic of Azerbaijan. Various years. Azerbaijan in Figures 1995–2017. Baku.

In the absence of a vibrant private sector, the public sector made use of SOEs as a vehicle to promote economic growth. Indeed, the reliance on extractive industry has helped achieve higher economic growth, which averaged around 13% during 2002–2013, and helped transform Azerbaijan into an upper-middle-income country. Although impressive, growth was largely driven by hydrocarbon resources (i.e., oil, oil products, and natural gas), which has made the economy vulnerable to external demand shocks.

6.3.1 Labor Market and Monthly Wages

SOEs dominate in employment in several sectors such as electricity, education, and water (Figure 6.3). By contrast, the manufacturing, trade, financial and insurance activities have low state employment. Sectors dominated by monopoly SOEs (Azerenerji, Azerishiq, Azersu, and Azerbaijan Railways) have also incurred large losses, suggesting a low level of productivity.

Figure 6.3: Azerbaijan's Labor Market and the State's Involvement, 2017

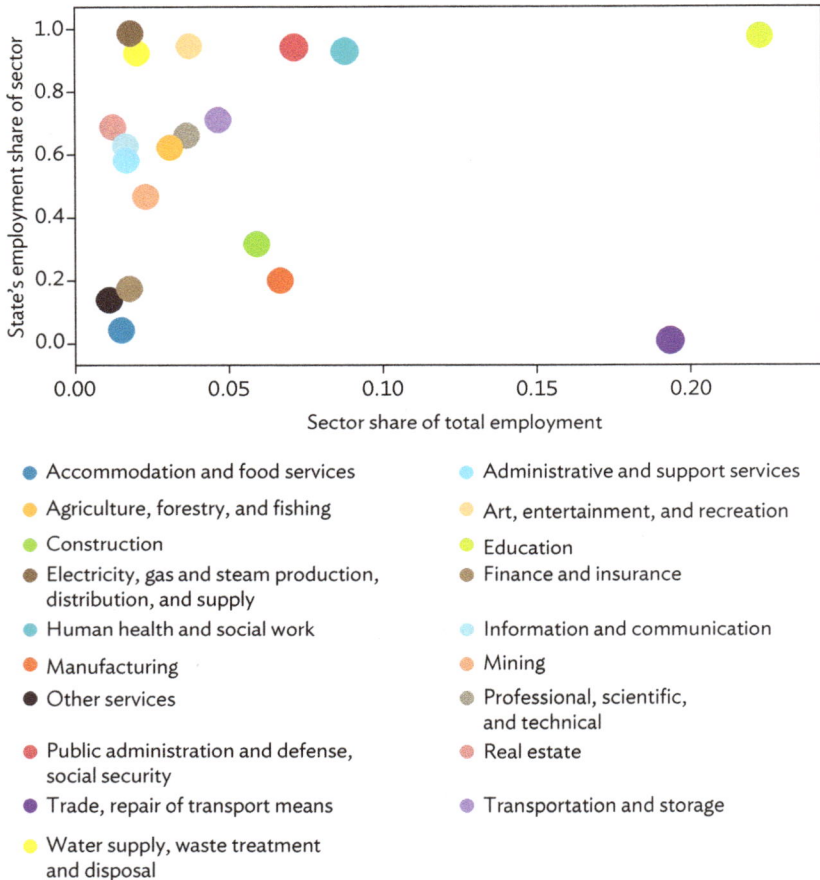

Source: State Statistical Committee of the Republic of Azerbaijan. Azerbaijan in Figures 2017. Baku.

However, private sector monthly wages are generally higher than state enterprise wages, and there is no clear indication that wages in sectors dominated by SOEs are higher than those in the private sector (Figure 6.4).

Figure 6.4: Private Sector Monthly Wages versus Public Sector, 2017

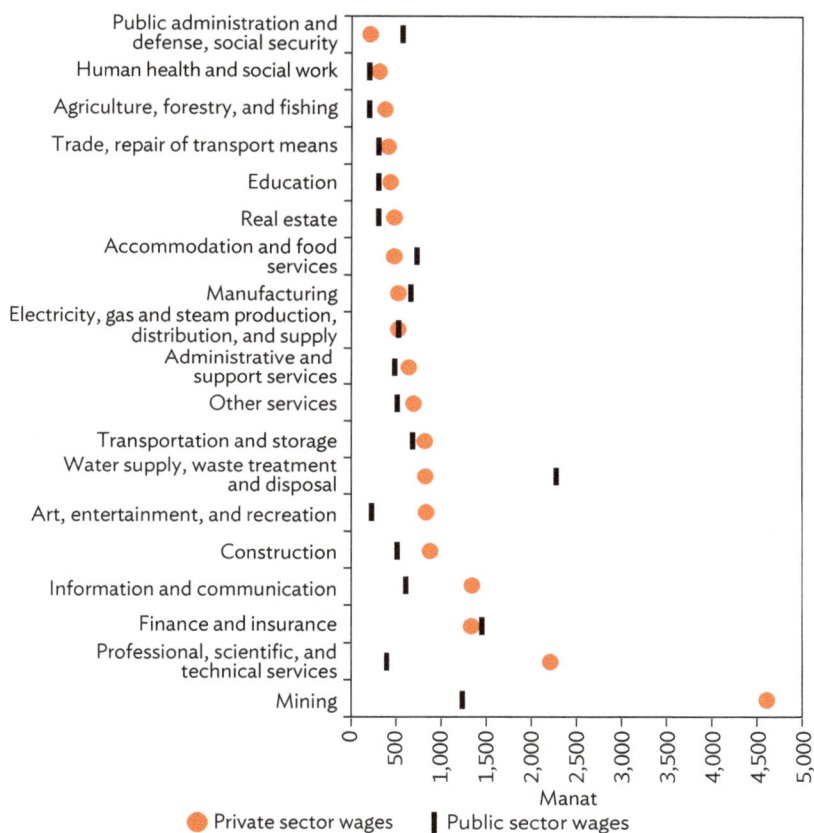

Note: Red circles are private sector wages; black bars represent public sector wages.
Source: State Statistical Committee of the Republic of Azerbaijan (2017a).

6.4   Performance of SOEs by Sector

SOEs play a critical role in delivering essential infrastructure and social services in Azerbaijan. As mentioned, the Government of Azerbaijan during the oil boom period invested heavily in infrastructure services at roughly 32% of GDP, bringing quality of services in line with regional peers (Figure 6.5). However, post-boom oil prices have declined significantly, leading to stark manat devaluation, which supported non-oil exports but also created large financial burdens on entities with significant foreign borrowings. Now more than ever, there is an urgent need to improve public sector efficiency and strengthen the performance of Azerbaijan's non-oil economy.

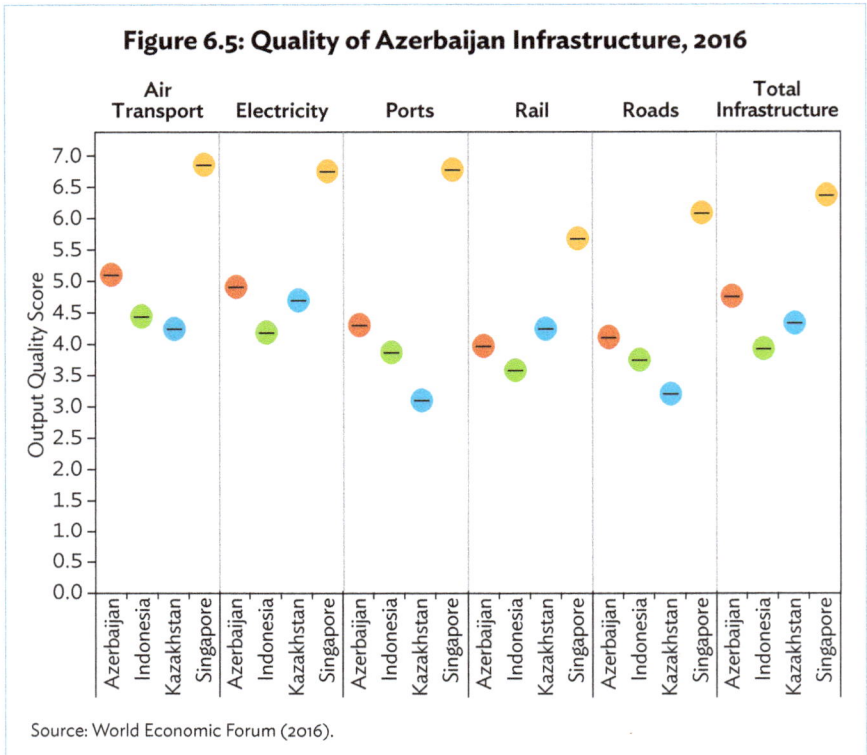

Figure 6.5: Quality of Azerbaijan Infrastructure, 2016

Source: World Economic Forum (2016).

We briefly describe the context of relevant sectors in which each major SOE operates, including their performance and the challenges they face. Financial metrics were used to assess individual SOEs. These should be, however, taken with caution because the management and pricing of the infrastructure services rendered by SOEs in Azerbaijan have in general not been guided by cost-recovery principles or financial sustainability targets. The policy choices that underpin these constraints are the underlying cause of recurrent operational losses and significant distortion in service provision.

As mentioned above, the current tariff policies and the existence of surplus labor do not allow for cost recovery, and SOEs have remained part of the employment and social policies arm of the government. This is gradually changing through sector reforms, but it is a reasonable explanation for why SOEs post operational losses systematically.

It is worth noting that losses because of underperforming SOEs are not merely because tariffs are not set to fully recover costs. These losses are also caused by poor corporate governance, inadequate financial management systems, and scant accountability of SOEs to shareholders. Combined, these factors create high levels of inefficiency independent of tariff levels.

Table 6.2 lists the major SOEs identified for this study. The Ministry of Finance was instrumental in providing supporting data.

Table 6.2: SOEs by Sector

SOE	Sector	Economic Role
Infrastructure SOEs		
State Oil Company of the Azerbaijan Republic (SOCAR)	Oil and gas	SOCAR is of high economic significance given its importance for the country's export revenue, tax revenue, employment, and providing oil and gas for domestic consumption.
Azerenerji	Power generation and transmission	Monopoly power generator and transmission company, with the potential to financially underperform.
Azerishiq	Power distribution	Monopoly power distribution company.
Azerbaijan Airlines	Passenger and freight airline, airports, air fuel provision, and air navigation services	The national flag carrier does not make its financial information public.
Azerbaijan Railways	Railway transport	A vertically integrated SOE that owns all rail infrastructure and related assets and is the only rail operator of both passenger and freight services. The company holds significant debt and received a government bailout in 2016 to restructure debt.
Azersu	Water supply and sanitation (except for Nakhchivan Autonomous Republic)	One of Azerbaijan's most vulnerable SOEs.
Baku Metropolitan	Underground rapid transit system in Baku	Receives significant subsidies from the state budget, which have increased over time.
State Agency of Azerbaijan Automobile Roads	National and regional roads	Has large debt and receives budget support.
Port of Baku	Ports	Strategic asset for trade in the region. Financial statements are not made public. Responsible for the Port of Alyat and Alyat Free Economic Zone.
Services SOEs		
Azercosmos	Satellite services	Strategic asset.
Azerpost	Postal services	Financial reports only available for 2009, 2015, and 2016.

Continued on next page

Table 6.2 continued

Azerbaijan Caspian Shipping Company	Marine merchant fleet, shipyards, and offshore support	Strategic asset for trade in the region. Plays connecting role in the Transport Corridor Europe Caucasus Asia. Provides marine transportation of goods and passengers in the Caspian Sea, and offshore support services for oil and gas operations.
Agrolizing	Agriculture machinery, cattle sale, and leasing finance	Sole provider of government-subsidized inputs and financing for operating equipment for the agriculture sector and one of Azerbaijan's most vulnerable SOEs.[a]
Government financial institutions		
International Bank of Azerbaijan	Banking	The country's largest bank defaulted in 2015 and received a bailout to restructure.

SOE = state-owned enterprise.
[a] Hashimova and Kadyrov (2017).
Source: Authors.

6.4.1   Oil and Gas Sector

Azerbaijan's transition from a low- to middle-income economy transpired on the back of a significant oil price boom from 2004 to 2014 and export-led growth. However, in late 2014 the price of Brent oil in world markets decreased by roughly 44%, causing substantial decline in economic growth within the country and putting pressure on its finance sector (Figure 6.6).

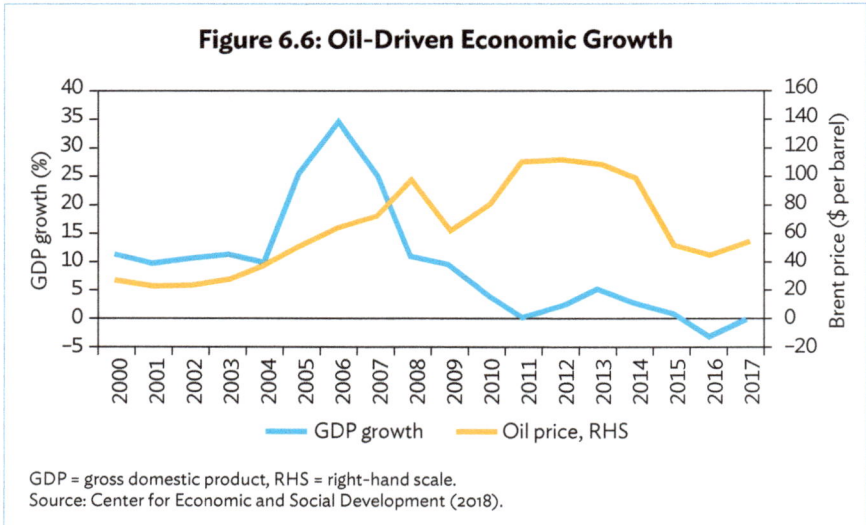

Figure 6.6: Oil-Driven Economic Growth

GDP = gross domestic product, RHS = right-hand scale.
Source: Center for Economic and Social Development (2018).

The decline in the oil and gas sector and subsequent changes in monetary policy (two devaluations in 2015) led to the need for increased transfers from the State Oil Fund of the Republic of Azerbaijan to support government countercyclical fiscal effort, and reductions in the current account and accumulated foreign reserves. Further, while the oil-boom period had allowed SOCAR, at SOE portfolio level, to offset the negative financial results of major SOEs in the non-oil sector, the decline in oil prices drastically impaired the capacity of the government to provide budget support to poorly performing non-oil SOEs providing essential infrastructure services. Figure 6.7 highlights the trends in profit margins and revenues of SOCAR during 2010–2016.

Figure 6.7: Revenue and Profit Margin of the State Oil Company of the Azerbaijan Republic, 2010–2016

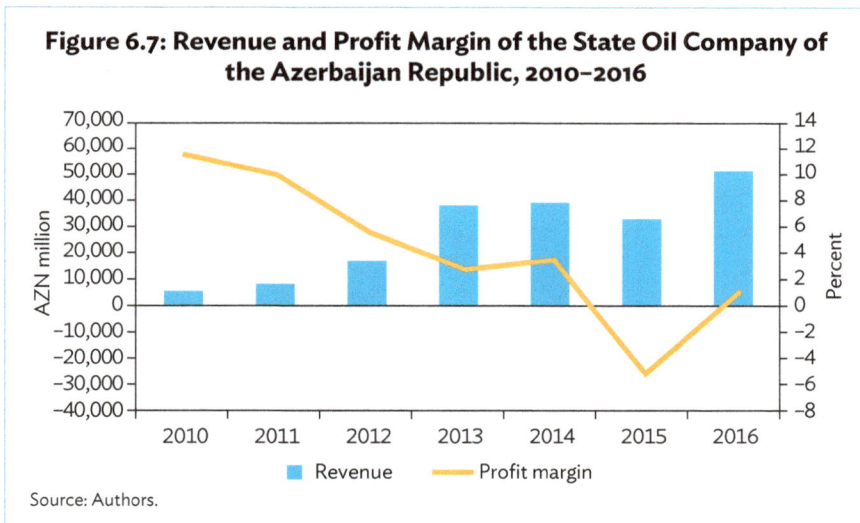

Source: Authors.

The currency devaluations of 2015 increased SOCAR's foreign debt exposure to a large extent and reduced its capacity to make interest repayments.

In March 2018, Fitch assigned a BB+ rating to SOCAR. SOCAR contributed roughly 34.2% of GDP in 2017 to the Azerbaijan economy and accounted for roughly 19% of corporate taxation.[6] Table 6.3 provides a summary of SOCAR's financial results against regional peers (Indonesian PT Pertamina and Kazakhstan's KazMunayGas) and emerging market benchmarks.

---

[6]   State Statistical Committee of the Republic of Azerbaijan. Azerbaijan in Figures 2017, Tax Contribution from Oil and Gas, and others.

Table 6.3: Financial Statistics of SOCAR, 2014–2016
(Average against peers, %)

	SOCAR	PT Pertamina	KazMunayGas	Emerging Markets
ROE	3.4	6.5	0.8	7.1
ROA	1.7	2.9	0.4	
EBITDA margin	4.0	14.1	(20.7)	20.7
ICR	4.1	5.6	Negative	2.0
EV: EBITDA	21.9	9.6	Negative	15.8
Debt: Capital	66.0	47.1	7.0	34.2
Debt: EBITDA multiple	15.2	4.5	Negative	5.4
Quick Ratio	1.1			

( ) = negative; EBITDA = earnings before interest, tax, depreciation, and amortization; EV = enterprise value; ICR = interest coverage ratio; ROA = return on assets; ROE = return on equity; SOCAR = State Oil Company of the Azerbaijan Republic.
Source: SOCAR. Financial Statements. Baku (Years: 2011–2016).

After the oil boom, SOCAR's return on equity (ROE); earnings before interest, tax, depreciation, and amortization (EBITDA) margin; and return on assets declined relative to private sector operators in the emerging market. Under the government's mandate, SOCAR was also required to undertake non-profile activities (i.e., noncommercial, social activities), which incurred costs of AZN143 million in 2015 and AZN148 million in 2016. Between 2014 and 2018, SOCAR was mandated by presidential decree to rehabilitate old local gas pipelines, receiving government contributions to capital of AZN1,122 million in 2016 and AZN858 million 2015.

6.4.2   Banking and Finance Sector

Reform and restructuring have been significant within the finance sector after the oil-boom period and the currency devaluations that increased foreign debt to GDP from 8.6% in 2014 to 22.8% in 2017. Azerbaijan's largest bank, the International Bank of Azerbaijan (IBAR), ceased repayments of foreign debts and filed for bankruptcy in May 2017 because of financial distress. The bank was required, under Presidential Decree 507, to reassess its policy on management, investment, and liquidity through the restructuring of $3.3 billion of its foreign debt (IBAR 2017). The restructuring caused the pass-through of the debt to special purpose vehicle Aqrarkredit, and the government stated the intention to privatize the bank in 2018. IBAR's systemic role in the finance sector adversely affected the country's financial stability.

Presidential Decree 507 required the rehabilitation of IBAR and preparation for its privatization after the financial trouble of 2015. The bank transferred over $3.3 billion in assets to Aqrarkredit to strengthen the balance sheet. Since 2015, significant reform has been undertaken within the bank to restructure and improve performance. As of January 2018, Moody's upgraded IBAR to B3 from a rating of Caa1. IBAR's key profitability metrics such as ROE increased significantly over the 3-year period, with return on equity improving from –140% in 2015 to roughly 80% in 2017 (a profit of AZN800 million). This wide range across the period of assessment resulted in a distorted average ROE across the period of –33%. Furthermore, IBAR's financial stability was strengthened—with significant deleveraging and improvement in the quality of capital held—and having reached a common equity tier 1 ratio of 20.8% in line with international standards, implied that the bank's quality of capital was adequate (Table 6.4). IBAR still faces several short-term challenges, with an open current foreign-exchange position of AZN3.2 billion.

Table 6.4: Financial Statistics of IBAR, 2015–2017
(Average against peers, %)

	IBAR	Azer Turk	BNI Indonesia	Halyk Bank	Emerging Markets
ROE	(33) (80 ROE in 2017, but average is skewed from default period)	3.8	13.7	25.3	20.5
ROA	0.01	1.0	2.0	3.5	2.0
NPL	8.5	9.4	2.9	9.9	4.0
CET1	12.9 (20.8 in 2017)	13.3	18.0	19.0	0.1
LCR	N/A	123.5	2.1	N/A	1.4
Debt: Capital	93 (89 in 2017)	88.5	82.9	86.3	81.0

CET = common equity tier, IBAR = International Bank of Azerbaijan, LCR = liquidity coverage ratio, N/A = not available, NPL = nonperforming loan, ROA = return on assets, ROE = return on equity.
Sources: Azer-Turk Bank. Financial Statements. Baku (Years: 2012–2016); IBAR. Financial Statements. Baku (Years: 2011–2016).

IBAR has underperformed financially against its peers in Kazakhstan, Indonesia, and benchmark private sector operators in emerging markets. However, this is expected given Azerbaijan's macroeconomic and financial environment over the past 3 years. Like Kazakhstan's Halyk Bank, IBAR holds a higher rate of nonperforming loans against international benchmarks (10.2%), although loan loss reserves have provisioned 15% of gross loans to mitigate this risk. IBAR has not publicly reported its liquidity coverage ratio, although Moody's in 2018 noted a significant cushion to respond to credit constraints. IBAR has progressed in removing bad assets from its balance sheet and restructuring its foreign exchange liabilities. Establishing a viable business model remains a key challenge for the bank. Without such model, it will be difficult to increase tangible returns on capital, develop sustainable lending opportunities, and attract private investment to IBAR.

6.4.3   Water and Waste Sector

The global financial crisis saw utility returns reduce rapidly internationally, as governments lowered tariffs to reduce financial pressures on households. Azersu uses underground and surface water sources to supply drinkable water, and its performance is driven heavily by the need to reconstruct water supply and sewerage systems across the country, except in the Nakhchivan Autonomous Republic. It operates in an environment where a large amount of capital expenditure is financed directly through the entity's balance sheet and through additional support from the government. As Azersu's assets are reaching the end of their life cycle, the quality of water supply services has reduced for end users, and operational inefficiencies are high.

From 2011 to 2014 the government funded over AZN2.7 billion of investments, roughly 9.8% of total government capital investment across this period. Investment within the sector has seen the supply of drinkable water increase from 25% to 65% between 2004 and 2015. From 2012 to 2016, Azersu's liabilities increased from AZN505 million to AZN970 million, with a 20% foreign exposure.

Table 6.5 outlines the financial performance of Azersu against peers. Given its negative equity position, we are unable to calculate metrics such as enterprise value multiples or return on equity. Azersu's operating margins, capital structure, and overall financial performance underperform against all peers, across all metrics. Azersu will require significant sector reform (e.g., cost-recovery tariffs and proper corporate governance) and performance-linked government support (in asset development and maintenance) to operate more sustainably.

Table 6.5: Azersu Average against Peers, 2014–2017
(%)

	Azersu	Jasa Tirta	Georgia Water and Power	Emerging Markets[a]
ROE	(170.0)	25.3	15.0	12.8
ROA	(52.0)	17.7	9.4	
EBITDA margin	(32.7) (21.6) in 2016	22.2	37.4	32.2
ICR	N/A	3.9	6.3	2.0
EV: EBITDA	N/A	3.9	7.4	18.2
Debt: Capital	100.0	30.9	37.4	34.1
Debt: EBITDA multiple	N/A	1.2	2.8	6.2

( ) = negative; EBITDA = earnings before interest, tax, depreciation, and amortization; EV = enterprise value; ICR = interest coverage ratio; N/A = not available; ROA = return on assets; ROE = return on equity.
[a] Damodaran Online. Emerging Market Multiples, Operating Markets, Return on Equity and Capital Structure. http://pages.stern.nyu.edu/~adamodar/New_Home_Page/datacurrent.html.
Source: Azersu. Financial Statements. Baku (Years: 2012–2016).

6.4.4   Power Sector

The power sector operates in a similar regulatory environment to that of the water sector, with the government's Tariff Council approving charges to consumers that are, by norm, not at cost-recovery levels. The electricity sector has been reformed considerably post-2015, with a presidential decree requiring all distribution assets of Azerenerji (electricity generation and transmission) to be transferred to Azerishiq (electricity distribution), to ensure that both entities focus and specialize on their allocated business areas.

Like the water sector, the power sector declined after the global financial crisis as the government eased the cost burden of essential economic services on consumers. More than half of Azerbaijan's 2014 installed capacity (56%) was generated by plants that have been operating for more than 30 years. Similarly, Azerishiq's distribution assets will soon reach the end of their life cycle and will require a large capital outlay to maintain or replace.

Responding to the need for capital outlay, the government made substantial investments in the sector (across generation, transmission, and distribution assets) from 2008 to 2014 as outlined in Figure 6.8. However, continued investment and financing will be a challenge for the sector.

As of February 2018, Azerenerji was rated BB/B by S&P, and Azerishiq was rated stable by Fitch at a BB+ rating. Table 6.6 outlines the financial results of Azerenerji and Azerishiq against Kazakh peer CAEPCO, Indonesian PT PLN, and emerging market benchmarks.

Figure 6.8: Public Investment in the Power Sector, 2008–2014
($ million)

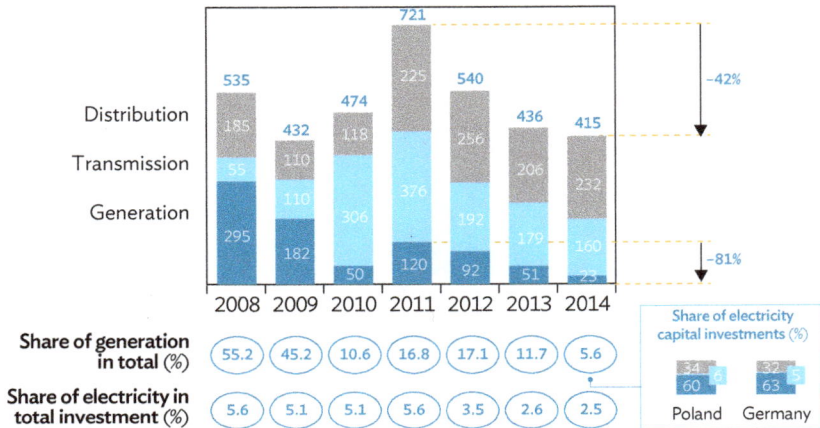

	2008	2009	2010	2011	2012	2013	2014
Share of generation in total (%)	55.2	45.2	10.6	16.8	17.1	11.7	5.6
Share of electricity in total investment (%)	5.6	5.1	5.1	5.6	3.5	2.6	2.5

Source: President of the Republic of Azerbaijan and the Ministry of Economy (2016e).

Table 6.6: Azerishiq and Azerenerji, 2014–2017
(Average against peers, %)

	Azerenerji	Azerishiq	PT PLN	CAEPCO	Emerging Markets[a]
ROE	(63.0)	(0.16)	(0.3)	4.8	12.4
ROA	(13.5)	(0.15)	(0.2)	2.6	
EBITDA margin	45.0	5.0	16.4	14.4	24.4
ICR	5.3	0.1	1.7	4.1	2.0
EV: EBITDA	11.1	27.6	33.0	16.9	14.0
Debt: Capital	73.5	42.0	33.5	49.8	47.0
Debt: EBITDA multiple	8.0	11.5	11.1	8.4	6.6
Quick Ratio	0.8				

( ) = negative; EBITDA = earnings before interest, tax, depreciation, and amortization; EV = enterprise value; ICR = interest coverage ratio; ROA = return on assets; ROE = return on equity.
[a] Damodaran Online. Emerging Market Multiples, Operating Markets, Return on Equity and Capital Structure. http://pages.stern.nyu.edu/~adamodar/New_Home_Page/datacurrent.html
Sources: Azerenerji. Financial Statements. Baku (Years: 2011–2016); Azerishiq. Financial Statements. Baku (Years: 2012–2016).

A significant proportion of Azerenerji's losses from 2014 to 2017 were incurred from impairment losses and asset replacement costs, given its positive EBITDA margin. This may be part of the reason why both entities have been earning below benchmark returns during 2014–2017. Azerenerji's capital structure suggests an excessive level of debt compared with benchmarks.

To support Azerenerji, which incurred a loss of roughly AZN1 billion in 2015 because of the manat devaluation, the government provided AZN457 million to ensure the company's balance sheet during this period of transition. Azerishiq was not incurring significant operating losses that create immediate alarm; however, its interest coverage ratio, enterprise value (EV): EBITDA and debt: EBITDA multiple suggested limited cash flow to cover interest obligations and excessive debt relative to operating returns.

In 2017, the government had to intervene to resolve issues among the power SOEs, particularly on payment for services, to ensure that impacts to consumers are minimized and to maintain the SOEs' financial stability (Reuters 2016 and News.Az 2017).

6.4.5   Rail and Road Transport Sector

Rail and road transport is a vital source of international trade via freight services and crucial for passenger transport within Azerbaijan. In 2016, freight services had grown to account for roughly 10% of total exports and playing a key role in strategic trade routes such as the North–South and East–West trade corridors.

However, a combination of excessive borrowing, lack of management autonomy, aging infrastructure, and below-cost tariffs saw Azerbaijan Railways (ADY) receive $600 million from the government to restructure debt. This was accompanied by technical assistance from the Asian Development Bank (ADB) to improve financial management, internal systems, and structures. These initiatives have enabled ADY to improve competitiveness, manage asset rehabilitation, improve productivity, and develop its broader corporate and financial strategy.

Table 6.7 compares the financial performance of Baku Metropolitan, Azerbaijan Railways, and the State Agency on Azerbaijan Automobile Roads against Indonesia's Kereta API, Kazakhstan's Kazakh Temir, and emerging market benchmarks.

Like ADY, Baku Metropolitan provides urban commuter transport services and is unable to cover operational costs because of below-cost tariffs. This creates financial stress on the business's capacity to cover staffing and amortization costs; thus, it required direct support from the budget to maintain operations, including AZN38 million in 2016. Even so, the company lost AZN78.7 million, a 280% increase from 2015.

Table 6.7: Financial Results of Transport Companies, 2014–2016
(%)

	Baku Metropolitan	Azerbaijan Railways	Kereta API	Kazakh Temir	Emerging Markets[a]
ROE	(2.3)	(59.0)	8.4	(13.3)	13.4
ROA	(0.02)	(22.5)	3.9	(3.9)	
EBITDA margin	24.0	(66.8)	27.2	12.1	20.9
ICR	N/A	N/A	8.0	1.8	2.0
EVM	N/A	N/A	6.1	32.9	17.3
Debt: Capital	31.8	69.8	59.4	53.6	19.1
Debt: EBITDA multiple	6.0	N/A	3.6	17.6	3.3
Quick Ratio	1.6	0.4			

( ) = negative; EBITDA = earnings before interest, tax, depreciation, and amortization; EVM = enterprise value multiple; ICR = interest coverage ratio; N/A = not applicable; ROA = return on assets; ROE = return on equity.
[a] Damodaran Online. Emerging Market Multiples, Operating Markets, Return on Equity and Capital Structure. http://pages.stern.nyu.edu/~adamodar/New_Home_Page/datacurrent.html
Sources: Azerbaijan Railways. Financial Statements. Baku (Years: 2014–2016); and Baku Metropolitan. Financial Statements. Baku (Years: 2012–2016).

Baku Metropolitan has also failed to attain commercial benchmarks but has not posted negative results to the level of those of ADY. A high debt: EBITDA ratio is driven by a low level of operating cash flows relative to peers. That is, although Baku Metropolitan's capital structure does not suggest excessive debt, its profitability or cash flow from operations could be improved.

6.4.6   Ports and Shipping Sector

Azerbaijan Caspian Shipping Company is a key SOE in the trade and logistics sector, instrumental in the operation of the East–West trade corridor. Azerbaijan's ports mostly serve as a transit destination, with 0.5 million tons of import–export goods volume in 2014 and 5.6 million tons of goods in transit—a transshipment ratio of 59% (President of the Republic of Azerbaijan and the Ministry of Economy 2016).

Azerbaijan Caspian Shipping Company outperforms international benchmarks, maintaining a low level of debt and obtaining sufficient returns on equity and assets. The business has sufficient operating cash flow to meet its interest obligations (based on its interest coverage ratio for 2015 as interest expenses were minimal in forward years), and in terms of its debt: EBITDA, the business has sufficient room to leverage further and keep in line with international standards. Table 6.8 presents the financial performance of Azerbaijan Caspian Shipping against Indonesia's Pelindo III and emerging market benchmarks.

Table 6.8: Ports and Shipping Financial Performance, 2014–2016
(%)

	Caspian Shipping	Pelindo III	Emerging Markets[a]
ROE	11.5	17.8	11.4
ROA	9.7	7.5	
EBITDA margin	43.0	27.2	14.8
ICR	12.2 (2015 value)	4.4	2.0
EV: EBITDA	6.5	9.3	15.6
Debt: Capital	10.5	57.8	27.0
Debt: EBITDA multiple	1.3	5.4	4.2

EBITDA = earnings before interest, tax, depreciation, and amortization; EV = enterprise value; ICR = interest coverage ratio; ROA = return on assets; ROE = return on equity.
[a] Damodaran Online. Emerging Market Multiples, Operating Markets, Return on Equity and Capital Structure. http://pages.stern.nyu.edu/~adamodar/New_Home_Page/datacurrent.html.
Source: Azerbaijan Caspian Shipping. Financial Statements. Baku (Years: 2014–2016).

6.4.7   Air Transport Sector

Azerbaijan Airlines (AZAL) dominates the air transport sector, providing domestic and international carrier services and is responsible for airport operations. Azerbaijan competes with many well-established industry leaders in the region such as Qatar and the United Arab Emirates. Skytrax has noted that the Heydar Aliyev International Airport is the best among all airports in the Russian Federation and the countries of the Commonwealth of Independent States. With the reconstruction of Nakhchivan International Airport in 2016, AZAL currently operates a fleet of about 30 aircrafts.

However, the airline has suffered large losses to equity and assets and its financial performance has fallen well below international benchmarks. AZAL is excessively leveraged at 94% as of 2016 and incurred also in 2016 a loss of AZN258 million and a depreciation and amortization cost of AZN142.9 million, placing significant financial stress on the business (Table 6.9).

Table 6.9: Azerbaijan Airlines Results Comparison, 2014–2016
(%)

	Azerbaijan Airlines	Garuda Indonesia	Air Astana	Emerging Markets[a]
ROE	(65.0)	(1.3)	(14.8)	10.3
ROA	(5.8)	(0.2)	2.4	
EBITDA margin	7.0	1.7	7.0	15.9
EV: EBITDA	17.9	24.2	12.7	24.6
Debt: Capital	94.0 (as of 2016)	73.1	77.9	47.8
Debt: EBITDA multiple	10.8	17.7	9.8	11.8

( ) = negative; EBITDA = earnings before interest, tax, depreciation, and amortization; EV = enterprise value; ROA = return on assets; ROE = return on equity.
[a] Damodaran Online. Emerging Market Multiples, Operating Markets, Return on Equity and Capital Structure. http://pages.stern.nyu.edu/~adamodar/New_Home_Page/datacurrent.html.
Source: Azerbaijan Airlines. Financial Statements. Baku (Years: 2014–2016).

6.4.8 Communications Sector

Numerous SOEs in Azerbaijan focus on providing communication services, among them Aztelkom, Azercosmos, and Azerpost. Azercosmos is the national satellite company and the first company in the Caucasus to operate a satellite. Azerpost is the national postal service and provides various e-financial and micro-crediting services. Table 6.10 outlines the performance of Azercosmos and Azerpost against Indonesia's PT Telkom, Kazakhtelecom, and emerging market benchmarks.

Table 6.10: Average Performance Benchmark of Azercosmos and Azerpost, 2014–2016
(%)

	Azercosmos	Azerpost	PT Telkom	Kazakhtelecom	Emerging Markets[a]
ROE	(82.7) (38.5 in 2016)	0.0 7.3 (2016)	17.9	7.0	12.9
ROA	(13.1)	(0.1)	20.1	4.8	
EBITDA margin	(40.0) (7.0 in 2016)	19.6	32.3	15.4	24.6
ICR	N/A	0.4	17.4	4.4	2.0
EV: EBITDA	N/A	9.6	4.1	14.8	13.7
Debt: Capital	84.5	41.4	41.3	31.7	28.0
Debt: EBITDA Multiple	N/A	2.3	1.7	4.7	3.8
Quick ratio	0.3	1.5			

( ) = negative; EBITDA = earnings before interest, tax, depreciation, and amortization; EV = enterprise value; ICR = interest coverage ratio; N/A = not available; ROA = return on assets; ROE = return on equity.
[a] Damodaran Online. Emerging Market Multiples, Operating Markets, Return on Equity and Capital Structure. http://pages.stern.nyu.edu/~adamodar/New_Home_Page/datacurrent.html.
Sources: Azercosmos. Financial Statements. Baku (Years: 2012–2016); Azerpost 2016 Financial Statement.

Azerpost performs poorly relative to its international peers and emerging market benchmarks but it is essentially breaking even. Similarly, Azercosmos has been performing below benchmarks and incurring operating losses, but it has improved greatly from 2014 to 2016, with its EBITDA (operating margin) improving from –34% in 2014 to 0.4% in 2016.

6.4.9 Agricultural Finance Sector

The Strategic Roadmaps for National Economy identifies agriculture as a priority sector for future development. According to the State Statistical Committee's Statistical Yearbook (2017), 36.7% of employment in the country was generated within the sector, and tertiary specializations within this area have been rising rapidly as a result of the need to develop qualified specialists (as productivity has been low).

Agrolizing has provided agricultural equipment to landowners through the means of leasing. The SOE was responsible for the social development of regions and had participated in numerous state-funded social programs that target the agriculture sector. Agrolizing has been underperforming relative to profitability benchmarks (ROE) and incurred financial losses between 2015 and 2017. Its net loss was AZN21 million in 2017, almost a 100% increase from its loss of AZN11 million in 2016. It has slowly deleveraged over the period of assessment to 42% debt (Table 6.11).

Table 6.11: Agrolizing Results, 2015–2017

(%)

	Agrolizing	Emerging Markets[a]
ROE	(5.4)	12.4
ROA	(2.7)	N/A
EBITDA margin	(12.4)	12.6
Enterprise Value: EBITDA	N/A	10.0
Debt: EBITDA	N/A	5.0
ICR	N/A	2.0
Debt: Capital	52 42 (2017)	N/A

( ) = negative; EBITDA = earnings before interest, tax, depreciation, and amortization; ICR = interest coverage ratio; N/A = not applicable; ROA = return on assets; ROE = return on equity.
[a] Damodaran Online. Emerging Market Multiples, Operating Markets, Return on Equity and Capital Structure. http://pages.stern.nyu.edu/~adamodar/New_Home_Page/datacurrent.html.
Source: Agrolizing 2016 Financial Statements.

Under Presidential Decree No. 413, dated 19 December 2018, the government opened the sale of machinery and cattle to farmers and to other suppliers. The decree stipulated that agricultural leasing will be financed through authorized banks, and envisaged also the gradual privatization of Agrolizing's agrotechnical extension services.

6.5 Fiscal Implications

As discussed, the policy choices constraining the management and operations of SOEs have a direct impact on the fiscal sustainability of the government, and in turn bring negative consequences for the economy.

Under the Strategic Roadmaps for National Economy, strategic targets 1 and 2 outline the need to strengthen fiscal sustainability and improve the efficiency of the public sector's role within the economy, specifically within the non-oil sector (SOCAR, Azerbaijan's major oil sector SOE accounts for roughly 34.2% of GDP). Economic diversification and performance improvements within the non-oil sector ensure fiscal sustainability of the State Oil Fund of the Republic of Azerbaijan's transfers and the government's fiscal position—linking both strategic targets 1 and 2 explicitly. Table 6.12 describes the ways in which SOE financial results impact the government's fiscal position.

Table 6.12: Government's Operating Budget, Balance Sheet, and SOE Financial Performance

Revenue	Expenditure
Dividend income from SOEs – requires profitability	Direct subsidies – underperforming SOEs require support from the government
Corporate tax revenues – currently, SOEs account for 23% of total tax revenues	Explicit government guarantees on debt – contingent liability: government must provision for explicit contingent liabilities expected to crystallize

SOE = state-owned enterprise.
Source: Author.

On the revenue side of the government's operating budget, SOE profitability can lead to increased budget revenues through corporate taxation and dividend income paid to the government. On the expenditure side, the government incurs the cost of providing budget support to public utility SOEs (such as Azersu) and subsidizing social activities. On the government's balance sheet, provisions for explicit guarantees are expensed annually; and non-guaranteed debt of systemically important SOEs can be an ultimate cost to the government as the collapse of such SOEs would not be socially affordable. Box 6.1 provides a practical example in the case of Estonia.

Box 6.1: Performance Improvement and Fiscal Position of SOEs in Estonia

Estonia was part of the former Soviet Union with a relatively high share of state participation in the capital of public and private companies, (19.0% and 0.2% of gross domestic product [GDP], respectively). The annual accounts of the state (available in Estonian on the website of the Ministry of Finance of Estonia) provide a good example of transparency by listing all companies with the participation of the central government, together with the state's share and companies' financial information. According to this list, the Estonian government was in 2014 full or majority owner of several principal infrastructure companies active in the energy sector (notably Eesti Energia and Elering), in the maritime transport sector (notably Port of Tallinn), in the railway sector (notably Estonian Railways), and in the air transportation sector (notably Estonian Air and Tallinn Airport).

The companies in state ownership have predominantly been profitable, which is reflected in the fact that dividends received by general government improved the budgetary position by 0.9% of GDP on average between 2005 and 2014, being a relatively stable source of income for the budget.

On the other hand, the national airline Estonian Air, in which the state owned 97% of shares, has experienced difficulties from 2000 onward, and the government made capital injections into the company for €17.9 million (0.1% of GDP) in 2010 and €30 million (0.2% of GDP) in 2011 to restore the stock capital of the company. These transactions were considered to have an unrequited nature, i.e., expenditure from the point of view of public finances. In addition, a debt cancellation toward Estonian Air was decided by the government in 2014, reducing general government's surplus in that year by €37 million (0.2% of GDP). The company went into liquidation in late 2015.

Estonia is a case of both SOE performance improving the budget position and the national airline becoming a significant fiscal drain.

Source: European Commission (2016).

6.5.1   Budget Support and Cross-Party Risk

The financing needs of SOEs are high, with most of them incurring financial losses and heavily financed by the government on an ad hoc ex post financing basis. Many large SOEs are highly important from social (e.g., water supply and sanitation, and power distribution), economic (e.g., Azerbaijan Railways), or strategic (e.g., SOCAR) perspectives. The government, therefore, favorably considers their financial needs and provides budget support when adverse events occur (Figure 6.9). In this context, it is important to keep in mind the two structural constraints that contribute to SOEs' financial underperformance:

tariff policies to keep services affordable, and retainment of significant labor surpluses by SOEs, making them implicit social protection and employment policy instruments. Removing these structural constraints should be a priority. This will require development of the targeted and fiscally more efficient explicit subsidy mechanisms.

Figure 6.9: Budget Support to SOEs, 2016 and 2017
(% of budget expenditure)

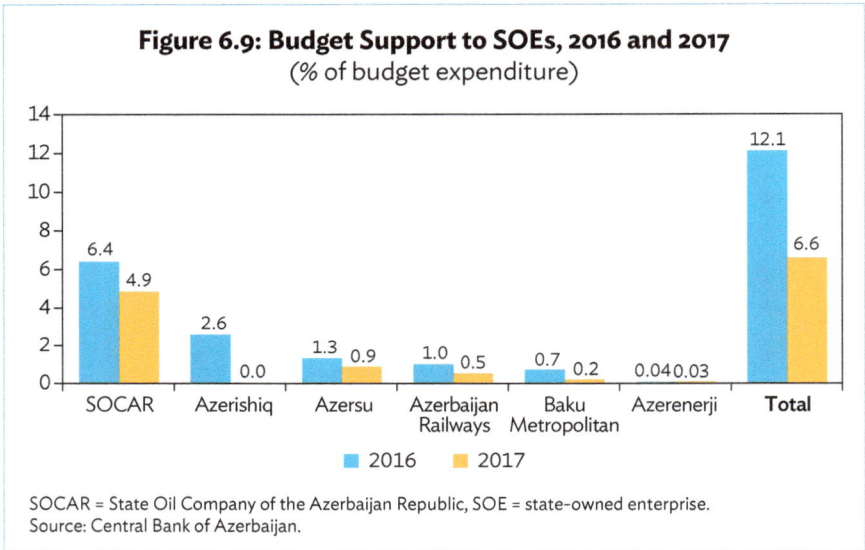

SOCAR = State Oil Company of the Azerbaijan Republic, SOE = state-owned enterprise.
Source: Central Bank of Azerbaijan.

In addition to providing direct budget support, the government in 2009 amended the Central Bank Law by allowing SOEs to finance debt from the Central Bank with a government guarantee as a way of stimulating the economy after the global financial crisis.[7] Specifically, the law allowed SOEs to obtain a guarantee from the Ministry of Finance (MOF) to borrow funds from domestic banks, which were receiving onlent financing from the Central Bank (more than $1.1 billion was provided to the International Bank of Azerbaijan [IBAR] from 2009 to 2010) (IMF 2010). However, the poor financial performance of many SOEs made them incapable of making repayments (Azeraliminium, Azerenerji, and AZAL), resulting in the government covering the costs of the Central Bank.[8] In April 2017, the 2009 amendment to the Central Bank Law was revoked.

---

[7]   Subsection 49.1 was added to the Central Bank Law, 19 June 2009 (in Azerbaijani).

[8]   http://sai.gov.az/upload/files/REY_ICRA-2015.pdf

The reliance of major SOEs on budget support and excessive debt is exacerbated by the many activities of SOEs with related parties. For example, SOCAR is the sole supplier of gas to Azerenerji for electricity production.

6.5.2   Fiscal Risk of SOE Underperformance

We measure the risk currently arising from the SOEs (based on the assessment period referenced respectively within earlier subsections) through an assessment of the factors in Table 6.13, before evaluating the overall risk of the SOE sector. These risks arise from several factors, including the following:

- Dependence of the sector on budget support—How would the sector perform without government support?

- Degree of guaranteed debt—What explicit level of debt is the government required to cover in the event of a default?

- Foreign exchange exposure—How exposed is the sector to exchange rate fluctuations?

- Financial performance—Is the sector profitable?

- Debt serviceability—Are operating cash flows sufficient to cover interest repayments?

6.5.3   Risk of SOE Underperformance to State-Owned Finance Sector

As the government is a majority owner in Azerturk Bank and IBAR, loan defaults would reduce the banks' assets and consequently the government's equity position. The Central Bank of Azerbaijan has reported that 81% of loans in Azerbaijan are from state-owned banks, implying that SOEs such as IBAR and Azer-Turk Bank dominate the sector; and SOEs hold 16% of all loans within the financial system.

In addition, the power, water, air transport, and rail sectors are particularly risky for state banks given their financial underperformance. Aqrarkredit's $3.3 billion debt should be included as a fiscal risk to the government. Although the former toxic assets of IBAR were transferred to Aqrarkredit, IBAR still has an exposure to the debt, as it is currently an equity holder in Aqrarkredit. Thus, even though the special purpose vehicle is off balance sheet for the government, if the debts cannot be reclaimed the government will incur this loss through a devaluation of IBAR's assets.

Table 6.13: Fiscal Risk Assessment from SOE Sectors

Sector	Guaranteed Debt Obligations and Liabilities to GDP (% of GDP, 2016)	Foreign Exchange Exposure	Financial Performance	Debt Serviceability
Oil and gas	58.42	High exposure to foreign exchange in short-term positions	Low risk (positive operating returns)	Low risk due to high operating cash flows in relation to service debt
Government financial institutions	23.23	High exposure to foreign exchange, but trend is declining	Moderate risk (positive operating returns)	Moderate risk
Transport	10.52	High exposure to foreign exchange (Azerbaijan Railways)	High risk (financial losses)	High risk
Air transport	3.94	Low exposure (exposure of 5% or less)	High risk	High risk
Ports and shipping	0.16	Low exposure	Low risk	Low risk
Communications	1.31	Low exposure	Moderate risk (operating losses of Azercosmos, breakeven of Azerpost)	Low risk
Power	6.38	Moderate exposure	Moderate risk (Azerenerji operational losses, Azerishiq breakeven)	Moderate risk
Water	1.61	Low exposure	High risk (Azersu financial losses)	High risk
Others	0.65	Low exposure	Low risk	Low risk

GDP = gross domestic product, SOE = state-owned enterprise.
Source: Author.

6.5.4   SOEs and Productivity Improvement

Inadequate fiscal support to SOEs has led to mismanagement and operational inefficiencies and adversely affected the size and quality of SOE services and contribution to the economy. There can be potential output losses because of the underperformance of the largest SOEs that are dominant in the provision of public infrastructure and infrastructure services. This is because improving power, transport, communication, and water supply and sanitation infrastructure spurs economic output. The direct effect of improved infrastructure is raising the productivity of land, labor, and other physical capital.

Improved productivity of SOEs could produce the following effects within the economy of Azerbaijan:

- Improved non-oil sector and economic diversification would improve the balance of payments. The major non-oil sectors will contribute a greater share of GDP and employment, reducing reliance on SOCAR (in terms of infrastructure delivery and employment) or the State Oil Fund of the Republic of Azerbaijan (in terms of transfers to the state budget).

- Increased demand for domestic credit. As economic activity improves, the demand for domestic financing will rise with investment.

- Increased investment. State support to struggling SOEs crowds out more growth-enhancing investment.

On the fiscal side, improved SOE productivity brings about additional benefits:

- Improved budget position. Increased corporate tax revenues and a broader tax base will reduce the budget deficit.

- Reduced need to provision for guaranteed debt. SOEs will require less secured debt from the government and the probability of default falls.

6.6   Reforms to Improve SOE Performance

The challenges of SOEs in Azerbaijan are not unrelated to SOE governance. The Organisation for Economic Co-operation and Development (OECD) Guidelines on Corporate Governance of State-Owned Enterprises (OECD 2015) are one standard against which SOE corporate governance could be assessed. The guidelines are widely used as an international benchmark to help governments align the management and regulation of their SOEs with standards used in the private sector. The guidelines take into consideration the special nature of SOEs as instruments of public and social policy. But they also emphasize that SOEs should operate in an environment that closely resembles the private sector. The OECD guidelines cover (i) legal and regulatory frameworks, (ii) the state acting as an owner, (iii) the equitable treatment of shareholders, (iv) relations with stakeholders, (v) transparency and disclosure of company information, and (vi) the responsibilities of SOE boards.

6.6.1   Azerbaijan SOEs and OECD Guidelines

Review of the legal framework and practices against the OECD Guidelines suggests that SOEs in Azerbaijan widely miss to meet the expectation of the guidelines. Even where legislation is available, the practice has shortcomings:

- The legislation does not clearly establish reasons for establishing SOEs and the objectives of such enterprises.

- A comprehensive, publicly available national SOE ownership policy is lacking.

- A centralized system of accountability of SOE performance is missing.

- The disclosure of information, performance monitoring, and financial oversight architecture require improvement. Monitoring of SOE financial and nonfinancial activity is largely fragmented.

- Insufficient and inconsistent publicly available information on SOE financial health, corporate governance, board composition, objectives, and other performance-related matters.

- There are no transparent rules for the nomination, appointment, remuneration, and dismissal of board members. There seems to be little board autonomy coupled with a lack of public information on board composition and qualifications.

The government has been taking steps to improve SOE governance to comply with OECD guidelines through implementation of reforms.

In 2016, the President decreed the Order to Promote Efficiency of Legal Entities with Controlling Shares in State Ownership.[9] Specifically, the order required improvements in corporate governance standards, establishment of supervisory boards and remuneration agreements, and rules for efficiency monitoring and performance assessments of SOEs. In addition, the Center for Analysis and Communication of Economic Reforms monitors the implementation of the SOE reforms embedded in the Strategic Roadmaps for National Economy and core sectors. In 2017, reform progress related to SOEs is illustrated within national targets 2.1 and 2.2 in Figure 6.10.[10]

---

[9] President of the Republic of Azerbaijan. Order No. 1.1.1–1.1.3 on Additional Measures to Promote Efficiency of the Work of the Legal Persons with Share Control Package in State Ownership. 5 September 2016.

[10] Center for Analysis and Communication on Economic Reforms. National Strategic Road Map Progress Update, 2018. https://azertag.az/store/files/2018/IYUL/Milli%20iqtisadiyyat_hesabat_.pdf (in Azeri).

Figure 6.10: 2017 Implementation Progress against National Road Map Targets, 2018

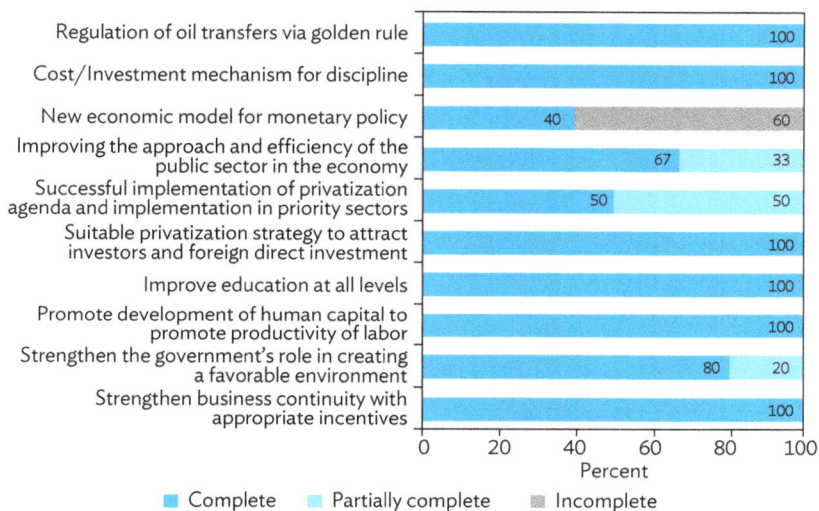

Source: Center for Analysis and Communication on Economic Reforms. National Strategic Road Map Progress Update, 2018.

Measures to improve the regulatory and legal framework for SOEs were established by the State Property Committee and the Ministry of Economy, and measures to improve the legal framework and management practices of businesses were developed (such as draft governance standards). In June 2019, a new set of SOE corporate governance standards was approved for application to all SOEs in Azerbaijan.

Between 1995 and 1999, several laws were adopted such as the Law on Privatization, Law on Insolvency and Bankruptcy, and Law on Transformation of State Enterprises into Joint Companies. In 2000, a law on the Debt of Privatized State Enterprises was implemented, but the extent of this law's application is not clear. The Insolvency Law is seldom used in practice, and the Privatization Law has been revised in 2000 and in 2007.

A special committee was established to monitor the revenue and expenditure of the largest 11 SOEs under Resolution 534 dated December 2016.[11] Details on reporting obligations were specified by the Law on Accounting (requiring

---

[11] Resolution of the Cabinet of Ministers of the Azerbaijan Republic No. 534 dated 30 December 2016 on the Estimates and Expenditures of Large State-Owned Enterprises.

International Financial Reporting Standards) and the 2017 Law on Internal Audit, which are applicable to public interest SOEs and the largest 20 SOEs.[12]

The State Property Committee and the Ministry of Economy successfully developed the database of SOEs, evaluated proposals to improve the regulatory and legal framework, and classified assets in priority sectors (SOEs) for privatization. Of the 40 SOEs identified as suitable for privatization, 11 out of 13 within the annual 2017 pipeline were privatized. In 2018, the government introduced significant restrictions on loans and state guarantees to SOEs and government financial institutions. It also strengthened institutional arrangements and business processes for appraisal and approval of such loans and guarantees.[13]

6.6.2 Assessments by the International Finance Corporation and European Bank for Reconstruction and Development

The International Finance Corporation (IFC) and the European Bank for Reconstruction and Development (EBRD) have conducted assessments of Azerbaijan's overall governance standards. The IFC study showed that the companies failed to follow corporate governance best practices, but also did not always comply with Azerbaijani legal requirements. For example, major shareholders participated in management of companies in 34% of the companies surveyed, even though the Civil Code prohibits this.[14] In some companies, management was involved in election and dismissal of supervisory board members and chairpersons, even though this practice violates Azerbaijani legislation.

The EBRD noted that the institutional environment promoting corporate governance in Azerbaijan should be strengthened. Relevant authorities need to play a more active role to promote governance practices and ensure that large corporations disclose their compliance against the existing nonmandatory corporate governance standards. Existing companies or SOEs pay little attention to requests by stakeholders, and international indicators show that corruption and misuse of funds remain an issue.[15]

---

[12] Resolution of the Cabinet of Ministers of the Azerbaijan Republic No. 636 dated 1 December 2016 on Approving Action Plan to Improve Financial and Business Performance Transparency and Efficiency of Large State-Owned Enterprises.

[13] Presidential Decrees No. 424, dated 24 August 2018, and No. 410 dated 18 December 2018.

[14] The Civil Code came into force on 1 September 2000 and provides that shareholders who own 20% or more of a company's charter capital may not participate in the management of the company (Article 107-10.7) (Government of Azerbaijan 2000).

[15] EBRD. Corporate Governance Sector Assessment. https://www.ebrd.com/what-we-do/sectors/legal-reform/corporate-governance/sector-assessment.html.

The IMF noted that SOE restructuring is important to reduce demands on the public purse and improve economic efficiency. Past devaluations, sluggish growth, quasi-fiscal activity, and poor governance have weakened the financial position of most SOEs, which required increased budget support. The IMF noted that the government agreed with the importance of adjusting tariff schedules to achieve viability and prioritizing investments to replace aging capital in the electricity, gas, water, railroad, and shipping sector SOEs. The IMF recommended that commercial and noncommercial activities be separated, and a commercial performance framework enacted. This would help to accelerate privatization.

Presently, no central authority is responsible for the evaluation of performance standards of SOEs and overall financial risk oversight and enforcement of noncompliant SOEs.

6.6.3   Initiatives to Strengthen Corporate Governance

The government recognizes that corporate governance rules should be established and enforced among Azerbaijan's SOEs to (i) improve their overall performance, and (ii) attract private participation in the economy.

Sectoral action plans—the Action Plan for Increasing Transparency and Efficiency in Financial Activities of the Large State-Owned Enterprises,[16] and Presidential Order 2300 dated 5 September 2016 On Additional Measures to Increase Efficiency in the Activities of Legal Entities Whose Controlling Block of Shares Belongs to the State—all emphasize the government's desire to instill a strong corporate governance culture in SOEs and enhance their performance.

The second goal of the Strategic Roadmaps for National Economy explicitly targets reforms to transform SOEs from being a burden on state budget to being development agents. The action plan focuses on 20 SOEs, with the aim of improving their transparency and efficiency of operations, to make them more attractive for privatization. Among major measures are establishing SOE boards in the 20 largest SOEs, creating a single database of these 20 large SOEs, and improving their transparency and accountability through quality financial reporting and public disclosure. The effects of these changes are yet to be demonstrated in practice.

---

[16]   Cabinet of Ministers of the Azerbaijan Republic. Resolution No. 636s dated 1 December 2016 on Approving Action Plan to Improve Financial and Business Performance Transparency and Efficiency of Large State-Owned Enterprises. Baku.

The government has subsequently sought the assistance of the EBRD, the World Bank, and ADB to support structural reforms. One of the key directions of ADB assistance focuses on restructuring Azerbaijan's SOEs by improving legal and institutional arrangements and strengthening private sector participation in economic activities. ADB has been supporting the government in improving governance and public-sector efficiency through the Improving Governance and Public-Sector Efficiency Program. Appendix A6.2 lists some of the policy actions that are being implemented under this program.

The EBRD in turn is working with the Ministry of Economy and the State Committee on Property Issues to improve SOE corporate governance. In particular, the EBRD will assist the state committee in implementing the action plan items and drafting model corporate documents of SOEs in line with international standards and best practices.[17] This initiative is part of pre-privatization enhancement of selected SOEs.

The World Bank was involved through technical assistance for Promoting Transparency and Efficiency of SOEs in Azerbaijan, developing a technical note on corporate governance of SOEs in Azerbaijan. The note outlined international good practice, summarized current practices in Azerbaijan, and provided recommendations to improve SOE corporate governance in Azerbaijan along six corporate governance areas: (i) the rationale for state ownership; (ii) the state's role and responsibilities as an owner; (iii) the role of SOE boards; (iv) accountability and performance monitoring; (v) SOEs' financial accountability, disclosure and transparency, including audit arrangements; and (vi) financial discipline and fiscal risks stemming from SOE operations. The World Bank has also provided support to the State Committee on Property Issues in developing a unified database for large SOEs regarding their financial, personnel, and accounting records.

The Cabinet of Ministers approved decrees on performance-based remuneration for management of SOEs (applicable to joint-stock enterprises) and regulation on procedures for assessment of SOE efficiency (that defines key performance indicators [KPIs]). The formalization of performance evaluation systems is a critical element in this endeavor as it will enable respective oversight agencies (e.g., FIMSA for financial SOEs and the Ministry of Economy for nonfinancial SOEs) to respond on time when it detects serious performance weaknesses revealed through KPIs. Additionally, the Cabinet of Ministers also approved new rules for corporate governance for SOEs. Box 6.2 highlights Georgia's experience on corporate governance and provides interesting insights about managing fiscal risks.

---

[17] Republic of Azerbaijan, Action Plan for Increasing Transparency and Efficiency in Financial Activities of the Large State-Owned Enterprises, Action Plan, Item 2, Azerbaijan 2015–2016.

Box 6.2: Georgia's Experience

According to the European Bank for Reconstruction and Development's Corporate Governance Sector Assessment, companies in Georgia exhibit better compliance with the recognized corporate governance standards than their peers in Azerbaijan. Georgia scores better on 3 out of 5 governance categories: structure and functioning of the board, internal control, and stakeholders and institutions (Figure B6.2.1).

Figure B6.2.1: Corporate Governance Performance of Georgia and Azerbaijan

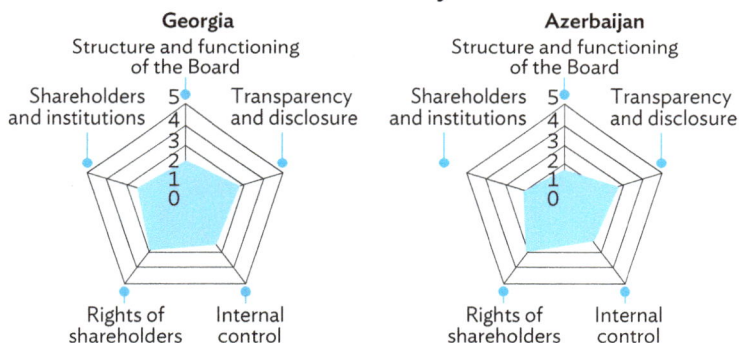

OECD = Organisation for Economic Co-operation and Development.
Note: 1 = Very Weak, 2 = Weak, 3 = Fair, 4 = Moderately Strong, 5 = Strong to Very Strong. The extremity of each axis represents an ideal score, i.e., corresponding to the standards set forth in best practices and international standards (e.g., OECD Corporate Governance Principles). The fuller the "web," the closer the corporate governance legislation and practices of the country approximate best practices.
Source: European Bank for Reconstruction and Development (2016).

These assessments do not evaluate state-owned enterprise (SOE) corporate governance specifically, yet the findings shed light on the state of corporate governance legislative advancement in the two countries as benchmarked against best practice.

Disclosure of fiscal risks in Georgia has improved substantially in the past 10 years. Since 2005, the Government of Georgia has been running programs aimed at safeguarding fiscal sustainability. The key milestone of the reform efforts has been the publication of a fiscal risk statement, beginning with the 2015 budget. The government started to disclose and analyze the fiscal risks it faces, including risks emanating from SOEs (public corporations).

The budget and the Fiscal Risk Statement disclose transfers between the government and Georgia's SOEs and include information on all direct transfers

Continued on next page

Box 6.2 continued

to SOEs (including subsidies, equity injections, and loans), as well as contingent exposures associated with non-debt guarantees (such as letters of comfort). Further, the state budget has an annex on analysis of macroeconomic risks that classifies SOEs by risk category.

Detailed information on the financial performance of most SOEs is published annually. The Fiscal Risk Statement includes aggregated summary income and balance sheet indicators for 65 SOEs—representing about three-quarters of the SOE sector. The statement also includes a detailed assessment of the financial performance of 10 major enterprises including key financial performance and risk ratios. The Ministry of Finance conducts and publishes an assessment of fiscal risks materializing from SOE activity, which involves assessing each SOE according to selected financial ratios and classifying them into different categories based on the degree of risk they pose. The Government of Georgia plans to further strengthen the fiscal management process by assessing more comprehensively all existing public–private-partnership-associated and contingent liabilities, developing a quantitative reporting of quasi-fiscal relationships, and expanding the analysis of contingent liabilities associated with SOEs.

Source: Authors.

Azerbaijan Railways Closed Joint Stock Company. The Azerbaijan Railways Closed Joint Stock Company (ADY) is exemplary among SOEs in the nonfinance sector in its pursuit of performance-enhancing restructuring to address its high debt. The Government of Azerbaijan considers the rehabilitation and recovery of the railway sector a crucial pillar of its strategy to diversify the economy. Given the strategic importance of the sector, the management of ADY has been implementing reforms since 2015. ADY management embarked on more radical reforms in management structure, business practices, and internal systems, and financial management and reporting supported by ADB's Railway Sector Development Program, whose anticipated outcome is to improve rail service delivery and financial viability of railway operations in Azerbaijan.

Among major contributing initiatives is the implementation of information technology systems to make cost accounting by service, freight traffic, operational efficiency level, procurement, and maintenance practices more transparent, and support the reform drive of ADY's senior management. ADB technical assistance for capacity development and reform support equips ADY with the capacity to undergo railway sector development reforms in management autonomy and governance, financial restructuring, reporting and control, operational efficiency, and corporate restructuring.

As ADY plans to attract the private sector to take over some of its functions (e.g., maintenance and management of infrastructure), the company is improving compliance with best-practice standards starting with the basics—financial management. The company is establishing a centralized procurement department and effective human resources management. It is restructuring the finance department, establishing proper accounting and reporting processes, consolidating financial control measures, centralizing the registry for all contracts, consolidating all bank accounts into a single-ledger bank account, and centralizing all payment-authorization responsibilities with the newly appointed chief financial officer. ADY has also introduced internal audit functions. It will start attracting independent auditors and disclosing its annual reports and statements publicly as required of it by the action plan. The experience of Lithuania's railway company, AB Lietuvos Geležinkeliai (Lithuanian Railways) can offer useful lessons to ADY in implementing structural and management changes that contribute to improved efficiency and performance (Box 6.3).

Box 6.3: Lithuania's Experience – Transformation from Inefficient to World-Class Railway Company

Political disintegration of the former Soviet Union triggered the economic collapse of Lithuanian Railways. Between 1990 and 2000, freight and passenger turnover dropped by 54% and 84%, respectively; profitability and productivity plummeted in tandem. For decades, the company lacked transparency and hid behind its social functions to justify poor performance results. However, as Lithuania was preparing to join the European Union, it embarked on reforms on all fronts, including in the railway sector.

The railway industry reforms initiated in 2000 have quickly transformed the decaying company, with dilapidated infrastructure and chronically dropping volumes. The reform process that emphasized introduction of good corporate governance principles, commercial orientation, and structural changes improved Lithuanian Railways' revenues by 93% during 2001–2009 (World Bank 2017).

Today, Lithuanian Railways is a commercialized state-owned company. Notable practices for Azerbaijan Railways (ADY) to note are as follows:

- **Well-defined purpose and objective.** Lithuanian Railways is a commercial enterprise with the principal purpose to generate added value from freight carriage by rail. Passenger transportation is a loss-generating function of the company, which Lithuanian Railways is obliged to perform on behalf of the state in the public interest. The dual objective of the company is clearly defined, and the company is compensated for the loss-generating function.

Continued on next page

Box 6.3 continued

- **Separation of accounts.** Lithuanian Railways plans to adopt a holding company structure. It will split into three separate companies: passenger transportation, freight transportation, and infrastructure management, all subsidiaries of the Lithuanian Railways which will remain 100% state-owned. This will allow the firm to operate in a more transparent and cost-effective manner.

- **Application of International Financial Reporting Standards.** The company exercises good practice in transparency and disclosure. It prepares and publicly discloses its audited financial statements according to the International Financial Reporting Standards. Reports with main financial and economic indicators are published on the company's website in four languages.

- **Investment in improved processes.** The modernization of equipment and systems, especially computerization and financial accounting, is a significant challenge to ADY given a delayed nonattendance to systems upgrades. On this front, Lithuanian Railways is more advanced as it continuously invests in developing its information technology. In 2015 alone, the company spent €4.8 million to expand the functional abilities of the financial accounting, business management, and accounting information systems.

- **Human resources.** ADY did not have a proper human resources management system in place or a performance-based system to incentivize better performance among its employees. By 2015, ADY was overstaffed and lacked qualified personnel to fill in positions in the information technology and accounting departments at the onset of its internal restructuring. While ADY acknowledges that finding talented workers with the relevant skills and innovative ideas is a problem, the pay at ADY is on average 30% less than in the transport sector. Lithuanian Railways, on the other hand, is one of the most attractive employers in Lithuania. Much attention is dedicated to the training, professional development, and requalification of its 10,000 employees. The company pays 30% more than the average salary in Lithuania. Performance-based pay helps ensure that the employees' skills and services remain relevant and of high quality.

Source: Authors.

International Bank of Azerbaijan. Since 2015, Azerbaijan's largest bank, the International Bank of Azerbaijan (IBAR), has undergone significant reform to restructure and improve performance. IBAR's key profitability metrics such as return on equity (ROE) have increased considerably over the 3-year period, with equity returns improving from –140% in 2015 to roughly 80% in 2017 (a profit of AZN800 million). Further, IBAR's financial stability has improved, with much deleveraging and improvement in the quality of capital held and reaching a common equity tier 1 ratio of 20.8% in line with international standards and implying that the bank's quality of capital is sufficient. IBAR still faces several short-term challenges, with an open current foreign-exchange position of AZN3.2 billion.

Reforms in management and governance of SOEs have resulted in several initiatives, including (i) the creation of a unified database of large state-owned companies which currently contains information on 20 large SOEs, with plans to include more; (ii) completion of improved accounting reporting in 18 of the 20 largest SOEs; (iii) the creation of the commission to oversee revenues and expenditures of large SOEs; (iv) the development of a draft regulation on SOE monitoring, which includes KPIs; (v) preparation by the Ministry of Economy of a draft regulation on performance-based remuneration system for SOE management; and (vi) adoption of Corporate Governance Guidelines and Standards for SOEs which will include procedures for efficiency assessments of SOEs.

6.7 Possible Ways Forward

It will be important to sustain the reforms initiated in 2017 to improve the financial oversight and transparency of SOEs. This could be done by adopting and effectively rolling out the SOE corporate governance rules and standards, conducting regular SOE performance monitoring and reporting, and implementing efficiency-enhancing sector-specific reforms.

Comprehensive, well-sequenced, and coordinated reforms at the macro, sector, and SOE levels will require addressing inherently complex and sensitive issues for the government, SOEs, and other stakeholders. In line with the OECD guidelines, and consistent with the initiatives already identified in existing laws and regulations but which are not enforced or complied with, we recommend a four-step approach, each step serving as a building block for the next and addressing country-specific challenges.

1.   Establish a clear ownership policy

Although the government in 2016 updated the list of SOEs to remain under state ownership, a clear ownership policy for SOEs with a fundamental division between commercial and noncommercial functions (e.g., policy, regulatory, social) should be developed. The noncommercial functions should either be vested in separate bodies to ensure that the commercial performance of

SOEs can be assessed, or if they remain the responsibility of SOEs, these non-profile activities be appropriately compensated through transparent subsidies (e.g., a "fee for service" model in which the government contracts for services) to avoid distorting commercial performance. It is also important to separate functions (e.g., policy and regulatory) that may lead to conflict of interest.

In using SOEs as instruments for social and public policy, governments compromise the commercial orientation of these enterprises by impacting their profitability and diminishing the autonomy of their decision-making. Investors are not attracted to enterprises that do not perform commercially, and market mechanisms are distorted and prevent private sector participation. It is standard procedure in several countries to review on a regular basis the rationale for each SOE's public ownership to determine whether state ownership is necessary or, alternatively, whether the SOE could be privatized. When well implemented and reviewed for relevancy on a regular basis, state ownership frameworks can positively affect competitive neutrality in the country while also optimizing the use of public resources and guiding ongoing SOE reforms.

2. Align legal and institutional frameworks with the state ownership policy

After establishing an ownership policy, all existing and proposed legislation on the one hand, and governance arrangements for SOEs on the other, should be reviewed to ensure that they reflect and are consistent with the ownership policy. In combination, the revised legislation, rules, and institutional arrangements should provide a clear governance framework for SOE performance to bring consistency and certainty in applying good corporate governance standards to SOEs and become the mechanism through which the ownership policy is implemented. This should be coupled with actions to professionalize SOE boards to strengthen the new governance and institutional framework. Government ministries or independent regulators will also be required to take on the policy and regulatory roles currently undertaken by SOEs.

The governance framework should clearly specify the roles and powers of government ministries and other bodies to direct SOEs in the delivery of services or otherwise undertake its functions. Ideally, the framework should specify outputs and not inputs in the same manner as legislation applies to the private sector. This means defining results—e.g., provision of standard potable drinking water to 95% of the population—rather than specifying how this is to be achieved. This ensures that SOE management has the autonomy to determine the most efficient way to deliver outcomes and also holds them accountable for those outcomes.

To professionalize SOE boards to lead SOEs, three complementary aspects are critical: a transparent process for the nomination, selection, evaluation, and dismissal of board members; a performance-based remuneration scheme; and legal extension of the board's powers to make independent decisions and have sufficient discretion free from government interference; the board should have sufficient autonomy to decide on its own internal governance framework. Currently, SOE boards in Azerbaijan lack decision-making autonomy, clearly established functions and responsibilities, and their expertise may not be relevant to the sector in which the SOE operates (as in the case of a politically appointed board). This is a consequence of legislative shortcoming, with no legislation governing SOE boards up to OECD standards.[18]

3.   Develop a commercial performance and monitoring framework

The government established in June 2019 an overarching commercial performance framework to govern how SOEs are to set targets to operate at more efficient levels. This framework establishes the principles around how SOEs will plan and coordinate with government to establish key short- to medium-term targets and objectives (such as a target rate of return or a credit rating); how their boards will disclose to the shareholders performance against these targets; and how the government, through the Ministry of Finance and the Commission on Large SOEs, will exercise oversight to monitor performance and disclose fiscal risk.

Currently, the role of the Commission on SOEs is focused on monitoring annual revenue and expenditure movements. This will now be complemented by the monitoring of forward projections of the SOEs' overall financial positions, including debt levels, capital structure, and dividends and no defined financial or nonfinancial targets. A process under which the commission transparently sets profitability targets for SOEs will be initiated and is to be repeated annually.

The implementation of this performance and monitoring framework with a range of overarching policies is expected to impose financial discipline on Azerbaijan's SOEs and create incentives to facilitate commercial management practices and outcomes. The framework and respective policies will clearly

---

[18] Although the Civil Code has several relevant provisions, it offers insufficient detail on the supervisory board and its function. The Corporate Governance Standards adopted in Azerbaijan in 2011 have provisions more closely aligned with the best practice; however, they are not legally binding or widely applied.

define KPIs and objectives of SOEs annually, and performance monitoring and reporting practices required from the government ministries and SOEs.

To ensure the success of the framework, government planning agencies must also use public investment management systems consistent with the commercial framework. That is, there must be an overarching sector strategy, allocation of institutional responsibility, and plan for project implementation. Before allocating projects to SOEs, the government should evaluate the economic, financial, and technical feasibility to prioritize projects. After projects have been screened for this criterion, the government should conduct analysis to identify the appropriate project structure (public–private partnership, directly budget financed, or SOE financed) to ensure the fiscal sustainability of both the government and SOEs and generate value for money.

The SOE boards must carry out regular public reporting of performance to assess individual board member and senior management remuneration. For example, in Azerbaijan, our analysis has shown that numerous SOEs have failed to disclose financial statements publicly. By contrast in Australia, disclosure requirements are a KPI and since remuneration is adjusted based on performance against these KPIs, the incentive is created to meet this target. Performance evaluation and bonuses should be justified and approved by the board of respective SOEs. Moreover, the salaries and bonuses of senior staff should be made publicly available.

4.   Prepare state assets for greater private sector participation

Privatization is a complex political and economic process. A precursor to any privatization policy that sets out principles for determining which categories of entities the government might consider for divestment is to follow the preceding three recommendations to transform SOEs into efficient commercialized entities. Once this is achieved, a comprehensive privatization policy can be developed.

There has been very slow progress toward privatization, despite its prominence in the strategic road map. To put this in perspective, consider that in 2015–2017, the revenue from privatization was only AZN124.1 million, which is more than AZN100 million short of the projected revenue from SOE sales (Table 6.14). The main source of this revenue came from the privatization of small SOEs, publicly owned facilities, rented nonresidential premises, and unfinished buildings.[19] No large SOE that could attract strategic investors has been privatized.

Table 6.14: Revenue from Privatization, 2015–2017
(AZN million)

	2015	2016	2017
A. Expected revenue from privatization	29.0	100.0	100.0
B. Actual revenue from privatization	24.1	31.2	68.8
C. Fulfillment rate (B/A)	83%	31%	69%

Source: Central Bank of Azerbaijan.

While at this time the government is not likely to privatize the strategically important SOEs such as SOCAR or Azerenerji, the privatization process of major SOEs in the finance sector, railway (some aspects), airlines, communication, agri-business, hospitality, and construction could be expedited. This would attract foreign capital and reduce fiscal burden.

The government has been preparing the finance sector for privatization. In July 2015, the government rehabilitated IBAR by transferring problematic assets to the state-owned credit organization CJSC "Aqrarkredit," which was required to enhance IBAR's privatization prospects.

The Cabinet of Ministers signed two decrees in December 2016 to support divestment initiatives: listing SOEs to be held in the public domain and those to be privatized in the medium term. Additionally, a web-based privatization portal has been established for transparency of privatization processes. The government acknowledges that it is necessary to restructure SOEs and privatize their noncore assets. Doing so will relieve the burden from the state's budget and balance sheet and allow SOEs to focus on maintaining core activities and assets. For example, Azerbaijan Railways (ADY) is planning to transfer into private hands some of its current operations, e.g., maintenance and management of rail infrastructure, which will allow the company to focus its resources on the primary services.

However, beyond privatizing small SOEs and selling off noncore activities, there are no signs that strategic investors are interested in larger assets and entities. The unattractiveness of SOEs may be the consequence of years of underinvestment; dependence on government subsidies (or on below-market-rate goods and services from other SOEs) and limited control over their own

---

[19] Republic of Azerbaijan Chamber of Accounts. Budget Reports (Years: 2015, 2016, 2017). http://sai.gov.az/1/reyler/.

financial health; weak or absent corporate governance culture; prolonged absence of commercial orientation of SOEs; and ad hoc tariff-setting practice. Attempting to privatize SOEs without first developing a privatization strategy can lead to delays, loss of value, or failure to complete transactions (so far, privatization in Azerbaijan has been conducted more on an ad hoc basis than guided strategically). Lack of a clear privatization strategy can explain why the target revenue from privatization (Table 6.14) was far from achieved.

To avoid these risks in the future, divestment strategies should include identifying which entities and assets are strategic to the needs of the sector and the national economy. State-owned assets and entities that are not strategic (those in which the state has no particular interest in how they are operated once they are divested) are easiest to deal with and the only consideration for them should be a speedy transaction involving the highest value that can be attained during divestment. Strategic assets and entities require a comprehensive approach, which should be established in an overall privatization strategy and conducted by a competent body. Privatization of SOEs should only proceed once the four recommended steps have been taken. SOEs operating within well-defined commercial frameworks and regulatory structures will reduce the risk of anticompetitive behavior with private ownership.

Appendix A6.1: Financial Metrics and Key Performance Indicators for SOE Analysis

Ratio	Calculation	Interpretation
Operating Efficiency		
EBITDA margin (%)	EBITDA divided by revenue	Measures the profitability of a business's core operations and varies by sector.
Valuation Multiple		
Enterprise Value (EV): EBITDA ratio or EV multiple (Value)	Assets minus cash divided by EBITDA

Note: the standard practice is to calculate enterprise value rather than utilizing the book value of assets. However, we use book value for a simple and consistent comparison. | Used as a valuation multiple and demonstrates the overall value of a business relative to the cash flow it generates. Used as a valuation metric and useful for peer comparisons to assess whether a business is overvalued (or undervalued) relative to peers.

Cannot be calculated with a negative EBITDA. |

Debt Sustainability and Management		
Debt: Capital (%)	Book value of liabilities divided by capital	Provides an indication of how the business is leveraged. Varies by sector, but excessive leverage and poor financial performance indicates risk.
Debt: EBITDA (Value)	Book value of debt divided by EBITDA	Indicates thebusiness's operating cash flow relative to its overall debt. A high ratio relative to peers implies a lack of cash flow and risk (EBITDA is a measure of net operating cash flows). Cannot be calculated when EBITDA is negative.
Quick ratio (Value)	Current assets divided by current liabilities	A higher ratio indicates (greater than 1 preferred) no short-term challenges in meeting liabilities.
Interest coverage ratio (Value)	EBIT divided by interest expense	Measures a business's ability to service interest obligations. A higher ratio is preferred. When EBIT is negative, the ratio cannot be calculated, but this does not mean the business cannot make interest repayments (they could be paid via cash balances).
Profitability Metrics		
Profit margin (%)	Net profit after tax divided by revenue	Measures profitability after tax and other expenses relative to revenue (varies by sector).

Continued on next page

Appendix A6.1 continued

Return on equity (before tax) (%)	Profit before taxation divided by equity	Profits received by equity holder before tax (before tax is useful when the government is the shareholder).
Asset Efficiency		
Return on assets (%)	Profit before taxation divided by asset value	Measures profitability after tax relative to the assets held (higher preferred, differs by sector).
Banking Sustainability Indicators (for financial SOEs)		
Nonperforming loans (%)	Gross value of loans nonperforming	A banking metric which measures the value of loans that are at risk.
Liquidity coverage ratio (%)	Ability of the bank to meet its short-term liquidity based on its assets and liabilities	A banking metric which measures the bank's ability to service obligations in a short-term period (Basel 3 benchmarks suggest 140%).
Common equity tier 1 (%)	Ratio of equity rated tier 1 to total bank assets	A measure of the quality of a bank's capital (Basel 3 benchmarks require a minimum of 14% tier 1).

EBITDA = earnings before interest, tax, depreciation, and amortization; SOE = state-owned enterprise.
Source: Authors.

Where ratios are blank or noted as N/A, data are unavailable, or the metric cannot be calculated due to negative operating cash flows.

Appendix A6.2: Policy Actions under the Improving Governance and Public-Sector Efficiency Program

- Legislative amendments to keep public debt and fiscal deficit to manageable levels by framing of guidelines for the borrowings of state-owned enterprises (SOEs) by imposing an upper limit.

- Comprehensive debt management strategic policy, including significant restrictions on the issuance of loans and state guarantees to SOEs.

- Complementing the guidelines for SOE borrowing (on their own risk, without state involvement or guarantee), for example by setting out clear annual borrowing limits for each SOE and specifying the approval process for SOE borrowings.

- Mandating the overall direction of SOE restructuring and privatization and approving an action plan on increasing transparency and efficiency in the management of the 20 large SOEs, including financial practices.

- Establishing a commission to monitor income and expenditure budgets of large SOEs, amending the existing rules related to SOE budget preparation and submittal to the government and increasing the monitoring of budget execution with a view to improve oversight and transparency in the large SOEs.

- Drafting and submitting for Cabinet of Ministers approval a comprehensive corporate governance standards/rules framework covering selection of directors, internal audit, accounting and financial reporting for all SOEs; in alignment with the Order of the President No. 2300 dated 5 September 2016.

- Approving a plan for implementation of international and national accounting standards to strengthen financial discipline in 20 large SOEs.

- Implementing the action item numbers 1, 5, 6, and 7 of the approved action plan for the large SOEs and submitting a report on action taken.[1]

---

[1] Item no. 1 of Action Plan: Submit proposals on transformation of large state-owned companies into the organization legal form defined by the legislation, as per institution.

Item no. 5 of Action Plan: To specify the current account payables of large state-owned companies based on the acts of reconciliation, approval of payment schedule, making payments in accordance with the schedule, and submitting the reports to the Ministry of Economy of the Republic of Azerbaijan and to the Ministry of Finance of the Republic of Azerbaijan, in this connection.

Item no. 6 of Action Plan: Formulation of a single database (finance, accounting, personnel records, etc.) in regard to large state-owned companies.

Item no. 7 of Action Plan: Making the annual financial reports and the consolidated financial reports public, together with the audit opinion, in the cases determined by law.

- Approving a complete set of standards to measure performance and monitor the financial efficiency of SOEs (introducing assessment criteria to assign ratings to SOEs and link managerial remuneration to performance of the SOEs) and approve the high-level institutional division of responsibilities for setting efficiency targets for SOEs and monitoring their financial/corporate performance (for both financial and nonfinancial SOEs).

- Establishing underpinnings of corporate governance for all SOEs (in line with, e.g., recommendations of the Network on Corporate Governance of State-Owned Enterprises in Asia [OECD 2010]) by requiring SOEs to engage certified chief accounting officers, and to be subject to more robust financial reporting practices and systems.

- The Commission annually monitors the budget of the selected SOEs and submits regular reports to the government with recommended actions.

- Approval of the Ministry of Finance of amendments to the SOE Borrowing Control Guidelines to bring them in line with the quarterly reporting requirements of the Ministry of Economy and budget preparation processes.

- Approval of (i) the Corporate Governance Standards/Rules for all SOEs (that are either joint-stock companies or limited liability companies), and (ii) rules for performance-based remuneration (bonuses).

- Approval of the institutional division of responsibilities for monitoring compliance with corporate governance rules for both financial and nonfinancial SOEs, including annual self-reporting requirements for SOEs.

- Approval of the amendments to the law on accounting to bring it in line with the International Financial Reporting Standards, and submission of a compliance report on the implementation of international accounting standards in at least 20 large SOEs.

Bibliography

Asian Development Bank (ADB). 2018. Study on State-Owned Reforms in the Asia Pacific Region. Fact-Finding Mission on Study on Azerbaijan State Owned Enterprise Reform. Aide-Mémoire. 16–20 April (internal).

Agrolizing. 2017. Financial Statement 2016. Baku.

ADB. 2019. ADB's New 5-Year Country Strategy Promotes Diversified and Inclusive Growth in Azerbaijan. News Release. Manila. https://www.adb.org/news/adbs-new-5-year-country-strategy-promotes-diversified-and-inclusive-growth-azerbaijan.

Azerbaijan Airlines. 2015. Financial Statement 2014. Baku.

_____. 2017. Financial Statement 2016. Baku.

Azerbaijan Caspian Shipping. 2015. Financial Statement 2014. Baku.

_____. 2017. Financial Statement 2016. Baku.

Azerbaijan Railways. 2015. Financial Statement 2014. Baku.

_____. 2017. Financial Statement 2016. Baku.

Azercosmos. 2013. Financial Statement 2012. Baku.

_____. 2015. Financial Statement 2014. Baku.

_____. 2017. Financial Statement 2016. Baku.

Azerenerji. 2011. Financial Statement 2011. Baku.

_____. 2013. Financial Statement 2012. Baku.

_____. 2015. Financial Statement 2014. Baku.

_____. 2017. Financial Statement 2016. Baku.

Azerishiq. 2013. Financial Statement 2012. Baku.

_____. 2015. Financial Statement 2014. Baku.

_____. 2017. Financial Statement 2016. Baku.

Azerpost. 2017. Financial Statement 2016. Baku.

Azersu. 2013. Financial Statement 2012. Baku.

_____. 2015. Financial Statement 2014. Baku.

_____. 2017. Financial Statement 2016. Baku.

Azer-Turk Bank. 2013. Financial Statement 2012. Baku.

_____. 2015. Financial Statement 2014. Baku.

_____. 2017. Financial Statement 2016. Baku.

Baku Metropolitan. 2013. Financial Statement 2012. Baku.

———. 2015. Financial Statement 2014. Baku.

———. 2017. Financial Statement 2016. Baku.

Center for Economic and Social Development (CESD). 2018. The Economy of Azerbaijan in 2017- Brief Overview. Baku: CESD Press. http://cesd. az/new/wp-content/uploads/2018/01/CESD_Research_Paper_ Azerbaijan_Economy_2017.pdf

Central Bank of the Republic of Azerbaijan. 2018. Statistical Bulletin. 2 (215). February. Baku.

European Bank for Reconstruction and Development. 2016. Corporate Governance in Transition Economies: Azerbaijan Country Report. May.

European Commission. 2016. State-Owned Enterprises in the EU: Lessons Learnt and Ways Forward in a Post-Crisis Context. Institutional Paper 31. Brussels.

Government of Azerbaijan. 2000. The Civil Code of the Azerbaijan Republic. Baku.

Hashimova, K. and Z. Kadyrov. 2017. The Current Situation and Problems of State-Owned Enterprises in Azerbaijan. Baku: Center for Economic & Social Development. http://cesd.az/new/wp-content/ uploads/2017/12/State-Owned-Enterprises-Azerbaijan.pdf.

Independent Evaluation Department . 2018. *Thematic Evaluation Study: State-Owned Enterprise Engagement and Reform*. Manila: ADB.

International Bank of Azerbaijan (IBAR). 2011. Financial Statement 2011. Baku.

———. 2013. Financial Statement 2012. Baku.

———. 2015. Financial Statement 2014. Baku.

———. 2017. Financial Statement 2016. Baku.

International Finance Corporation (IFC) and the State Secretariat for Economic Affairs. 2005. Company Corporate Governance in Azerbaijan: Survey Results 2005. Baku.

International Monetary Fund (IMF). 2010. Republic of Azerbaijan: 2010 Article IV Consultation—Staff Report; Public Information Notice on the Executive Board Discussion; and Statement by the Executive Director for Azerbaijan. IMF Country Report. No. 10/113. Washington, DC. https://www.imf.org/external/pubs/ft/scr/2010/cr10113.pdf.

———. 2019. Republic of Azerbaijan: 2019 Article IV Consultation—Press Release; Staff Report; and Statement by the Executive Director for Azerbaijan. IMF Country Report. No. 19/301. Washington, DC. https:// www.imf.org/~/media/Files/Publications/CR/2019/1AZEEA2019001. ashx.

News.Az. 2017. Azerenerji to Attract AZN 360 to Pay Tax Due. 4 May. https://news.az/articles/economy/121395.

Organisation for Economic Co-operation and Development (OECD). 2005. *OECD Guidelines on Corporate Governance of State-Owned Enterprises.* Paris.

_____. 2010. Policy Brief on Corporate Governance of State-Owned Enterprises in Asia. Paris.

_____. 2015. *Guidelines on Corporate Governance of State-Owned Enterprises, 2015 Edition.* Paris.

President of the Republic of Azerbaijan and Ministry of Economy. 2016. *Strategic Road Map for the Prospects of the National Economy of the Republic of Azerbaijan.* Baku.

Reuters. 2016. Azerenerji Owes SOCAR $350 Million. https://af.reuters.com/article/africaTech/idAFFit982648.

State Oil Company of the Azerbaijan Republic (SOCAR). 2011. Financial Statement 2011. Baku.

_____. 2013. Financial Statement 2012. Baku.

_____. 2015. Financial Statement 2014. Baku.

_____. 2017. Financial Statement 2016. Baku.

State Statistical Committee of the Republic of Azerbaijan. 2017a. Azerbaijan Fact of Facts 2017. Baku.

_____. 2017b. Azerbaijan in Figures: GDP Contribution by Sector. Baku.

_____. 2017c. Azerbaijan in Figures: Tax Contribution from Oil and Gas and Others. Baku.

_____. 2018. Azerbaijan in Figures 2018. Baku.

Taghizadeh-Hesary, F., N. Yoshino, C. J. Kim, and A. Mortha. 2019. A Comprehensive Evaluation Framework on the Economic Performance of State-Owned Enterprises. *ADBI Working Paper.* No. 949. Tokyo: ADB Institute.

World Bank. 2016a. *Strategic Road Map for the Development of the Oil and Gas Industry of the Republic of Azerbaijan.* Baku.

_____. 2016b. *Strategic Road Map for the Development of Logistics and Trade in the Republic of Azerbaijan.* Baku.

_____. 2016c. *Strategic Road Map for the Development of Financial Services in the Republic of Azerbaijan.* Baku.

_____. 2016d. *Strategic Road Map for the Development of Utilities (Electricity and Thermal Energy, Water and Gas Supply) in the Republic of Azerbaijan.* Baku.

_____. 2017a. *Railway Reform: Toolkit for Improving Rail Sector Performance.* pp. 445–452. Washington, DC. http://documents.worldbank.org/ curated/en/529921469672181559/Railway-reform-Toolkit-for- improving-rail-sector-performance.

_____. 2017b. Republic of Azerbaijan: Corporate Governance and Ownership of State-Owned Enterprises. Technical Note. November Washington, DC. http://documents.worldbank.org/curated/ en/741211532553730650/pdf/AUS 0000257-Ajarb-PUBLIC-2018- JUNE-AZE-Final-Technical-Note-AZ-SOEs-FINAL.pdf.

World Economic Forum. 2016. *The Global Competitiveness Report 2016–2017.* Geneva. http://www3.weforum.org/docs/GCR2016- 2017/05FullReport/ TheGlobalCompetitivenessReport2016-2017_ FINAL.pdf.

CHAPTER 7

State-Owned Enterprises in Viet Nam

Alexander Ewart*

7.1   Introduction

Viet Nam has made substantial advances since the reunification of the North and South in 1975. Economic growth has broadly been inclusive with significant reduction in poverty and improvements in access and quality of services. Viet Nam reached middle-income status in 2009 and the country is now ranked 48th out of 157 countries in terms of human capital index, second in the Association of Southeast Asian Nations (ASEAN) behind Singapore.

In the decade following independence, Viet Nam's economic reform commenced with the introduction of the "Doi Moi" policy in 1986, which introduced the concept of a socialist-oriented market economy supporting different ownership categories, promoting exports, and actively engaging in attracting foreign direct investment (FDI).

Viet Nam's economic growth has been impressive with an average gross domestic product (GDP) growth rate of approximately 7% between 1991 and 2016. The country has been transformed from one of the poorest in Southeast Asia to lower-middle-income status (World Bank 2013).

Viet Nam became a full member of ASEAN in 1995 and subsequently participated in the ASEAN Free Trade Agreement in 1997. It joined the World Trade Organization in 2007; signed the EU–Viet Nam Free Trade Agreement in June 2019, which will be presented to the National Assembly for ratification, and has joined the Comprehensive and Progressive Agreement for Trans-

* The completion of this chapter was enhanced considerably by the support and assistance of Vu Van Tuan. His appreciation of the nuances in official communications and his ability to obtain hard to find data was a valuable contribution to the overall development process.

Pacific Partnership in January 2019. It is now considered to be one of the most open economies in Asia.

Viet Nam's accession to the World Trade Organization in January 2007 boosted FDI inflow. By July 2018, there were a total of 26,214 FDI projects with a total registered capital of $333.03 billion and disbursed capital of $182.22 billion from investors from 129 countries, according to the Foreign Investment Agency.[1]

Despite opening domestic manufacturing and production to the private sector and the successful wooing of international investors, the government has consistently viewed state-owned enterprises (SOEs) as the primary focus of production in Viet Nam. Under the planned economy instituted after reunification in 1975, SOEs proliferated across the country with more than 12,000 SOEs in existence by 1986. The role of SOEs has changed over time: local and national companies acting as the foundation for industrial and economic development; being the conduit for much-needed foreign currency; supporting Viet Nam's regional and international expansion; and, in some cases, being true global players with multiple international investments.

Key industry sectors include

- coal, oil, and gas;
- rice, coffee, and rubber;
- food processing and fish processing;
- textiles and garments; and
- electronics and mobile telephony.

SOEs continue to be the main players in each sector with the exception of electronics and mobile telephony.

Access to foreign investment, international markets, as well as the international development community, has supported the transition from a primarily agricultural economy to a more dynamic and productive manufacturing and service economy.

However, having attained lower-middle-income status, being a low-cost labor center with a constantly increasing labor market supplying the manufacturing

---

[1]   Ministry of Planning and Investment of the Socialist Republic of Vietnam. Foreign Investment Agency. http://www.mpi.gov.vn/en/Pages/tinbai.aspx?idTin=40423&idcm=122.

sector, is neither sustainable nor conducive to creating the additional added value required to support further growth and development.

While growth has been steady and impressive, Viet Nam is now facing a more challenging future due to rising public debt, constraints in the financial market because of significant levels of nonperforming loans and burgeoning SOE debt, and the underperformance of SOEs.

The reform of SOEs is one of the five targets of the plan for economic restructuring from 2016 to 2020 (Government of Viet Nam 2016):

1. Developing the domestic private sector and continuing to attract FDI;

2. Restructuring of the state sector: restructuring SOEs, public investment, the state budget, and the public services sector;

3. Restructuring the financial market with the emphasis on restructuring credit institutions and the securities market;

4. Modernizing the planning of economic sectors and regions toward improving productivity, quality, and efficiency in connection with promoting international economic integration; and

5. Restructuring major factor markets, including the land use rights market, labor market, and science and technology market.

7.2   Definitions

The definition of SOEs and aspects of SOE reform differs among countries. The key definitions applicable to Viet Nam are as follows:

State-Owned Enterprise (Government Definition)

The Law on Enterprises (2014), implemented with effect from 1 July 2015 defines an SOE as an enterprise in which the state owns 100% of the charter capital.[2]

While the government continues to report on the reform of SOEs, the numbers from 2016 onward cannot easily be directly compared with those in earlier years in which SOEs were defined as enterprises in which the state owned 50% or more of the capital or controlled more than 50% of the votes.

---

[2] Government of the Socialist Republic of Vietnam. Law No. 68/2014/QH13 on Enterprises. 26 November 2014. Ha Noi.

State-Owned Enterprise (General Statistics Office Definition)

The General Statistics Office (GSO) of Vietnam continues to define SOEs as being

- enterprises with 100% of state capital operating under the control of central or local government agencies;
- limited companies under management of central or local government; or
- joint-stock companies with domestic capital, of which the government owns more than 50% of the charter capital.

As the GSO has so far maintained its definitions, comparisons with previous GSO data are still possible.

The differing definitions and reporting make the analysis of SOE performance and contribution to the economy over time after 2015 challenging. It is also not unusual for both definitions to be used in the same analysis by different government agencies and/or ministries.

State-Owned Enterprise Reform

In Viet Nam, SOE reform relates to

- the reform of the regulatory and legislative environment in which SOEs and equitized SOEs operate;
- the reform and restructuring of the mechanisms of SOE oversight, reporting and monitoring, and evaluation;
- the reform of enterprises from one legal form to another legal form;
- the restructuring of individual SOEs to improve efficiencies, effectiveness, performance, finances, internal structures, etc.;
- the change in ownership of individual enterprises—transfer, sale, merger, and equitization; and
- the closure of individual enterprises through closing down or bankruptcy.

Equitization

Equitization is the Government of Viet Nam's preferred form of reform for SOEs. Equitization (and the process of equitization) is currently defined within

Decree No. 126/2017/ND-CP of 16 November 2017.[3] The key points to note are as follows:

1. Equitization refers to the conversion of 100% SOEs to joint-stock companies through

    a)   issuing additional shares in order to increase charter capital while keeping current state capital unchanged;

    b)   selling part of current state capital or both selling part of state capital and issuing additional shares to increase charter capital; or

    c)   selling the entire state capital available at the enterprise or both selling the entire state capital and issuing additional shares to increase charter capital.

2. Shares sold at an initial public auction are available to all investors whether they are organizations or individuals, domestic or foreign.

3. There are defined share purchase options available to the labor union of the equitized enterprise and management and employees.

4. Strategic investors—generally, an initial offering of shares to strategic investors (domestic or foreign) is only available to enterprises in which the state proposes to retain more than 50% of the shares.

Appendix A7.3 provides an expanded definition of equitization.

7.3   SOE Reform

7.3.1   Early Stages

In the early years, SOE reform proceeded very slowly. The government's preferred form of SOE reform is "equitization"—the process of converting 100% SOEs into joint-stock companies, which was launched in mid-1992, but by the end of 1997 only 17 enterprises had been equitized. By the start of this century there were still more than 6,000 SOEs. In the mid-1990s, the government organized a number of SOEs into 17 general corporations (GCs) reporting to the Prime Minister (GC 91s) and 77 special GCs under line

---

[3]   Government of Viet Nam. Decree No. 126/2017/ND-CP of 16 November 2017 on conversion from state-owned enterprises and single-member limited liability companies with 100% of charter capital invested by state-owned enterprises into joint-stock companies. Ha Noi.

ministries and provincial people's committees (GC 90s). In 2002, these 94 GCs included 1,605 member SOEs, representing 28% of all SOEs, yet 65% of the capital of all SOEs (Figure 7.1).[4]

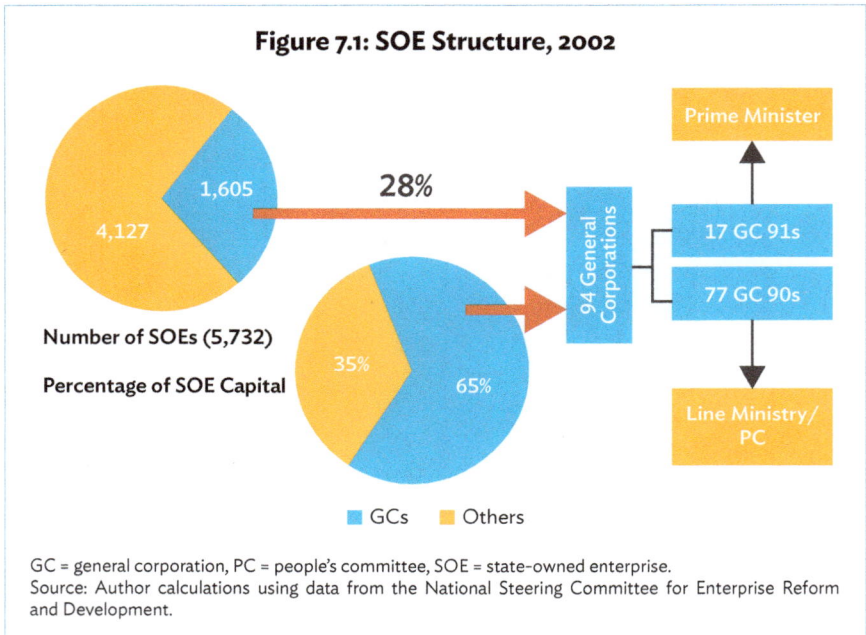

Figure 7.1: SOE Structure, 2002

Number of SOEs (5,732)

Percentage of SOE Capital

■ GCs   ■ Others

GC = general corporation, PC = people's committee, SOE = state-owned enterprise.
Source: Author calculations using data from the National Steering Committee for Enterprise Reform and Development.

The National Steering Committee for Reform and Development also reported that 64% of SOEs (3,328) were administered by local/provincial government and 36% (1,903) by central authorities (primarily line ministries).

At the same time, the government was ambitious for the role of the larger GCs and wanted to replicate the apparent success of Japan's keiretsus and the Republic of Korea's chaebols, in Viet Nam. Thus from 2005 onward, the government created state economic groups (SEGs) by grouping large SOEs and GCs that were supposed to form strong, strategically linked corporations that would be more able to compete with international companies in Viet Nam and more importantly in the regional and international arena. The SEGs were created by the government specifically to become large diversified holding companies.

---

4   National Steering Committee for Enterprise Reform and Development and Ministry of Finance Statistics. Vietnam Pilot Restructuring Project for Three General Corporations: VINATEX, VINACAFE, and SEAPRODEX. World Bank Grant No. TF050047.

Concurrently, the government recognized the importance of a capital market and developed the Ho Chi Minh Stock Exchange, primarily as a vehicle for equitized SOEs to raise capital and reduce the reliance on the state budget but also to support the development of the burgeoning private sector.[5] The Ho Chi Minh Stock Exchange was launched in 2000 and the Hanoi Stock Exchange was launched in March 2005. Figure 7.2 shows the progress of listing from 2000 to 2015.

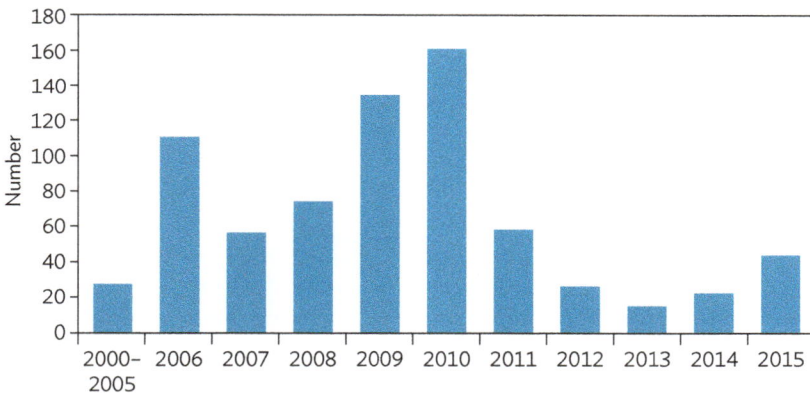

Figure 7.2: Stock Market Listings, 2000–2015

Source: Author.

Viet Nam's peak years for listing on the stock markets (2009 and 2010) were not as a result of economic or corporate strength but because of tax incentives (3 years tax free) available to companies that listed by the end of 2010.

State Economic Groups

From 2005 to 2010, 12 SEGS were established with the Prime Minister's approval. Some SEGs—Viet Nam Industry and Construction Group, Viet Nam Housing and Urban Development Group, and Viet Nam Shipbuilding Industry Group—failed to fulfill their set objectives after a period of experimentation and were transformed into corporations, which left the nine SEGs in Table 7.1.

---

5   The development of IPO regulations and early support for listings was provided by ADB (2000).

Table 7.1: State Economic Groups

1. Bao Viet Financial Insurance (Bao Viet)	6. Vietnam National Chemical Group (Vinachem)
2. Vietnam Electricity Group (EVN)	7. Vietnam National Textile and Garment Corporation (VINATEX)
3. Vietnam National Coal-Mineral Industries Group (Vinacomin)	8. Vietnam Military Telecommunications Group (Viettel)
4. Vietnam National Post and Telecoms (VNPT)	9. Vietnam National Oil and Gas Group (PVN)
5. Vietnam Rubber Group (VRG)	

Source: Author.

Four of these SEGs are still among the largest five companies in Viet Nam by revenue (see Table 7.6).

The weaknesses of SEGs were eventually highlighted by their inability to create more value together than they did separately, a massive expansion into noncore activities outside the core competencies, weak management centrally, and poor oversight of the many subsidiaries and affiliated companies (World Bank 2012). This resulted in a number of criticisms of the way SOEs in general were being managed and operated, including the Economic Forum of the National Assembly recommending that it should no longer be appropriate that SOEs be considered the foundation for industrial and economic development and that restructuring of the SOE sector was to be a top priority of the government in the Socioeconomic Development Plan for 2011 to 2015 and accompanying Social Development Strategy 2011–2020.

This led to a number of decrees and decisions including Prime Minister Decision No. 929,[6] which sets out the objectives of restructuring as focusing on SEGs and state corporations to achieve a more reasonable structure that focuses on key sectors and provides essential public products, services to society, and national defense and security, and plays the core role to motivate state economy to perform its leading role as an important material force so that the state orients, regulates the economy, and stabilizes the macroeconomy and to improve competitiveness, and return on equity (ROE) for trading enterprises.

Many SEGs (and GCs) had taken advantage of weak oversight and transparency in the system, and expanded operations beyond their core competency. The government then followed Prime Minister Decision No. 929 with a decree

---

[6] The Socialist Republic of Vietnam. Prime Minister's Decision No. 929/QD-TTg dated 17 July 2012 on approval of the scheme on restructuring of state-owned enterprises, focusing on economic groups and state-owned corporations in period 2011–2015. Ha Noi.

for restructuring of SEGs that commit all SEGs to divest from five "high-risk" noncore activities (banking, insurance, real estate, securities trading, and investment funds) by 2015 thereby helping to reduce risks, including potential fiscal bailout arising from unregulated activities and poor transparency.[7]

Decision No. 929 and Decree No. 71 can be seen as responses to lessons learned from the very public $4 billion scandal of Vinashin. Weak oversight, "self-assessment" in reporting to the government, poor transparency, and significant expansion into noncore areas of no competence and wanton mismanagement of state capital resulted in the collapse of a major SOE and imprisonment (and, for some, the death sentence) for the leadership of the enterprise.

These changes to the regulatory and legislative environment created a new sense of urgency into the SOE reform agenda. By 2015, additional reform legislation had been approved and introduced, including the Law on Enterprise (2014), the Law on Investment and Management of State Capital (2014), and Prime Minister's Decision No. 37/2014/QD-TTg (2014) defining the level of state ownership by category of SOEs.

SOE Efficiency

There is evidence that SOEs tended to absorb a very large share of aggregate investment, yet their contribution to real GDP and aggregate employment has been disappointing and low relative to private enterprise and FDI (ADB 2016a). When SOEs compete with private sector companies, they do so on a favored basis receiving preferential access to capital, land, and public procurement opportunities, making it difficult for private sector competitors to invest and grow (ADB 2016a).

In 2000, the average ratio of turnover to capital (a proxy for the productivity of capital) in SOEs was 1.6 compared with 8.8 for the enterprise sector as a whole. However, by 2009 the average ratio of turnover to capital for the SOEs fell to 1.1 while it increased to 21.0 for industry. So, while the enterprise sector as a whole was getting better at using capital more economically, the SOEs were using it more extravagantly (World Bank 2012).

Although SOEs continue to account for just less than 30% of GDP and about 40% of total investment, their share of economic activity has not changed since 1990 (World Bank and MPI 2016).

---

[7] Government of Viet Nam. Decree No. 71/2013/ND-CP on investment of state capital in enterprises and financial management of enterprises of which 100% charter capital is held by the state. Ha Noi.

Figures 7.3a and 7.3b show that, although SOEs had higher fixed capital and long-term investments compared with the private sector and foreign investors (Figure 7.3a), the efficiency with which these investments generate revenue is lower as shown by its low net turnover as share of long-term assets (Figure 7.3b).

Figure 7.3a: Fixed Capital and Long-Term Investment by Entity, 2010–2016
(VND trillion)

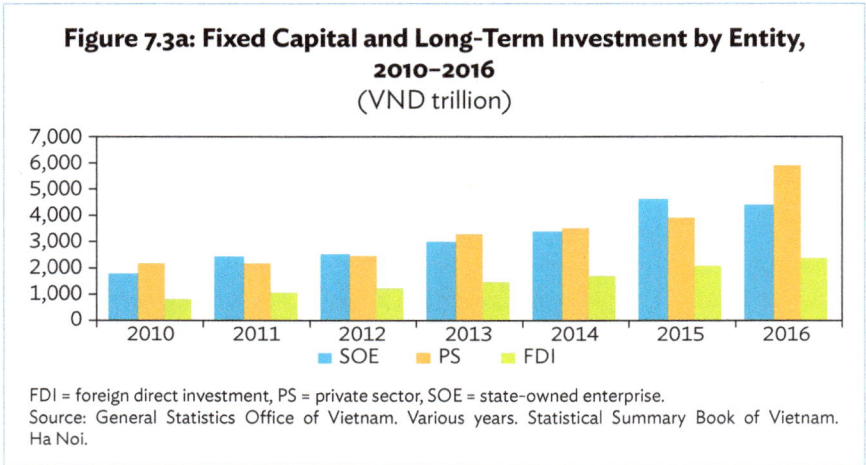

FDI = foreign direct investment, PS = private sector, SOE = state-owned enterprise.
Source: General Statistics Office of Vietnam. Various years. Statistical Summary Book of Vietnam. Ha Noi.

Figure 7.3b: Net Turnover as Percentage of Long-Term Assets, 2010–2016
(%)

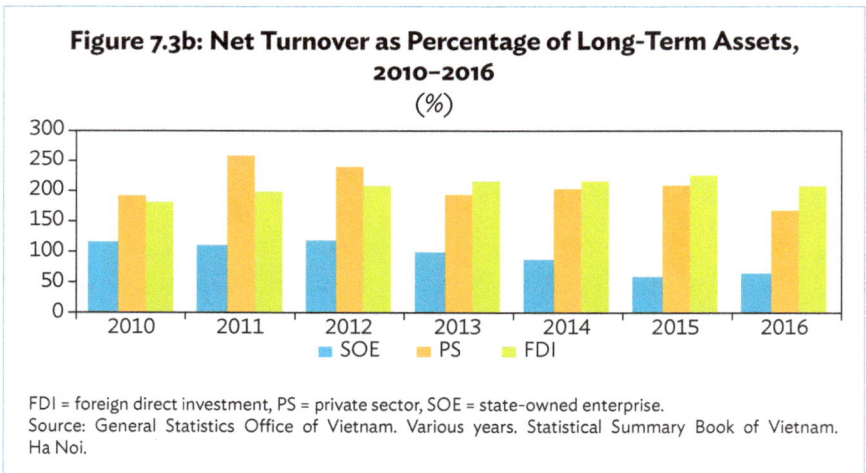

FDI = foreign direct investment, PS = private sector, SOE = state-owned enterprise.
Source: General Statistics Office of Vietnam. Various years. Statistical Summary Book of Vietnam. Ha Noi.

Although their numbers are decreasing, SOEs use up an increasing amount of scarce capital in the Viet Nam economy. However, the underperformance of these companies manifest itself in lower and declining efficiency. More importantly, SOEs produce lower (and declining) levels of output than the private sector, acting as a drag on economic growth.

Between 2000 and 2008, the turnover-to-employee ratio in SOEs increased from 0.6 to 1.7. During the same period, the turnover-to-employee ratio for the overall enterprise sector increased from 2.7 to 16.3, indicating that labor productivity between SOEs and the rest of the enterprise sector widened from 1:4 in 2000 to 1:10 in 2008 (World Bank 2012).

In 2015, the ROE of SOEs was only 2.1%, far lower than the 5.5% of foreign-invested enterprises. Investment effectiveness of SOEs was also lower than that of Viet Nam's domestic private enterprises and foreign-invested enterprises, with the incremental capital output ratio in the 2011–2016 period of SOEs being 1.6 and 1.86 times higher than those of domestic private enterprises and foreign-invested enterprises, respectively. In addition, during the 2011–2016 period, the ROE ratio of all SOEs was down by 39%, and their return on assets decreased by 30% (Vietnam Investment Review 2018).

In addition, Figure 7.4 highlights that SOEs continue to pay their employees significantly more than both the domestic private sector and the FDI sector, making it more difficult for the more efficient private and FDI sectors to attract skilled labor.

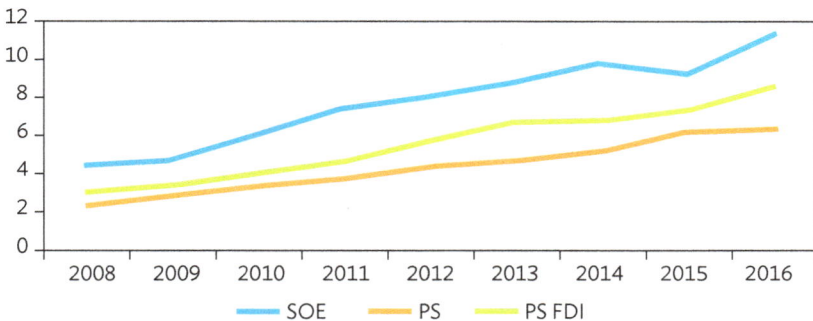

Figure 7.4: Average Salary, 2008–2016
(VND million per month)

FDI = foreign direct investment, PS = private sector, SOE = state-owned enterprise.
Source: General Statistics Office of Vietnam. Various Years. Statistical Summary Book of Vietnam. Ha Noi.

The differential between SOE wages and the private sector also appears to be increasing rather than decreasing. In 2016, SOEs were, on average, paying 178% per month more than the domestic private sector and 134% more than the FDI sector.

7.3.2   Recent Situation

Overview

Overall economic outlook in recent years appears to be optimistic as GDP growth during 2017 reached 6.81%, the highest rate since 2007. Macroeconomic stability was maintained. Inflation was kept under control. Credit growth was about 19%. State foreign exchange reserves reached the all-time high of $52 billion. International credit-rating agencies raised Viet Nam's ratings on banking activities from stable to positive. State budget revenue increased significantly. The industry and construction sectors grew 8%. The services sector grew by 7.44%. Exports touched $213.8 billion. Total import–export turnover reached nearly $425 billion, the highest level ever. Export surplus reached $2.7 billion. The total newly registered and increased capital of FDI was nearly $30 billion, up 44.2% year-on-year. Disbursed capital reached $17.5 billion, up 10.8% year-on-year, and 126,700 new enterprises were established.[8]

SOE Numbers and Data

The analysis and reporting of statistics on SOEs in Viet Nam are not straightforward. Different ministries and other sources issue contradictory numbers and a variety of other issues impact the analysis:

- When the government indicates that there are 583 SOEs, this relates to the 100% owned first-tier SOEs. However, many of these enterprises will have second- and third-tier subsidiary enterprises that are also in effect, SOEs. For example, the Vietnam Electricity (EVN) is (and for the foreseeable future will remain) a 100% SOE. But EVN has at least nine subsidiaries that are 100% owned. These enterprises are properly registered legal entities operating in the market and as their capital is 100% owned by the state, it is reasonable to consider that they too are SOEs. This situation is replicated with many SOEs to a greater or lesser degree.

- When the Ministry of Finance (MOF) reports the value of key financial indicators as the total for SOEs, e.g., equity, assets, profit, and remittance to state budget, we have assumed for the purposes of this chapter that these figures relate to the sum totals of the assets, equity, etc. for the 100% owned parent company SOE and do not include

---

[8] Based on the discussion of the delegates attending the meeting, the Cabinet members and the conclusion of the Prime Minister at the government's meeting with provinces and the government's regular meeting held on 28 and 29 December 2017. VGP News. The Government's Regular Meeting in December 2017. http://news.chinhphu.vn/Home/The-Governments-regular-meeting-in-December-2017/20181/33012.vgp.

consolidated results for the SOE and its 100% owned subsidiaries or its joint-stock company subsidiaries—i.e., it is assumed that the numbers relate to the stand-alone 100% SOEs.

Taking the above caveats into consideration, Table 7.2 provides an overview of the current situation in Viet Nam.

Table 7.2: Number of SOEs, 2011–2018

2011	2015	2016	2017	2018
1,369	806	583	562	490

SOEs = state-owned enterprises.
Note: As per the Ministry of Finance definition of state-owned enterprises being 100% owned.
Source: Ministry of Finance (2018).

At the end of 2016, there were 7 SEGs, 67 GCs, 17 one-member limited liability companies operating as holding companies, and 492 independent SOEs under line ministries and people's committees (Government of Viet Nam 2018). However, each of these companies may well have a number of 100% owned subsidiaries, making the total number of SOEs that are 100% owned by the state significantly larger.

There was a significant reduction in the number of SOEs between 2011 and 2015 as a result of equitizations, sales, mergers, and liquidations. However, the apparent reduction in the number of SOEs between 2015 and 2016 is primarily accounted for by the change in the state's definition of an SOE as highlighted above.

The report also indicates plans to reduce the number of SOEs from greater than 500 to around 150 by the end of 2020. These enterprises will primarily be lottery companies, public utility companies, and three large corporations— Vietnam National Oil and Gas Group, Vietnam Electricity Group, and the Viettel Group.

Enterprises with 100% state capital will only exist in 11 industry sectors, focusing on key sectors that provide essential products and services for society, and those of strategic importance to national defense and security.[9] The key sectors are national defense mapping services, manufacture and sale of explosives, electricity distribution, railways and railway infrastructure,

---

[9] As classified in Prime Minister of the Socialist Republic of Vietnam. Decision No. 58/2016/QD-TTg of 28 December 2016 on criteria for classification of wholly state-owned enterprises, partially state-owned enterprises and list of state-owned enterprises undergoing restructuring in 2016–2020, which replaced Prime Minister's Decision No. 37/2014/QD-TTg of 2014. Ha Noi.

air traffic and safety services, maritime safety, public post, lottery businesses, publishing, manufacture of currency and gold bullion, and credit instruments (see Appendix A7.4).

Financial Highlights

Table 7.3 summarizes the 2016 financial highlights from MOF (2018).

Table 7.3: 2016 Financial Highlights

Indicator	VND billion	$ billion
Total equity	1,398,183	62.760
Total assets	3,053,547	136.991
Total liabilities	1,628,649	72.340
Total revenue	1,515,821	68.004
Profit before tax	139,658	6.266
Total remittance	251,845	11.300

Note: The numbers above relate to the 583 state-owned enterprises that are 100% state owned.
Source: Ministry of Finance.

From Table 7.3, we can deduce the following:

The average debt ratio (liabilities/assets) at 53.34% indicates a minor propensity for borrowings to finance assets. However, this average figure hides the range of the debt ratio in the SOE sector. There are a number of larger SOEs in which the debt ratio is between 70.35% (EVN) and 101% (Vietnam Expressway Corporation), which makes them more financially vulnerable and more difficult to restructure through equitization.[10]

The total assets of enterprises that are targeted for restructuring must be revalued. It has been found that the valuation can result in a restatement of asset values of up to 100%. This has the potential to blur the debt ratio: when the asset value goes up, the debt ratio goes down and makes the company look less vulnerable than it might be.

Total remittance of enterprises to the state budget increased by 2% and according to MOF the majority of SOEs made profits.

---

[10] EVN and Vietnam Expressway Corporation. 2017 Financial Statements. Ha Noi.

Contribution to Gross Domestic Product and Employment

The SOE data relating to contribution to GDP (Table 7.4) and employment (Table 7.5) are based on General Statistics Office (GSO) data and therefore relate to enterprises in which the state has >50% of the equity or >50% of the control.

Table 7.4: Contribution to GDP, 2010–2016

	2010	2013	2014	2015	2016
No. of SOEs	3,281	3,199	3,048	2,835	2,662
GDP ($ billion)	171.22	186.21	193.24	205.28	220
SOE (%)	29.34	29.01	28.73	28.69	28.81
Collective (%)	3.99	4.03	4.04	4.01	3.92
Private (%)	6.9	7.78	7.79	7.88	8.21
Household (%)	32.07	31.71	31.5	31.33	30.43
FDI (%)	15.15	17.36	17.89	18.07	18.59

FDI = foreign direct investment, GDP = gross domestic product, SOE = state-owned enterprise.
Source: General Statistics Office of Vietnam. Various years. Statistical Summary Book of Vietnam. Ha Noi.

The major difference between private and household enterprises is one of business registration. Household businesses are not limited liability companies and cannot engage in import/export activities. They are relatively large retailers, hotels, restaurants, and many other commercial/industrial businesses as well as the more obvious small-scale café, hairdresser, print shop, etc.

The SOE share of GDP has remained relatively stable despite the government's policy of continued equitizations and the average annual GDP increase of 6.02%. This highlights that the largest companies have yet to be equitized (as at the end of 2016) and that the government's equitization targets are not being met.[11]

The table also highlights very clearly that the largest contribution to GDP continues to come from household business and that the private sector has yet to become the driving force that is expected of it. Between 2010 and 2016, FDI grew by 156.2% and the private sector by 148% when it would be expected that the private sector growth rate would be higher given its smaller starting base.

---

[11] The General Statistics Office continues to use the old definition for an SOE as being more than 50% state owned.

Table 7.5: Contribution to Employment, 2010–2016
(%)

	2010	2011	2012	2013	2014	2015	2016
Non-state	86.1	86.2	86.3	86.4	85.7	86.0	85.8
SOE	10.4	10.4	10.4	10.2	10.4	9.8	9.8
FDI	3.5	3.4	3.3	3.4	3.9	4.2	4.4

FDI = foreign direct investment, SOE = state-owned enterprise.
Source: General Statistics Office of Vietnam. Various years. Statistical Summary Book of Vietnam. Ha Noi.

Table 7.5 appears to show the relative stability and importance of employment contribution by SOEs, despite the number of equitizations. However, SOE employment statistics are not accurate in that SOEs include the employee numbers for all subsidiaries in which they own 30% or more of the equity. In theory, this means that an enterprise that is owned equally by three SOEs will have its employee numbers counted three times. The capacity for double (or triple) counting of employees among SOEs is significant.

There is an expectation that SOEs will list on the stock exchange within a short period after their initial public offering (IPO), though this is not happening at the rate the government would like. Figure 7.5 shows the number of listings on the stock exchange in 2014–2018. By the end of March 2019, 756 companies were listed on the Hanoi Stock Exchange and the Ho Chi Minh Stock Exchange.

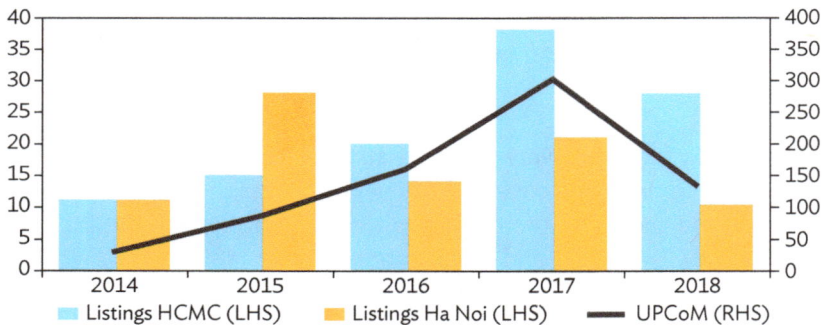

Figure 7.5: Listings on the Hanoi Stock Exchange and the Ho Chi Minh Stock Exchange, 2014–2018
(Number)

HCMC = Ho Chi Minh City, LHS = left-hand scale, RHS = right-hand scale, UPCoM = Unlisted Public Company Market.
Source: Author.

In addition, 811 companies were registered on the Unlisted Public Company Market (UPCoM) on the Hanoi Stock Exchange. It is the UPCoM that has become the more popular vehicle for initially registering recently equitized SOEs. The market capitalization of the Hanoi Stock Exchange at the end of May 2018 was $7.1 billion while the Ho Chi Minh Stock Exchange had a market capitalization of $71.8 billion.[12]

The merger of the two stock exchanges has been proposed since 2011. A merger plan was presented to the Prime Minister in 2018 in which the merger would be completed by 2020.

SOE Size and Importance

The Viet Nam Report in conjunction with Viet NamNet publishes an annual ranking of Vietnamese companies (using similar metrics to the Forbes 500 report) each year. Table 7.6 shows the rankings for 2018 (Viet NamNet 2018).

Table 7.6: VNR500 Top-10 Companies, 2018

No.	Company	State Share (%)
1	Samsung Electronics Vietnam	0
2	Vietnam Electricity (EVN)	100
3	Vietnam National Oil and Gas Group (PVN)	100
4	Viettel Group	100
5	Vietnam National Petroleum Group	76
6	Vingroup Corporation	0
7	Vietnam Bank for Agriculture and Rural Development (VBARD)	100
8	Bank for Investment and Development of Vietnam (BIDV)	100
9	Honda Vietnam Company	0
10	Vietnam Airlines Joint Stock Company	86

Source: Author.

While Samsung has been the largest company for 3 years, 2018 marked the first time three private companies appeared in the top 10 and the first time that a Vietnamese private company (Vingroup) appeared in the top 10. Despite the inclusion of private sector companies, the table highlights the continued dominance of SOEs in the economy. However, while the ranking is based on size it is not indicative of the relative efficiency of performance of these companies.

---

[12] Hanoi Stock Exchange. https://hnx.vn/en-gb/hnx.html; and Ho Chi Minh Stock Exchange. https://www.hsx.vn/.

Benefits of Equitization

The summary of results of operation of 350 post-equitization enterprises in 2015 shows that compared with the previous year, the average profit before tax increased 49%, the budget contribution increased 27%, charter capital increased 72%, total assets increased 39%, revenue increased 29%, and income per capita increased 33% (Government of Viet Nam 2018).

The consolidated results of the operations of 273 enterprises having shares and contributed capital of the state in 2016 showed that total assets increased by 7%, total equity increased by 14%, pretax profit increased by 54%, the total amount payable to the state budget increased by 24% compared with 2015, and average ROE was 18%. The average ROE of equitized companies is significantly higher than that of 100% SOEs (MOF 2018).

This analysis concurs with earlier studies undertaken by the Central Institute of Economic Management that SOEs' performance improves post equitization. Indicators, such as turnover, profit, value added, and laborers' income increased rapidly after equitization (CIEM 2002, 2005). The 2002 study also inferred that "if the entire SOE sector was reformed and grew as the equitized enterprises did, Viet Nam's growth rate could be 0.6–0.7 percentage points per year higher" (World Bank 2012); and appears to support the Government of Viet Nam's focus on equitization as the key reform tool for SOEs.

Debt

The issue of debt is fundamental to successful SOE reform. The government no longer has the capacity or the appetite to increase its debt burden. There are three forms of debt influencing SOE reform: the level of public debt, SOE debt, and nonperforming loans.

Public debt is defined by MOF as government debt, government-guaranteed debt, and local-government debt, as regulated by the current law. The Government of Viet Nam has set a ceiling of 65% in relation to the ratio of public debt to GDP. Viet Nam's economic growth rate has been increasing since 2012 (5.25%) and in 2018 GDP growth reached 7.08% while the level of GDP exceeded $240 billion.

According to MOF, Viet Nam's ratio of public debt to GDP stood at 58.4% at the end of 2018 (Figure 7.6).

Figure 7.6: Public Debt to GDP, 2013–2018
(%)

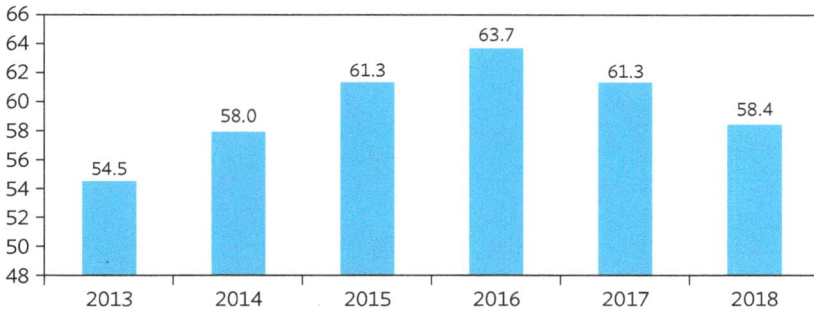

GDP = gross domestic product.
Sources: Ministry of Finance; author.

A large proportion of the public debt is as a result of foreign currency-denominated loans to SOEs (and equitized SOEs) that are guaranteed by the state. This is one of the key reasons for the government's determination to restructure the SOE sector.

SOE debt. A major constraint on transforming SOEs, SEGs, and GCs in Viet Nam has been the inherent financial weakness in many of them. These SOEs have historically relied on extensive borrowing from the government and state-owned commercial banks to finance their operations. Many of the large SEGs and GCs have very high debt, with stressed debt-to-equity ratios. This has severely constrained their ability to service their debts and contributed to the high number of nonperforming loans in the banking system.

Figure 7.7 shows that the source of SOE investments is not internal resources but is more likely to be from the state budget and borrowings from the banks. The level of SOE capacity to use internal resources as a source of investment and/or raise capital from the market is impacted by its equitization, level of continued state investment in the enterprise, and the efficiency and effectiveness of the company.

High indebtedness also implies that SEGs and GCs are ill-equipped to deal with risks and will not have the financial capacity to fund capital investments. The problem is exacerbated because much of the SOE debt is high cost and short term but used to fund long-term investments (ADB 2014).

Figure 7.7: Source of State-Owned Investments, 2001–2017
(%)

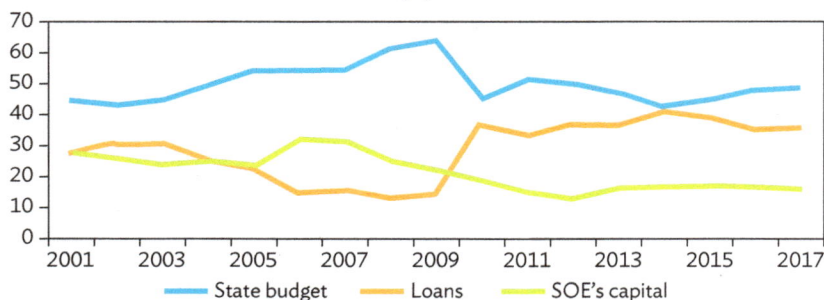

SOE = state-owned enterprise.
Source: General Statistics Office of Vietnam. Various years. Ha Noi.

Debt has a substantial impact on the performance of SOEs and their capacity to restructure and to raise capital, and because the level of debt and much of it being guaranteed by the government in foreign currencies have a very significant impact on the economy and the government's borrowing capacity.

According to the Government of Viet Nam, SOE debt is equivalent to $64.10 billion in 2015 (approximately 33% of GDP) and $66.03 billion in 2016 (approximately 32% of GDP).

It is assumed that these figures relate to 100% owned SOEs. If the debt for enterprises in which the state has 51% or more of the invested capital is included, the number will be significantly larger. Some of this SOE debt will also be included in the public debt, as it will have been guaranteed by the government.

According to the MOF, since SOEs are one-member limited liability companies, they therefore have to bear responsibility for the borrowed capital that has not been guaranteed by the state. If they cannot repay the debt, they would have to be dissolved in accordance with the law on bankruptcy. The non-guaranteed debts of SOEs are not subject to the Law on Public Debt Management.

Viet Nam has two state debt trading companies—Debt Asset Trading Company and the Vietnam Asset Management Company (VAMC). While VAMC is responsible for handling bad debts of commercial banks and financial institutions, the Debt Asset Trading Company is responsible for settlements of bad debt owed by SOEs in the pre- and post-equitization processes. By the end of 2017, the Debt Asset Trading Company managed debts worth nearly VND20.6 trillion.

Nonperforming loans have been of concern in Viet Nam for the past 15 years. In many respects, nonperforming loans (NPLs) have been fueled by the SOE sector, which has had privileged access to borrowings and the greatest access to credit. In an effort to stem the rise of NPLs, VAMC was established in 2013. VAMC swapped NPLs at cost from banks in exchange for VAMC-issued "special bonds" that provide collateral for borrowing from the central bank.

According to SBV, the ratio of reported NPLs in the banking system fell to 1.89% of total outstanding loans in December 2018, down from 3.2% at the beginning of 2015, as banks stepped up NPL resolution through debt collection and the sale of collateral. This improvement partly reflects the increasing strength of the economy and the recovery of the property market. However, the improvement is partly due to the transfer and warehousing of NPLs at VAMC. All NPLs on bank balance sheets and warehoused with the VAMC, combined with bank loans deemed at high risk of becoming NPLs in the near term, were estimated at 5.85% of all outstanding loans in 2018, down from the 10.1% in December 2016.

NPLs reduce capital resources for lending, result in lower bank profitability, lead to misallocation of capital, and drag on economic growth. In Viet Nam, it has been argued that economic growth is constrained by resource misallocation between SOEs and non-SOEs. In particular, commercial banks lend to underperforming SOEs at unnaturally low rates, thus preventing profitable non-SOEs' access to credit and suppressing economic growth via credit misallocation. While there is only limited data about NPLs for SOE lending, it is considered that the soundness of the banking sector in Viet Nam has been deteriorated by the weak SOE sector (IMF 2017).

The figures in Table 7.7 apply only to SEGs and GCs yet not all SEGs and GCs are 100% owned SOEs. The total for the whole SOE sector will be higher.

Table 7.7: Value of Nonperforming Loans in State Economic Groups and General Corporations

(million)

	2015 $	2016 $
State economic groups	850.8	714.0
General corporations	476.3	511.3
Total	**1,327.1**	**1,225.3**

Source: Ministry of Finance.

In 2017, the Government of Viet Nam issued Resolution No. 42/2017/QH14 of the National Assembly which enables assets used as collateral for NPLs to be seized and sold to settle the debt. This has resulted in a flurry of activity in NPL resolution by both the VAMC and the banks, particularly in instances where the collateral involves real estate. It is perceived to be such a positive step forward that banks are actually buying back their debt from the VAMC and taking action to seize collateral.

7.4   Key Issues, Challenges, and Observations for Continuing Reform

The Government of Viet Nam and the ministries (particularly the Ministry of Planning and Investment and MOF) have been active in producing decrees and decisions to support/guide the implementation of laws and the SOE reform process—more than 100 since 2011.[13] However, there is a vast difference between developing the tools to support the reform process and the implementation of successful reform. The government's year-end report for 2017 concluded that economic restructuring and transforming the growth model and the quality of growth remained slow. Labor productivity and competitiveness were not satisfactory. Room for fiscal and monetary policies was limited amid huge demand for resources for investment development, social security, national defense, and security. *Production and business efficiency of many state-owned enterprises remained low.* Urban management and development were still limited and inadequate. Environmental pollution recovery remained slow.[14]

At present the Government of Viet Nam is focused on

- restructuring the structure and process of oversight, management, and control the state has over SOEs and enterprises in which there is state capital;

- reducing the number of SOEs, primarily through equitization as that is believed to generate the greatest level of return on the state's investment in enterprises while reducing the burden on the state budget; and

- further divestment of state capital in enterprises already equitized.

---

[13] Most recent are the Action Plan of the Government of Viet Nam on the Implementation of the Resolution No. 12-NQ/TW 2017 of the 5th Central Committee on Implementation of Restructuring, Renovating and Improving the Efficiency of the SOEs; and the government's Resolution No. 97/NQ-CP in 2017.

[14] Based on the discussion of the delegates attending the meeting, the Cabinet members and the conclusion of the Prime Minister at the government's meeting with provinces and the government's regular meeting, held on 28 and 29 December 2017. VGP News. The Government's Regular Meeting in December 2017. http://news.chinhphu.vn/Home/The-Governments-regular-meeting-in-December-2017/20181/33012.vgp.

Achieving these three objectives means contending with a number of challenges some of which are common across the three objectives.

7.4.1   Oversight and Management

Until late 2018 Viet Nam followed a fragmented decentralized model of oversight and management of its SOEs. Some of the larger SEGs and GCs reported to the Prime Minister, larger national SOEs reported directly to their respective industry line ministry, and many SOEs were under the ownership and management of the 63 provincial governments. A key issue with the oversight and management of SOEs was the conflicting interests of those in charge. Line ministries were both owners with a vested interest in SOEs, yet also regulators in the sectors in which the SOEs operate.

In November 2018, the Commission for the Management of State Capital (CMSC) was established as the key driver for reforming the way in which the Government of Viet Nam maintains oversight, management, and control over state capital invested in enterprises.[15] This is the most significant change in oversight by separating the regulatory and ownership functions, and bringing most of the management of state capital in enterprises under one agency.

The following will be transferred to the CMSC:

- The parent companies of 21 of the largest corporations in key industry sectors in Viet Nam;

- 100% SOEs or enterprises in which the government has controlling shares, as decided by the Prime Minister periodically; and,

- The State Capital Investment Corporation (SCIC) – previously reporting to the MOF. The SCIC will be the representative for enterprises transferred from line ministries and provincial people's committees (except for any mentioned above).

The following *shall not be* transferred to the CMSC:

- Enterprises under the MOF, as agreed with the Prime Minister;

- Enterprises under the State Bank of Vietnam and state-owned credit institutions;

---

[15] Government of Viet Nam. Decree No. 131/2018/ND-CP dated 29 September 2018 on the functions, tasks, powers and organizational structure of the Commission for the Management of State Capital at enterprises provided guidance for implementation. Ha Noi.

- Construction lottery companies in provinces and cities directly under the central government;
- Enterprises involved in defense, security, and production and supply of public products and services; and
- Enterprises under the Hanoi People's Committee and Ho Chi Minh City People's Committee.

The CMSC is not simply focused on SOEs but on the management of state capital with the responsibility to proactively manage the state's representation in the enterprises transferred to it, including the parent companies of 21 large SEGs and corporations (see Appendix A7.5) most of which have already undertaken an IPO, or are planning for an IPO, and are not therefore SOEs under the current definition.

The SCIC, a key institution in the management of state capital in enterprises, reports to the CMSC. Initially, the SCIC took on the responsibility for SOEs that were not under a GC and did not fall naturally into a specific line ministry, or were smaller and less financially viable, and destined for 100% divestment rather than retention. More recently, it became responsible for the state's investment in enterprises that have been equitized to below 50% state ownership, irrespective of size and viability (e.g., Vietnam Dairy Products Joint Stock Company (Vinamilk), a large and very successful enterprise) and is managing a portfolio of over 500 enterprises operating in various industrial and commercial sectors.

The Government of Viet Nam is planning to equitize or otherwise alter the ownership model of around 350 enterprises by the end of 2020. Whenever an IPO takes place, the remaining state capital in the enterprise will be managed by the SCIC. Adding another 300+ enterprises to the SCIC's responsibility may add significant strain to its resources.

Conversely, the government has reduced the SCIC's financial management role. The Support Fund for Enterprise Reorganization and Development and the Support Fund for Enterprise Reorganization at Parent Companies of SEGs and GCs are directly managed by the MOF with effect from 10 December 2017.[16]

---

[16] In accordance with Clause 4 Article 39 of Decree No. 126/2017/ND-CP dated 16 November 2017.

Decision 58[17] provides the details of 103 SOEs undergoing restructuring that will remain 100% owned SOEs, of which at least 75 will not be transferred to the CMSC. If Decision 58 remains as the primary indicator for the number of SOEs, then there is an inference that under the current plan, the CMSC will initially have responsibility for the 21 large enterprises (including the SCIC and its portfolio of enterprises) plus another 28 SOEs. It is however, possible for new SOEs to be established at the order of the Prime Minister.

To be effective the CMSC needs to be staffed by individuals with business analysis skills who are able to analyze and report on the performance of individual SOEs with both the Government of Viet Nam and the enterprise management. Many of the enterprises will be underperforming and in need of support that is more comprehensive than simply ensuring regulatory and legal compliance.

In particular, the 21 large SEGs/corporations that are to be transferred to the new committee will require operational and financial restructuring. Complexities inherent in operational and financial restructuring of these large enterprises are extremely challenging and have already stretched the capacity of the leadership and management. A special kind of expertise is required and it is unlikely that staff currently employed in SOE renovation and reform in line ministries will have the requisite skills and expertise. There is, therefore, a challenge to ensure that the new structure is not only organizationally effective but that it is operationally effective too.

Recommending that some SOEs are not transferred to the CMSC appears contrary to improved corporate governance. Some of these enterprises will be under the ownership and management of those that regulate them.

7.4.2   SOE Debt and Nonperforming Loans

Many large SEGs, GCs, and enterprises in which the state has an investment are significantly overburdened with debt, including many of the 21 enterprises to be transferred to the CMSC. Among Vinacomex, Vinacomin, Vietnam Airlines, and Vietnam Expressway Corporation, the debt ratio[18] ranges from 80% to more than 100%. EVN, which has a debt ratio of approximately 70%, has the largest total debt of any SOE at $15 billion. Nonperforming loans of

---

[17]   Prime Minister of the Socialist Republic of Vietnam. Decision No. 58/2016/Qd-Ttg criteria for classification of wholly state-owned enterprises, partially state-owned enterprises and list of state-owned enterprises undergoing restructuring in 2016–2020. Ha Noi.

[18]   Total liabilities divided by total assets.

the SEGs and GCs are more than $1 billion. Such levels of debt create major problems for the enterprises in terms of their capacity to perform efficiently, restructure, raise capital, and find strategic investors. Significant levels of debt can also be seen in enterprises that have attempted to equitize but which the market has rejected.

7.4.3   Institutional Capacity

The Government of Viet Nam is making strenuous efforts to increase the rate and attractiveness of SOE equitizations and has had some significant successes in the recent past—e.g., Petrolimex and PV Oil, whose IPOs have been oversubscribed, yet the pace of equitization is still slow and behind schedule.

There were more than 500 SOEs, 100% owned, at the end of 2017 and earlier targets of 60 to 70 equitizations in a year have not been achieved. A planned reduction from >500 to around 150 SOEs in 3 years is a very ambitious target. The government considers 2018 a key year in the country's restructuring plan of SOEs, targeting to equitize at least 85 SOEs in the year, 64 of which being large companies. This, of course, does not take into account the enterprises from previous years that are still in the process of equitization but which have not reached the IPO stage.

In November 2018, the Ministry of Finance announced that only 11 SOEs were equitized in the first 9 months of the year, making it unlikely that the country's target to complete the equitization of at least 85 SOEs in 2018 could be achieved.

The divestment process during the period was also sluggish. Under the plan, 135 SOEs had to undergo the divestment process in 2017 and 181 in 2018. But by November 2018 the state had divested capital from only 31 firms, 13 of which conducted the process in 2017 and 18 did so in 2018 (Vietnam Investment Review 2018).

Although the process has been determined as a key policy, one of the major blockages is the institutional capacity to undertake enterprise valuations, especially in relation to large SOEs with complex structures, significant debt, and operations in various industries. According to the State Audit Office of Vietnam, legal regulations concerning enterprise evaluation have many flaws, with regard to land-use rights, brand values, the selection of evaluation firms, and determining the market value of SOEs' assets.

Decree No. 126/2017/ND-CP (Decree 126) has been developed partly to clarify some of these issues and is significant in that it introduces a more transparent structure and methodology for preparing enterprises for their IPO.[19] It introduces book building as an optional IPO pricing tool that is hoped will allow for more market-sensitive pricing. It also provides much more detail in terms of how the valuation is calculated. But while Decree 126 is perceived as being a progressive change, particularly to the IPO prices achieved, there is still some doubt as to the effectiveness in speeding up the process.

If the institutional capacity required to support the ambitious targets is not in place then the targets will continually fail to be achieved, irrespective of the exhortations of government agencies and ministries.

7.4.4   Internal Capacity

The Government of Viet Nam has approved the restructuring plans of many SEGs, GCs, and individual SOEs during the years since Decision 929 and continues to push for further restructuring and reform.[20] There is a clear intent to ensure that individual corporate restructuring is comprehensive and encompasses the organizational structure, management, production and business activities, strategy, marketing, financial restructuring, and results in performance improvement including profitability and return on equity.

However, restructuring plans are general, not strongly market based and contain information relating to past achievements and some future intentions designed to achieve whatever outcomes the SOE believes will be acceptable to its owners and the government, rather than being based on commercially sound assumptions. Strategies to support the restructuring plans are not clearly articulated. To date, SOE management have focused on the preservation of state capital rather than increasing the value. The development of robust, factually based restructuring plans that have credible financial analysis and projections underpinned by sound and understood assumptions is completely new to the management of SOEs (ADB 2014).

In approving SOE restructuring plans, line ministries and people's committees ensure that the SOEs under their supervision have complied with all the

---

[19] Government of Viet Nam. Decree No. 126/2017/ND-CP on conversion from state-owned enterprises and single-member limited liability companies with 100% of charter capital invested by state-owned enterprises into Joint-Stock Companies. Ha Noi.

20 Prime Minister of the Socialist Republic of Vietnam. Decision No. 929/QD-TTg dated 17 July 2012 on approval of the scheme on "restructuring of state-owned enterprises, focusing on economic groups and state-owned corporations in period 2011–2015. Ha Noi.

regulations surrounding the development and submission of a restructuring plan, and that associated equitization plans and/or valuations are developed as per the state regulations. It is not their role, nor do they have the capacity to provide commercial judgment as to the quality or appropriateness of the restructuring plans, nor each SOE's potential to achieve the implementation of the restructuring plan. This is an issue that could be replicated in the new committee unless the staff recruited are much more business oriented and experienced.

There is a clear and obvious disconnect between the aspirations of the government and the capacity of those who have to implement. Direct restructuring planning and implementation support to the SOEs' leadership and management should be a priority if the Government of Viet Nam wishes to achieve its restructuring targets.

7.4.5   Infrastructure

Based on a study on the quality and competitiveness of infrastructure conducted by the World Economic Forum in 2018 (Figure 7.8), Viet Nam ranked 75th out of 148 countries, well behind regional competitors Malaysia (32), Thailand (60), and Indonesia (71) (World Economic Forum 2018). The poor quality of infrastructure services provided by Viet Nam SOEs drives up the cost of doing business, inhibits private sector investment, and diverts government funds away from more productive activities.

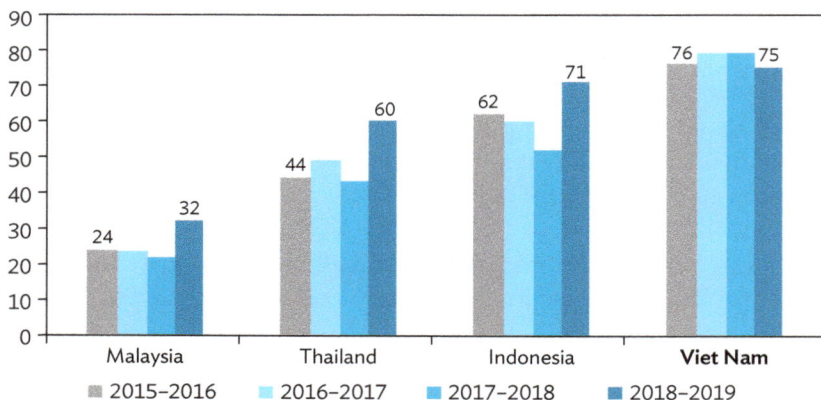

Figure 7.8: Quality of Infrastructure, 2015–2019

Source: World Economic Forum. Various years. Global Competitiveness Report. Geneva.

Viet Nam's ranking appears to be slowly improving in comparison to significant declines among regional competitors. However, the overall ranking of 75th place hides much worse rankings in terms of quality of roads, road connectivity, air transport services, electrification rate, and reliability of water supply, all of which are critical to strong manufacturing and efficient production. These are fundamental infrastructure needs to continue to attract FDI and are critical to the development of a strong domestic sector.

Infrastructure is also at the heart of the SOE sector yet it is these large economic groups and general corporations that have the weakest performance, greatest level of debt, and are the least effective. The development of good quality and sufficient infrastructure is therefore a challenge made more difficult for the government to overcome.

7.4.6   Productivity and Innovation

Productivity and innovation will eventually have to become the main drivers of growth. That will require policies to tackle the stagnation in productivity and long-term investments, especially in urban infrastructure and innovation capabilities. What explains the stagnation in productivity? Public investment is not as efficient as it needs to be because of uncoordinated and often incoherent investment decisions of a fragmented state structure. There also is little doubt that most SOEs are inefficient producers (World Bank and MPI 2016).

Simply reducing the state's capital in inefficient SOEs through equitization and divestment, however, will not provide the solution to the issue. The SOEs and large enterprises (SEGs and GCs) in which the government plans to retain a controlling stake are among the least efficient and, because of their size, are a disproportionately large part of the problem.

According to the Global Competitiveness Reports in 2018/19 (Figure 7.9), Viet Nam ranked 82nd out of 140 countries in terms of innovation—a drop of 10 places in comparison to 2017. While the region appears to demonstrate a trend implying that it is becoming less innovatively competitive in comparison to other countries, Cambodia, a strong competitor to Viet Nam, has shown consistent improvements from being ranked 121st in the world in 2015 to 96th position in 2019.

Figure 7.9: Innovation Ranking, 2015–2019

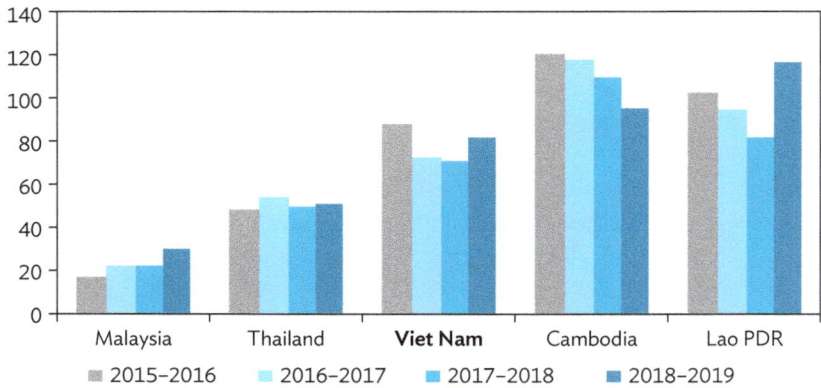

Lao PDR = Lao People's Democratic Republic.
Source: World Economic Forum. Various years. Global Competitiveness Report. Geneva.

The issue of innovation and its impact on the future is already on the government's radar, and ministries have been directed to take responsibilities in developing a report on the current status and impact scenarios of the Fourth Industrial Revolution for Viet Nam. On that basis, the Ministry of Science and Technology shall develop a draft resolution on enhancing capacity to access the 4th Industrial Revolution and submit it to government for approval in 2018.[21]

Innovation as a driver of growth will be achieved by enterprises able to capitalize on, and be at the forefront of, an increasingly accelerating pace of change. These enterprises are most likely to be dynamic small and medium-sized enterprises with rapid decision-making capabilities and are connected to the needs of their customers and have access to capital. They are least likely to be large bureaucratic organizations with a strict hierarchy of delegated authorities, typified by SOEs.

FDI companies tend to be larger and more efficient producers with good access to capital. However, FDI companies also tend to be investors in manufacturing processes that capitalize on lower costs of production, especially labor. While FDI brings many positive benefits to Viet Nam, FDI companies are not likely to be the key drivers of innovation.

---

[21] Based on the Government of Viet Nam's resolution effective from the government's regular meeting of 28 and 29 December 2017. VGP News. The Government's Regular Meeting in December 2017. http://news.chinhphu. vn/Home/The-Governments-regular-meeting-in-December-2017/20181/33012.vgp.

Where SOEs can contribute to, and help expand the innovation economy, is through supporting the development of innovation companies as spin-offs from the main SOE or partnering with innovative small and medium-sized enterprises as users and conduits to markets and customers. For example, the State Bank of Vietnam (SBV) has participated in the Fintech Challenge Vietnam, a combined event to promote and catalyze financial inclusion in Viet Nam, which was organized by the SBV and the Mekong Business Initiative (a program funded by ADB and the Australian government) with two co-organizers—the Vietnam Banks Association and the Fintech Vietnam Club.

7.4.7   Reform versus Control

While thousands of equitizations have taken place, SOE reform efforts often continue to target the sale of minority noncontrolling stakes in these companies, with the government remaining as the largest shareholder. By only partially divesting its ownership, and retaining majority control and decision-making authority, private sector strategic partners have had a limited ability to reshape these companies into globally competitive enterprises.

While state ownership has shrunk in commercial sectors of the economy, government plans have continued to emphasize the importance of retaining control over many "strategic sectors" particularly those sectors related to public infrastructure and service delivery (i.e., electricity, water supply, telecommunication, postal, ports, and airports). These sectors are prone to natural monopolies and oligopolies, so in many cases a continued government role may be necessary. However, while some of these SOEs have been partially equitized, few operate on strict commercial terms with management independence, profit orientation, hard budget constraint, and accountability for results. These characteristics are essential for improved SOE performance as it forces SOEs to meet their costs of capital and divest any activities that are not commercially viable. Improving SOE performance in these sectors will rely not only on partial equitization but on overhauling the government's competition policies, regulatory oversight, and corporate governance standards to lift accountability for results. Unfortunately, progress on this front has been slow.

In a number of cases, the Government of Viet Nam (through the SCIC) has continued to retain 36% of the equity in equitized entities long after the equitization, and in industry sectors that are not normally considered strategic or protected. This includes at least two high profile examples: Vinamilk and

Saigon Alcohol Beer and Beverages Corporation (Sabeco), the major brewer. By retaining 36%, the government retains the right of veto in relation to board resolutions, board appointments, etc. While these two listed companies in particular have been very successful, it is not always the case. It is valid to question why the state continues to retain control over enterprises that are truly and comprehensively commercial in nature, or which are financially weak. Appendix A7.1, a case study on Southern Waterborne Joint Stock General Corporation, demonstrates the issues surrounding continued majority government control in SOEs.

7.4.8 Public Service Obligations

Complicating the task of reforming service delivery SOEs is the difficulty in judging their performance, given their competing often complex mandates. For example, some infrastructure SOEs make substantial profits while providing reasonably priced services. But often, outside of public view, this occurs at the cost of absorbing large amounts of scarce capital stock on which they provide very low returns, acting as a drag on economic growth. Similarly, profitability within some service providers comes at the expense of limited coverage, with service delivery focused on high-density, low-cost regions. The profitability of other SOEs is often eroded by a requirement to deliver services into non-commercially viable regions. These activities, often referred to as public service obligations (PSOs), also include delivering services at below cost-recovery levels or to remote populations where commercial services are often not commercially viable. If properly identified, contracted, and funded, delivering these PSOs should not reduce SOEs' profitability. The reality, however, is that PSOs in Viet Nam continue to be haphazardly imposed, rarely costed, and unfunded. As a result, infrastructure SOEs are forced to operate with conflicting mandates, making it very difficult for SOE management and directors to exercise their responsibilities in a fiscally responsible, efficiency-promoting manner (ADB 2016b).

The net result in some cases is that the returns on investment are too low to attract private sector investment (especially FDI), thereby creating a cycle of continuing investment demand that has to be publicly funded to the detriment of the overall efficiency of the state budget.

This is typified by comparing the performance of Vietnam Electricity (EVN) with other energy companies across ASEAN in 2015.

EVN is one of the largest SEGs and one of the largest electricity companies in the region. However, as we can see from the following charts, EVN suffers from PSOs relating to price setting and delivery across the nation. Not only is EVN suffering but it is clear from the charts that its performance is extremely poor in relation to other electricity providers in the other ASEAN countries.

EVN's return on equity (ROE) of 1.9% and return on assets of 0.58% are only just greater than Indonesia (Figure 7.10).

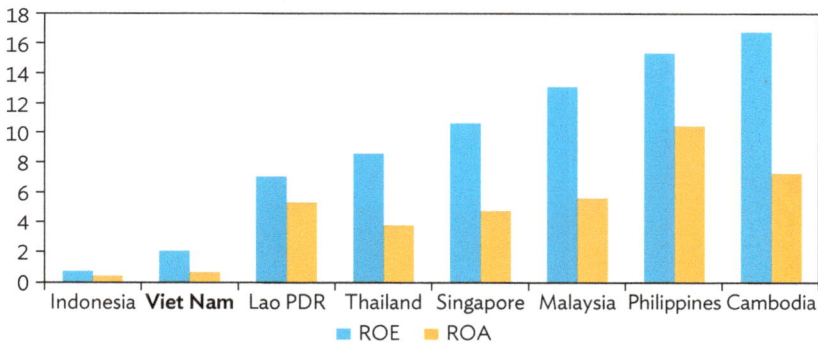

Figure 7.10: Performance of Vietnam Electricity and ASEAN Energy Companies, 2015
(%)

ASEAN = Association of Southeast Asian Nations, Lao PDR = Lao People's Democratic Republic, ROA = return on assets, ROE = return on equity.
Source: Author, based on financial data derived from audited accounts and annual reports for Vietnam Electricity and other electricity providers.

EVN has the lowest end-user tariff—this is reflected in the level of debt, current ratio of less than 1, and the lowest level of gross profitability in the region (Figures 7.11a–7.11c).

The data for 2012 to 2014 contain very similar results. The figures in the charts appear to demonstrate that EVN is in a vicious circle of having insufficient liquidity to reduce its debt burden in any meaningful way, has limited opportunity to invest in the business; and with a current ratio that has reduced to 0.82, is in danger of being unable to manage its obligations, and is dependent on borrowings.

Figure 7.11a: Vietnam Electricity Liabilities, 2012–2016
($ billion)

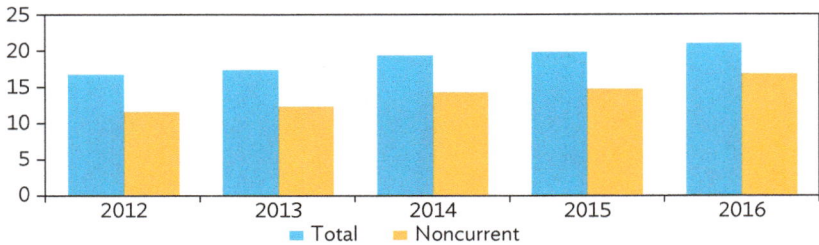

Sources: Vietnam Electricity. Various annual reports; Author.

Figure 7.11b: Liabilities to Assets and Current Ratios, 2015
(%)

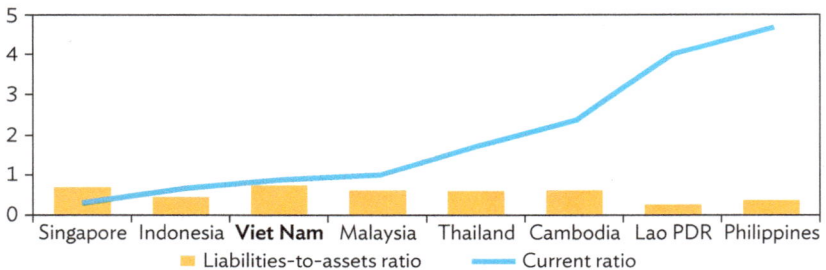

Lao PDR = Lao People's Democratic Republic.
Source: Author, based on financial data derived from audited accounts and annual reports for Vietnam Electricity and other electricity providers.

Figure 7.11c: Gross Profitability and Average End-User Tariff, 2015

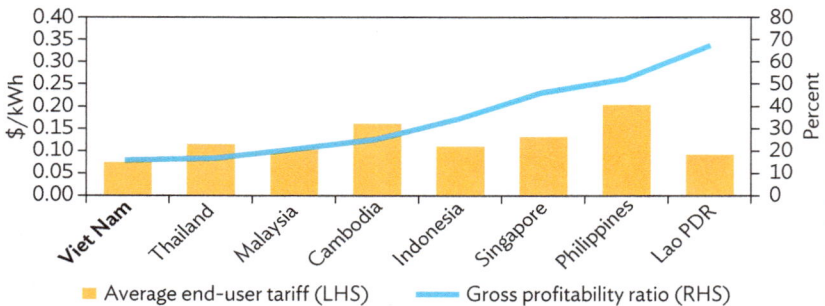

kWh = kilowatt-hour, Lao PDR = Lao People's Democratic Republic, LHS = left-hand scale, RHS = right-hand scale.
Sources: Author, based on financial data derived from audited accounts and annual reports for Vietnam Electricity and other electricity providers; Average end-user tariffs sourced from electricity providers and the World Bank.

This highlights the complexities and challenges in assessing the performance of enterprises that are providing services that are directly linked to PSOs and at a pricing level over which they have little control. It is difficult to determine the performance level that is a result of management capacity and how much is impacted by external factors.

EVN is one of the companies that will transfer to the CMSC. It is therefore a prime example of the rationale for recruiting individuals who are highly skilled in business analysis and strategy within the CMSC, can understand the issues at EVN, and can drive the restructuring to reduce the state's burden.

7.4.9   The Reform Process

Should restructuring occur before or after equitization? In a perfect world, SOEs would be restructured and operating at optimal performance before equitization, thereby generating the greatest value back to the state when the SOE equitized. The reality is, however, rather different. SOEs do not have the internal capacity or the financial and other resources to restructure without the financial support they plan to raise from the components of restructuring (equitization and divestment). Neither do they generally have the support from professional advisers (an added cost to the business) and/or strategic investors.

As comprehensive restructuring can take 3 to 5 years and more, it is more pragmatic for the SOE to ensure that they have the best possible restructuring and implementation plans and demonstrate that low-cost but high-impact changes are being implemented during the period between the acceptance of the restructuring and implementation plans and the equitization.

For most SOEs, the equitization process will take 18 months or so, primarily due to the time taken for the valuation. During this process there are some aspects of restructuring that have to be put on hold, e.g., the divestment of any subsidiaries or assets that are being included in the valuation. It is, therefore, critical that the restructuring plans are developed not only on the basis of real market conditions and accurate projections but also along realistic implementation timescales that take the equitization process into account. Appendix A7.2, a case study on Construction Corporation No. 1, highlights these issues.

A comprehensive monitoring and evaluation framework was developed to support performance management of individual SOEs at line ministry and owner level. The framework also provides key performance indicators

(KPIs) to monitor the overall progress of the SEGs and GCs going through restructuring.[22]

Despite some high-profile success stories, overall in total, IPOs had not been particularly successful in the past 2 years. Generally, the SOEs are unprepared in terms of pre-equitization restructuring and find it difficult to attract potential shareholder and strategic partner interest in the IPO. If there is uncertainty and a lack of clarity as to future plans it is difficult for potential investors (at any level) to understand the long-term benefits of investing.

7.4.10 Slow Pace of Reform Implementation

While progress had been made and new targets set, a number of barriers still exist to realizing the full benefits of SOE reform. First, the pace of SOE equitization had slowed considerably. This reduced momentum is partly explained by the quick wins of earlier reform efforts, which targeted the comparatively uncomplicated sale, or closure, of small loss-making enterprises. In contrast, many remaining SOEs were and continue to be much larger, with equitization made more challenging by limited progress on resolving their complex ownership and management structures and unclear financial and debt obligations. These challenges, as well as those related to SOE transparency and corporate governance more generally, have also made it more difficult to find strategic investors willing to participate in IPOs of SOEs.

SOE reform and restructuring targets, including equitizations, have failed to be achieved each year since 2013 when the Government of Viet Nam began the restructuring of larger SOEs, and not all equitized SOEs were immediately successful. While a lack of intuitional and internal capacity has contributed to the results, the government recognized other relevant issues:

- Directive 04/CT-TTg issued by the Prime Minister on the restructuring and renovation of SOEs in 2016–2020 requires the SOEs to list their shares on the stock exchanges within a year after their IPOs. Statistics of the Ministry of Finance (MOF) showed that as of 15 November 2018, 677 SOEs were already privatized but not listed on exchanges.
- The transparency at SOEs was also limited, with only 42% of 622 SOEs submitting reports to the Ministry of Planning and Investment to be publicized on the national enterprise portal in 2017, a slight increase from 38.9% in 2016, the ministry's statistics showed (Vietnam Investment Review 2018).

---

[22] The road map and the monitoring and evaluation framework were developed under ADB (2014).

- Equitization has not actually changed the capacity or motivation of management. Information disclosure is not implemented uniformly, financial information is not transparent, and enterprises are not registered for trading and listed on the stock market.

- The supervision by state owners of enterprises after equitization is often ineffective: some tend to interfere in the production and business activities of enterprises.

- The perception and visions of many committees, government agencies, and SOEs are affected by local interests and short-term thinking. Some leaders fear that they will no longer hold leadership positions after equitization, so they hesitate to equitize or ask the state to continue holding the dominant share after equitization.

- After being approved for restructuring, the implementation in many ministries, sectors, provinces, state economic groups, and corporations is passive and ineffective.

- Investors are wary of share auctions at IPO due to the fear that the stocks after auction may be difficult to trade after the IPO.

In effect, there is a level of passive resistance that the Government of Viet Nam either finds difficult to surmount or does not have the political will to deal with.

The contradictions actually occur at all levels as the following suggest:

> In 2011, the Economic Forum of the National Assembly recommended that it should no longer be appropriate that SOEs be considered the foundation for industrial and economic development [...].

In 2012, the Prime Minister acted on this resolution with Decree 929:

> SOEs [...] play the core role to motivate state economy to perform its leading role as an important material force so that the State orients, regulates the economy and stabilizes the macro-economy and to improve competitiveness, and return on equity (ROE) for trading enterprises.

The SCIC's mission and primary objective are

> to represent the state capital interests in enterprises and invest in key sectors and essential industries with a view to strengthening the dominant role of the state sector while respecting market rules.[23]

---

[23] SCIC. http://www.scic.vn/english/.

Implementation of individual SOE restructuring is also hindered by legal impediments that include:

- Article 12 of the Law on Securities, Article 9 Decree No. 58/2012/ ND-CP dated 20/7/2012 of the Government (Decree 58), the offer for sale of stocks to the public must satisfy the condition that the enterprise has no loss in the financial statement of the year preceding the year of auction and has no aggregated loss arising; and

- the Enterprise Law whereby according to Article 59 and Article 120 of the Law on Enterprise, when the Member Council (in limited liability companies) or the BOM (in joint-stock companies) approves decisions on merger (or other restructuring) transactions, the parent company as the "related party" is not permitted to vote on the resolution. While this is protecting the rights of minority shareholders, it frequently results in the situation that when the parent company holds controlling shares at the subsidiary company but has no right to vote, the remaining shareholders are reluctant to approve the decision.

The government's program of reform via equitization continued its slow progress in 2017, with 69 SOEs planned to have their IPOs and the state planning to collect around $1 billion from the IPOs. However, only 21 SOEs held their IPOs, the state collected only 22% of its target and retained significantly more than 53% of the total chartered capital that it intended to retain.

As some IPOs were either fully or even oversubscribed, there must have been a number of IPOs that were very unsuccessful. The unsuccessful IPOs have an impact on the capacity of the SOEs in question to implement their corporate and financial restructuring, which then has an impact on the whole SOE reform and restructuring process.

On the other hand, SOE reform continues to include mergers, closures, bankruptcy, and the divestment of state capital from previously equitized companies. The Steering Committee for Business Renovation and Development reported that for the first 11 months of 2017, the state collected approximately $1.1 billion from divestments of state capital. The most significant divestment by value was approximately $900 million gained through the SCIC reducing the state's holdings in Vietnam Dairy Products Joint Stock Company (Vinamilk) to 36% (yet remaining the largest shareholder).

In December 2017, the Ministry of Industry and Trade sold a controlling interest of Saigon Beer, Alcohol and Beverage Corporation (Sabeco) to ThaiBev corporation for $4.8 billion yet retained a 36% shareholding in Sabeco.

7.4.11 Corporate Governance

The mere size and prevalence of state ownership/investment in commercial enterprises in Viet Nam makes efficient governance of SOEs of all types and enterprises in which the state has an investment, an important facet of overall economic performance. For the enterprises themselves, good corporate governance practices open the way to strong efficiency gains, improvements in performance, and the ability to compete with private competitors. At a more macro level, improvements in the governance of SOEs and enterprises with state capital will promote growth through improved economic performance and increased productivity. It should lead to a more transparent allocation of resources and enhanced investment and job creation. It will facilitate access to capital (both debt and equity).

In the early stages of reform, SOE boards were almost completely dominated by insiders—the government approved all senior positions; there was almost no performance management linking performance to reward; there were no independent nonexecutive board members; and it was normal for the positions of chair of the board and general director to be held by the same person. Transparency and disclosure were nonexistent. SOEs effectively self-assessed when reporting back to government. Corporate governance was only an issue for, and applied to, listed companies that were required to follow the obligations of the exchange.

The most comprehensive changes to corporate governance have come via the Enterprise Law and Decree No. 71/2017/ND-CP (Decree 71) that came into effect on 1 August 2017 and is applicable to public companies.[24] A public company is a joint-stock company defined in Clause 1 Article 25 of the Law on Securities. This means that the new decree applies to listed companies; companies that have had an IPO but not listed; and a company that has shares owned by at least 100 investors excluding professional securities investors, and which has paid-up charter capital of VND10 billion or more. This encompasses almost all enterprises in which the state has an investment and will apply to every SOE that equitizes in the future. It does not, however, apply to SOEs that remain 100% state owned.

Decree 71 goes further than any other previous legislation on corporate governance. It builds on the provisions of the Law on Enterprises and introduces more stringent regulations. It is closer to the Organisation for Economic Co-

[24] Government of Viet Nam. Decree No. 71/2013/ND-CP on investment of state capital in enterprises and financial management of enterprises of which 100% charter capital is held by the state. Ha Noi.

operation and Development guidelines than has been seen in Viet Nam before. Examples of the reach of Decree 71 are as follows:

- A corporate governance charter must be approved by the shareholders.

- Reports on the operations of the audit committee, other board committees, and the performance of the board and executives are to be available to shareholders.

- The chairman must not also be the director/general director (to be enforced on 1 August 2020).

- A member of the board of directors cannot simultaneously be a director of more than five other companies.

- A member of the board must be assigned with the responsibility for corporate governance.

- At least one-third of the board must be nonexecutive members and depending on the organizational structure, one-fifth must be independent.

- The salaries of the general director and other management must be disclosed in the annual financial report.

- An internal audit committee must be established for all relevant companies.

Concomitant to Decree 71, the MOF launched an internal audit handbook (coauthored by the MOF and the World Bank). This serves as a source of reference to establish an internal audit function with clarity in structure, policies, and procedures and presents the relationship between internal audit, corporate governance, risk management, and internal control.

The decree also directs the MOF to provide

- a sample charter which public companies can use to formulate their own charter; and

- a model of internal regulations on corporate governance, which public companies can use to formulate their own internal regulations.

Yet the decree does not apply to companies that are currently 100% SOEs. There is inconsistent and poor understanding about corporate governance among SOE leadership and management leading to limited corporate governance policies and strategies (ADB 2016a). Will the Government of Viet Nam develop a decree for corporate governance in SOEs that is as progressive as Decree 71?

7.4.12   Risk Management

Awareness of risk management in Viet Nam has been improving, yet risk management is only a legal requirement in the banking, insurance, and securities sectors. This requirement includes risk management structure, methodology, risk reporting, and monitoring. For other sectors and other types of companies, the requirement for risk management is generic and not compulsory.

Generally, SOEs and equitized SOEs do not have a risk function. There is a lack of documented risk assessment results or risk management policies. Risks are dealt with in an ad hoc manner, as and when they occur, rather than using a risk-based approach to identify, quantify, and manage risks in a systematic manner as part of the planning process.

Many SOEs have a large network of subsidiaries and affiliates. Subsidiaries are managed via "capital representatives" reporting directly to senior management of the parent companies. The capital representative reports to the parent company on a periodic basis, normally via quarterly meetings. However, the capital representatives tend to check on compliance rather than performance. There tends not to be any mechanism with sufficient tools/guidance to effectively and frequently monitor and track and evaluate the performance and future risk of subsidiaries/affiliates.

There is confusion among SOE management as to whether risk management, internal control, and internal audit are subsets of corporate governance or each a discipline of its own; and even whether corporate governance is a form of management style.

7.5   Proposals for Continuing Reform

7.5.1   Support to Internal Capacity Development

The government has identified SOE reform as crucial in its ability to achieve the economic and social targets of its Socioeconomic Development Plan, 2016–2020. A recurring theme of this chapter is that equitizing SOEs is, and will remain, a key Government of Viet Nam reform strategy. It is important but will not be enough. Resources have to be applied to SOEs that remain so that they can be restructured to make them efficient, productive, and net contributors to the budget and the economy.

The internal competency and capacity of senior SOE management has proven to be critical to SOE reform. Moving from a controlled business environment to a more market-led and competitive environment in which the company does not have the privileges, benefits, and protection enjoyed by state enterprises, requires very different business skills and mindset.

In the past, the focus of SOE management has often been on preserving the value of state capital. Management skills have, therefore, been more aligned to internal planning and compliance with state regulations, rather than strategy, marketing, human resources management, and corporate governance. While restructuring plans of SOEs comply with the law and the requirements of the "owners," they tend to lack focus and attention to full commercial considerations.

Capacity building is essential to improve SOEs to be equitized, and those already equitized who are unable to fulfill their full potential. Improvements in restructuring planning is important but equally so is the competency and capacity to implement the restructuring. Unless the leadership and management have the means to improve their performance, it will not happen.

Capacity building is equally critical for the 100% SOEs that will remain, as they are the largest, most challenging, and most problematic. Unless these enterprises are reformed, the problems will continue ad infinitum.

7.5.2   Strengthening the Rights of Strategic Investors

While government has moved recently to ease restrictions on foreign ownership of domestic corporations, many investors continue to be deterred by perceived weaknesses in the rights of minority shareholders. The issue of strategic investors and the state's share is potentially of great importance to the overall success of an SOE's restructuring. Strategic investors are brought in because they bring with them some inherent advantages (knowledge, experience, internal capacity, technology, financial resources, etc.) from which the SOE can benefit; it is therefore critical that those benefits can be exploited. When the state retains not just a portion of equity, but often a controlling equity, there is a distinct danger that it will put off some strategic investors.

Even when a strategic investor does commit to investing in an SOE, those advantages may be lost if the strategic investor does not have the power to implement the capacity, technology, and financial resources it brings to the venture to the extent required to optimize the restructuring and future development of the enterprise. Being a strategic investor brings with it certain obligations such as being locked into the deal for a minimum of 3 years and providing resources to develop the business, yet it does not bring the rights that would normally be associated with being a strategic investor such as acquiring the majority share or even having the right of veto if holding less than 35%.

The state wishes to capitalize on the potential growth in equity value after equitization, so there is a case to consider that an enterprise's charter could be amended to provide the strategic investor with controlling voting rights or at least the right of veto, thereby allowing commercial and strategic decisions to be made in a timely manner and based on what is good for the enterprise and maximizing shareholder value. As a result, the state would eventually be able to sell its remaining shares at the optimal value.

7.5.3   Support to Private Sector Development

SOEs that are equitized become part of what is currently a weak domestic private sector that is also in need of policy attention. As the Government of Viet Nam is retaining what is often a controlling interest in the parent company of an equitized SOE, and because of the change in definition of an SOE, the state is, in reality, becoming the largest investor in the private sector. For example, if we look at EVN which is, and will continue to be, a 100% SOE, and Petrolimex, an ex-SOE that has equitized, listed on the Ho Chi Minh Stock Exchange, and is the fifth-largest company in Viet Nam (2017), we can see the real reach and influence that the state has in the private sector (EVN 2018, Petrolimex 2018).

The examples in Table 7.8 only show the first-tier subsidiaries. However, any of the first-tier subsidiaries could be a holding company with one or more subsidiaries. The situation is replicated across SOEs and equitized/listed enterprises in which the state has equity.

Table 7.8: EVN and Petrolimex Subsidiary Ownership, 2018

	EVN	Petrolimex
State share in parent company	100%	75.87%
Subsidiary ownership	Number of Enterprises	Number of Enterprises
100%	9	47
50% but less than 100%	6	20
Less than 50%	3	4
Total	**18**	**71**

EVN = Vietnam Electricity.
Source: Author.

There is, therefore, a vested interest in the state ensuring a more competitive and productive domestic private sector. This will involve strengthening the institutional foundations of the market economy, with emphasis on protecting property rights and enforcing competition policies. A stable, well regulated, and inclusive finance sector and transparent and functioning land markets will also be crucial. A more capable and confident domestic private sector will deepen links with foreign firms, enabling the transfer of technology and know-how that are critical for higher productivity growth. More rewarding participation in global value chains will also come from a stronger services sector and more extensive transport and network connectivity across the country and with trading partners. Commitments under major international trade agreements offer a real opportunity to carry out many demanding and politically sensitive reforms (ADB 2016b).

7.5.4   Increasing the Depth of Equitization

There remain a significant number of SOEs, or enterprises in which there is state capital, that deliver no essential public services and operate in sectors of the economy where private sector competition would lead to more efficient production.

Any decision to partially equitize SOEs that are deemed to be of some importance to the state is likely to result in ineffective restructuring and conflicting commercial objectives. It will also give the impression that the state is seeking control and financial return rather than pure SOE reform and will have an impact on the perceived attractiveness of the SOE to potential investors.

Nguyen Duc Kien, vice chairman of the National Assembly's Economic Committee, stressed that slow equitization "has been seriously affecting investors, especially foreign ones who are eager to purchase more stakes from SOEs. Over the past years, though 96.5% of SOEs have been equitized, only 8% of the state's capital has been transferred to private investors," Kien said (Vietnam Investment Review 2017).

Reducing government ownership and allowing fully commercial, market-driven companies to emerge should be the central priority of SOE reform efforts. If an SOE is operating as a commercial enterprise competing in clearly defined market sectors, it should be fully equitized and fully join the private sector.

While transition costs (such as labor retrenchment) need to be carefully managed, removing all government ownership and control of these entities would lead to significant productivity, employment, and growth gains for Viet Nam's economy.

Taking this view allied to the apparent lack of institutional capacity to manage the targeted levels of equitizations would allow the Government of Viet Nam to focus more on the quality of equitizations and IPOs rather than the quantity.

Equitization targets need to focus on the sale of more than 50% of SOE equity as a minimum, but ideally toward removing all government ownership and/or involvement in their operations.

7.5.5   Strengthening Institutional Capacity

It is not only the current wave of equitizations that are failing to achieve targets, it is an issue that has been prevalent since 2013. The frequency and diversity of legal revisions may have inhibited SOE management and the relevant institutions from implementing restructuring and reform while the regulatory landscape is constantly changing. However, in the current period it is more the size and complexity of the SOEs going through the equitization process that is challenging the capacity of the agencies involved. Without the capacity, equitization success will continue to be inconsistent.

7.5.6   Increase Provisioning for the Cost of SOE Restructuring

Uncertainty in the size of SOE liabilities means that the government needs to adequately provide for the cost of restructuring SOEs. There is, however, a lack of provisioning in the budget. ADB's Strengthening Support for State-Owned Enterprise Reform and Corporate Governance Facilitation Program has shown that as equitization plans are developed, initial cost estimates typically rise due to opaque accounting practices and a lack of transparency that initially hide the true extent of liabilities accumulated by SOEs. Allocating resources to identify SOE liabilities and then providing adequate budget provisioning to cover whatever portion cannot be transferred with the SOE sale, will be an essential step in allowing equitization plans to be carried out more smoothly (ADB 2016a).

7.5.7   Improve the Safety Net

As the SOE reform process deepens, and uncompetitive SOEs are faced with closure, it is possible that opposition to reform will intensify. This situation can be mitigated if extensive and genuine consultations and discussions are undertaken between all stakeholders so that everyone understands the objectives of the reforms and the underlying rationale for policy change.

Some SOEs are not divesting 100% of the equity in poorly performing subsidiary enterprises, but are reducing their equity stake to 36%. There is often no strategic reason for retaining any equity in such companies, but there is a concern that if the equity is diluted to <36%, the new owners will have a more commercial outlook and there will be large-scale redundancies. It is understood that this could result in negative perceptions of SOE restructuring and add to the burden on the social welfare system at a time when it is likely to be already stretched. By retaining 36% of such companies the SOE shareholder can have the right of veto and ensure that the new owners cannot impose redundancies on the company.

The issue is whether state capital is better placed in a poorly performing company that is perhaps unable to contribute tax payments and dividends to the state budget or whether the government should use the capital to strengthen the social safety net in terms of its provisions to support and retrain workers displaced during the shake-up of state-invested enterprises.

Strengthening the social safety net for people impacted by SOE restructuring could be supported with the recent significant gains of almost $6 billion from the divestment of equity in Sabeco and Vinamilk to the Support Fund for Enterprise Reorganization and Development.

7.5.8   Public Service Obligations

Reduce the complexity and conflicting mandates of service delivery SOEs. To generate improved service delivery outcomes, infrastructure SOEs need to have the same commercial discipline imposed on them as private corporations. They need clear commercial objectives that can drive incentives for enhanced efficiency and performance. Any PSO which they are required to deliver but which cannot be done on a fully commercial basis should be clearly mandated and publicly disclosed. Over time, the related costs of delivering these PSOs should be covered by the budget in a fully transparent manner. Having done this, service delivery SOEs can be made fully accountable for their financial performance, with an independent board of directors pursuing a commercial mandate. This will be essential to placing service delivery SOEs on a stronger commercial footing, while improving transparency, accountability, and ultimately the quality of service delivery.

7.5.9   Enforcing Governance Compliance

While the legal framework for SOE governance has improved, implementation has been uneven—particularly in regard to increased transparency and disclosure of enterprise finances and operations. For instance, new laws require the public disclosure of information related to SOE corporate performance,[25] including on enterprise websites (as recommended under ADB's Strengthening Support for State-Owned Enterprise Reform and Corporate Governance Facilitation Program) yet compliance does not seem to be monitored; nor are penalties for noncompliance imposed.

Further, although many SOE restructuring plans have been approved, there is little information on the process in which these plans were developed and their content made available to the public (ADB 2016b). This lack of information raises uncertainties for the private sector and civil society. Greater information disclosure would significantly improve investor confidence and public perceptions.

Post equitization, there is a requirement to list on the stock exchange. Because of the lower levels of corporate governance standards among SOEs, the Unlisted Public Company Market (UPCoM) was established with less stringent governance requirements to enable equitized SOEs to register on UPCoM, allowing them time to improve their governance and transparency, and then go to a full listing. However, there are now more than 740 companies registered on UPCoM some of which have been there for 5 years. The Government of Viet Nam should move to direct many of these companies to go for a full listing.

It is also recommended that the government develop a decree for corporate governance in SOEs that is as progressive as Decree 71.

---

[25] Government of the Socialist Republic of Vietnam. Decree No. 87/2017/ND-CP Financial Supervision, Performance Assessment and Disclosure of Financial Information of SOEs and State-Invested Enterprises; Circular No. 200/2015/TT-BE on Guidelines for Certain Details Regarding the Supervision of the Investment of State Capital in Enterprises and Regarding the Financial Supervision, Performance Assessment and Financial Information Disclosure in State-Owned and State-Invested Enterprises; and Decision No. 36/2014/QD-TTg on Regulations for Information Disclosure of 1MLLC SOEs.

7.5.10 Director Appointments

Introducing a transparent, fully skills-based director appointment process can also be instrumental in improving the performance of SOEs. Even though the government is likely to retain ownership of some service delivery SOEs for the foreseeable future, they should still be managed by skilled directors who make decisions in the best commercial interests of the SOE, its owners, and key stakeholders. At present, the appointment of members of the board of management, its chair, and the general director is determined by an authorized state body. In addition, there is often a lack of clear separation of authority and responsibility between the board of management and the board of directors. This creates difficulties in allocating duties and responsibilities and the related authority over operational matters between the chair, the board of management, and the general director, as well as accountability for their actions. The board of management and the board of directors are often uncertain over the strategic direction of the holding company and their operational relationships with fellow subsidiaries and affiliates, or how to create an effective grouping that will grow sustainably. When SOE directors are selected on the basis of their party membership, political education, political influence, and length of public service, the government's ability to hold them accountable for performance is also diminished. The introduction of a strict set of guidelines on skills-based director appointments would help to strengthen the ability of SOEs to enhance their management capacity.

Not only qualifications and skills are required but those appointed to a board must have the time and resources to manage their responsibilities, have a clear understanding of the objectives of an enterprise's management and the owners, while being committed to adding value for all stakeholders.

7.5.11 Benchmarking and Performance Monitoring

Experience has shown that policy debate over the efficiency of SOE service delivery is blurred by a lack of information and evidence-based analysis on the performance of SOEs compared with alternative service delivery models. There is broad domestic consensus that reform is needed and that corporatization and competition can play an important role in improving the efficiency and effectiveness of infrastructure service delivery. However, equally, there is a lack of information and evidence-based analysis to assess past and ongoing reforms, and to inform future policy actions.

Industry sector benchmarking would identify which companies are outperforming the sector in terms of specific key performance indicators

(KPIs) and which are not achieving the KPIs. The more successful companies can then be analyzed to identify how or why they are outperforming specific KPIs and the same would apply to the enterprises not achieving the KPIs. The output of the analysis would be recommendations on business practices and management behavior to enable companies that are not performing so well on specific KPIs to improve.

It is also vital that private sector performance data are taken into account— SOE reform implies that many of the current SOEs will evolve into joint-stock companies and ultimately have very little, if any, state ownership. This means that current SOEs have to perform as well as any other competitors in the same industry, irrespective of ownership. Ultimately, benchmarking should include comparison with regional and international norms to establish how truly competitive Viet Nam's SOEs are. While Viet Nam has yet to introduce such a system it is quite common in other countries in the region.

The establishment of industry KPIs based on a comprehensive review of industry performance makes monitoring and evaluating enterprise progress much more accurate and effective and provides a clearer demonstration of where state capital is being used effectively and where it is being utilized less effectively. It also creates a much more powerful performance management tool for both the owners and management of an enterprise.

The reporting systems should give the ownership entity a true picture of the SOE's performance or financial situation, enabling it to react on time and to be selective in its intervention.

For SOEs with no comparable entity against which to benchmark overall performance, comparisons can be made concerning certain elements of their operations and performance. This benchmarking should cover productivity and the efficient use of labor, assets, and capital. This benchmarking is particularly important for SOEs operating in sectors where they do not face competition. It allows the SOEs, the ownership entity, and the general public to better assess SOE performance and reflect on their development (OECD 2015).

7.5.12 Performance Evaluation

It is not just the enterprises that require monitoring and evaluation but also the management. The implementation of KPIs and a competency-based human resources system would enable clear performance evaluations and enhanced recruitment and succession planning.

It would also ensure a much more open and transparent process based on required qualifications, experience, and capabilities.

7.5.13   The Commission for the Management of State Capital

The CMSC and the reform of oversight and management of SOEs and state capital invested in enterprises provide a unique opportunity for the Government of Viet Nam to transform the way in which it relates to SOEs and become an informed and active owner, setting and monitoring the implementation of broad mandates and objectives for SOEs, including financial targets, capital structure objectives, and risk tolerance levels.

The rationale and government appetite for SOEs change periodically but it is a fact that they will endure. It is, therefore, critical to ensure that the state's investment is secure and that it is delivering the returns (financial and nonfinancial), which the state and other stakeholders, including the people, require of SOEs. SOEs of the future must be more actively managed and deliver abundant value to the economy and society.

The CMSC should take this opportunity to rewrite the rules and recruit professional, skilled people who have the experience and credibility to push the restructuring and reform of the key enterprises under its oversight. It is their responsibility to support them to become sector leaders.

7.5.14   Changing the Definition of SOEs

The change to 100% state owned as being the definition of an SOE has proved to be confusing in terms of analysis of trends and performance, both domestically and against international SOEs. It is against the international norm.

The Government of Viet Nam should reconsider the way in which SOEs and enterprises in the state continue to own in excess of 50% are defined. It would make analysis and comprehension of SOEs and SOE performance by the government and stakeholders more transparent if the definition returned to the international norm and the GSO.

Appendix A7.1: Case Study – Southern Waterborne Joint Stock General Corporation

This mini case study focuses on the issues surrounding state-owned enterprise (SOE) reform and the impact (both planned and unplanned) reform can have on an SOE. The Southern Waterborne Joint Stock General Corporation (Sowatco) is a relatively small enterprise with turnover peaking at around $49 million in 2013. However, the size of the SOE is less important than the lessons that can be learned from the positive and negative impacts SOE reform can have on individual enterprises. This case study offers a good example of how focusing on the financial figures only and not the background of the company can result in a misleading analysis.

Sowatco was established in 1975, reporting to the Ministry of Transport. Sowatco is involved in three key areas of operation: waterborne transport, port operations—Long Binh Port and VICT, and mechanical engineering and shipbuilding.

From 1975 to 1996 (the period of reunification and development of around 12,000 SOEs), Sowatco became the leading waterborne transport SOE for Southern Viet Nam, operating in a closed command economy and focused on maintaining the value of state capital and in delivering local water transport services.

Table A7.1.1 shows that the company spent 30 years under government control before becoming fully privatized. For Sowatco, at least half of this period was a time of an almost constantly changing business and regulatory environment in which there was never any certainty regarding direction, financial resources, ownership, and capacity to grow. Besides maintaining the value of the state capital, Sowatco aimed to ensure compliance with the ever changing legal and regulatory framework. In some respects, Sowatco has been a guinea pig for the various stages of SOE reform in Viet Nam, which in some cases has proved to be a resounding success, yet in many others has been a long and difficult journey.

Table A7.1.1 also highlights the position and the activities that have influenced Sowatco's development during the SOE reform process, and the periods of inactivity and inertia caused, to a great extent, by the reform process.

Table A7.1.1: History of Events and Reform Lessons

Year	Events Timeline	How Reform Can Inhibit Progress
1996–2003	• Established as a general corporation 90 in 1996. • Seven other SOEs in similar sector(s) grouped with Southern Waterborne Joint Stock General Corporation (Sowatco). Becomes one of the smallest general corporations (GCs) of the 94 created at this time. Like many other SOEs, Sowatco has to find alternative sources of revenue to fund the "core business." In Sowatco's case, this included a subsidiary that profited substantially from the export of labor.	Sowatco was operating as a GC. Although GCs are called "corporations," they were not corporations in the international sense of corporate entities. GCs did not have rights over their member SOEs in the same way as a parent company owning a majority of the stock in its subsidiaries. The current legal framework neither requires nor allows GCs to make many strategic decisions and be accountable for these decisions, and the current level of capitalization is not sufficient to replace or upgrade installations and equipment to ensure products that have high export value added. In addition, the relationship between GCs and their members is only administrative, and the relationships between members of the same GC have not been clearly defined, so that the level of cooperation between the members is still low and often competitive rather than cooperative. The lack of clear relationships between the Government of Viet Nam authority and GC management, practical legal issues on state capital and how it is owned and managed, plus the conflicting interests and opinions of the main stakeholders exacerbate the situation. Institutional overlap, partly due to the decentralized system, stresses the importance of the maintenance of state capital as a fixed obligation of "parenting" an SOE, and favors inertia rather than proactive action.[a]
2003–2007	• In 2003, Sowatco became one of the first GC 90s to be given permission to operate under the pilot holding company model. At that time, the holding company was composed of the parent company, 7 subsidiary companies, and 3 joint venture (JV) companies. • Aging assets in the logistics business, logistics operating in domestic market only. Port can only handle small-scale river traffic, Sowatco providing a transfer service from larger ships to port. • Alternative revenue–generating businesses, e.g., provision of labor and trading becoming more important to the business. • Access to banking finance is limited and interest rates are rising.	Sowatco operating under the "pilot" holding company model. During this period, there was significant confusion regarding responsibility and accountability between the "holding company" and its "subsidiaries" and the line ministries to whom the parent company reported and the line ministries to which the "subsidiaries" may have been reporting to, and the regulatory and legislative environment was still being drafted. This resulted in considerable inertia while guidelines were developed by various state agencies. The Ministry of Transport (MOT) and the Ministry of Finance (MOF) unsure of what a "holding company" is and can or cannot do. Everyone is waiting for guidelines. Results in considerable uncertainty for Sowatco.

Continued on next page

Table A7.1.1 continued

Year	Events Timeline	How Reform Can Inhibit Progress
2007–2009	• MOT recommends reform by equitization. But no initial public offering (IPO)/listing. • Equitization results in the Government of Viet Nam keeping 66.58%. CUBE Investments from Hong Kong, China take 29.8%; remaining 3.62% goes to staff and unions. • CUBE not an active "strategic partner" and MOT has no capacity to provide professional oversight and management; still has to follow state model and direction. • Sowatco financing longer-term projects with expensive short-term loans with interest rates of up to 15.8%.	Sowatco, under the guidance of the MOT, was preparing for its initial equitization. The equitization plan and valuation has to be developed on the status of the company at a specific date. The process of developing the plan, obtaining approval, and the valuation would take around 18 months; during this time, no divestments, mergers, acquisitions, or other changes that may have an impact on the valuation can occur. The equitization did not include an IPO/listing so there is no opportunity to raise additional capital from the market. Equitization receipts go to "owner"/the Support Fund for Enterprise Reorganization and Development.
2010–2011	• Introduction to and participation in the Strengthening Support for State-Owned Enterprise Reform and Corporate Governance Facilitation Program of the Asian Development Bank (ADB). • Operational revenue generation mediocre but bottom line healthy from returns from investments in real estate JV and other noncore businesses. • Borrowing rates as high as 16.95% by 2011. ADB provides $2.47 million long-term debt restructuring over 25 years at much reduced interest rate thus providing some debt relief and improvements to cash flow to finance capital investments. • ADB also providing up to $700,000 in Asian Development Fund support for management training and restructuring support from international consultants. • Introduction to and commencing implementation of modern/demand economy management concepts. • But still following state model.	MOT decides Sowatco should list on Unlisted Public Company Market (UPCoM). This involved hiring an independent consulting organization to value the company (using the asset evaluation methodology). In the overall scheme of things, this process was relatively quick but still took around 4 months.

Continued on next page

Table A7.1 continued

Year	Events Timeline	How Reform Can Inhibit Progress
2011	• Shares registered for trading on UPCoM. • Initial price on UPCoM is VND10,200 (against par of VND10,000).	Government of Viet Nam steadfastly keeps shareholding (as does CUBE).
2010–2015	• Trading becoming even more the focus to generate cash to support logistics. • By 2012, trading was generating 84% of total revenue at a margin of 4.13% while logistics (the "core business") was only contributing 15.19% of total revenue and operating at margin of −2.33, meaning that trading was simply keeping the operational business afloat rather than providing additional resources for any significant investment in logistics. • By the end of 2014, the balance had improved—69.67% of revenue from trading at a margin of 5.66% and 30.33% revenue from logistics at 1.46%. But total sales had plummeted by 71.5%. The key trading contract (distribution of lubricants) had not been renewed as the supplier opened its own plant and distribution network in Viet Nam. • Share value on UPCoM dips as low as VND3,200. • Financial position still "sound" only due to the noncore investments.	Sowatco, with support from Ernst and Young, developed a restructuring plan as required by the Prime Minister and MOT and the Strengthening Support for State-Owned Enterprise Reform and Corporate Governance Facilitation Program of ADB. The plan was approved in January 2013. The period of planning and obtaining approval for the restructuring plan is generally a period in which there is little dynamic activity. Decision No. 929 and Decree No. 71 are announced, directing the divestment of noncore assets to counter the flagrant excesses of large state economic groups (SEGs) like Vinashin. But against the law to sell underperforming companies at below book value and more importantly for Sowatco, noncore businesses were providing the "bottom line," which was keeping the company solvent. Deliberation as to whether MOT should continue to be Sowatco's "owner." In terms of its financial position (as opposed to the rationale for its establishment), Sowatco is not really a transport and logistics company but more of a trading company. Decided that Sowatco should move to the State Capital Investment Corporation (SCIC).
2015	• Preparation for full privatization (but continue to list on UPCoM. • Government of Viet Nam (SCIC) at last decided that it was time to sell off all shares in Sowatco.	The SCIC decide that the state will divest all its equity in Sowatco. Sowatco looks for a strategic partner who could take 35% or more of the equity and commences dialogue with one or more potential strategic investors. The Prime Minister eventually decides against any sale to a strategic investor and decrees that the divestment will be by public auction. The process including the timing and the base price at auction was managed and controlled by the SCIC with almost no involvement by Sowatco. The process took 12 months from start to finish.

Continued on next page

Table A7.1.1 continued

Year	Events Timeline	How Reform Can Inhibit Progress
2016	• Sowatco fully privatized. • Public auction on 18 January 2016 was oversubscribed by 11.31%. The sale of 44,675,400 shares raised VND626,802,600,000 at an average price of VND14,030 per share. The Government of Viet Nam and CUBE sold all shares. • At the end of the IPO and immediate post-IPO transactions, SOTRANS, an experienced and dynamic logistics company, becomes the main shareholder.	
2016–2018	• Positive impact of being free of state control and having a dynamic strategic partner/owner is realized. Commercially focused decision-making down from 2 to 3 months under the state control to 48 hours now that fully privatized. • Business restructured, noncore businesses being divested and trading wound down. Divestment of real estate JV with book value of $14.4 million realized $38 million that has been reinvested in the development of Long Binh Port and larger container ships. • Proper implementation of management techniques and corporate governance as recommended in 2011. • Shares trading at VND13,500 per share and providing significant dividends.	

[a] World Bank. 2003. *Vietnam Pilot Restructuring Project for Three General Corporations: Vinatex, Vinacafe and Seaprodex.* Washington, DC.
Source: Author.

Table A7.1.2. Key Financial Indicators, 2012–2017
(VND billion)

	2012	2013	2014	2015	2016	2017
Total operating revenue	759.1	1,023.6	489.9	216.0	210.0	182.5
Gross profit	26.9	41.4	21.5	49.1	27.0	35.6
Revenue from financial activities	38.8	43.6	29.1	17.6	75.4	616.6
Net profit after tax	25.3	37.2	45.5	67.1	63.2	509.3
Gross profit margin (%)	3.6	4.0	4.4	22.7	13.1	19.5
Net profit margin (%)	3.3	3.6	9.3	31.0	30.1	279.1
Return on equity (%)	2.8	4.1	4.9	6.9	6.3	43.2
Return on total assets (%)	2.1	2.8	4.1	6.0	5.4	37.3
Total liabilities to equity	0.4	0.5	0.2	0.2	0.2	0.1

Sources: Sowatco audited financial statements; author's calculations.

Although the figures in Table A7.1.2 above clearly demonstrate that Sowatco was, in relative terms financially sound, the numbers hide the true picture of an SOE that was generating revenue and profit from noncore activities, which enabled it to continue operating in the core business for which it was established. The multiple changes to Sowatco and the reform process and the economic conditions of the time inhibited the company from implementing meaningful change to both the internal structures and the corporate structure and new investments in logistics that could have resulted in efficient and profitable operations of its core business.

Current Status

Sowatco, as part of the SOTRANS group (which benefits from the extension of its logistics value chain), will focus on the development of the logistics business, particularly the development of Long Binh Port as a "feeder port." This means that the 22 hectares will be developed as warehousing so that container ships can drop off at Long Binh and smaller boats can then transport the contents via the river to Ho Chi Minh City. It has been building and operating larger container ships resulting in greater operational efficiencies. The development of Long Binh Port is being financed by the proceeds of the divestment of the joint venture with Keppel Land. The group is now one of the top logistics companies in Viet Nam.

Lessons Learned

A key lesson from this case study is that there is no one approach that fits all in SOE reform. While the government was making positive moves toward SOE reform and improved governance through revisions to the legal and regulatory system (e.g., Prime Minister's Decision No. 929[1] issued in July 2012 followed by Decree No. 71[2]), Sowatco's position would have been negatively affected had it implemented (or been able to implement) the divestment of noncore businesses. These businesses were keeping Sowatco afloat and without them the company was in danger of possible collapse and the state would have lost its investment. By keeping the noncore businesses for as long as possible, Sowatco was able to have a relatively favorable listing with the average share sold at VND14,200 (a premium of 42%) and the state was able to make a good return.

---

[1]   Prime Minister of the Socialist Republic of Vietnam. Decision No. 929/QD-TTg dated 17 July 2012 on approval of the scheme on "restructuring of state-owned enterprises, focusing on economic groups and state-owned corporations in period 2011–2015. Ha Noi.

[2]   Government of Viet Nam. Decree No. 71/2013/ND-CP on investment of state capital in enterprises and financial management of enterprises of which 100% charter capital is held by the state. Ha Noi.

The length and complexities of the various reform and restructuring processes have a negative effect on the performance and development of an enterprise.

There have been concerns regarding the Government of Viet Nam's preference to retain a controlling interest in equitized companies. In the case of Sowatco, the company is no longer dependent on the state and will be profitable in its core business of transport and logistics. The revised strategy proposed by the new investor and the board of directors would appear to offer Sowatco an enhanced future outside the constraints that the SOE/state-invested sector continues to suffer from.

Appendix A7.2: Case Study – Construction Corporation No. 1

Construction Corporation No. 1 Company Limited (CC1) located in Ho Chi Minh City, was founded in 1979, as a state-owned enterprise (SOE) under the Ministry of Construction (MOC). CC1 was made a general corporation (GC) in 1995. Between 2011 and 2006, CC1 experienced 90% growth, with turnover growing to $150 million and it was regarded as one of the leading construction companies in the south of Viet Nam. CC1 was a diverse group with 9 subsidiaries in which they held between 50% and 100% of the equity and investments of 14% to 50% equity in an additional 13 other affiliate companies. The subsidiaries and affiliate companies operated in various sectors within and out of the core business:

- energy, infrastructure, industrial and civil engineering construction;
- design consultancy, investment consultancy;
- import and export and trading (machinery and equipment, building materials);
- investment in urban services and housing development projects, industrial manufacturing, infrastructure, production of construction materials, construction equipment, and financial investments;
- investment and trading in tourism and hotels, entertainment services (water parks), advertising services;
- manufacturing and trading in pure water, bottled mineral water; and
- training and skills development and foreign languages for laborers before being sent to work in other countries.

Despite its impressive revenue growth, by 2011 the group had debts of $160 million, with loan interest rates of up to 23%; a high debt–equity ratio and low current ratio, and was constantly renegotiating short-term loans for long-term projects. There was no long-term "big picture" strategy and group companies were competing against each other rather than complementing and supporting each other. There were weaknesses in the relationships and financial linkages between the parent company and subsidiaries. Reporting by the subsidiaries was slow and cumbersome as was performance monitoring by the parent.

The owners (MOC) were focused on ensuring compliance with internal reporting systems and were unable to provide direction or sound commercial advice/support, despite being the agency that approves the appointment of the chairman and general director.

Prime Minister's Decision No. 929[3] issued in July 2012 followed by Decree No. 71[4] provided the impetus for CC1 to develop a restructuring plan to be approved by both the MOC and the Prime Minister. The Ministry of Finance also recommended that CC1 make a competitive bid to join the second phase of the Strengthening Support for State-Owned Enterprise Reform and Corporate Governance Facilitation Program of the Asian Development Bank (ADB 2014). The program aimed to support the Government of Viet Nam in realizing SOE reform through improving the corporate and management structure and financial position of GCs; as well as improving transparency, accountability, professionalism, commercialism, profitability, and operational efficiency, leading to equitization and listing.

The motivation to join this reform initiative was initially that ordinary capital resources (OCR) could be provided to restructure a significant portion of the GC's short-term, high-interest debt with cheaper long-term debt, thereby providing a much-needed release of operational cash flow that could be utilized more effectively in improving the overall business performance of the GC.

However, the GC benefited in more ways than just debt restructuring. The level of OCR to be awarded was based on an in-depth diagnostic review of the company's restructuring plan, internal capacity, long-term sustainability, forecast improvements in key financial ratios, and the ability to repay. The future equitization and listing of the enterprise was also a key consideration.

Complexities inherent in operational and financial restructuring are difficult and stretched the capacity of CC1's management. The CC1 restructuring plan appeared ambitious and based on MOC/Government of Viet Nam expectations rather than reality; it lacked rigorous market analysis; and the linkages between proposed divestments, business developments, and financial projections were disjointed. There was little development of organizational and corporate restructuring and no plans as to how corporate governance and risk management would be improved.

Crucial was the involvement of international consultants, provided under ADB's Capacity Development Technical Assistance 8016, in the process who were able to support CC1 to produce an improved and coherent restructuring

---

[3]   Prime Minister of the Socialist Republic of Vietnam. Decision No. 929/QD-TTg dated 17 July 2012 on approval of the scheme on restructuring of state-owned enterprises, focusing on economic groups and state-owned corporations in period 2011–2015. Ha Noi.

[4]   Government of Viet Nam. Decree No. 71/2013/ND-CP on investment of state capital in enterprises and financial management of enterprises of which 100% charter capital is held by the state. Ha Noi.

plan based on robust market analysis, documenting a realistic forward pipeline; a detailed plan of divestment of noncore and nonessential investments; and accurate financial analysis and forecasting.

Not only did the consultants provide in-depth support in restructuring planning but they also supported significant capacity building at senior management level, thus enabling a more comprehensive plan that encompassed clear changes to be made to governance practices, risk management, and organizational structures.

The key objectives of CC1's revised restructuring plan were as follows:

- Equitize the parent company in 2015. It was anticipated that this would enable an increase in equity thereby widening the opportunity for commercial fund raising from the market. The Government of Viet Nam planned to retain 51%.
- Restructure the business lines and focus on core competencies.
- Increase ownership of strategic subsidiaries and affiliates, particularly DakrTih Hydropower JSC, and create a new design company.
- Restructure the internal and organizational and corporate structure.
- Dilute equity in four nonstrategic subsidiaries to below 50%, and divest all equity in two associates.
- Introduce improvements to corporate governance.
- Restructure a significant proportion of the debt using OCR loans.

The revised plan was comprehensive, coherent, and credible. The financial forecasts, based on realistic future projections that factored in approximately $100 million of OCR, indicated that key ratios would improve and the company would become more stable. ADB agreed to provide $105 million in OCR to restructure approximately 65% of CC1's total debts. Asian Development Fund (ADF) support of $4 million was also agreed.

CC1 commenced implementation of the plan, including preparation for equitization and ultimately registration on the Unlisted Public Company Market (UPCoM).

However, all was not plain sailing. CC1 and MOC had originally targeted 2015 for CC1's equitization with MOC deciding the state would retain 51%. As can be seen in Table A7.2.1 there were significant delays and changes to the equitization plan.

Table A7.2.1: CC1 Equitization Process

Action	Plan	Actual
Closing date of accounts for valuation for equitization	30 June 2014	30 June 2014
Approval of valuation by Ministry of Construction (MOC)	2014	10 March 2015
Present equitization plan to MOC		24 April 2015
Approval of equitization plan by MOC	May 2015	
MOC submits equitization plan to Prime Minister	15 June 2015	
Approval of equitization plan by Prime Minister	July 2015	28 October 2015
Sell shares to strategic investor by negotiation	November 2015	Did not happen
Initial public offering (IPO)	June 2015	October 2016
Register on Unlisted Public Company Market	6 months after IPO	July 2017

Source: Construction Corporation No. 1 Company Limited.

When the equitization/initial public offering (IPO) eventually took place, some 27 months after closing the accounts for valuation purposes, the final ownership structure was as per Table A7.2.2 below.

Table A7.2.2: CC1 Ownership Structure after Equitization
(%)

Shareholder	Planned Share of Equity	Actual Share of Equity
Government	51.0	40.5
Staff	2.2	2.2
Strategic investor	38.0	
Corporate investor	7.0	19.0
Corporate investor		15.0
Corporate investor		11.0
Initial public offering	12.8	12.3
Total	**100.0**	**100.0**

Sources: Construction Corporation No. 1 Company Limited and Unlisted Public Company Market.

There are a number of points to note regarding the delays, the final shareholding structure, and the performance of the enterprise during this period.

- Initially there were delays, particularly relating to the speed of activity and approvals by MOC, the "owners," and other agencies.
- Generally, an initial offering of shares to strategic investors before the IPO is only available to enterprises in which the state proposes

to retain more than 50% of the shares. CC1 had identified a strategic partner interested in taking 38% of the equity, which provides some control through the right of veto on board resolutions, etc. Strategic investors are brought in because they bring with them some inherent advantages (knowledge, experience, internal capacity, technology, financial resources, etc.) from which the SOE can benefit. When the state retains not just a portion of equity, but often a controlling equity, there is a distinct danger that it will put off strategic investors.

However, eventually MOC decided to retain only 40% of the equity at equitization, which meant that there could be no prior offering to strategic investors, and that MOC would continue to appoint three members of the board. The IPO therefore became less attractive to strategic investors and more about commercial investors.

• Originally, the IPO had been expected to take place in June 2015 and then it was hoped for September 2015, which would have been within the regulated 18 months of the closing of the accounts for the purposes of the valuation. Because the IPO took place 27 months after the valuation, a special dispensation from the Government of Viet Nam would have had to be obtained.

• Investors must have confidence in the financial and nonfinancial information reported for IPO and equitization purposes. The older the data, the less and less reliable it will be viewed by the market and its credibility will be questioned. This leads to a less successful IPO/equitization, which is detrimental not only to CC1's restructuring but also to the overall image of SOE equitization and restructuring. The financial indicators of CC1 are reported in Table A7.2.3.

Table A7.2.3: Financial Indicators, 2012–2016

	2012	2013	2014	2015	2016
Total revenue (VND billion)	3,515.0	3,031.0	4,681.1	5,593.3	6,584.0
Gross profit (VND billion)	713.4	552.8	706.2	792.6	728.0
Net profit after tax (VND billion)	223.1	99.3	306.9	297.9	211.1
Gross profit margin (%)	20.3	18.2	15.1	14.2	11.1
Net profit margin (%)	6.4	3.3	6.6	5.3	3.2
Return on equity (%)	16.8	6.2	14.7	13.5	11.9
Return on assets (%)	3.0	1.4	3.2	2.8	2.3
Liabilities to equity (%)	4.7	3.6	3.5	3.7	4.3
Current ratio (%)	1.2	1.0	1.0	1.1	1.2
Asset utilization (%)	73.4	60.1	83.4	96.6	154.8

Sources: CC1 Audited Financial Statements; Unlisted Public Company Market; and author.

- Due to the constraints of the OCR debt guarantee mechanism of Vietnam Development Bank relating to the issue of collateral, CC1 was unable to take advantage of the whole $105 million OCR and $4 million in ADF support. Ultimately, the level of support agreed was $57.38 million OCR and no ADF, which resulted in

  o   less debt being restructured and therefore less freed-up cash flow; and

  o   the need to utilize internal resources to support the internal restructuring, upgrading of financial and information and technology systems, and the capacity building the ADF had been planned for.

- The plan to repurchase shares in DakrTih Hydropower JSC has not happened due to the limitations of the agreement on OCR support. This has had a negative effect on CC1's financial results. Had the purchase taken place, DakrTih would have been consolidated into the group accounts; instead CC1 is simply receiving dividends, which changes the nature of the financial picture.

- The total time taken for the equitization was 27 months and the negotiation surrounding the OCR took more than 12 months, which is a lengthy period of uncertainty and inertia that had a negative impact on decision-making and performance.

However, irrespective of the overall performance, efficiency gains have been made in both revenue and gross profit per employee as can be seen from Table A7.2.4 below.

Table A7.2.4: Employee Efficiency Gains, 2012-2016
(VND million)

	2012	2013	2014	2,015	2016
Revenue per employee	1,424.4	1,223.6	2,014.6	2,517.1	3,254.7
Gross profit per employee	289.3	223.2	303.9	365.6	359.9

Note: Revenue per employee has grown by 128% and gross profit by 24%.
Sources: CC1 audited financial statements; author's calculations.

Current Situation

Under Decree No. 131/2018/ND-CP dated 29 September 2018, CC1 should transfer from MOC to the State Capital Investment Corporation (SCIC) (under the Commission for the Management of State Capital at Enterprises [CMSC]). The SCIC should take ownership of the state's shares and it is assumed to ultimately divest the total equity held by the state. Under the decree, the CMSC came into operation on 29 September 2018 and the transfer of all companies should have been achieved by 13 November 2018. However, by the end of October, MOC has not provided any detailed information to CC1 with regard to when or how this might happen.

MOC had indicated that they are planning to sell the remaining state's equity in CC1 by the end of 2019. It is unclear as to whether the changes in "ownership" will have an impact on that plan.

So, CC1 continues to be in a state of uncertainty, which has a negative impact on the company and individual morale, planning, implementation, and performance.

Lessons Learned

As highlighted in the main text, a key issue in successful restructuring and reform through equitization has been the time taken for the equitization process. This is very apparent in the case of CC1 where inactivity and inertia, due to the length of the process, had a significant impact on the company. Although recent legislation has been introduced to speed up the process, the results for 2017 and 2018 indicate that there are still issues with institutional capacity.

The capacity of the "owner" to manage the reform and restructuring process is also an important factor in the process. Clarity with regard to how much equity will be retained and a clear indication of the path to total divestment of the state's shares is critical for the management in planning and implementation and raising additional capital. The state's involvement in individual enterprises is an important factor in attracting strategic partners.

The mindset of the company management and leadership and the company's overall culture has shifted to be more dynamic and market focused but the benefits of this change cannot be capitalized on without an absolute change of ownership from the state to being 100% publicly owned.

Appendix A7.3: Definition of Equitization

Equitization is the Government of Viet Nam's preferred form of reform for state-owned enterprises (SOEs). Equitization (and the process of equitization) is currently defined within Decree No. 126/2017/ND-CP of 16 November 2017.[5] Key points to note are as follows:

1. Equitization refers to the conversion of 100% SOEs to joint-stock companies (JSC) through

    a. issuing additional shares in order to increase charter capital while keeping current state capital unchanged;

    b. selling part of current state capital or both selling part of state capital and issuing additional shares to increase charter capital; or

    c. selling the entire state capital available at the enterprise or both selling the entire state capital and issuing additional shares to increase charter capital.

2. Unless there has been an agreement to sell directly to one or more interested parties, there will be an initial public auction (initial public offering [IPO]) available to all investors whether they are organizations or individuals, domestic, or foreign. Shares offered at public auctions should account for at least 20% of the charter capital.

3. The labor union of the equitized enterprise can purchase shares not exceeding 3% of the charter capital, provided that they are retained for 3 years from the date of equitization. The selling price of shares offered to the labor union shall be the par value of VND10,000 per share.

4. Management and employees are entitled to purchase up to 100 shares for each year working in state sectors for a discounted price equal to 60% of the par value of VND10,000 per share. The shares must be retained for 3 years. Management and employees committing to work for at least 3 years with the enterprise post equitization can buy between 200 and 500 additional shares each year (up to a maximum of 2,000 to 5,000 shares) at the public auction starting price.

5. Strategic investors—generally, an initial offering of shares to strategic investors is only available to enterprises in which the state proposes to retain more than 50% of the shares.

---

[5] Government of Viet Nam. Decree No. 126/2017/ND-CP on conversion from state-owned enterprises and single-member limited liability companies with 100% of charter capital invested by state-owned enterprises into joint-stock companies. Ha Noi.

A strategic investor may be a domestic or foreign investor having a plan to assist the enterprise in new technology exchange, provide training, enhance financial capacity, enhance enterprise management, provide materials, and develop the market.

Strategic investors can invest directly with the agreement of the enterprise and the "representative authority" before the IPO. However, if there are at least two potential strategic investors and the total number of shares subscribed by strategic investors is more than the number of shares offered to strategic investors, an auction for strategic investors will be held after the IPO with the starting price equal to the average successful bid of the IPO. Strategic investors must hold the shares for 3 years.

6. Within 5 working days from the deadlines for payment by the bidders, the auctioneering organization shall transfer the revenue earned from the IPO to the equitized enterprise in order to settle redundancy policies and make payment for equitization expenses. The remainder shall be transferred to the Enterprise Assistance and Development Fund.

Appendix A7.4: 11 Key Sectors in which 100% State-Owned Enterprises Will Remain

State-Owned Enterprise Industry Sectors	
1 Mapping services for national defense and security	7 Public postal services
2 Manufacture and sale of industrial explosives	8 Lottery business
3 Electricity distribution, national electricity system dispatching, management of electrical grids, multipurpose hydropower and nuclear power playing a significant role in socioeconomic development, and national defense and security	9 Publishing (excluding printing and publication)
4 Management of national and state-invested municipal railroad infrastructure, coordination of state-invested national and municipal railroad traffic	10 Printing and manufacture of notes and gold bullion and golden souvenir
5 Air traffic services, aeronautical information services, and search and rescue services	11 Credit instruments for socioeconomic development, services for banking system, and credit institution safety
6 Maritime safety (excluding dredging and maintenance of public navigable channels)	

Appendix A7.5: Corporations to Be Transferred to the Commission for the Management of State Capital

Corporation	Total Assets (VND trillion)	Ownership by Government	Sector/Field	Debt Ratio	Governing Body
State Capital Investment Corporation	66	100%	Finance		Ministry of Finance
Vietnam Electricity	692	100%	Energy/Power	70.4	Ministry of Industry and Trade
Petrolimex	54	76%	Energy/Petrol	62.1	Ministry of Industry and Trade
PetroVietnam	770	100%	Energy/Oil and gas	44.0	Ministry of Industry and Trade
Vinachem	57	100%	Chemicals		Ministry of Industry and Trade

Continued on next page

Appendix A7.5 continued

Corporation	Total Assets (VND trillion)	Ownership by Government	Sector/Field	Debt Ratio	Governing Body
Vinacomin	140	100%	Energy/Coal	83.6	Ministry of Industry and Trade
Vinataba	18	100%	Tobacco		Ministry of Industry and Trade
CIPM	37	100%	Transport/Transport Infrastructure		Ministry of Transport
ACV	47	95%	Transport/Airport		Ministry of Transport
VEC	78	100%	Transport/Transport Infrastructure		Ministry of Transport
Vietnam Airlines	96	86%	Transport/Airlines	83.2	Ministry of Transport
Vietnam Railways	21	100%	Transport/Railway		Ministry of Transport
Vinalines	30	100%	Transport/Maritime		Ministry of Transport
Vinacafe	2	100%	Agriculture		Ministry of Agriculture and Rural Development
Vinafor	5	51%	Agriculture		Ministry of Agriculture and Rural Development
Vinafood I	11	100%	Food		Ministry of Agriculture and Rural Development
Vinafood II	8	51%	Food		Ministry of Agriculture and Rural Development
VRG	70	75%	Agriculture		Ministry of Agriculture and Rural Development
Mobifone	28	100%	Information Technology and Telecommunication		Ministry of Information and Communications
VNPT	89	100%	Information Technology and Telecommunication		Ministry of Information and Communications
VTC	3	100%	Information Technology and Telecommunication		Ministry of Information and Communications

References

Asian Development Bank (ADB). 2000. *Technical Assistance to Viet Nam for State-Owned Enterprise Diagnostic Audits.* Manila.

_____. 2014. *Socialist Republic of Viet Nam: Strengthening Support for State-Owned Enterprise Reform and Corporate Governance Facilitation Program.* Consultant's report. Manila (TA 8016-VIE).

_____. 2016a. What's Next for SOE Reform in Viet Nam? July (internal).

_____. 2016b. *Socialist Republic of Viet Nam: Strengthening Support for State-Owned Enterprise Reform and Corporate Governance Facilitation Program.* Manila (TA 8387-VIE).

Central Institute of Economic Management (CIEM). 2002. Firm Level Survey. Ha Noi.

_____. 2005. Report of the Study on Post-Equitization of State-Owned Enterprises. Ha Noi.

Vietnam Electricity (EVN). 2018. *Vietnam Electricity Annual Report 2017.* Ha Noi. https://en.evn.com.vn/userfile/User/huongbtt/files/2018/2/AnnualReport2017.pdf.

General Statistics Office of Vietnam. Various years. Statistical Summary Book of Vietnam. Ha Noi.

Government of Viet Nam. 2016. Summary Report No. 460/BC-CP on Economic Restructuring Plan for the Period 2016 to 2020. 18 October. Ha Noi.

_____. 2018. Report No. 217/BC-CP on the Implementation of Policies and Laws on Management and Use of State Capital at Enterprises and Equitisation of State Enterprises in the 2011–2016 Period. Ha Noi.

Hanoi Stock Exchange. https://hnx.vn/en-gb/hnx.html.

Ho Chi Minh Stock Exchange. https://www.hsx.vn/.

International Monetary Fund (IMF). 2017. Viet Nam: Selected Issues. IMF Country Report No. 17/191. Washington, DC.

Mekong Business Initiative. https://www.mekongbiz.org.

Ministry of Finance (MOF). 2018. *Report on Reorganization and Restructuring of SOEs and Enterprise Development in 2017.* Ha Noi.

Ministry of Finance of the Socialist Republic of Vietnam. http://www.mof.gov.vn/webcenter/portal/mof/r/m/trangchu?_afrLoop=25735120959868222.

Ministry of Planning and Investment. Ministry of Planning and Investment of the Socialist Republic of Vietnam. Foreign Investment Agency. http://www.mpi.gov.vn/en/Pages/tinbai.aspx?idTin=40423&idcm=122.

Organisation for Economic Co-operation and Development (OECD). 2015. *OECD Guidelines on Corporate Governance of State-Owned Enterprises.* Paris.

Petrolimex. 2018. *Petrolimex Annual Report 2017.* https://www.petrolimex.com.vn/details/reports/petrolimex-annual-report-2017.html.

Socialist Republic of Vietnam. Government Portal. http://chinhphu.vn/portal/page/portal/English.

State Capital Investment Corporation. http://www.scic.vn/english/.

VGP News. The Government's Regular Meeting in December 2017. http://news.chinhphu.vn/Home/The-Governments-regular-meeting-in-December-2017/20181/33012.vgp.

Vietnam Investment Review. 2017. Foreign Investors Point Out Difficulties and Solutions for SOE Equitisation. Ha Noi.

_____. 2018. 667 SOEs Equitized but Yet Listed 21 November. https://www.vir.com.vn/667-soes-equitized-but-yet-listed-64012.html.

Viet NamNet. 2018. VNR500 Report 2017. http://www.vnr500.com.vn.

World Bank. 2012. *Vietnam Development Report 2012: Market Economy for a Middle-Income Vietnam.* Washington, DC.

_____. 2013. *Vietnam Development Report 2013: Skilling Up Vietnam.* Washington, DC.

World Bank and Ministry of Planning and Investment of Vietnam (MPI). 2016. *Vietnam 2035: Toward Prosperity, Creativity, Equity, and Democracy.* Washington, DC.

World Economic Forum. Various years. Global Competitiveness Report. Geneva.

_____. 2018. *The Global Competitiveness Report 2018.* Geneva.

www.ingramcontent.com/pod-product-compliance
Lightning Source LLC
Chambersburg PA
CBHW082348230326
41599CB00058BA/7148